Law and Social Change

Law and Social Change

2nd edition

Sharyn L. Roach Anleu

Los Angeles | London | New Delhi
Singapore | Washington DC

First published 2000

Reprinted 2001, 2002, 2003, 2005, 2006, 2008
Second edition published 2010

SAGE Publications Ltd
1 Oliver's Yard
55 City Road
London EC1Y 1SP

SAGE Publications Inc.
2455 Teller Road
Thousand Oaks, California 91320

SAGE Publications India Pvt Ltd
B 1/I 1 Mohan Cooperative Industrial Area
Mathura Road
New Delhi 110 044

SAGE Publications Asia-Pacific Pte Ltd
33 Pekin Street #02-01
Far East Square
Singapore 048763

Library of Congress Control Number: 2009922683

British Library Cataloguing in Publication data

A catalogue record for this book is available from the British Library

ISBN 978-1-4129-4559-2
ISBN 978-1-4129-4560-8 (pbk)

Typeset by C&M Digitals (P) Ltd, Chennai, India
Printed by CPI Antony Rowe, Chippenham, Wiltshire
Printed on paper from sustainable resources

Mixed Sources
Product group from well-managed
forests and other controlled sources
www.fsc.org Cert no. SGS-COC-2953
© 1996 Forest Stewardship Council
FSC

Contents

Preface to First Edition

This book grew from a dual interest in the interface between sociology and law and in the apparent increasing reliance on law as a route for social change. Until very recently the sociology of law was not an established subdiscipline; sociology was conscious of the law as a social institution and law was conscious of the social conditions in which it operated, but there was relatively little interaction between the two disciplines. This has changed. There is now a vast sociological literature on legal institutions, especially those in industrialized western nations, greater consideration of the relationships between law and non-legal forms of social control and dispute processing, and increasing discussion of the role of law and legal discourse in everyday life.

There is an enormous amount of attention being given to law – both as legislation and as judicial decisions – as a source of social change. Litigation and lobbying for legislative change are strategies that social movements adopt across the full political spectrum. Governments also rely on legislation to implement various social welfare programmes and, more recently, international laws are an important aspect of the constitution of the international community and the possibilities of global governance or regulation. In the wake of a reliance on law to further desired social transformations, there is widespread disillusionment regarding the persistence of inequalities and the resistance of social institutions and actors to changed legal environments. Many therefore would suggest that law is an ineffective source of social change and does not readily translate into altered social practices. However, the effects of new legislation or new judicial interpretations of social life are difficult to evaluate precisely, and it is rather naive to expect that legal change will directly and simplistically translate into the expected social changes. The expectation that law will have anticipated results belies positivistic reasoning, that is, that one set of changes in the law directly causes the anticipated change.

This book provides a sociological examination of law, surveys current theoretical debates and examines socio-legal research. It goes beyond a discussion of contemporary legal institutions to include a consideration of the relationships between law and other aspects of social life. The focus is on broad and general patterns grounded in specific examples. Overwhelmingly, examples are taken from the common-law legal systems, but there is also considerable attention paid to comparing the legal systems of Europe and Asia. There is also some coverage of current discussions of globalization and the role of law in an international context.

Chapter 1 examines the idea of law and introduces some legal concepts. In discussing the interface between sociology and law, it provides a brief overview of legal theories, including positivism, legal realism and natural law. Chapter 2 investigates the `classical' sociological theorists – Durkheim, Weber and Marx – and their analyses of the interconnections between social and economic transformations and the nature of law, legal thought and legal relations. This theoretical legacy has influenced diverse contemporary theories of law. Chapter 3 examines contemporary debates in theories of law, including systems theory, juridification, law and discipline, critical legal theory, feminist legal theory, and legal pluralism.

Chapter 4, the first of the substantive chapters, examines the legal profession. It addresses the concept of profession, then examines the nature of legal work and discusses changes to the legal profession that have occurred over the past three decades across a number of different societies. Chapter 5 deals with the social practices involved in the emergence, identification and processing of disputes, which can include adjudication, mediation, conciliation and negotiation. It examines the alternative dispute-resolution movement and assesses its role and functions within the legal/justice system, specifically the relationships between different forums for resolving disputes and the social conditions under which certain kinds of dispute settlement emerge. Social control, a concept that has a long history within sociology, is the topic of Chapter 6, which focuses on the connections between legal and nonlegal control. This chapter looks at the criminal trial, including what happens in the shadow of the courtroom, for example negotiations between lawyers and plea bargaining. The chapter also discusses the role of the judge, sentencing, the aims of punishment and the role of victims in the criminal justice process, and finally explores new developments in crime management and prevention.

The next two chapters address some specific and very contemporary issues. Chapter 7 looks at feminism and legal reform and investigates the ways in which legal mobilization is one strategy that social movements, here women's movements, pursue as a route for social change in the areas of employment and sex discrimination, rape and domestic violence, pornography and reproductive issues. The central argument is that it is naive to expect that simply reforming statutes will directly transform discriminatory social practices and enduring attitudes towards women. Viewing law as a complex of diverse and often contradictory legislation, judicial decisions and administration, it is not surprising that advances in one area may be thwarted by legal and other impediments in a different area. Chapter 8 examines the significance of law in contemporary discussions of rights and citizenship. In this context, there is debate about the efficacy of the nation state and its capacity (or willingness) to accord rights and social justice to many of its citizens. The chapter examines new discussions of human rights, globalization and the rise of international law. It also addresses the phenomenon of war crimes trials, both regarding the post-World War II cases as well as those being pursued more recently in special tribunals. It also investigates the role of law in the transformation of eastern Europe following the demise of the Soviet political and economic regimes. Finally, Chapter 9 – the conclusion – provides an overview of the central arguments and ties together the underlying themes of the book.

There are numerous people to thank regarding the emergence and development of this book. They have been very helpful in establishing its direction and form. First, I am extremely grateful to Professor Malcolm Waters for discussions with me about this project in its early stages. Malcolm has been central in encouraging and maintaining my sociological imagination and this l appreciate. Secondly, I wish to record my great appreciation to Kathy Mack for extending my interest in and knowledge about the operation of the criminal justice process. Thirdly, I appreciate the very reliable and competent research assistance provided to me by Elizabeth Birkett, Margaret Cameron and Megan Morgan. A special thanks goes to Megan for her helpful editorial assistance, checking of the bibliography and preparation of the index. I would also like to thank Flinders University for financial assistance and its Faculty of Social Sciences for secretarial support, especially to Anne Kelly for the final typing of the bibliography. I extend great appreciation to Gillian Stern for her encouragement of this project, her extremely professional approach and patience regarding the deadline. I also appreciate the astute and very helpful comments made by the reviewer of the manuscript. My thanks also to Miranda Nunhofer, Seth Edwards and others at Sage for their assistance and input throughout the production process. Ultimately, I am indebted to Oliver, Tristan, Lucinda and Edmer for their help, which assumed various forms.

Preface to Second Edition

It is ten years ago now, almost to the very day, that I was putting the finishing touches to *Law and Social Change*. One decade on I am now completing the second edition. Much has changed in that time span. There have been significant and momentous events in terms of politics, financial markets, labour markets, migration, wars, and terrorism, all with international and local reverberations. Perhaps, the biggest set of changes for discussions of social change and law has been the vast scholarship – theoretical development and empirical investigation – on the topic of globalization. The second edition accordingly spends more time discussing social change through the conceptual lens of globalization. Moreover, information about some of these changes has become more accessible (i.e. for those with access to computers and the internet) on web pages; so URLs have been a much more important resource in writing the second edition. The format of the book parallels the first edition and retains the same chapters with various degrees of change, revision and updating.

Any book is the product of many more contributors than the author. This edition has benefited from the suggestions, insights and fresh perspectives of the four anonymous reviewers who I am unable to thank by name.

I would like to thank Rose Williams for her expertise with the bibliography, final formatting and index, and Carolyn Corkindale for her expert research assistance and capacity to track down articles not readily available to me. I also thank Edmer Anleu and Patricia Roach for carefully reading the final draft and detecting those errors I could no longer see. Countless sociology of law students in the Department of Sociology at Flinders University helped me hone ideas and think about interesting and useful issues in the teaching and learning context. During a period at the International Institute for the Sociology of Law (Oñati, Spain), in 2008, I was able to see the final version of the second edition emerging, and I thank Carlos Lista, Susana Arrese Murguzur and the other staff for their assistance during that period. I acknowledge the Faculty of Social Sciences (Flinders University) for a grant to complete the research, writing and manuscript preparation. I appreciate the patience and advice of Jai Seaman, Chris Rojek and Mila Steele at SAGE and the efforts of Imogen Roome in the production phase. I wish to thank Kathy Mack for helping me create the space to effectively complete this project and appreciate the efforts of Oliver, Tristan and Lucinda, whose assistance, as before, assumed various forms.

Bridport, Tasmania
January 2009

List of Figures

1 Introduction: the Meanings of Law

Law is a social phenomenon and has been of interest to sociology since the early days of the discipline. However, much discussion of law has been and remains monopolized by legal practitioners and legal theorists who primarily focus on legal doctrine; they are concerned to analyse patterns, directions and inconsistencies in judicial thinking and decision making. They attend to social factors in discussing the kinds of values reflected in judicial statements and the ways in which judges resolve practical, everyday dilemmas in deciding cases. The enduring emphasis is on analysing appellate cases. Indeed, the sociology of law is more often taught in law schools by law academics (albeit with a strong interest in the social sciences and/or social science training) than in sociology departments. For many sociologists, law is derivative of broader (or more authentic) sociological concerns, for example social control and deviance, or is treated within other substantive areas such as labour relations, the welfare state and social policy, crime, bureaucratic organizations or contemporary family relations. Many sociological definitions of law stress its normative character and are concerned with the responses to behaviour that violates laws. Sociological discussions of law are often limited to discussions of the criminal law, its operation and administration.

Law and sociology are often presented as two distinct disciplines and bodies of knowledge. For example, Cotterrell – a socio-legal theorist – seeks to understand 'the nature and effects of confrontations between such different fields of knowledge and practice as those of law and sociology ... [that have] quite different historical origins or patterns of development, social and institutional contexts of existence, and social and political consequences' (Cotterrell, 1986: 9–10). Another commentator disagrees that the common law can be considered a social science because of the two disciplines' different epistemological approaches: the former relies on adjudication to discern 'facts' and on precedent to resolve present disputes, while the latter relies on 'positivity', the constitution of knowledge via empirical research and the deployment of statistical analyses (Murphy, 1991: 185–200).

Certainly, the development of law and sociology in western societies occurs within different institutions and bodies of knowledge (as professionally defined). However, they have very similar subject matters: both are concerned with social relationships, values, social regulation, obligations and expectations arising from particular social positions and roles, and the linkages between individuals and society. Almost any aspect of social life can be subject to legal regulation and judicial statements do have similarities with social theory (and often read like social theory). Nonetheless, the substance of law in western democratic societies primarily deals with the regulation of property relationships and the enunciation and protection of property rights. Sociology is more interested in a wider array of social relationships and investigates inequality and power at both structural and interpersonal levels. While jurists are concerned primarily with the activities of courts, especially the process of legal reasoning, sociologists are more interested in the interconnections between law and changing social institutions, political structures and economic conditions and the relationships between legal institutions and other forms of dispute resolution, social control or regulation. At a more individual or micro level, social researchers investigate how various actors – including lawyers, judges, social activists and people in everyday life – experience, use, interpret, negotiate and confront law, legal institutions and legal discourse (Silbey, 1991: 826–9; Travers, 1993).

Social change

Social change is a term sociologists use to describe usually large scale transformations, such as industrialization and the shift from rural agrarian, feudal or traditional societies to modern, industrial societies, the emergence of capitalism, democratization, and most recently globalization. These changes are associated primarily with economic conditions and market forces and have consequences for political, social and cultural activities. Indeed, the formative period of sociology as a distinct discipline was characterized by large-scale economic, political and social transformation. Key nineteenth century social theorists focused on social change at a macro level such as capitalism and its contradictions (Karl Marx), rationalization (Max Weber), and the increasing division of labour (Emile Durkheim) (Arjomand, 2004: 321). More specific theories of social change address the implications of overall, abstract changes for human social relations, the lives and experiences of individuals and their everyday social environments, school, work/employment, families, social control and so on (Hallinan, 1997). Especially during the twentieth century, governments often relied on the law as a route, or resource, to implement desired social change. In part this reflected aspirations for the welfare state and its social reform agenda, including the statutory implementation and bureaucratic administration of social programmes.

A distinction is often drawn between revolutionary social change and evolutionary social change. Revolutionary social change tends to derive from inequalities of various kinds and resulting conflicts which spawn political action, both within and beyond the recognized political institutions. Evolutionary change occurs 'naturally' as populations grow, and societies become more complex (Abercrombie et al., 2006: 351–2). A third kind of social change can be imposed from external sources, as in the case of colonization.

In thinking about societies and social change, an analytical distinction between structure and action is often made. Social structures are patterns of actions and behaviour that exist over and beyond the activities and purposes of individuals but in turn depend on individual action for their reproduction and continuation (Sewell, 1992: 3). The idea of structure suggests a fixed, observable, enduring entity, such as a whole society or part thereof, for example the legal system, or the system of inequality. Social structure constrains human activity limiting the scope for human agency, individual choice, responsibility, motivation or intention. This image of structure is most obvious in structural-functionalist accounts that conceptualise society or social organization as constituted by different parts undergirded by the logics of integration and stability. Any change seems to be the natural process of evolution and progress, often toward modern societies characterized by the replacement of tradition and custom by science and rationality (Etzioni, 1966). Either way, social change can bring about instability, conflict and dislocation (see Parsons, 1951).

Weber (1978) observed the relationship between structure and action as paradoxical. For Weber 'paradox is the defining characteristic of modern life; that is the *inevitable* consequence of all social action in modernity' (Symonds and Pudsey, 2008: 229, emphasis in original). Human action establishes and reproduces social structures which in turn confine, or even undermine, that action despite the intentions or motivations of actors. Organizational contexts and everyday routines can militate against the realisation of original goals or the purposes of the social structure. In an important early essay Robert Merton articulates 'the problem of the unanticipated consequences of purposive action' (1936: 894). Purposive action is conduct which involves motives and some degree of choice between various alternatives or competing options. For many reasons individuals cannot or do not foresee all the possible consequences – positive, neutral or negative – of their conduct and choices, and thus these are unanticipated.

One significant example of where unanticipated consequences often occur is bureaucratic organization. Putting aside cultural and social variation in the bureaucratic form, Weber's ideal type of bureaucracy is the quintessential example of legal-rational authority: it is bounded by rules, authority is hierarchical and it is oriented to the achievement of one or more identifiable goals, for example, welfare provision, education, justice, or profit. These overarching goals can become displaced from the everyday conduct and choices of employees, in turn limiting the ways that overall goals can be achieved, or redefining or undermining these (Merton, 1968: 249–60). Vaughan (1999) describes the 'dark side' of bureaucratic organizations which present possibilities for mistakes, misconduct and disaster with potentially adverse societal consequences. Her (1998) research shows that the National Aeronautic and Space Agency's (NASA) decision to launch the Challenger space shuttle followed a gradual increment of seemingly minor problems without major damage, which engineers defined as separate, local and within acceptable risk but which ultimately resulted in its explosion after takeoff in 1986.

The example of bureaucracy is significant for understandings of law and social change because the organizations established to implement legal change usually assume some or all of the elements of the bureaucratic form. A new statute may not be translated into the expected or desired social change because of the structures of implementation, especially if these involve a bureaucratic organization, which entails contextual or local practices, values, and viewpoints. An excellent example of this is recent research on hate crimes (discussed in Chapter 8 below). This phenomenon might be characterized as the gap between law on the books and law in action (Jenness and Grattet, 2005).

The notion of 'structuration' conveys a dynamic relationship between structure and agency (Giddens, 1976; Sewell, 1992). Social structures, constituted by rules and resources, constrain human agency but also provide opportunities or capacities for creativity, reinterpretation or innovation, which constitute structural change. Human agents are knowledgeable and competent, can mobilize resources (which can vary in accessibility), and are not viewed as over-determined by their location in the social structure. 'To be an agent means to be capable of exerting some degree of control over the social relations in which one is enmeshed, which in turn implies the ability to transform those social relations to some degree' (Sewell, 1992: 20).

Understanding law and social change will be complex. Broadly defined, as a set of shared or at least accepted rules governing social interaction, law is a social institution but the way in which law is organized or manifest in different societies varies. Considerable research in the sociology of law attends to legal institutions: the legal profession, police, courts, legislation, and judicial decisions. Many socio-legal studies focus on issues, such as guilty pleas, criminal courts, lawyering or legal services, employment, divorce and family law, within the bounds of nation states and then make comparisons across nation states. Until recently, the legal system was viewed as the primary repository of law and attention was paid to the demarcations between criminal and civil law, the operation of various dimensions of law on citizens, the organization of national courts, and the division of labour between legal personnel: police, the legal profession, the judiciary. Conceptually, legal processes have now been uncoupled from the legal institutions or organizations in which they are typically nested: police do not monopolize policing; governance is not synonymous with governments; law operates within and beyond the legal system; and legal norms and understandings pervade everyday life (Ewick and Silbey, 1998).

Social change and law

Nineteenth century social theorists described a central role for law in understandings of social change. Henry Maine (1888) described social change in terms of the move from status (inherited and prescribed) to contract (individual and voluntary, at least in theory and only available to some members of the society). For Durkheim the prevailing type of law is an indication of the type of society and changes in law signal the nature and type of social change. Weber's typology of law and legal thought implies evolutionary development and the extension of western rationality and Marx saw law as inevitability intertwined with capitalist economic relations and therefore an impediment to class struggle and revolutionary social change (see Chapter 2).

In the twentieth century, much sociology examined social change within sovereign nation states with clear territorial boundaries and law was viewed as an instrument or vehicle for the implementation of social and economic policy (Dror, 1968). The dominant conception of society was of a bounded system with clearly identifiable and separate subsystems: the legal system, the economic system, the cultural system, the industrial system, the nation state and the family (Beck and Lau, 2005: 527; Giddens, 1990: 64). The systematic study of social change from the mid-twentieth century onwards, particularly in the United States, was aided by the public availability of nationally representative longitudinal data sets collected by federal, state and private agencies (Hallinan, 1997: 3).

At least in the context of the US, and other states with independent judiciaries, a constitutional tradition and the rule of law, the state can be seen as 'fundamentally legal' (Skrentny, 2006: 214). Understanding the nation state requires an engagement with law and legal concepts, such as legality, which can enable and constrain state actions (2006: 213–4). In a discussion of the American state Skrentny shows that the relationship between law and the state varies over time and by issue. Sometimes there is no role at all for law and the courts. At other times, there can be a negative role of reducing progressive social options by limiting welfare benefits and safeguarding business/employer dominance through enforcing property rights in a way that spurs on economic development and large enterprises. Sometimes there is a positive role for law with the expansion of welfare rights in the 1960s and 1970s (2006: 218).

There is often a perception, either implicit or explicit, that social change is tantamount to social progress (Connell, 1997: 1519–21). Social movement activists lobby parliaments to enact new legislation and they initiate or support litigation in the quest to have particular judicial decisions overturned. Relying on law as a source of social change is not the sole province of either liberal, radical or conservative politics (Ginsburg, 1981: 541–7). Numerous commentators point out the limitations of a simplistic instrumental approach to legal and social change: the one does not necessarily nor easily translate into the other. However, as suggested above, just considering statutory change or decided cases may not simply translate into anticipated, practical changes.

Increasingly, the study of law and understandings of law and social change will go beyond national legal institutions and focus more on transnational law and legal institutions, which have expanded in size and number since World War II, and significantly in the past decade or so, especially in the wake of the September 11 (2001) attacks in the United States. Some commentators suggest that the sovereign nation state is losing its relevance and regulatory capacity in a global context where a raft of multinational conventions and bilateral agreements bind nation states, where non-state transnational entities such as the International Monetary Fund or the World Bank influences government decisions and domestic policies, and the voluminous movement of capital, commodities and people across national borders increases interdependence especially economic: 'The major factor contributing to the denationalization of law would be the declining role of the state in the world' (Glenn, 2003: 843). Others conclude that: 'Globalization certainly poses new problems for states, but it also strengthens the world-cultural principle that nation-states are the primary actors charged with identifying and managing those problems on behalf of their societies. Expansion of the authority and responsibilities of states creates unwieldy and fragmented structures, perhaps, but not weakness' (Meyer et al., 1997: 157). The relationships between nation states, globalization and law are discussed further in Chapter 3.

This book adopts a very wide conception of law; it does not restrict its attentions to the activities of the courts or to legal doctrine. It examines various sociological and socio-legal theories of law; considers the legal profession, which in many ways is the gatekeeper to the legal system, with practitioners having considerable leeway and influence in determining legal outcomes; looks at dispute processing and the role of legal institutions and actors; social control, including the operation of the criminal justice system; and social movement activism, especially regarding women and current debates about human rights and their legal recognition. At the same time, the discussion pays attention to conventional sociological concerns, for example the theories of Durkheim, Weber and Marx and their comments on the role of law and legal institutions. The book addresses:

(a) the social conditions under which laws emerge and change;
(b) the extent to which law can be a resource to implement social change;
(c) the kinds of values or worldviews that laws incorporate; and
(d) the ways in which laws shape social institutions and practices and vice versa.

While Durkheim, Marx and particularly Weber theorized the role of law in society and its interconnections with other institutions, it was not until the 1960s that a distinct subdiscipline on the sociology of law emerged (Schwartz, 1965: 1). Contemporary research on law in society is multidisciplinary, receiving input from sociologists, political scientists, anthropologists, philosophers, legal scholars and others. Often analyses of law are equated with the discussion of familiar and culturally specific legal institutions, for example the courts and tribunals, judges, the jury system, legislation, the police, the legal profession and prisons. Anthropologists point out that to restrict the discussion of law to familiar legal institutions results in ignoring other forms of law and socio-legal arrangements. In his ethnography of the Trobriand Islands (north-east of New Guinea), Malinowski (1961) adopted wide conceptions of law and legal forces as binding, reciprocal obligations and suggested that law and legal phenomena are not located in special, separate enactments, administration or enforcement mechanisms. He observed: 'Law represents rather an aspect of their tribal life, one side of their structure, than any independent, self-contained social arrangements. ... Law is the specific result of the configuration of obligations, which makes it impossible for the native to shirk his [sic] responsibility without suffering for it in the future' (Malinowski, 1961: 59).

Socio-legal research is inevitably shaped by the kind of legal system being studied. In western capitalist societies, and their former (and present) colonies, two predominant kinds of legal system exist: common or case law and civil[1] or code law systems. Along with cricket and the railways, the common law is a legacy of British imperialism, although its history is longer than that of colonialism. At its heart, the common law is constituted by previous decided cases. Legal reasoning is based on precedent and courts are structured hierarchically. Anglo-American legal systems are adversarial. at its simplest, adversarialism means that two opponents/parties present their cases; in Criminal law it is the prosecution versus the defendant(s) and in civil cases it is a complainant versus the respondent. The truth (that is, the facts) is supposed to emerge from the examination and cross-examination of witnesses by defence and prosecution lawyers and any other evidence adduced. Of course, the facts of a case are not raw data but rather those items that have been selected and classified in terms of legal categories (Berman, 1968: 198; Geertz, 1983). The judge adjudicates, that is, acts as a neutral arbiter who applies the appropriate legal rule to the facts as they emerge, or are divined by a jury. The judge decides in favour of one party, or one side, with little scope for compromise: the criminal defendant is convicted or acquitted; the respondent is judged to be negligent or in breach of contract and ordered to pay the plaintiff damages, or is found not liable.

In the countries of continental Europe and their former colonies, the legal systems are more codified and there is not the same reliance on a prior judicial decision to determine outcomes. Most of the laws are in a more or less permanent, organized and written form. The two major acts of codification of modern times are the French civil code *(Code Napoléon)* of 1804 and the German civil code *(Buergerliches Gesetzbuch)* of 1900. The former has provided the basis for the legal systems of countries in the Middle East, Africa and Latin America, while the latter has influenced the Japanese civil code and the pre-communist Chinese legal regime (McWhinney, 1968: 214). These systems are sometimes termed inquisitorial, as the judge has more scope to question the adversarial parties directly and may even have a role in the investigation of crime.

Legal theory

Before considering sociological discussions of law, the following section outlines various strands of legal thought that are often discussed by jurists and legal theorists.[2] Much jurisprudence is primarily concerned with the nature of legal reasoning and specifying the relationships between judicial decision making and the law (Davies, 2008: 37–49). Legal theory generally addresses abstract questions about the nature of laws and legal systems and the relationship of law to justice and morality. Legal change is seen as deriving from the judicial interpretation of new legislation and the logical application to new circumstances of legal rules formulated in prior decided cases, that is, via legal reasoning.

In common-law countries, legal reasoning is often equated with the intellectual processes whereby judges (especially those in higher courts) reach conclusions in deciding cases (Berman, 1968: 197; Fuller, 1978: 363–81). In this context, legal change is an incremental, continuous process in which small changes to the law arising from extended judicial interpretation contribute to the law's evolution (Davies, 2008: 56–64). In more codified systems, legal reasoning is usually identified with the processes by which the rationality and consistency of legal doctrines are maintained.

Formally, legal reasoning strives for a consistency that is achievable only if similar cases are decided in a similar way resulting in similar outcomes. As Davies notes: 'Common law theory is a way of thinking which rests on the idea that there is something inherently *necessary* and right about the process of legal reasoning which emerges in decided cases' (Davies, 2008: 49, emphasis in original). Legal reasoning differs from ordinary or natural reasoning processes and can only be acquired through a legal education. The law, then, is not knowable by those without a thorough legal education and training in legal reasoning, general legal concepts and legal logic (Dietrich, 2005; Gordley, 1984).

The most pervasive form of legal logic is that of analogy, which entails the comparison of similar and dissimilar examples. The common-law tradition stresses precedent, so that lower courts view themselves as inextricably bound by the decisions of courts superior to them in the judicial hierarchy (McHugh, 1988a: 118). Reasoning by analogy involves comparing the facts of different cases, identifying the principle or rule underlying the decision in a prior (relevant) case – that is, the *ratio decidendi* (the reason for deciding) – and applying this to the new facts. Alternatively, the facts of a case are distinguished so that the same legal principle does not apply. Reasoning by analogy uses inductive rather than deductive reasoning from legal rules; the idea is that when the facts are determined, then the process of logical reasoning produces the correct outcome. The reasons for the decision precede the decision. As cases are distinguished on their facts, changes are incremental and evolutionary; the common law develops as judges apply existing rules to new, but analogous, situations (Berman, 1968: 197–200; Bourdieu, 1987: 822–3; McHugh, 1988b: 15–18; McWhinney, 1968: 212–3).

Rather than being a mechanical, value-free process, legal reasoning involves interpretation and assessment; *ratios decidendi* are often ambiguous, amorphous and contradictory, and must be identified or constructed. Reasoning by analogy involves elasticity: judges can interpret precedents expansively or narrowly in order to achieve a particular outcome. This is especially true given the tendency of judges to provide individual reasons for their decisions, so that even though the majority of a final appellate court may reach the same decision, their reasons can be different. Thus the *ratio decidendi* may follow the decision and rationalize a particular outcome. Identifying the facts and discerning the legal rules to reach the 'correct' legal outcome often entail value judgements, policy decisions and the manipulation of arguments that are not informed by the system of legal rules. Legal reasoning is but one type of argumentative technique (Kennedy, 1990: 43–5). Nevertheless, the lower courts may have little discretion to deviate from established rules without risking an appeal process overturning their decisions. The opportunity for judicial law making or activism increases as cases proceed along the judicial hierarchy (McHugh, 1988a: 118). As Bourdieu suggests: 'judicial decisions can be distinguished from naked exercises of power only to the extent that they can be presented as the necessary result of a principled interpretation of unanimously accepted texts' (1987: 818).

A perennial question among judges and legal theorists is whether judges make or find the law (McHugh, 1988b: 15). This is an unanswerable question: because of the equation between common law and judges there is no extra-judicial way of discerning the common law. Whether judges (and others) view judicial decision making as making or finding the law, the law is what judges say it is, until a judge in a higher court disagrees with (and overrules) an earlier decision. The view that judges declare and apply the law with little scope for judicial activism or law making is known as positivism or legal formalism.

Positivism or legal formalism

Legal positivists view the law as a formal, logical system of legal rules. Positivism involves an adherence to legalism, that is, the process of subjecting human behaviour to the governance of rules. Positivism has been the predominant philosophy of law since the nineteenth century. Austin, who devised one of the first systematic theories of legal positivism, defined law as the command of a sovereign and wrote: 'Considered as a whole, and as implicated or connected with one another, the positive laws and rules of a particular community, are a system or body of law' (Lloyd and Freeman, 1985: 231). Austin sought to show what the law really is, as opposed to moral or natural-law notions of what law ought to be. This reflects a quest for law to be scientific and impermeable to personal values or individual manipulation.

For the positivist, law is a discrete or autonomous system of logically consistent concepts and principles that have no relevant characteristics or functions apart from their possible validity or invalidity within the system. In determining whether a statute is law, judges must determine whether it is valid, that is, whether the legislative process conformed with procedural and substantive rules. The process of judicial decision making, or adjudication, involves finding, declaring and applying the correct legal rule or principle to the facts of a particular case, regardless of the consequences. Issues of economic inequality, social reform or moral values are outside judicial competence and are issues for the legislature. Once laws are passed, questions of their justness are beyond the scope of law but lie in the realm of philosophy, religion or politics. A law does not cease to be law because it is perceived by some as unjust or because it conflicts with some values, and the converse – the assertion that a rule is morally appropriate – does not render it a legal rule (Hart, 1980: 51; Lloyd and Freeman, 1985: 64). In this context, legal theory is concerned overwhelmingly with doctrinal analysis and the force of law is viewed as deriving from such textual sources as statutes, precedents or constitutions (McHugh, 1988b: 25). Hart (1961) analyses the law in terms of primary rules, which he terms rules of obligation, and secondary rules, which are the rules about rules, such as rules of recognition and adjudication. Thus, he makes a distinction between duty-imposing and power-conferring rules. He also acknowledges that occasionally there will be situations where there is no clear or settled rule – which he terms 'a penumbra of uncertainty' – where the outcome cannot be the result of deductive reasoning, but where judges have some discretion (Hart, 1980: 55). In contrast, Ronald Dworkin argues that the law is a 'seamless web' of principles that, despite the absence of an explicit legal principle on an issue, ensures that there is a right way of deciding a case and that constrains judicial discretion and creativity (Davies, 2008: 115–19; Lloyd and Freeman, 1985: 411–3, 1121–6).

Hans Kelsen proposed a 'pure theory of law', which he considered to be a science and not a politics of law (Stewart, 1990: 274). He wanted to describe what the law is rather than what it ought to be. For Kelsen, the multiplicity of legal norms constitutes a system when the validity of each norm can be traced to its final source, which he termed the *Grundnorm*. This basic norm provides the overall rationale for and unity of the legal system. The legal system is a hierarchy of norms, with legal acts and rules traceable to norms at still higher and more abstract levels and the *Grundnorm* providing the major premise of the entire system. The validity of any law is determined solely through a process of authorization to higher norms and ultimately to the basic norm. Legal norms are not valid by virtue of their content; a norm becomes a legal norm only because it has been constituted in a particular fashion. The highest point of a legal order is the constitution, then general norms are established by legislation that determines legal organizations and procedure (Stewart, 1990: 285–8).

Kelsen's approach has been criticized because of its rigidity and ambiguity surrounding the nature and identity of the basic norm (Lloyd and Freeman, 1985: 330–6; Stewart, 1990: 274, 295–7). More generally, positivism has come under scrutiny because the legal system can never be contained fully within such a closed logical structure. Positivism tends to ignore the human dimensions of the legal process, whereby interpretation inevitably entails value commitments with individual judicial biases and broader social factors affecting decision making. From a positivist viewpoint, there is little opportunity for judicial activism or scope for the common law to be a source of transformative social change. While there has been a rejection of rigid formalism, formalistic assumptions remain in some sociological and contemporary theories or conceptualizations of law, particularly in systems theory (see for example Luhmann, 1992).

Legal realism

Legal realism is often counterpoised to positivism because of realists' attack on the certainty of legal rules and rejection of any proposition that judicial decision making is free of values and politics. Realists argue that there is a basic legal myth, namely, that legal rules are certain and that their application to specific cases is essentially a rational, mechanical task to be performed by the courts. Whereas the conventional view of the adjudicative process is that judges apply rules to the facts of a case in order to reach a decision, in reality the decision is the outcome of a wholly unpredictable interaction between the stimuli bearing on the judge at the time and the judge's personality. Far more important than legal rules or precedents is the intuitive flash of understanding or hunch that may inspire and motivate a judge to reach a particular decision (Duxbury, 1991: 181–4). Legal realists will assert, with various degrees of emphasis, that judges make rather than find the law; judicial decision making is not the rational application of pre-existing rules but the rationalization of decisions by assertions of legality.

The central concern of legal realists is with law in action rather than law on the books. Holmes formulates the concept of law as: 'The prophecies of what the courts will do in fact, and nothing more pretentious [for example a system of reason], are what I mean by the law' (Holmes, 1897: 460–1). Since the law is always human, it cannot be absolute, determinate or omnipotent. It is indistinguishable from human action – that is, judicial behaviour – and has no existence beyond it. Legal realism has been more developed in the US, where courts traditionally assume a greater role in public policy formulation and social change than is the case in the UK or Australia (Brigham, 1996: 56–61; Brigham and Harrington, 1989: 41–2; Lloyd and Freeman, 1985: 682; Tunc, 1984: 168–70). This perspective reached its zenith in the 1920s and 1930s and was revived during the 1980s with the emergence of the Critical Legal Studies movement, which incorporates many realist assumptions (see Chapter 3).

Realists criticized the case method of legal education that was introduced into American law schools in the 1870s and is now generally adopted as the basic form of legal training in many universities. The case method requires the legal scholar to demonstrate how reported decisions can be explained in terms of fundamental principles implicit in the common law. Realists argued that this approach deals with law on the books rather than with the everyday, irrational workings of courts and legal practices. They advocated greater practical training for lawyers who should experience legal practice in law offices before completing their formal education (Duxbury, 1991: 177, 186–8).

A central problem with the realist approach is relativism, an issue that became particularly salient during the rise of totalitarianism in Europe during the 1930s and 1940s. If there is no independent or external means of evaluating law, outside what judges say it is, then it is impossible to evaluate the kinds of decisions that judges make that support totalitarian regimes. Legal realists rejected the charge of relativism and amoralism and viewed the flexibility in law as providing opportunities for courts to be engaged in progressive social reform. Many legal realists played an active part in developing and advancing President Roosevelt's programme of social engineering and expanding the welfare state in the New Deal in America during the 1930s.

Legal realists tend to adopt an asocial and behaviourist view of courts. Their primary concern with the behaviour of judges downplays questions about the origin of judicial power and the relationship between the legal profession and the judiciary, as well as the relationships between political and economic institutions and the legal system (Brigham and Harrington, 1989: 42–6). Realists also tend to discount the limitations on judicial activity. Judges do not operate in a vacuum guided only by their personal predilections, but are constrained by statutes, procedural rules, appellate cases, and the chance that their decisions will be appealed and overturned by a higher court. Certainly, within these constraints judges do experience latitude in interpreting the meaning of statutes and prior binding judicial decisions. Ironically, the focus on judicial behaviour encourages psychological research and psychology aspires to values of scientism and positivism, perhaps even more so than do judges.

Natural law

Natural-law theories assume the existence of certain fundamental moral and universal principles that establish absolute standards of justice that can be discovered by human reason (Lloyd and Freeman, 1985: 93–9). Statutes and judicial decisions are evaluated in terms of higher (secular or religious) value commitments regarding justice, fairness, rights and humanity. Versions of natural-law theory have existed since ancient Greece and were developed in Roman Catholicism. Scholastic philosophy as expounded by St Thomas Aquinas was highly rationalistic, as it relied heavily on truth as elicited by logic and deductive reasoning but, at the same time, its premises were not chosen on rational grounds but were instead given by the beliefs of Christian ideology (Lloyd and Freeman, 1985: 80).

For natural-law theorists, when substantive laws deviate from higher principles they are unjust laws and, *ipso facto,* not legally binding. This poses a dilemma regarding potential conflicts between enacted law and the dictates of natural law. It raises the question of how citizens should act when their governments impose legal obligations that are contrary to natural law. The cruelty and inhumanity of Nazi policies and actions during World War II brought about a renewed interest in natural law. The atrocities perpetrated by the Nazis highlighted the dangers of extreme relativism and the separation of law from morality or values, as many of these actions had been carried out according to German laws. Some contemporary secular discussions of universal human rights provide current examples of natural-law theory (see Chapter 8).

A few sociologists have attempted to offer an elaboration of natural law and avoid the positivist disavowal of values. Selznick identifies some secular natural-law principles, especially respect for others as human beings, and suggests that the chief tenet of natural law is that arbitrary will is not legally final. He argues that natural-law inquiry presumes a set of ideals or values, including reason, legalism or the rule of law, and the considerable sociological and anthropological research identifies and analyses norms and the systems of norms, thus revealing their complementarity (Selznick, 1982: 18). It is impossible in describing any legal system to avoid identifying values to be realized, that is, ideals that imply natural law. Selznick suggests the importance of sociology in providing knowledge regarding generalizations about human nature that are universal in social organization and pervasive in human values, despite the effects of social environment and the diversity of cultures. He lists such motivating forces as the search for respect, including self-respect, for affection, and for a cessation of anxiety, and the enlargement of social insight and understanding, reason and aesthetic creativity (Selznick, 1982: 25). He then advances the proposition that: 'Legal norms or principles are "natural law" to the extent that they are *based upon* scientific generalizations, *grounded in* warranted assertions about men [*sic*], about groups, about the effects of law itself' (Selznick, 1982: 32, emphasis in original). In other words, sociologists are able to identify dominant human values, which he asserts relate to a notion of human dignity, and it is these values that must inform the legal order. On this assessment, arguably all legal systems would be contrary to natural law, especially as experienced by nonproperty owners, women, ethnic minorities and other marginalized segments of the population.

More recently, Turner has proposed a minimalist theory of rights from a foundational account of human embodiment. He suggests a universal requirement for protective rights given the frailty of the human body and the precariousness of social institutions. A moral proposal that human beings have a claim to an irreducible dignity *qua* humans underlies his argument. However, he specifies that the protective rights for which he argues are not strictly human rights but are more appropriately called natural rights, as distinct from individual rights granted by national governments (Turner, 1993: 4–5)

Even though natural law and positivism are contrasted as polar opposites, it is not true that the former eschews legalism or rationality. Fuller, in departing from other natural-law traditions, goes so far as to argue that the moral basis of modern natural-law theory is the enterprise of subjecting human conduct to the governance of rules, which is a formalist contention (Kaye, 1987: 314; Lloyd and Freeman, 1985: 129–33). Natural-law theories leave unanswered questions about determining the nature of humanity, especially in light of the range of human sentiments that are possible. There are difficulties in accepting the assertion of universal moral principles or conceptions of human rights, especially when these are being promulgated only by western societies.

Conclusion

While 'law' or 'the law' is often a taken-for-granted concept, the above discussion highlights the complexities of law. The term 'law' can include legal doctrine, types of norms, such institutions and actors as courts, lawyers, judges, clients and citizens, and the activities and values of groups or individuals, including social movements, that espouse a legal ideology and are oriented to the legal system as a set of resources to effect social change or settle disputes. When contemplating the role of law in social change, these numerous dimensions of law must be taken into account.

The purpose of this book is to address some of these dimensions. It does so by discussing various sociological conceptions and theoretical approaches to law. Chapter 2 examines the various approaches to and comments about law made by Durkheim, Weber and Marx.

Notes

1. The term civil law is also used in common-law countries to describe laws regulating conflicts between persons (individual and corporate), for example tort, contract, property, constitutional, administrative and family law, as distinct from criminal law where the conflict, in legal terms, is between a person and the state.

2. For an excellent discussion of legal theory see Davies (2008).

2 Law in Classical Social Theory

The formative sociological theorists were all concerned with social change and in varying degrees with the ways in which law is implicated as both a product and a catalyst of change. As many stressed the primacy of economic changes and market relations, a focus for their discussions was the extent to which law (and other social institutions) is autonomous from economic forces. Durkheim's discussion of law occurs within his analysis of social differentiation and complexity; Weber seeks to identify the relationship between law and rationality; and Marx identifies connections between capitalism and law.

Law and the division of labour: Durkheim

Durkheim's interest in law is secondary to his overriding concern with social solidarity and the scientific study of society. He seeks to analyse law in a general way in order to reveal principles of social organization and collective thinking. Durkheim tends to conceptualize law as derivative from and expressive of a society's morality (Lukes and Scull, 1983: 1–4; also see Smith, 2008a). For Durkheim, social solidarity is the social phenomenon binding individuals together to create a society that exists *sui generis*. Social solidarity has a life of its own and is more than the sum of its constitutive parts. Social life is constituted by social facts, the characteristics of which are external to the individual, they exercise constraints on people and provide sanctions for nonconformity, and they are independent of the actions of particular individuals but exist throughout the social group (Lukes, 1975: 8–15). The most important social facts are 'collective representations' and Durkheim comments:

> While one might perhaps contest the statement that all social facts without exception impose themselves from without upon the individual, the doubt does not seem possible as regards religious beliefs and practices, the rules of morality and the innumerable precepts of law – that is to say all the most characteristic manifestations of collective life. All are expressly obligatory, and this obligation is the proof that these ways of acting and thinking are not the work of the individual but come from a moral power above him [*sic*]. (Durkheim, 1974: 25)

Even though social life is experienced as an objective reality, it is not directly amenable to empirical observation and scientific study. This presents a significant problem for Durkheim's aspirations for a positivistic sociology. He observes that in science we can know causes only through the effects that they produce and, in order to determine causes precisely, the scientific method selects only those results that are the most objective and the most quantifiable. Durkheim asks: 'Why should social solidarity prove an exception?' (1984: 26–7). He proposes that solidarity is a social fact that can only be known thoroughly through its social effects and can be measured. Durkheim says:

> [S]ocial solidarity is a wholly moral phenomenon which by itself is not amenable to exact observation and especially not to measurement. To arrive at this classification, as well as this comparison, we must therefore substitute for this internal datum, which escapes us, an external one which symbolizes it, and then study the former through the latter. That visible symbol is the law. (Durkheim, 1984: 24)

Durkheim's interest in the evolution of societies and the implications of the increasing division of labour for social solidarity means that he is concerned to identify and classify different types of social solidarity. Where the society or social type is relatively small, there is only a rudimentary division of labour, members are relatively homogeneous in needs and interests, the social structure is relatively simple and there is a dominating collective consciousness, mechanical solidarity prevails. On the other side, where the society has a relatively large population, a complex division of labour causing interdependence between the specialized component parts, greater differences between individuals and a relatively weak collective consciousness, organic solidarity dominates. The method is clear and simple: in order to discern the type of solidarity, it is necessary to distinguish and examine the types of law, specifically: 'Since law reproduces the main forms of social solidarity, we have only to classify the different types of law in order to be able to investigate which species of social solidarity correspond to them' (Durkheim, 1984: 28).

The next methodological question is how to classify and measure different types of law. Durkheim defines legal precepts as rules of behaviour to which sanctions apply. He then makes a bold assumption and claims that 'it is clear that the sanctions change according to the degree of seriousness in which the precepts are held, the place they occupy in the public consciousness, and the role they play in society' (1984: 28). Different legal rules are then measured according to their sanctions, which are of two main types: repressive and restitutive.

Repressive sanctions entail the imposition of suffering or disadvantage on the perpetrator of a crime. The purpose of the sanction is to deprive offenders of their life, fortune, honour, liberty or other possessions. Repressive sanctions are usually contained in the criminal or penal law. An offence against an individual offends the entire society and the criminal law reflects this. Penal law is an expression of the shared outrage against acts that offend the collective morality and, where mechanical solidarity prevails, there is only a collective morality. Repressive law corresponds to what is at the heart and centre of the collective consciousness, indeed: 'an act is criminal when it offends the strong, well-defined states of the collective consciousness' (Durkheim, 1984: 39). An act does not offend the common consciousness because it is criminal but the converse: the act is a crime because it is condemned. Durkheim observes: 'Crime is not only injury done to interests which may be serious; it is also an offence against an authority which is in some way transcendent' (1984: 43). Ironically, crime serves to reinforce and strengthen the collective consciousness. The common expression of anger enhances social solidarity by reaffirming agreement on social norms. In primitive societies law is wholly penal or repressive in character; it is the people assembled together who mete out justice.

Restitutive sanctions aim to restore the *status quo ante,* they do not necessarily imply any suffering on the part of the offender, who may be an individual or corporate citizen. The aim of the sanctions is to reestablish relationships and restore the previous state of affairs that have been disturbed through the actions or inaction of one of the parties to the relationship. Rules with restitutive sanctions are not established directly between the individual and the society but between limited and particular sectors of society, for example between and among individuals, associations, companies or governments, which they will link together. Examples of laws with restitutive sanctions include civil law, tort, commercial law, and contract, as well as laws that concern personal status, for example family law, administrative and constitutional law. Violation of these relationships and the obligations thereby established generally does not offend the entire collective consciousness, instead it inconveniences or harms only the plaintiff or complainant. In civil law cases the judge awards damages or orders a specific performance to complete the requirements of the obligation; the sanctions are neither penal nor expiatory. The losing plaintiff is not disgraced nor is their honour impugned. While repressive law tends to stay diffused throughout society, restitutory law sets up for itself ever more specialized bodies, for example consular courts and industrial and administrative tribunals. The institutions of the civil law are more specialized than those of the criminal law.

Restitutive law nevertheless remains connected, albeit weakly, to the *conscience collective:* it does not just involve private actors. While restitutive law does not intervene by itself and of its own volition but must be initiated by one or more of the parties concerned, it is society that lays down the law through the body representing it. Society is not absent: if a contract has a binding force it is society that confers that force. 'Every contract therefore presumes that, behind the parties binding each other, society is there, quite ready to intervene and enforce respect for undertakings entered into' (Durkheim, 1984: 71). However, contract law does not enforce all the obligations between private parties, only those that conform to the rules of law, that is, obligatory force only attaches to those contracts that themselves have a social value. In the law of contract agreements can be null and void if they contravene the criminal law, entail coercion or conflict with public policy.

The reliance on restitutive laws to regulate many and various types of social relationship indicates organic solidarity: law becomes a way of coordinating the differentiated parts of the society and integrating their diverse needs, interests and expectations. As societies expand, the collective consciousness must transcend all local diversities and become more abstract, thereby leaving more scope for individual variations. As a result, transgressing restitutive laws does not evoke the same strong sentiments as violating repressive laws. The evolution of societies from those characterized by mechanical solidarity to those where organic solidarity dominates is indicated by a drift towards more and more restitutive law, while repressive law regulates a smaller quantity of offences and range of relationships.

Durkheim's tight definitional alignment of types of law with types of sanctions is difficult to maintain in practice. The distinctions between criminal and civil law are not necessarily clear. Some kinds of behaviour may be subject to both kinds of laws/sanctions simultaneously. For example, a medical practitioner who causes the death of a patient may be sued in the civil courts for breach of duty and negligence as well as be subject to criminal proceedings for manslaughter or murder. Secondly, some civil laws have repressive and even penal sanctions, for example corporate law may provide for prison sentences for company directors who lie to shareholders; and courts can specify that some orders for damages are punitive, not just aimed at restoring the status quo. Thirdly, civil sanctions are increasingly being used to achieve criminal-law aims, especially crime prevention in some jurisdictions (Cheh, 1991; Green, 1996; Roach Anleu, 1998).

Durkheim anticipates some of these complications when he examines not only the effects of the division of labour on legal patterns but also the growth of governmental power, which he now regards as autonomous from the division of labour. He attempts to articulate general tendencies and suggests that throughout history punishment has passed through two kinds of changes: quantitative and qualitative. He formulates the law of quantitative change as: 'The intensity of punishment is the greater the more closely societies approximate to a less developed type – and the more the central power assumes an absolute character' (Durkheim, 1973: 285). Durkheim qualifies this by saying that a complete absence of limitations on governmental power does not exist empirically. Traditions, religious beliefs and resistance on the part of subordinate institutions and individuals place constraints on governmental power; however, they are not legally (either in written or customary law) binding on the government.

The degree to which a government possesses an absolutist character is not linked to any particular social type. Absolutist governments can be found in a very simple, primitive society or in an extremely complex society. This is why Durkheim seeks to distinguish the two causes of the evolution of punishment: the nature of the social type and of the governmental organ. Accordingly, the movement from a primitive type of society to other, more advanced types may not entail a decline in punishment (as might be anticipated following Durkheim's earlier references to the division of labour), because the type of government counterbalances the effects of social organization. With the advent of the Roman Empire governmental power tended to become absolute, the penal law became more severe and the number of capital crimes grew. During feudal times punishment was much milder than in earlier types of society, until the fourteenth century, which marks the increasing consolidation of monarchical power. Durkheim says that 'the apogée of the absolute monarchy coincides with the period of the greatest repression'; during the seventeenth century the galley was introduced, countless corporal punishments emerged, and the number of capital crimes increased because the crimes of *lèse majesté* expanded (1973: 293). Historical research in England documents the enormous expansion of capital crimes during the eighteenth century (Hay, 1975: 18–26; Thompson, 1975: 190–218). Reforms in the late eighteenth and early nineteenth centuries introduced greater leniency into the penal system, suppressed all mutilations, decreased the number of capital crimes and gave the criminal courts more discretion and autonomy from the government.

Durkheim specifies the law of qualitative change as follows: 'Deprivations of liberty, and of liberty alone, varying in time according to the seriousness of the crime, tend to become more and more the normal means of social control' (1973: 294). Punishments become less severe with the move from a primitive to an advanced society. Primitive societies almost completely lack prisons and, where these exist, they are not punishments, but forms of pre-trial detention for those accused of crimes. Durkheim explains this absence in terms of a lack of need. In relatively underdeveloped societies, responsibilities are collective so that when a crime occurs it is not only the guilty party who pays the penalty or reparation, it is also the clan or kin group. If the perpetrator disappears, others from the kin group or clan remain. It is not until the late eighteenth century that imprisonment – that is, a deprivation of liberty that can vary in length according to the seriousness of the offence – became the basis of the system of control and the use of capital punishment declined. Governmental/political power became more centralized, elementary groups lost their identity, and responsibility became individual (Durkheim, 1973: 295–9; also see Foucault, 1979; Smith, 2008b). For Durkheim, this development did not emanate from greater humanity or altruism but 'it is in the evolution of crime that one must seek the cause determining the evolution of punishment' (1973: 300).

Durkheim identifies two forms of criminality: religious criminality, which is directed against collective things, for example offences against public authority and its representatives, mores, traditions or religion; and human criminality, which only injures the individual, including theft, violence and fraud. The penal law of primitive societies consists almost exclusively of crimes of the first type; but as evolution advances religious forms of criminality diminish, while outrages against the person increase. The two kinds of criminality differ because the collective sentiments they offend are different, thus the types of repression cannot be the same. Offences of the first type are more odious because they offend a divine power exterior and superior to humanity. In the second type, as there is not the same social distance between the offender and the victim, the moral scandal that the criminal act constitutes is less severe and consequently does not call for such violent repression: both the perpetrator and the victim are citizens with associated individual rights. In contemporary times, crimes against the person constitute the principal crimes and offences against collective things lose more and more of the religiosity that had formerly marked them. So crimes directed against these collectivities – for example, the family and the state – partake of the same characteristics as those that directly injure individuals and punishments become milder. 'The list of acts which are defined as crimes of this type will grow, and their criminal character will be accentuated. Frauds and injustices, which yesterday left the public conscience almost indifferent, arouse it today, and this sensitivity will only become more acute with time' (Durkheim, 1973: 307).

In a later essay, Durkheim offers some thoughts on juridification. 'Each day the involvement of law in the sphere of private interests becomes greater. ... Superior animals have a nervous system more complicated than that of the lower animals; similarly, in so far as societies grow and become more complicated, their conditions of existence become more numerous and complicated, and this is why our legal codes grow in front of our eyes' (Durkheim, 1986: 350). On the one hand, it seems that the strictly individual or personal sphere of life will continue to diminish but, as with progress, the increasing separation of human personality from the physical or social environment creates more liberty at the same time as increasing social obligations.

Problems

Numerous problems exist with Durkheim's exposition of law and its connections with social structure. The following points identify some of the main issues.

First, Durkheim's rendition of legal and social change is too simple and neat to properly reflect social reality. One consequence of this is that Durkheim's conception of law remains very undeveloped. While his view of laws and sanctions tends to conceptualize differences in terms of dichotomies, with the understanding that intermediary types emerge during the process of evolution, there is very little articulation of what these intervening types look like. Durkheim devotes little attention to the institutional structure of law: the organization and actions of those who interpret, formulate, make, apply or use the law. The organization and interrelations between police departments, legislatures, corrections, the legal profession, organizational pressures and career aspirations, as well as legal culture and ideology, do not figure in Durkheim's primary concerns. Often the aims and practices of these organizations and actors are in continual conflict; they are not integrated and the importance of negotiation and the processing of cases demonstrates how fluid, inconsistent and contradictory law can be. Only in 'Two laws of penal evolution' does Durkheim begin to examine the independent role of political action and political structures, and thereby acknowledge the state as separate from the collective conscience (Durkheim, 1973: 286–9).

Secondly, in Durkheim's scheme, as law is an indicator of social solidarity, there is little scope for investigating conflicts or the discontinuity between them. Such a situation is an aberration, exceptional and pathological for Durkheim. He recognizes that customs might be out of step with the law, they might modify the law in practice or be an antidote to rigid formalism, but assures us that normally customs are not opposed to law (Durkheim, 1984: 25–7). This stance, then, is not very helpful in analysing colonial legal regimes and the imposition of western European law on indigenous normative systems. He pays little attention to the possibility of plural legal systems that can coexist and even cooperate. Durkheim's overcommitment to a unilinear, evolutionary theory of legal and social change closes off opportunities to theorize alternative models of development and to articulate the various relationships between law and morality (Jones, 1981: 1014).

Thirdly, Durkheim emphasized the external, constraining and controlling aspects of law, thereby precluding a systematic inquiry into its positive or enabling aspects as a set of procedural rules permitting individuals and groups to act in certain ways. Nevertheless, he recognized the importance of regulatory law in highly differentiated societies as a mechanism for coordinating different segments of society.

Fourthly, little evidence supports Durkheim's claims that repressive sanctions prevail in primitive societies and that as societies evolve the dominant type of sanction becomes restitutive. Critics identify Durkheim's empirical errors as stemming from his lack of anthropological data, his incorrect treatment of the material from ancient societies and an undue emphasis on the religious nature of early law (Barnes, 1966; Faris, 1934; Sheleff, 1975).

Anthropological studies point to the predominance of restitutive laws and sanctions in pre-industrial societies and show that the management of crime does not necessarily involve the collectivity and expression of penal sanctions (Merton, 1934: 324). Diamond indicates that in the early stages of development repressive law is restricted to a very few serious offences and early law involves a regulated or part-regulated system of private vengeance or feuding. The rise of repressive law parallels the emergence of economic class divisions and state formation (Diamond, 1951). On the basis of a cross-cultural survey of 51 societies, Schwartz and Miller tentatively conclude that their findings contradict Durkheim's major thesis that penal law predominates in simple societies. They found that restitutive sanctions – mediation and damages – which Durkheim believed to be associated with an increasing division of labour, are found in many societies that lack even a rudimentary specialization (Schwartz and Miller, 1964). The research suggests that the division of labour is a necessary condition for punishment but not for mediation (Schwartz, 1974). They conclude that an evolutionary sequence occurs in the development of legal institutions, but the direction seems to be the reverse of that which Durkheim predicted. Similarly, an examination of punishment in 48 societies finds that the severity of punishment does not decrease as societies become more concentrated and complex; rather, greater punitiveness is associated with higher levels of structural differentiation (Spitzer, 1975a: 903).

Following Sir Henry Maine's argument in *On Ancient Law* that law progresses from status to contract (Lloyd and Freeman, 1985: 895–7), Durkheim argued that 'the prominence given to penal law would be the greater the more ancient it was' (Durkheim, 1984: 97). In defining the area of the criminal law, Maine uses the criterion of harm caused to another, which also incorporates the area of tort law. Maine indicated that Roman law, the laws of the Germanic tribes and Anglo-Saxon law all allowed for compensation: the person harmed normally proceeds against the wrong doer via a civil action and, if successful, receives damages (Sheleff, 1975: 20–1). Historical research in early modern Europe also demonstrates that repressive sanctions involving violence and barbarism were exceptional and only exacted for specific types of serious offences and certain categories of offender, whereas civil actions were far more common as a legal remedy for harm done (Lenman and Parker, 1980: 14).

In tribal societies, religious systems and legal systems were so intertwined as to be almost synonymous. Malinowski conceptualizes law as a system of mutual obligations that constitute definite rules constraining behaviour. He argues that these obligatory rules are 'not endowed with any mystical character, not set forth in "the name of God", not enforced by any supernatural sanction but provided with a purely social binding force' (Malinowski, 1961: 51). The rules of law are the obligations of one person and the rightful claims of another. Explicitly contrasting Durkheim's views, Malinowski asserts: 'We may therefore finally dismiss the view that "group sentiment" or "collective responsibility" is the only or even the main force which ensures adhesion to custom and which makes it binding or legal' (Malinowski, 1961: 55).

Finally, Durkheim's view of the law as a reflection and index of social solidarity assumes that the nature of the law is determined internally, that is, within the structure of the society in question, and not imposed from outside. Many studies of colonial regimes, however, document the imposition of law in an attempt to effect rapid social change, usually modernization.

In light of the above, we might ask why Durkheim's ideas on law are important. This is a potent question, especially as Durkheim's ideas are empirically unverified and by his own positivistic standards this is a problem in itself. The following are some suggestions.

First, Durkheim's ideas on law are important arguably because it is Durkheim who formulated them. As many sociologists consider Durkheim's writings to be a central foundation of sociology, everything he wrote merits attention. One commentator goes so far as to suggest that Durkheim's writings 'remain the last neglected continent of classic theory in the sociological study of law' (Cotterrell, 1991: 924).

Secondly, Durkheim offers a way of thinking about law and morality that is sociological, as he examines the connections between legal forms and other major dimensions of social life. Discussions of law and legal institutions have traditionally been the domain of jurists, legal historians and philosophers. Rather than viewing law and morality as ideational systems, Durkheim points towards the connections between law and other dimensions of social structure, especially social complexity and individualism, even though his version of the connections is too simplistic and rigid. His writings highlight the importance of examining the implications of broader social changes in social organization and collective sentiment for types of law. Even some critics of Durkheim's views on the evolution from repressive to restitutive law wish to salvage these, suggesting that law is probably 'the outer symbol of the nature of a society' (Sheleff, 1975: 45).

Thirdly, Durkheim's discussion of law offers a good starting point for a sociology of punishment, which surprisingly is a relatively recent subdiscipline (Garland, 1990: 1; Smith, 2008a: 335–7; 2008b). This leads to an examination of the ways in which punishments reflect or are interconnected with other aspects of social structure rather than solely linking them with an ethical system, or an assumption that punishment is the nonproblematic response to criminal deviance (Spitzer, 1975a: 634). A sociology of punishment must investigate how social controls interrelate with political, economic and ideological dimensions of social organization and social change, rather than treating punishment as emergent and spontaneous or imposed (Jones, 1981: 1019; Spitzer, 1979: 208). Examining the connections between the types and severity of punishments and such broader social changes as a weakening *conscience collective,* or increasing individualism, becomes the focus of investigation rather than simply assumed. Durkheim's approach also emphasizes the expressive, emotional and symbolic elements of punishment, and the way in which it can be a realm for expressing collective values and concerns. This is an antidote to approaches that emphasize only the instrumental, purposive and control dimensions of punishments (Garland, 1990: 4–8; Rock, 1998; Smith, 2008b).

Law and rationality: Weber

Law was a central aspect of Weber's education and his career as well as his sociological theory. Weber studied law during the height of German historical jurisprudence and was always interested in the complex relationship between legal development and economic history, which distinguishes his approach from idealist legal theory, on the one hand, and economic determinism, on the other (Turner, 1981: 318–23). Weber taught commercial law and legal history at the University of Berlin, but moved to the newly created chair of economics at the University of Freiburg in 1894 (Hunt, 1978: 94–5; Rheinstein, 1954: xxxii–xxxiii). His major analysis of law (*Rechtssoziologie*) is contained in *Economy and Society* (Weber, 1978). Parsons goes so far as to suggest that 'the core of Weber's substantive sociology lies ... in his sociology of law' (Parsons, 1971: 40), and Kronman observes that 'his lifelong interest in the law is reflected in nearly everything he wrote' (Kronman, 1983: 1). Even so, it is only in the last few decades that Weber has been taken seriously as a sociologist of law.

In elaborating a theory of law, Weber pursues his general methodological concern to develop a value-free scientific approach to society, especially to normative and value-laden phenomena. His analysis of law also reflects an interest in comparative sociology and in adopting multi-causal, pluralist explanations (Gerth and Mills, 1977: 55–65; Parsons, 1964b: 8–29). It is sometimes said that Weber's sociology is shaped by its debate with Marxist approaches and a denial of economic determinism; however, that is less relevant to a discussion of law given Marx's sparse writings on the topic (Birnbaum, 1953; Hunt, 1978). Arguably, Weber's approach to law is positivist: he is at pains to provide systematic, formal definitions and to develop a classificatory scheme that implies evolutionary potential (Parsons, 1971: 43; Trubek, 1986: 583–7). At the same time, he demonstrates how legal forms are shaped by economic and social forces and vice versa.

Weber's discussion of law is intimately linked with his concern to explain the distinctiveness of the West, in particular the pervasiveness of rationality in economic and social life. He identifies four main kinds of social action:

1 Traditional conduct is performed in the way it is simply because it has always been carried on in that way.
2 Emotional action is determined by passions and feelings.
3 Value-rational *(wertrational)* action is oriented to value systems – religion, ethics or aesthetics, for example – and is regarded as proper regardless of its immediate practical consequences.

4 Purposively rational *(zweckrational)* action is oriented to a practical purpose and is determined by rational choice. Modern capitalism constitutes the prototype of purposively rational conduct, as it involves conduct oriented towards profit and rational choice as the means to achieve that end. Rheinstein asserts that Weber makes an explicit connection between rationality in economic activity and in legal thought: 'The categories of legal thought are obviously conceived along lines parallel to the categories of economic conduct. The logically formal rationality of legal thought is the counterpart to the purposive rationality of economic conduct' (Rheinstein, 1954: lviii).

Weber distinguishes legal rules from other normative systems, including morality and convention. He writes: 'An order will be called law when conformity with it is upheld by the probability that deviant action will be met by physical or psychic sanctions aimed to compel conformity or to punish disobedience, and applied by a group of men [*sic*] especially empowered to carry out this function' (Gerth and Mills, 1977: 180, emphasis deleted, also see Weber, 1978: 313–4; Parsons, 1947: 127). Weber does not define legal norms in terms of their substance but in terms of their administration: the existence of a specialized enforcement staff (themselves bound by legal rules) distinguishes legal norms from convention or morality. Law is more than the use of coercion to achieve certain ends; it involves a recognition that the agents of the law act with legitimacy, that is their sphere of authority is bounded or defined by legal rules, which distinguishes legal compulsion from other forms of coercion or domination. Those people subject to legal regulation consider compliance obligatory. Recognizing the legitimacy of law or the obligation to conform with legal sanctions does not imply that the law being enforced is consensually agreed on, appropriate, just or reasonable. It is the form of a norm, not its substance, which identifies it as law. To the extent that sanctions are applied in accord with a system of rules, law is said to be rational (Kronman, 1983: 30; Trubek, 1986: 727).

Typology of law

Weber constructs a typology of law based on different modes of legal thought. He addresses the process of legal thought in general and recognizes that legal systems can be dominated by such figures as priests, professors, consultants or judges. This typology is an example of an ideal type, that is, a hypothetical construct that involves the theoretical enumeration of all the possible characteristics against which empirical material may be compared. The concept of rationality is central to the typology of law. Both law making – the establishment of general norms that assume the character of rational rules of law – and law finding – the application of established norms and legal propositions deduced via legal thinking to concrete facts or particular cases – can be rational or irrational and can vary in terms of being formal or substantive. Weber's typology of law has four main variants, as illustrated in Figure 2.1.

Formal irrationality In a legal system characterized by formal irrationality, law makers and law finders apply means that are beyond the control of reason.

Formal irrationality	Substantive irrationality
A prophetic revelation Oracle Lay magistrates, juries	Kadi justice Tyrant
Formal rationality	Substative rationality

(a) External: English common law
(b) Logical:
    German civil law
    Continental codified legal systems
	Socialist regimes
	Talmud
	Church law

Figure 2.1 Weber's Typology of Law

Recourse to the pronouncements of an oracle or a prophetic revelation, for example, determines legal outcomes.

Substantive irrationality   In this situation, decisions are influenced by concrete factors of the particular case evaluated in terms of ethical, emotional or political values rather than general norms. Law makers and law finders deal with particular cases arbitrarily or in terms of their own conscience based on emotional evaluations. Examples include decisions of the tyrant or the *kadi* (the Middle eastern Islamic judge in the marketplace), who apparently renders decisions without reference to general rules but assesses the particular merits of individual cases (Weber, 1978: 976–8). Weber also considers aspects of the English common law to be irrational, especially the role of the jury in determining questions of fact and the process of decision making guided by human emotion, intuition and persuasion, rather than by logical thought and reasoning. Arguably, in actuality neither the *kadi* nor the common-law judge administers justice according to an arbitrary whim or fancy without considering or being guided by broader values, be they legal, religious or other. Judicial case law requires some degree of consistency that is evidence of rationality. As no two cases are identical, it is impossible to follow precedent except by following the principle on which previous decisions were based (Hunt, 1978: 108–10).

Substantive rationality   A legal system characterized by substantive rationality occurs where legal decisions are made by reference to rules that reflect value commitments or ethical imperatives, for example a set of codified religious rules or a political ideology. An example is Jewish Talmudic law or Church Canons, where a central issue is the interpretation of scripture in the light of general principles articulated as part of the religious value system. The implementation of welfare policies, collectivist goals or social justice policies via legislative programmes and principles that determine, or at least influence, judicial pronouncements is also an example of substantive rationality.

Formal rationality   This is the most sophisticated form of systematization. A law is formally rational insofar as significance in both substantive law and procedure is ascribed exclusively to operative facts, which are determined not from case to case but in a generically determined manner. 'All formal law is, formally at least, relatively rational. Law, however, is "formal" to the extent that, in both substantive and procedural matters, only unambiguous general characteristics of the facts of the case are taken into account' (Weber, 1978: 656–7). Two kinds of formalism can be distinguished:

1 *Extrinsic:* where the legally relevant characteristics are of a tangible, observable nature, they are perceptible as sense data and include the utterance of certain words, and the execution of a signature. The reasons relevant in the decision of concrete, individual cases are reduced to one or more legal propositions, which usually depend on a prior or concurrent analysis of the facts of the case as to those ultimate components that are regarded as relevant by the judge. The most important example of extrinsic systematization is the common law found in England and its former colonies, which operates primarily on a case-by-case accretion of legal principles. For Weber, extrinsic formal rationality tends to exhaust itself in casuistry, case-by-case quibbling about facts and the meaning of words, which draws practitioners towards ethical rather than purely procedural judgements.

2 *Intrinsic:* here, the legally relevant characteristics of the facts are disclosed intrinsically via the logical analysis of meaning and, accordingly, definitely fixed legal concepts in the form of highly abstract rules are formulated and applied (Weber, 1978: 657). Weber confines most of his discussion of formally rational law to this type, drawing on the example of Pandectist German law, which was based on an original set of Roman principles from the sixth century. Only the modern code systems developed out of Roman law and produced through the legal science of the Pandectists reflect, to any really significant extent, attitudes and methods of a formally rational sort (Kronman, 1983: 78; Weber, 1978: 657). Law making and law finding can be logically rational insofar as they proceed on the basis of generic rules that are neither determined by any religious, ethical, political or other system of ideology, and nor do they regard as relevant the observance by the senses of formalized acts, but are formulated by the use of generic concepts of an abstract character (Rheinstein, 1954: xlix). The legal propositions are integrated to form a logically clear, internally consistent and theoretically gapless system of rules. All situations of fact must be capable of being logically subsumed within the system (Weber, 1978: 655–6).

Weber maintains that present-day legal science, at least in those forms that have achieved the highest measure of methodological and logical rationality produced through the legal science of the Pandectist Civil Law, proceeds from the following five postulates:

1 Every concrete legal decision must be the application of an abstract legal proposition to a concrete fact situation.
2 It must be possible in every concrete case to derive the decision from abstract legal propositions by means of legal logic.

3   The law must constitute a gapless system of legal propositions or must at least be treated as if it were a such a gapless system.

4   Whatever cannot be construed rationally in legal terms is legally irrelevant.

5   Every human social action must be visualized as either an application or an execution of legal propositions or as an infringement thereof, since the gaplessness of the legal system must result in a gapless legal ordering of all social conduct (Weber, 1978: 657–8).

Law and change

Weber's typology of law is not just a descriptive classification but also implies evolutionary legal development, with formally rational law being the most advanced type. Weber proposes that the general development of law and legal procedure passes through the following stages:

(a) charismatic legal revelation through 'law prophets';

(b) the empirical creation and finding of law by legal honoratiores. This entails the creation of law through an adherence to precedent, that is, judicial law;

(c) the imposition of law by secular or theocratic powers, that is, legislative law;

(d) the systematized elaboration of law and professionalized administration of justice by persons who have received their legal training in a learned and formally logical manner (Weber, 1978: 882–3).

Weber views developments in contemporary western law as moving from substantively rational law to formally rational law, but argues against any specifically economic causation. He recognizes that there are multiple causes for particular types and degrees of rationalization in law. Nevertheless, logically formal rationality is not evident in other legal systems and is a peculiar product of western civilization. This raises questions about the influence of rational law in the development of modern capitalism and the extent to which economic factors determine the development of law (Hunt, 1978: 118; Kronman, 1983: 118–37). 'Has perhaps, the rise of formal rationality in legal thought contributed to the rise of capitalism; or has, possibly, capitalism contributed to the rise of logical rationality in legal thought?' (Rheinstein, 1954: 1). While Weber acknowledges a link between the distinctiveness of modern capitalism and the salience of the logically formal rationality of legal thought, the precise nature of the relationship remains unclear. He vehemently denies economic determinism and priority, yet notes the indirect influence of economic factors. He states that all purely economic influences occur as concrete instances and cannot be formulated in general rules, but also recognizes that: 'certain rationalizations of economic behavior, based upon such phenomena as a market economy or freedom of contract, and the resulting awareness of underlying, and increasingly complex conflicts of interests to be resolved by legal machinery, have influenced the systematization of the law' (Weber, 1978: 655).

For Weber, law constitutes a sphere of relative autonomy, influenced in its development by economic forces, but in turn influencing economic and other social processes. Developments in economic and legal rationality are parallel; there is no direct causation in either direction. However, the nature of the relationship and interpretations of Weber's articulation of the relationship are the source of a great deal of academic controversy, especially following some commentators' assertions that the logically formal rationality of legal thought is the counterpart to the purposive rationality of economic conduct (Ewing, 1987: 492). Debate on the relationship between legal and economic rationality focuses on the empirical case of England, which experienced the first historical onset of modern capitalism. Yet, the English legal system has never been as formally rational as in Germany, where capitalism emerged later. The English legal system constituted by the common law has been highly durable (and transportable) and was not a fetter to the development of economic rationality.

The common law is an admixture of various stages of legal development, namely:

1 Jury trial and royal courts indicate the retention of oracular methods with appeals to the sentiments of the layperson; the verdict is delivered as an irrational oracle without any statement of reasons and without the possibility of substantive criticism. The notion that a jury decision had to be unanimous indicates the reliance on a collective subjective response to the facts as presented. 'Irrational kadi justice is exercised today in criminal cases clearly and extensively in the "popular" justice of the jury' (Weber, 1978: 892).

2 The adversarial trial procedure is also an outgrowth of the oracle. The judge is bound by formalism, rules and procedures and can only respond to material presented by the parties, unlike the continental inquisitorial system where the judge has more scope for intervention.

3 A lay magistracy, especially in the administration of the criminal law, exhibits many of the elements of *kadi* justice. Magistrates are not bound by the same degree of formalism as higher courts; there is more informal justice, greater scope for value judgements and the inclusion of nonlegal, subjective evaluations to determine outcomes. This is particularly true of the patriarchal and highly irrational jurisdiction of justices of the peace who deal with the numerous daily troubles and misdemeanours of many ordinary people. Cases before the central courts are adjudicated in a strictly formalistic way, with a high cost for litigation and legal services. This denial of justice aligns with the interests of the propertied, especially the capitalistic classes (Weber, 1978: 814, 891).

4 The precedent system is a form of substantive irrationality comparable to *kadi* justice because: 'formal judgements [are] rendered, not by subsumption under rational concepts, but by drawing on "analogies" and by depending upon and interpreting concrete "precedents". This is "empirical justice"' (Weber, 1978: 976). Reliance on precedent is irrational: it is inductive, it generates empirical propositions from particular facts, and allows the inclusion of extra-legal factors into the judicial process due to its emphasis on facts rather than on general principles of law. Nonetheless, a process of internal rationalization does take place, so that precedents that are grounded in facts become a system of general and abstract principles important in determining the outcome of subsequent cases, although their origin is empirical not logical. Weber concludes:

Even today, and in spite of all influences by the ever more rigorous demands for academic training, English legal thought is essentially an empirical art. Precedent still fully retains its old significance. ... One can also still observe the charismatic character of law finding ... In practice varying significance is given to a decided case not only, as happens everywhere, in accordance with the hierarchical position of the court by which it was decided but also in accordance with the very personal authority of an individual judge. (Weber, 1978: 890)

English law finding is not, like that of the European continent, the application of legal propositions logically derived from statutory texts, but the logical derivation of legal propositions from previous decided cases. While English common law is less highly rationalized in the systematization of legal doctrine, it has been even more highly developed on the procedural side (Parsons, 1971: 42). In explaining the unique character of English law, Weber identifies two key factors:

(a) the role of the legal profession; and
(b) the political framework within which the common law developed.

The dominant role of the craft-like English legal profession, characterized by a highly practical orientation to the law with an associated instrumentalism in the utilization of technical skills to advance clients' interests, resulted in a very pragmatic jurisprudence. This form of legal training was also linked closely with the class structure. Training for the profession was monopolized by lawyers from whose ranks, particularly barristers, the judiciary were recruited. Moreover, lawyers actively serve the interests of the propertied, and particularly capitalistic, private interests who turn to the law for property conveyance and the resolution of contractual and other disputes (Weber, 1978: 892). The profession's pecuniary interest in preserving its technical skills was an obstacle to the rationalization of law. The failure of all efforts at a rational codification of law, including the failure to receive the Roman law at the end of the Middle Ages, resulted from the successful resistance by centrally organized lawyers' guilds, which retained legal training as a practical apprenticeship. Rationalization of the law could not occur, because concepts formed are constructed in relation to the actual events of everyday life and are distinguished from each other by external criteria, rather than by general concepts formed through abstraction or a logical interpretation of meaning. Lawyers' guilds successfully resisted all moves toward rational law, including for a time those from the universities that threatened their social and material position (Weber, 1978: 891–2). In Germany, scholars driven by the requirements of oral and written teaching to conceptual articulation and the systematic arrangement of legal phenomena dominated legal thought. On the European continent, legal uniformity was not achieved by a national legislature nor a national supreme court, but by scholars of university law schools.

In a radical tone, Weber comments that capitalism could manage a less rational and less bureaucratic judicature and trial process because this enabled a widespread denial of justice to economically weak groups, thus converging with capitalists' interests. The high time and financial costs of property conveyancing – a function of the economic interests of the lawyer class – exerted a profound influence on the agrarian structure of England in favour of the accumulation and immobilization of landed wealth (Weber, 1978: 977). The centralization of justice in the higher courts in London and the extreme costliness of legal action and lawyers' fees amounted to a denial of access to the courts for those with inadequate means. This illustrates the clear class dimensions of English law: the development of law in the hands of lawyers who, in the service of their capitalist clients, invented suitable forms for the transaction of business, and from whose midst judges were recruited who were strictly bound to precedent (and therefore conservative). Here Weber gives considerable importance to the value of economic factors, almost instrumentally, in shaping the development of English law. He notes that the resilience of the common law is illustrated in the Canadian situation, where the two kinds of administration of justice confront one another but the common law prevails. This leads him to conclude that: 'capitalism has not been a decisive factor in the promotion of that form of rationalization of the law which has been peculiar to the continental West' (Weber, 1978: 892).

Evaluations of Weber's sociology of law point out that the so-called England problem illuminates the contradictions and ambiguities in his conceptual scheme (Albrow, 1975: 22; Kronman, 1983: 1204; Turner, 1981: 330–5). Hunt suggests that Weber's treatment of the 'England problem' exposes a weakness in his substantive, as opposed to his conceptual, sociology. He fails to advance any coherent solution to the problem that he recognizes, but seeks to explain it by identifying discrete and historically specific causes, bearing no direct relationship to his conceptual sociology (Hunt, 1978: 127). He holds two mutually inconsistent positions: the English legal system has a low degree of calculability, but within the central courts that dealt largely with capitalist classes and their disputes there emerged a high level of calculability arising from the formal requirement of the bindingness of precedent (Trubek, 1972: 746–8). Later, Trubek suggests that the tension in Weber's sociology of law arises from his commitment to the superiority of rational legal thought, but pessimism regarding the cultural implications of formal legalism and the denial of substantive justice (Trubek, 1986: 587–93). Some historians disagree with Weber's argument that going to law was the sole domain of the wealthy, propertied classes and show that legal instruments and the courts were used by people from various occupations and classes to both avoid and settle disputes in early modern England (Brooks, 2004; Churches, 2004).

To be fair, Weber's schema is an ideal type and we should expect to find empirical deviations. He is careful to disclaim any economic reductionism and carefully identifies the ways in which the English legal system incorporates elements of formal rationality. To an extent, debates about the empirical validity of Weber's conceptual scheme and his handling of the so-called English problem are artefacts, arising from commentators' assertions about Weber's alleged enthusiasm for the proposition that forms of legal rationality directly correlate with types of economic rationality. All along, Weber is much more guarded against economic determinism and sees economic influences as indirect and mediated by political circumstances and internal legal developments. Ewing disputes the claim that Weber was determined to find a relationship between the extreme rationalization in legal thought, which found its clearest expression in the logically formal rationality of German Pandectist law, and the purposively rational action of capitalist economic relations (Ewing, 1987: 488–91), and Turner suggests that 'it would be perfectly possible to make Weber's position coherent by dropping the assumption that there is an affinity between capitalism and formal, rational law' (Turner, 1981: 350).

Ewing distinguishes Weber's sociology of legal thought from his sociology of law and suggests that: 'For Weber, the "legal order" that was relevant to the rise of capitalism was not a particular type of legal thought but a social order in which law facilitated capitalist transactions by contributing to the predictability of social action' (Ewing, 1987: 498). It did this through contract. With the extension of the market, legal transactions, especially contracts, become more numerous and complex. The kinds of contracts recognized and enforced by the law are affected by diverse interest groups and, in an increasingly expanding market, those with market interests constitute the most important group. Their influence predominates in determining which legal transactions the law should regulate (Weber, 1978: 669–81). 'The present-day significance of contract is primarily the result of the high degree to which our economic system is market-oriented and of the role played by money' (Weber, 1978: 671–2). Bourgeois interests promoted formal legal rationalization in the sense of establishing guaranteed rights, and the evolving body of case law enforced contractual agreements, thereby enhancing predictability in social and economic relations (Ewing, 1987: 500–1). This facilitates market relations by enhancing calculability and the opportunity for rational calculation in relation to the actions of others.

Ambiguity persists around the idea of legal rationality, which is the most important concept in Weber's sociology of law. When he says that a particular legal institution or mode of thought is particularly rational, at least four meanings are discernable: it suggests a system governed by rules or principles; it designates the systematic character of a legal order; a method of legal analysis; and control by the intellect (Kronman, 1983: 72–5). A larger problem for Weber's sociology of law is the empirical impossibility of formally rational law; it is impossible to contemplate law as uninfluenced by religious or other values or political ideology. Indeed, the concept of rationality is profoundly value oriented; Weber explicitly considers rational legal behaviour and thought as superior and more advanced compared with irrational legal thought (Hunt, 1978: 100). It is no coincidence that Weber, a fervent nationalist, saw the German legal system as the most rational. When discussing English law and the formally rational aspects of it – namely the central courts and binding precedent – he himself shows how unjust this formal system is, as it excludes many people without means from access to justice or legal resources, thereby perpetuating class divisions and illustrating the affinity in interests between lawyers, judges and capitalists. This generated a dual legal system: one kind of law for the rich, and another kind – the irrational *kadi* justice of the lower courts – for the poor.

Law, class and capitalism: Marx

The legal system and law were not specific objects of inquiry for Marx. Indeed, Marx comments that he only pursued law 'as a subordinate subject along with philosophy and history' (McLellan, 1977: 388). Neither he nor Engels wrote on law directly, and they did not offer theories of law, or even a definition; however, many of their writings and concerns dealt with issues of law. Marx's comments on law are scattered throughout material that he wrote alone and with others, thus it is often difficult to disentangle some of his views from those of Engels, whose aims were often more political. The incompleteness, diversity and interweaving with other topics have been the cause of various and often incompatible interpretations of Marx's views on law. Some commentators observe that Marxist theories of law, crime and deviance are at best tenuous and at worst impossible. As Marx does not offer a theory or even a concept of law – since his concern was with concepts of the mode of production, the class struggle, the state and ideology – any attempt to generate a Marxist sociology of law is revisionist and necessarily distorts Marx's original arguments (Collins, 1982; Hirst, 1972).

Nevertheless, considerable scholarship seeks to retrieve Marx's and Engels' writings on law and demonstrates that a Marxist approach to law, especially an understanding of the relationship between law and economic relations, is possible and useful (Cain, 1974; Cain and Hunt, 1979: ix; Vincent, 1993). Marx's fragmentary writings are the source of many critical approaches to deviance and crime that experienced a resurgence during the 1970s (see for example Quinney, 1978; Spitzer, 1975b; Taylor et al., 1973). In the 1990s degrees of disillusionment existed regarding Marxist theory, especially in light of the dismantling of the communist governments of eastern Europe and the way in which laws were used as instruments of repression in those regimes, which, in the post-communist era, are now adopting constitutional democracies (Krygier, 1990; Sajo, 1990; Scheppele, 1996).

Generally, Marx's treatment of law insists on establishing its class character and class specificity (Cain and Hunt, 1979: 62). Two different orientations towards law are discernible.

First, a simplified view considers the class character of law as a controlled instrument that protects and advances the interests of the bourgeois class. An example of this conception is contained in the political tract, *The Communist Manifesto*:

> Your very ideas are but the outgrowth of the conditions of your bourgeois production and bourgeois property, just as your jurisprudence is but the will of your class made into a law for all, a will whose essential character and direction are determined by the economical conditions of existence of your class. (Marx and Engels, 1948: 140)

Earlier, Marx and Engels stated that the bourgeoisie 'has converted the physician, the lawyer, the priest, the poet, the man [*sic*] of science, into its paid wage labourers' (Marx and Engels, 1948: 123). The law, as a set of concepts, the recognition of rights and the activities of lawyers operating in the service of the bourgeoisie, is determined by capitalist economic relations.

Secondly, there is a more complex and sophisticated rendering of law as an integral part of economic relations that cannot be reduced directly and simply to class interests and does not only reflect economic conditions (Cain and Hunt, 1979: 63). The increased interest in developing Marxist theories of law indicates wider concerns within Marxian scholarship to reject ~~economic determinism~~ (reductionism) and instrumentalism in favour of a more dynamic or dialectical approach, where there is interaction between the economic structure and such social institutions as law, education, religion and the state (Chambliss, 1979: 7–8; Jessop, 1980: 339–41; O'Malley, 1987: 75–9).

In tracking Marx's more complex rendition of law, it is important to note that various phases are discernible in his theoretical development and political purpose that affect the kinds of approaches that he adopted towards law. Roughly, Marx's positions on law and crime can be classified into three distinct kinds (Hirst, 1972: 30).

1840–42: The Kantian–Liberal critique of law

Marx advances a position of rationalism and universalism and espouses radical democratic and egalitarian views. He contrasts positive law and official morality founded on mundane interests with the true, universal and free necessity of laws and morality founded on reason. In a newspaper article defending the freedom of the press, Marx says:

> Laws are rather positive, bright and general norms in which freedom has attained to an existence that is impersonal, theoretical, and independent of the arbitrariness of individuals. ... Thus it [law] must always be present, even when it is never applied ... while censorship, like slavery, can never become legal, though it were a thousand times present as law. ... Where law is true law, i.e. where it is the existence of freedom, it is the true existence of the freedom of man [sic]. (McLellan, 1977: 18)

This is a conception of true law as natural law and superior to bourgeois law, which violates natural rights and undermines natural human equality. One of Marx's most important early statements on law is an article that he published in 1842 in the *Rheinische Zeitung,* a newspaper of which he was editor until the paper was suppressed due to its blatant criticism of the government. The article entitled 'Debates on the law on thefts of wood' deals with a debate in the Rhenish parliament regarding a proposal to make the law prohibiting thefts of wood more stringent. The collection of fallen wood had been a customary right and unrestricted, but laws facilitating the transformation of common land to private property rendered such gathering of wood theft. The extension of the definition of theft to include fallen wood was part of the general attempt under capitalism to privatize all property. The specific proposal would circumvent the courts and enable the gamekeeper to be the sole arbiter of an alleged offence and the sole authority to assess any damage.

Marx considered that the state should defend customary law and communal interests against the pragmatism and self-interest of the bourgeoisie (McLellan, 1977: 20–1). He argues (almost like a criminal defence lawyer) that the gathering of fallen wood and the theft of wood are essentially different: the objects concerned and thus the actions in regard to them are different; in the case of fallen wood nothing has been separated from property, it is fallen not felled wood. The owner possesses only the tree but the tree no longer possesses the branches that have fallen from it; the frame of mind, that is the intention of gathering fallen wood, is different from that involved in cutting down trees or branches. '[I]f the law applies the term theft to an action that is scarcely even a violation of forest regulations, then the law *lies,* and the poor are sacrificed to a legal lie' (Marx, 1975: 227, emphasis in original). The legal distinctions being made are shaped by class interests. Marx rhetorically asks: 'If every violation of property without distinction, without a more exact definition, is termed theft, will not all private property be theft?' (Marx, 1975: 228). He refers to the partiality in the content of law despite impartiality in its form. Even though the rule of law means a universal rather than an unequal application to all classes, the effect or substance of the law is biased in favour of bourgeois class interests:

> The Assembly ... repudiates the difference between gathering fallen wood, infringement of forest regulations, and theft of wood. It repudiates the difference between these actions, refusing to regard it as determining the character of the action, when it is a question of the interests of the infringers of forest regulations but it recognises this difference when it is a question of the interests of the forest owners. (Marx, 1975: 228)

He continues: 'We demand for the poor a *customary right,* and indeed one which is not of a local character but is a customary right of the poor in all countries. We go still further and maintain that a customary right by its very nature can only be a right of this lowest, propertyless and elemental mass' (Marx, 1975: 230, emphasis in original). Thus Marx shows how legislation – that is, positive law – abrogates the customary rights of the propertyless by offering a transcendental, universal view of law and reason and a conception of natural rights in which private property violates the rights of others, and legislation, protecting the interests of the bourgeoisie, is not collective but contravenes natural law (Hirst, 1972: 30–3). Marx advocates distributive justice *vis-à-vis* property and calls for a more radical democratic state to uphold fundamental rights and freedoms. So here legislation is implicated in direct oppression, which is applied by the bourgeois class to control the propertyless or in order to advance its own economic interests and protect its own property.

1842–44: The Feuerbachian period   *The Economic and Philosophical Manuscripts of 1844* are the most important here, where Marx discusses alienated labour, private property and communism, as well as the relationship of capitalism to human needs, and criticizes Hegel's abstract philosophy (McLellan, 1977: 75). Law ceases to be an important element in Marx's argument and the conceptual structure of the *Manuscripts* reduces all particular phenomena – for example the law, the state, the family and religion – to the essential contradiction in society, between the essence of labour as a self-realizing human activity and its alienation in an object, private property (Hirst, 1972: 33). 'Religion, family, state, law, morality, science, and art are only particular forms of production and fall under its [capitalism's] general law. The positive abolition of private property and the appropriation of human life is therefore the positive abolition of all alienation, thus the return of man [*sic*] out of religion, family, state, etc. into his [*sic*] human, i.e. social being' (McLellan, 1977: 89).

1845–82: The formation and development of historical materialism   Commentators identify the mid- to late 1840s as a key turning point in Marx's analyses. In 1844 he met Engels, with whom he subsequently collaborated, and in 1848 a series of popular revolts across Europe left Marx disenchanted with the revolutionary potential of the working class. He developed a materialist conception of history that emphasizes the way in which the productive forces or economic relations of production both constrain and enable social change and social action. These economic forces exist beyond the history of ideas and lie outside the will or intention of individuals.

One of Marx's clearest statements on law was written in this period and is contained in the Preface to *A Critique of Political Economy,* published in 1859. This Preface is also taken as a central statement on two dimensions of social structure, the substructure (economic foundations) and the superstructure, which includes legal, political, religious, aesthetic and intellectual institutions, indeed every facet of life not subsumed within the economic substructure. The relationship between the substructure and the superstructure has been the focus of considerable academic debate. The Preface is widely acknowledged as the starting point for a Marxist approach that seeks to relate law to the economic structure of society (Cain and Hunt, 1979: 48; Collins, 1982: 17; Stone, 1985: 47). Marx writes:

> [L]egal relations as well as forms of state are to be grasped neither from themselves nor from the so-called general development of the human mind, but rather have their roots in the material conditions of life, the sum total of which Hegel ... combines under the name of 'civil society' ... [T]he anatomy of civil society is to be sought in political economy ... In the social production of their life, men [*sic*] enter into definite relations that are indispensable and independent of their will, relations of production which correspond to a definite stage of development of their material productive forces. The sum total of these relations of production constitutes the economic structure of society, the real foundation on which rises a legal and political superstructure and to which correspond definite forms of social consciousness. (McLellan, 1977: 389)

Marx did not propose that economic relations determine the law or that laws are subservient tools of the bourgeoisie, but that legal relations are rooted in 'material conditions', thus juxtaposing his materialist orientation with idealism and the philosophy of law. The key to understanding the legal superstructure lies within the production relations themselves, which are essentially class relations in capitalist society (Young, 1979: 135). Marx recognized that laws in capitalist society favour bourgeois interests, as they are entirely congruent with the goals and conditions of capitalism. While granting primacy to economic relations, he does not argue that they determine legal and political institutions, but that the latter are based on the former; the relations of production are the foundation of legal and political institutions and ideologies. This is not a reductionist argument. It suggests that the economic structure sets parameters on the limits of variation of the superstructure, but it does not specify the cause or origin of superstructural forms or the ideologies that correspond to them (Hirst, 1972: 36). The argument does not deny that legal and political institutions can alter economic relations, thus opening up the potential for a dynamic conception of social and legal change.

The distinction between substructure and superstructure has led to debates about the relationship between economic relations and the legal system and a view of the law as relatively autonomous but not disconnected from economic forces (Cain and Hunt, 1979: 48–51; Chambliss, 1979; Collins, 1982: 77–93; Thompson, 1975). Stone proposes that the notion of legal superstructure contains two distinct but related concepts: one that Engels termed 'essential legal relations' and the other, law or judicial practice (Johnstone and Wenglinsky, 1985: 49). Essential legal relations include legal conceptions that are central to a capitalist economic order, such as property, contract and credit. A general theme in Marx's writing subsequently developed is the notion that bourgeois law is the legal expression of the commodity exchange relationship; it presupposes a free and equal juridical person defined by the idealized characteristics of an individual engaged in a contractual exchange (Sumner, 1979: 292). Nevertheless, Marx's notion of law remains ambiguous. Later in the Preface he states:

> At a certain stage of their development, the material productive forces of society come in conflict with the existing relations of production, or – what is but a legal expression for the same thing – with the property relations within which they have been at work hitherto. ... With the change of the economic foundations the entire immense superstructure is more or less rapidly transformed. In considering such transformations a distinction should always be made between the material transformation of the economic conditions of production, which can be determined with the precision of natural science, and the legal, political, religious, aesthetic, or philosophic – in short, ideological forms in which men [*sic*] become conscious of this conflict and fight it out. (McLellan, 1977: 389–90)

This passage suggests a more economic determinist view of law, where a change in economic foundations transforms the entire superstructure, and there seems to be little scope for institutions of the superstructure to ameliorate economic conditions or to resist or delay change stemming from a change in the substructure. Marx also maintains that economic conditions are not the site of class struggle, but that this occurs within the superstructure. Young proposes that the conflict of which people become conscious in law is not the economic contradiction within production relations, but the conflict between class interests (Young, 1979: 136). The two conflicts are related but distinct. First, phenomena and changes within the legal superstructure arise from phenomena and changes in class relations at the level of the social relations of production. Secondly, law can affect these class relations in a dual process; law is an 'ideological form' by which people conceptualize and experience class relations and law is a means by which people can maintain or alter those relations.

Ideology is an important concept in Marx's writings and in the Marxist theorization of law. For Marx ideas, including politics, law, morality, religion and metaphysics, are produced by human actors within the conditions of a definite development of the productive forces in a society. The concept of ideology refers to ideas or forms of consciousness that are shaped by material conditions. In the *German Ideology*, Marx and Engels write:

> The ideas of the ruling class are in every epoch the ruling ideas: i.e., the class which is the ruling *material* force of society is at the same time its ruling *intellectual force*. The class which has the means of material production at its disposal, consequently also controls the means of mental production, so that the ideas of those who lack the means of mental production are on the whole subject to it. (Quoted in Cain and Hunt, 1979: 116, emphases in original)

Marxist theories of ideology use the term in various ways to indicate that the law reflects class interests, thus distorting reality and shrouding the real interests of non-dominant groups. Such concepts as equality, freedom and justice that form part of legal ideals in capitalist society in effect serve to reproduce unequal class relations. Sumner, while eschewing economic determinism, considers law to be 'a conjoint expression of power and ideology. ... Law is a public, ideological front which can often conceal the true workings of a social formation' (1979: 267). However, he denies that law is simply an instrument in the hands of the dominant class and says that: '[L]aw is only an instrument of class rule through the mediating arenas of politics and ideology ... it is not just an instrument of class rule' (1979: 268). While law does not directly reflect unified class interests, neither does it represent the plurality of all views: 'it is a much closer reflection of class inequality than other forms [for example music or literature]' (1979: 270). The idea that the law reflects or distorts social reality or that it entails 'false consciousness' assumes some pre-given relationship between the real and its ideological representation, and removes the empirically important issue of the association between ideas and interests (Hunt, 1985: 13, 21).

In his later writings, for example *Critique of the Gotha Programme* published in 1875, Marx rejected the notion that socialism is a matter of distributive justice. His ideas were founded on an analysis of the mode of production, the relations of production and the productive forces, which enforce a definite mode of distribution in a given social formation. He also rejected the egalitarianism of 'equal rights' and was not interested in abstractions like equality, but in the social relations generated by capitalist and socialist societies (Hirst, 1972: 37–8; McLellan, 1977: 564–70). He considered equality or equal rights to be bourgeois rights, thereby inevitably perpetuating inequality where class differences prevail. While not using this language, Marx recognized the distinction between formal and substantive equality:

> This equal right is an unequal right to unequal labour. It recognizes no class differences, because everyone is only a worker like everyone else; but it tacitly recognizes unequal individual endowment and thus productive capacity as natural privileges. It is, therefore, a right of inequality, in its content, like every right. [He elaborates that not all workers are equally situated; some have families and varying numbers of dependants] ... To avoid all these defects, rights instead of being equal would have to be unequal. (McLellan, 1977: 568–9)

In his defence speech at the trial of the Rhenish District Committee of Democrats, Marx expresses a complex view of law in which he echoes some of his earlier natural law presuppositions as well as recognizing that legislation can be the expression of sectarian interests and not resonate with actual social conditions. He stated:

> Society is not founded upon the law; this is a legal fiction. On the contrary, the law must be founded upon society, it must express the common interests and needs of society – as distinct from the caprice of the individuals – which arise from the material mode of production prevailing at the given time ... [Bourgeois society] merely finds its legal expression in this Code [Napoléon]. As soon as it ceases to fit the social conditions, it becomes simply a bundle of paper. (McLellan, 1977: 274)

In addition to social class and the law, it is important to investigate the relationship between the law and the state (Jessop, 1980). The state develops after irreconcilable antagonisms have arisen, when it becomes necessary to have a power seemingly above and independent of civil society, whose function is the alleviation of conflict and the maintenance of order. Marx and Engels appeared to be arguing that the capitalist class as a whole, in order to maintain its dominant position, gradually creates a set of linked organizations (the state) with the dual purpose of protecting their common interests, such as the formulation of clear rules for commercial transactions, and of protecting them against external threats from other classes or states. The idea that the law is above or untainted by class politics and divisions, exemplified in the rule of law ideology, gives the illusion that all members of society are protected by the general law, that all have equal legal rights by virtue of the social contract.

Law, legislation and capitalism

Debate still exists on Marx's interpretation of the role of law in the transition from feudalism to capitalism. Hindess and Hirst (1977) suggest that law is one of the 'conditions for existence' for the development and reproduction of the capitalist mode of production. They argue that it is a necessary, indispensable and independent presence with specific effects that are necessary and precede the transition from feudalism to capitalism. Marx and Engels' writings suggest that the emergence of a capitalist mode of production requires a generalized system of commodity production with circulation based on exchange value, and the creation of 'free labour' or the separation of agricultural workers from the land in such a way that they become available for industrial employment. When members of the bourgeois class gained control of the political institutions, specific legislation was passed to destroy feudal land tenure, displacing agricultural labourers and thereby creating the landless poor who became the potential 'free' labour force for capitalist production. Law also provides the necessary contractual framework within which labour power is itself transformed into a commodity (Cain and Hunt, 1979: 634). These processes were historically facilitated by coercion and violence, as in many cases of enclosure; however, law also expedited the whole process in developing sophisticated systems of property law, contract, tort and criminal law (Cain, 1974: 145). In *Capital* Vol. 1, Marx writes:

The advance made by the 18th century shows itself in this, that the law itself becomes now the instrument of the theft of the people's land, although the large farmers make use of their little independent methods as well. The parliamentary form of the robbery is that of Acts for enclosures of Commons, in other words, decrees by which the landlords grant themselves the people's land as private property, decrees of expropriation of the people. (Quoted in Cain and Hunt, 1979: 74)

An outcome of these policies was an increase in begging, robbery and vagabondage. The rise in legislative and punitive severity was aimed at suppressing vagabondage and forcing displaced people to work for very low wages. The process of land enclosure and clearance paralleled the growing severity of laws against vagrancy and a refusal to work became a criminal offence. Their combined effect drove the expropriated population towards the labour market and induced the forms of labour discipline required for the capitalist organization of production (Chambliss, 1964).

Marx and Engels also identified the complex ways in which legislation, particularly in England from the fifteenth to the nineteenth century, had a determining role in a general, historical process. Significant legislation included the Reform Act of 1832, which extended the property qualification for the franchise; the Poor Law Amendment Act of 1834, which incarcerated the indigent poor into large workhouses; and factory legislation that regulated the employment relationship and work conditions (Young, 1979: 149–62). Marx and Engels do not advance a conspiracy theory that the bourgeoisie pre-mediates the use of legislation to secure its interests, nor do they argue that all legislation favours the interests of the bourgeoisie to the detriment of the working class. Each piece of legislation had its own specific historical context incorporating contradictory features and effects. Despite facilitating capital accumulation, these laws often recognize workers' rights and represent a cost to factory owners. The *Factory Acts* passed in the first half of the nineteenth century governed the hours of labour and restricted work by women and children. This disadvantaged segments of the bourgeoisie, as it decreased the size of the labour pool and increased wages. However, Marx suggested that the legislative protection of labour, while 'protecting the working-class both in mind and body', facilitates capitalist expansion and accumulation because it 'hastens on the general conversion of numerous isolated small industries into a few combined industries carried on upon a large scale' (quoted in Cain and Hunt, 1979: 88). Implementing such reforms is expensive and small-scale capitalists lose their profit margin and competitive edge and thus are unable to continue.

Conclusion

Of the three sociological theorists examined in this chapter, only Weber viewed law as a central topic of inquiry. Nonetheless, each of the theorists explored the relationships between law – including legal thought, legal institutions and actors – and such other dimensions of social structure as the level of differentiation, the nature of social relationships and economic relations. Not surprisingly, their general views on social change and social organization influenced their commentaries on law. Durkheim's attention to law was subsumed within his general focus on the division of labour, social solidarity, the collective consciousness and evolutionary social change. For Weber, changes in the types of legal action and legal thought are inevitably intertwined with broader processes of rationalization. He saw changes in the direction of law linked with economic conditions, but did not advance an economic reductionist conception of law. Marx's discussion of law is the most fragmentary and reflects several shifts in his thinking. His early writing held out more prospects for legislation to facilitate justice, but later emphasized the materialist dimensions of social institutions, including law. The differing perspectives formulated by Durkheim, Weber and Marx, as well as their actual observations on law and social change, have influenced the development of contemporary theories, which are the topic of the next chapter.

3 Contemporary Social Theory and Law

Current social theories of law are diverse, often highly abstract, and it is difficult to corral them into clear statements about general themes or to identify unambiguous theoretical directions. Continuing concerns remain with the nature of law in modern societies alongside new attention to the effects of increasing social plurality and complexity. There is disenchantment with the nation state, first in the sense that social control or regulation is no longer monopolized by national governments and second, that the interventionist state reliant on legislative programmes to implement social goals has partly failed in all its forms, ranging from the polities of the former Soviet bloc to the liberal-democratic welfare states. Social justice and reform via legal intervention and the legislative/administrative establishment of programmes that aimed to ameliorate various inequalities and injustices have not completely occurred. Trends toward internationalization in business transactions, the movement of populations, a concern for human rights and globalization can mean that national legal processes are less dominant and less isolated. These tendencies have led to new theories that uncouple law from the activities of nation states and their legal institutions.

Contemporary legal theories also grapple with problems of subjectivity: the role of legal actors, the constitution of law in everyday life, and the distinctiveness of law as a form of social control and regulation. Particularly, following Weber it is surprising that the sociology of law has not consumed the same theoretical (or empirical) interest among sociologists as has social stratification or deviance and crime, at least until very recently. Current socio-legal theories describe the way in which law transposes nonlegal issues and ideas into legal problems and concepts, examines law's relationship to other interests, values and institutions, and proposes the special role of law in the social structure.

This chapter canvasses diverse, contemporary theories of law, commencing with systems theory. It then examines issues of juridification, considers the legal arena as a site of contestation and explores the relationship between law and other forms of regulation and discipline. The chapter addresses critical theories of law as developed by Marxists and feminist legal theorists, and finally considers theoretical developments around the notion of legal pluralism.

Systems theory

Undoubtedly, the most influential systems theorist in sociology has been Talcott Parsons, who unfortunately spent little time discussing the legal (sub)system *per se,* but for whom law constitutes a central component of social structure. Like Marx, Parsons' thoughts on law are scattered widely throughout his writings. Law is an important component in Parsons' overall systems theory, and at the same time he paid attention to legal actors and to the everyday dilemmas confronting legal professionals deriving from their institutional location (see Chapter 4). For Parsons, 'law should be treated as a generalized mechanism of social control that operates diffusely in virtually all sectors of the society' (Parsons, 1962: 57). He stresses that law, while being one type of social control, is located primarily at the institutional level and, following Weber, treats law 'as a set of prescriptions, permissions, and prohibitions bearing on social action and more or less systematically organized' (Parsons, 1978: 33; see also Parsons, 1962: 57). Parsons' writing on law provides a starting point for Luhmann and Habermas, even though their theories proceed in opposite directions. All three share a view of social evolution as a differentiation of social systems accompanied by the pre-eminence of universalistic, secular values (Deflem, 1998: 779–83; Holton, 1987).

According to Parsons, every society confronts four subsystem problems: Adaptation, Goal attainment, Integration and pattern maintenance or Latency (AGIL). Within this scheme, law features as the integrative mechanism: 'the primary function of the legal system is integrative' (Parsons, 1962: 58; and see 1978: 32–5, 52). Law mitigates conflict and facilitates social interaction; it regulates the relations of the differentiated parts to each other. Only by adhering to a system of rules can social interaction occur without breaking down into overt, chronic conflict. Considering the high level of structural differentiation and pluralism in modern societies, the legal system becomes especially significant because 'it can mediate between the normative and cultural orders which have become so important in a complex society and the vast complex of especially economic and political interests which are the primary focus of centrifugal pressures' (Parsons, 1976: 119). That the law is integrative means that it must have relationships, interaction and exchange with the other subsystems.

Parsons identifies four main problems that must be solved before a rule system can regulate social interaction:

1 It must have a basis of *legitimation* in order to obtain compliance/conformity.
2 It must solve the problem of *interpretation,* regarding which abstract legal rules govern particular situations and define specific rights.
3 It must provide *sanctions* to follow nonconformity, specify by whom they are applied, and which can range from pure inducement to coercion.
4 It must establish *jurisdiction* to determine to what circumstances a given rule or complex set of rules applies (Parsons, 1962: 58–9).

Along with bureaucratic organization, money and markets and democratic institutions, a universalistic legal system is fundamental to the structure of the large-scale and highly differentiated modern type of society. Parsons finds that law has its strongest place in a pluralistic, liberal society where many different kinds of interest must be balanced against each other and coexist (Parsons, 1962: 72). The development of certain kinds of law has adaptive or survival advantages for the society, which are not present in other kinds of society with different legal systems or legal processes. Specifically:

> [O]ne can identify the development of a general legal system as a crucial aspect of societal evolution. A general legal system is an integrated system of universalistic norms, applicable to the society as a whole rather than to a few functional or segmental sectors, highly generalized in terms of principles and standards, and relatively independent of both the religious agencies that legit-imize the normative order of the society and vested interest groups in the operative sector, particularly the government. (Parsons, 1964a: 351)

One important dimension of the emergence of a formal, secular, general, autonomous legal system is some kind of codification of norms under principles that are not directly moral or religious (although they generally continue to be grounded in religion), and the formalization of procedural rules that define the situations in which judgements are to be made on a societal basis, especially by courts (Parsons, 1964a: 353). Analytically, the legal system is not to be regarded as a political or religious phenomenon that is concerned with fundamental problems of value orien-tation involving basic decisions for the system as a whole. Nonetheless, behind proper procedure and the due authorization of law-making bodies lies the deeper set of questions of ultimate legitimation, namely a value system. Law provides a focal point for the relations between religion and politics as well as other aspects of society (Parsons, 1962: 62, 72). Indeed, Parsons remarks on the high level of lawyers' participation in all levels of government, including the legislature, which means that they interact with the power system and its coercive sanctions (Parsons, 1976: 118–19). This is also true today: the current President of the USA, Barack Obama, and his wife, Michelle, are both lawyers. Parsons also admits that the differentiation of secular government from religious organization has occurred unevenly, even in the modern world. He cites the example of the USA as the location of the furthest example of secularization, indicated by the legal commit-ment to the separation of church and state. Even so, some US states retain the death penalty as a criminal sanction, which reflects fundamentalist Judeo-Christian values and a pre-modern level of social development.

While Parsons does not go as far as Durkheim's argument that law reflects the *conscience collective* (the shared beliefs and values of a collectivity), he does observe that law flourishes when a certain type of social equilibrium is obtained, when the most fundamental questions of social values are not at issue and when the issues of enforcement are not too acute. Echoing Durkheim, he suggests that: 'This is partic-ularly true where there are strong informal forces reinforcing conformity with at least the main lines of the legally institutionalized tradition' (Parsons, 1962: 71).

Following Weber, he recognizes pre-modern examples of law – especially religious law – which resisted the generalization of legal principle. Roman law failed to become a generalized legal system not because of any intrinsic defect in legal content, but because of the failure to integrate the immense variety of peoples and cultures within the Empire or to maintain the necessary economic, political and administrative structures. Nevertheless, Roman law became the cultural reference point for significant later developments (Parsons, 1964a: 352).

Interestingly, Parsons does not view the English common law as posing a problem for his conceptual scheme and evolutionary view of history. The organizational independence of the judiciary, its emphasis on the protection of personal rights, the recognition of private property, freedom of contract and protection of contractual interests (more strongly than continental law), the adversarial system and its procedural protections led Parsons to conclude (without any hint of disappointment, in contrast to Weber) that the English common law constituted the most advanced case of a universalistic normative order and was probably decisive for the modern world. He states unequivocally: 'This general type of legal order is, in my opinion, the most important single hallmark of modern society. So much is it no accident that the Industrial Revolution occurred first in England' (Parsons, 1964a: 353).

Other systems theorists, following Parsons, examine the interrelationships and exchanges between the various subsystems and contemplate the impact of the activities or change in one subsystem – for example economics or politics – on such other subsystems as law, and vice versa (Evan, 1990: 48–53). Bredemeier, for example, examines the outputs of the legal system in exchange for such inputs as goals from the political system (goal attainment), knowledge from the adaptive system and, from the pattern maintenance system (religion and education), conflict and esteem (Bredemeier, 1962: 89).

A recent revival in systems theory has been brought about in large part by Luhmann, who spent time at Harvard University with Parsons in 1960–1 but whose work remained relatively unknown among the English speaking world until the 1980s. Luhmann both studied law at university and practised as a lawyer. He also worked as a civil servant, a major career route for lawyers in Germany, and later held a professorship in sociology. His *Rechtssoziologie* (literally translated as the sociology of rights/law; the German word *rechts* means both law and rights) was published in 1972, but not translated into English until 1985 and published as *A Sociological Theory of Law* (Luhmann, 1985).

Luhmann's basic argument is that under conditions of extreme social differentiation and pluralism (differentiation is primarily horizontal rather than the vertical differentiation of stratification), the legal system (and other subsystems) becomes relatively autonomous, not interdependent, and is able to reproduce itself independently. To make this argument he relies on systems theory, models of law and society derived from biology, and evolutionary/universal conceptions of change. In particular, Luhmann introduces the notion of *autopoiesis* (literally, self-production), which conceptualizes biological systems as units that persistently reproduce their unity from their own elements and thus become autonomous and independent of their external environments. Luhmann's approach departs from earlier systems theories; his concern is not to conceptualize systems as input–output models or to specify exchange relationships between various subsystems. Instead, he devotes almost exclusive attention to the closure of the legal system and its self-referentiality or the means by which its own identity and integrity are self-produced (King, 1993: 219; Teubner, 1984: 384). Even though the units of the system increasingly organize themselves (self-referentially) and society comes to lack a central subsystem that regulates all others, legitimation is not necessarily a problem because 'there is the possibility of order without Order' (Wolfe, 1992: 1730). Systems self-reproduce and coexist.

Luhmann commences with a theoretical view of society as a functionally differentiated social system, with the legal system as one of its functional subsystems (Luhmann, 1986: 112). Each subsystem is autonomous: 'functional subsystems of society are always self-referential systems: They presuppose and reproduce themselves. They constitute their components by the arrangement of their components and this "autopoietic" closure *is their unity*' (Luhmann, 1986: 112, emphasis in original). All such systems have to live with the inherent improbability of combining closure and openness; closure and openness are reciprocal not contradictory (Luhmann, 1985: 281–4; 1986: 122; 1988a; 1988b: 19–23; 1992: 1429–34). The unity of the system is produced by the system itself and the notion of operational or systemic closure does not mean empirical isolation or cognitive closure. Luhmann clarifies that the issue is not how a system can exist without external influences, but 'what kind of operations enable a system to form a self-reproducing network which relies exclusively on self-generated information and is capable of distinguishing internal needs from what it sees as environmental problems' (Luhmann, 1992: 1420).

Luhmann distinguishes social autopoiesis from its biological origins by identifying communication as the basic element of the former and by defining social systems as systems of meaning, not groups of people. These systems of meaning exist independent of individual action, but individuals are reconstructed or interpreted as epistemic subjects within different social meaning systems (King, 1993: 219, 228; Luhmann, 1988b: 16–19; 1992: 1422–5). Social systems as networks of meaning produce their own meaning: they construct the environment and perform their operations on the environment that they themselves have constructed. The central mechanism in this process is the use of binary codes to interpret and select information. Politics distinguishes between government and opposition, economics distinguishes payment from non-payment, morality separates good from bad, and science is built on the difference between truth and falsehood. In the case of the legal system, social events derive their meaning through the law's unique binary code of lawful/unlawful, legal/illegal (Luhmann, 1988a: 154–7; 1992: 1427–9). The legal system distinguishes norms from facts and in so doing actually constructs the difference and, *ipso facto,* its own legal data. Even the 'facts of a case' that are relevant for legal attention are not facts in general, or facts for everybody. 'Facts are constructions, statements about the world, and careful sociological investigations show that scientific facts and facts which serve as components of legal or political-administrative decision making differ in remarkable ways' (Luhmann, 1992: 1429–30). Communications that code social acts according to the law's binary code may be seen as part of the legal system regardless of their location.

Since systems use different coding and different procedures for validating reality, thereby constructing their external environments, they are unable to communicate directly with one another, in the sense that they cannot transmit meaning directly, only via their own unique codes (King, 1993: 220). Law cannot deal directly with economic policy, medical dilemmas, moral values, political philosophy or family life, but it produces parallel legal communications on all these issues and through this production nonlegal issues are transposed into legal questions and communicated as lawful/unlawful or legal/illegal. Accordingly, communications with other systems cannot be reproduced by law as legal communication, but must first be transformed or refracted as law if they are to become law.

Even though law is a normatively closed system, it is simultaneously a cognitively open one. It is open to cognitive information and input from its external environment as it responds to various substantive economic, political, scientific, social or other issues. However, it can only deal with these issues by transforming them into its own legal categories, which entails the selection of information according to legal (not political, moral, scientific or other) criteria (Luhmann, 1986: 117). Law's response to external social, economic and political change indicates its permeability but, more importantly, the idea of autopoiesis shows how it transforms the dictates of change to its environment into its own legal forms and legal remedies. Thus, law does not respond to an environment that in some way has a direct impact on it, but to an environment that law itself constructs intellectually in its own terms and understands in terms of its own communicative criteria (Cotterrell, 1992: 67). Legal autonomy means that law reproduces itself but is not insulated from its environment. External demands and changes are neither ignored nor unproblematically incorporated into law. Changes are filtered selectively into legal structures according to their own legal logic of development. Wider social pressures influence legal development to the extent that they affect legal constructions of reality; they therefore modulate legal change, which follows its own logic (Teubner, 1983: 249).

There is an inevitable tautology in the idea that the legal system reproduces itself by legal events and only by legal events. That the law produces law and nothing else is hardly a surprising conclusion. Luhmann acknowledges that: 'the reference to the normative framework of the law serves to establish circularity within the system: decisions are legally valid only on the basis of normative rules because normative rules are valid only when implemented by decisions' (Luhmann, 1986: 115; also see Rottleuthner, 1988: 117–18). For example, legislative attempts to change law will be mediated by the law's decisions on whether the legislation is valid, that is, whether the legislature acted within its constitutionally (legally) defined jurisdiction, or even whether the legislature has been properly (legally) constituted by a proper (legal) election.

This systems theory of law is neither formalist – it does not view legal change as the insulated unfolding of law's own internal logic – nor instrumentalist, which gives little credence to the legal sphere that is viewed as totally incoherent and manipulable. For Luhmann, legal change is evolutionary. He describes the continuing differentiation and functional independence of law, with the motor of evolutionary change being the increasing complexity of society (Luhmann, 1985: 83, 106–7, 168–9). Luhmann employs a three-stage evolutionary scheme that distinguishes among (a) segmented, (b) stratified, and (c) functionally differentiated societies, and for each type of social organization he posits a corresponding type of legal order (Teubner, 1983: 244).

Teubner, another proponent of autopoietic theory, refers to 'evolutionary co-variation' and 'co-evolution' to describe and explain the relationship between legal and social changes (Teubner, 1983: 246, 249). He formulates three dimensions of law:

(a) it is an autonomous epistemic subject that constructs a social reality of its own;
(b) it is not produced through the intentional actions of actors, but law as a communicative process constitutes human actors as semantic artefacts, and;
(c) its simultaneous dependence on and independence from other social discourses is the reason that modern law is permanently oscillating between cognitive autonomy and heteronomy (Teubner, 1989: 730).

Teubner follows Luhmann's notion of reflexive law, but attempts to go further and to reformulate the role of the law in relation to the other specialized social subsystems (Teubner, 1986: 8). He describes the current situation as a 'crisis' of legal and social evolution. The emergence of the welfare and regulatory state placed greater stress on substantively rational law, that is, on law as an instrument for purposive, goal-oriented intervention (Teubner, 1983: 240). Responding to the crisis in legal formalism that has led to calls for such alternatives as delegalization and informalism, a conundrum appears to the systems theorist: 'It is not possible to inaugurate functional equivalents outside of the system because being an equivalent includes them in the system' (Luhmann, 1986: 120). Replacing legal functions or legal actors with alternatives is impossible, even though remedies may be available. The political system cannot replace the legal system and the legal system cannot replace the economic system, as functional subsystems are unable to solve the core problems of other systems (Luhmann, 1986: 120).

The partial failure of the welfare state, which relies on legal intervention to facilitate social change, has taken up the considerable attention of contemporary systems socio-legal scholars. For proponents of autopoiesis theory, it is not surprising that law seems relatively unsuccessful when it is employed to achieve various economic or social policy aims, because law cannot directly intervene, or even communicate with those systems. Teubner suggests that the limits of regulation are defined by the limits of self-reproduction: 'A regulatory action is successful only to the degree that it maintains a self-producing internal interaction of the elements in the regulating systems, law and politics which is at the same time compatible with self-producing internal interactions in the regulated system' (Teubner, 1984: 386, emphasis deleted). If regulation does not conform to the conditions of the structural coupling of law, politics and society, it inevitably ends in regulatory failure. Regulatory law is ineffective because it overreaches the limitations that are built into the regulatory process: the self-referential elements of the systems are jeopardized. Regulation can fail in three ways:

1   *Incongruence of law, politics and society*: here the regulatory action is incompatible with the self-producing interactions of the regulated system. The regulatory action becomes irrelevant and the law is ineffective, as it creates no change in behaviour.

2   *Overlegalization of society*: regulatory action influences the internal interaction of elements in the regulated field so strongly that their self-production is endangered. Thus law destroys other patterns or systems of social life.

3   *Oversocialization of law*: here the self-producing organization of the regulated area remains intact, while the self-producing organization of the law is endangered. The law is 'captured' by politics or economics, for example, resulting in the self-production of law's normative elements becoming overstrained (Teubner, 1984: 386–7; 1987: 6–13).

Systems theory has generated considerable attention and criticism. Autopoietic theories indicate a return to abstract, grand theorizing and some commentators castigate the lack of empirical referents, especially as the central models are taken largely uncritically from biology. First, even if their assumptions are relevant to other animal species or to information theory, they may not be directly applicable to human society; and secondly, it is not taken for granted that such nonhuman, or nonliving, systems as biological organisms or computers operate self-referentially in the way that Luhmann supposes (Wolfe, 1992: 1731). Concepts are reified and autopoietic systems theory is tautological and becomes impossible to refute through empirical examples (Münch, 1992: 1464). It is a truism to assert that the legal system only produces law, and many social theorists earlier observed the ways in which law transforms the everyday world into legal relations. Teubner responds that such approaches are not scientific theories but strategic models of law, and that the theory of self-referential systems is a heuristic device (Teubner, 1984: 376–7, 384). Even so, following the dictates of this approach it is not possible to envisage an empirical situation that would not support the perspective. Finally, there is no culture or history in a view of law as an autopoietic system; law is not mediated by culture or everyday practices, but is only affected by structural differentiation and evolution.

Juridification

Habermas

Like Parsons, Habermas is interested in the integrative role of law in complex, secular societies. Following Weber, he focuses on rationality in law, but views rationality as more expansive than purposive rationality. Habermas decries the way in which normativity, and therefore, in his view, the legitimacy of law, disappears in models of law that stress its formal, rational, positivistic and systemic properties. He is particularly critical of Luhmann's self-referential conception of law, which eschews values and meaning as nonlaw, even though their descriptions of modern society are very similar.

Habermas distinguishes between the lifeworld and social systems. The lifeworld refers to spheres of meaningful social interaction and communication, based on a taken-for-granted cultural stock of knowledge that is intersubjectively shared. It is constituted by the totality of interpretations presupposed by the members as background knowledge, and is formed from relatively diffuse but always unproblematic background convictions relying on reciprocal recognition, thus enabling routine social activities (Habermas, 1984: 13, 70–3, 82; 1987: 119–52; 1996: 80). Communicative action – that is, 'the interaction of at least two subjects capable of speech and action who establish interpersonal relations' – depends on the use of language oriented to mutual understanding (Habermas, 1984: 86). Ideally, the maintenance of the lifeworld and undistorted, uncoerced communicative action results in social integration. However, communicative action becomes thwarted because of the ever-present potential for disagreement and dissension. The chances of conflict increase due to differentiation and pluralization (Habermas, 1996: 21–3). Habermas also attends to systems, especially the economy and the state. Action coordinated via money and power differs from communicative action because it only aims at purposive rationality: the economy is oriented towards monetary profit and the political system towards power.

In this schema law operates as a medium, it is both connected to the economy and state and to the lifeworld, which is not characterized by purposive rationality but by practical reason, with an emphasis on morality, personal autonomy and communication. Money and power are connected to the lifeworld via legal institutionalization and the concerns of the lifeworld are conveyed to economic and political realms via legal discourse (Deflem, 1996: 8; Habermas, 1987: 256–82; 1996: 40). As Habermas suggests:

> The legal code not only keeps one foot in the medium of ordinary language, through which everyday communication achieves social integration in the lifeworld; it also accepts messages that originate there and puts these into a form that is comprehensible to the special codes of the power-steered administration and the money-steered economy. To this extent the language of law ... can function as a transformer in the society-wide communication circulating between system and lifeworld. (Habermas, 1996: 81)

Law is implicated in all three resources of integration, namely communicative action on the part of citizens who exercise their legal rights and freedoms in everyday life, as well as making possible the establishment and regulation of economic markets (via property, contract and corporation laws) and governmental bodies (via administrative law).

Law, then, is two things at once: it is a type of cultural knowledge understood as texts composed of legal propositions and their interpretations, as well as an institution, that is, a complex of normatively regulated action (Habermas, 1996: 79). Legal and moral rules appear simultaneously as two different but mutually complementary kinds of action norms. Both are forms of cultural knowledge, but in addition law has a binding character at the institutional level (Habermas, 1996: 105–7). Law exists in the lifeworld, which is also the location of morality, and law requires justification, especially in complex societies, which entails value commitments. By emphasizing the positivity, legalism and formality of modern law, Habermas argues that Weber assumes that all individuals behave strategically, that is, that legal subjects utilize their private autonomy in a purposive-rational manner. This orientation displaces the problem of justification, for example: 'The catalog of basic rights contained in bourgeois constitutions, insofar as they are formally set down, together with the principle of the sovereignty of the people, which ties the competence to make law to the understanding of democratic will-formation are expressions of this justification that has become *structurally necessary*' (Habermas, 1984: 261, emphasis added). To the extent that modern law becomes a means for political domination, there emerges a need for legitimation, that is, a principled mode of justification, via a constitution, for example, that can be understood as the expression of a rational agreement among all citizens (Habermas, 1984: 262).

Because Weber viewed the rationalization of law in terms of purposive-rationality, questions regarding the institutional embodiment of moral practical rationality are inverted: they now appear to be a source of irrationality, or at least severely weaken the formal rationalism of law. Habermas considers that Weber confused an appeal to the need to justify legal domination with an appeal to particular values. Weber viewed societal rationalization explicitly from the perspective of purposive rationality, thereby denying value-rational aspects of action, which means that at the level of economic and political subsystems only the aspect of purposive-rational and not that of value-rational action is supposed to have structure-forming effects. His conceptions of modern law and legal domination are so narrow that the need for a principled, rational mode of justification is jettisoned in favour of emphasizing the positivity, legalism and formality of law. As such, the rationalization of law is no longer measured against the inner logic of the moral-practical sphere of value, as is that of ethics and life conduct; it is directly connected to the progress of knowledge in the cognitive-instrumental sphere of value (Habermas, 1984: 254, 262–8).

Even though law exists in both the lifeworld and the social system, its operation is not always positive and it is not just a medium; to some extent it has a life and logic of its own. Habermas describes tendencies toward increasing regulation by law or juridification *(Verrechtlichung)*, which is the general tendency towards an increase of written law evident in modern society. He identifies four epochal juridification processes/stages, characterized by new legal institutions.

1 The *bourgeois state,* which in western Europe developed during the period of absolutism in the form of the European state system. This formed the political order that enabled the transformation of early modern feudal society into capitalist market society; introduced important principles of statutory law and the concept of the legal person; and established private law or the code of civil law to regulate transactions between legal persons, while public law authorizes a sovereign state power with a monopoly on coercive force and is the sole source of legal domination.

2 The *bourgeois constitutional state,* which assumed an exemplary form in the monarchy of nineteenth-century Germany, entailed the constitutional regulation

of executive authority. As private individuals, citizens are given actionable rights in terms of life, liberty and property interests against the sovereign, though they do not yet democratically participate in forming the sovereign's will.

3   The *democratic constitutional state*, which spread in Europe and in North America post-1789. Constitutionalized state power was democratized and (some) citizens, as citizens of the state, were provided with rights of political participation. Now there is a democratically assured presumption that laws express a general interest and procedures are established for parliaments to enact legislation that allows for public debate on law and legal change.

4   The *social and democratic constitutional state*, which was achieved through the labour and welfare movements during the twentieth century. Shorter working hours, the freedom to organize unions, social security and factory acts indicate juridification in the world of paid work, as such issues had previously been part of the prerogative of the owners of the means of production (Habermas, 1987: 356–62).

This view of juridification is state-centred, but Habermas also describes the juridification of everyday life, which he refers to as the colonization of the lifeworld (Habermas, 1987: 318–31). Juridification results from the legislative programmes of the welfare state, which offer protection to citizens against the inhumane effects of the capitalist market and provide such rights and freedoms *vis-à-vis* the state as universal (albeit limited) education or health schemes. The impact of the welfare state is paradoxical: its development enhances autonomy by cushioning the effects of an unregulated market, but the creation of legislation and bureaucracies to administer legal entitlements (usually in the form of monetary compensation) results in greater intervention in the lifeworld (Habermas, 1987: 361–73). Habermas observes that: 'From the start, the ambivalence of guaranteeing freedom and taking it away has attached to policies of the welfare state' (Habermas, 1987: 361, emphasis deleted). Social services established to provide expert or therapeutic assistance constitute further incursions into the lifeworld of citizens (see also Foucault, 1979). While this type of juridification aims to facilitate social integration, disintegration occurs within the lifeworld as situations and relationships come to be calculated in terms of money and power. The medium of the law can actually inhibit the aims and rationale of the lifeworld. For example, laws and administrative regulations stemming from educational policy on schools and teachers may actually undermine education by fettering the teacher's discretion and pedagogical initiative. On one side, juridification grants protection and recognizes individual rights; on another it inhibits freedom and creativity. Specifically:

> The more the welfare state goes beyond pacifying the class conflict lodged in the sphere of production and spreads a net of client relationships over private spheres of life, the stronger are the anticipated pathological side effects of a juridification that entails both a bureaucratization and a monetarization of core areas of the lifeworld. (Habermas, 1987: 364)

Increasingly, the family, for example, is viewed as sets of legal relations and associated rights, protections and obligations. While such formalization is often seen as emancipatory, giving individual family members greater (legal) identity and rights, by breaking up the traditional structures of domination it can also create new forms of dependence and domination in the form of state intervention and payment (Glendon, 1989: 291–313).

Juridification of the lifeworld means legally supplementing a communicative context of action through the superimposition of legal norms. 'It is the medium of the law itself that violates the communicative structures of the sphere that has been juridified' (Habermas, 1987: 370; also compare with Luhmann, 1986; and see Deflem, 1996: 10–12). All this suggests an increasing disillusionment with the emancipatory potential of law and a sense that it aligns more with purposively rational action and less with the practical reason of the lifeworld. Surprisingly, Habermas does not jettison his expectations regarding the positive role of the legal institutions, nor reassess his defence of Enlightenment reason.

Earlier concerns with rationality, the legitimation of law and juridification establish the foundation for Habermas's most expansive treatment of law: *Between Facts and Norms* (1996). This was originally published in German as *Faktizitat und Geltung*, which translates literally as 'facticity and validity'. Habermas's overarching concern is to develop a theory of democracy that allows public participation and deliberation and that can be sustained in a highly pluralistic and differentiated society. He regards law, particularly the form existing in constitutional democracies, as central to ensuring deliberative democracy. His social theory of law is located between the fact of social differentiation and the norm of democracy, and he views law as mediating between normative demands of reason and the empirical facts of power and complexity (Bohman, 1994: 898–9). Habermas's quest to articulate a normative account of law continues and he articulates a reconstructive approach encompassing both 'the sociology of law and the philosophy of justice' (Habermas, 1996: 7).

Habermas rejects legal philosophers' lack of empirical grounding and inattention to legal institutions and criticizes social theorists', especially systems theorists', refusal to acknowledge values in the legal sphere. He argues that the rule of law and democracy are conceptually related, not just historically associated. The legitimacy of law derives from democratic procedures that create an open, tolerant, discursive and well-informed environment for political will formation. The core of democratic legitimacy is not metaphysical, but is the outcome of discursive conditions under which all citizens can shape, without coercion or distorted beliefs, the decisions that affect or interest them. Ideally, norms derive their legitimacy via the full agreement of citizens (Bohman, 1994: 903; Habermas, 1996: 449). Thus 'the establishment of the legal code, which is undertaken with the help of the universal right to equal individual liberties, must be *completed* through communicative and participatory rights that guarantee equal opportunities for the public use of communicative liberties' (Habermas, 1996: 458, emphasis in original). This is not an argument for direct participatory democracy, but one that seeks to embed radical democratic principles in an account of the political and legal institutions of modern constitutional democracies (Bohman, 1994: 897).

As society becomes more complex, shared background assumptions and overlapping lifeworlds diminish. Greater pluralization and the increasing individualization of life histories fragment common identity and community. The problem for modern societies becomes: 'how the validity and acceptance of a social order can be stabilized once communicative actions become autonomous and clearly begin to differ, in the view of the actors themselves, from strategic interactions' (Habermas, 1996: 25). In a secular, pluralistic society, normative orders must be maintained without shared religious worldviews. The increasing need for integration overtaxes the integrative capacity of communicative action. Because modern societies are heterogeneous, conflict resolution must accommodate various subgroups, each of which has its own self-understanding and unique set of shared background assumptions. The reduction of shared lifeworlds, combined with greater scope for individuals to pursue their interests according to the dictates of purposive rationality, jeopardizes social coordination (Rehg, 1996: xvii–xix). Modern law takes into account this tension by acknowledging private rights that define the legitimate scope of individual liberties and the pursuit of private interests. Citizens must recognize this system of abstract rights if they wish to regulate interactions and social relationships by means of legitimate positive law. A legal order must be legitimate by granting equal liberties to all citizens and the rights of each person must be reciprocally recognized (Habermas, 1996: 31–2; Rehg, 1996: xxvii).

Legal validity simultaneously defines freedom and is based on coercion, so that the same law can regulate actors acting instrumentally as well as those acting communicatively. Habermas says: 'for the person acting strategically, it [legal validity] lies at the level of social facts that externally restrict her range of options; for the person acting communicatively, it lies at the level of obligatory expectations that, she assumes, the legal community has rationally agreed on' (Habermas, 1996: 31). Actors can consider legal norms as commands that constrain their actions and that they contemplate strategically in order to determine the calculable consequences of possible rule violations. Alternatively, they can take a performative view and approach legal norms as valid and comply because of respect for the law (Habermas, 1996: 448). Modern law regulates action and can be enforced by sanctions. At the same time it has legitimacy, which attracts respect and compliance without coercion. This dual nature is possible because modern law grants liberties and rights to all and is built on citizen participation in the democratic process of law making. Habermas's model of deliberative democracy relies on citizen input in public forums, informal associations and social movements. Laws draw their legitimacy from a legislative procedure based on the principle of popular sovereignty. Modern law is especially suited for the social integration of diverse, plural and individualistic societies, as it provides rights that secure for citizens their political autonomy (Habermas, 1996: 83). Habermas thus evinces a modernist faith in the rule of law for the protection of all citizens. The rule of law and adherence to a discourse of legal rights are strongly criticized by critical legal theorists and feminists for reflecting a dominant worldview and not taking sufficient account of the fluidity of law and local or particular differences.

Bourdieu

While not a systems theorist, Bourdieu investigates the way in which law and lawyers translate everyday issues into legal problems requiring legal remedies. His is a dynamic, fluid and flexible notion of law that militates against an objectified, reified conception of law and legal process. He takes the law to be a constitutive force in modern liberal societies and considers that the juridical field, like any social field, is oriented by a set of internal protocols and assumptions, characteristic behaviours and self-sustaining values (Terdiman, 1987: 806). The idea of field is less rigid than that of system, although, like Luhmann, Bourdieu is able to argue that the law transforms nonlegal conflicts into its own concepts and discourse and it is not dominated by other social systems (especially the state). However, he gives far more recognition to the role of legal actors.

Bourdieu observes that the dominant jurisprudential debate about law has been between formalist and instrumentalist approaches. Formalism views law as autonomous from social values, economic contingencies or political influence, and conceptualizes law as an organic, closed system constituted by sets of interrelated laws and doctrines. Instrumentalism considers law to be a reflection of economic or political interests or as a tool to be used in the service of dominant groups, particularly the bourgeois/capitalist class or men/patriarchy. Law is an instrument of domination based on an economic or a gender hierarchy. While law might appear to be universal, abstract and equally applicable to all members of society, in reality it reflects and reproduces social inequalities and specific worldviews.

Bourdieu argues that these two antagonistic approaches ignore the constitution of the juridical field, which in practice is relatively independent of external determinations and pressures. The social practices of the law are the product of the functioning of a field whose logic is determined by:

(a) the specific power relations that give it its structure and order the competitive struggles over competence occurring within it;
(b) the internal logic of juridical functioning that constantly constrains the range of possible actions and, thereby, limits the realm of potential juridical solutions (Bourdieu, 1987: 816).

For Bourdieu, law is the outcome of struggles among different legal actors, who compete with each other for control of the right to determine the law. Within the juridical field, confrontation occurs among actors possessing differing degrees of technical competence, which is essentially the socially recognized capacity to interpret a corpus of texts as sanctifying a correct or legitimized vision of the social world. The law is an outcome of this process:

> The development of a body of rules and procedures with a claim to universality is the product of a division of labour resulting from the competition among different forms of competence, at once hostile and complementary. ... The

> practical meaning of the law is really only determined in the confrontation between different bodies (e.g. judges, lawyers, solicitors) moved by divergent specific interests. Those bodies are themselves in turn divided into different groups, moved by divergent (indeed, sometimes hostile) interests, depending on their position in the internal hierarchy of the body, which always corresponds rather closely to the position of their clients in the social hierarchy. (Bourdieu, 1987: 821–2)

Competition between interpreters is limited by the fact that judicial decisions can be distinguished from naked exercises of power only to the extent that they can be presented as the necessary result of a principled interpretation of unanimously accepted texts. Law can exercise its specific power only while the arbitrariness at the core of its functioning remains unrecognized (Bourdieu, 1987: 818, 844). The idea of legal authority, the hierarchical authority of higher courts, *stare decisis,* or following the decisions *(ratio decidendi)* of higher courts to determine the resolution of new cases, all suggest the disinterested nature of lawyers' work. The juridical use of the passive voice and impersonal constructions, the identification (or construction) of 'legal facts' from individual circumstances, the recourse to fixed formulas (legal tests) providing little scope for individual variation, and exhortations to be finding the law all contribute to a rhetoric of impersonality, impartiality, neutrality and objectivity.

The core idea of *stare decisis* gives the impression that principles in previous cases determine present outcomes, thus rendering the decision apparently the result of a neutral and objective application of juridical procedures. As Bourdieu observes: 'the legal tradition possesses a large diversity of precedents and of interpretations from which one can choose the one most suited to a particular result' (Bourdieu, 1987: 833). Judicial decision making may be motivated by extra-legal considerations and the decision may precede the reasoning, thus becoming a justification of the decision rather than the reason for it. The legal technique of distinguishing cases on their facts and extending or restricting precedent ensures that cases can be used in many different ways. Nonetheless, the rhetoric of autonomy, neutrality and universality is not simply an ideological mask, but expresses the whole operation of the juridical field and especially the work of rationalization to which the system of juridical norms is continually subordinated (Bourdieu, 1987: 820–32).

Bourdieu attends to the special linguistic and social power of the law to do things with words, its reproduction, continuation, and legitimation in the eyes of those under its jurisdiction. This is the law's 'power of form', inherent in its constitutive tendency to formalize and to codify everything that enters its field, again a sign of the law's impartiality and neutrality. Law's symbolic power of naming enables it to create the things that it names, particularly social groups. Even so, the efficacy of law is not unbounded but limited by the degree to which it is socially recognized and this depends on some correspondence with real needs and interests (Bourdieu, 1987: 838–41; Terdiman, 1987: 809).

Bourdieu cautions against being misled by the exalted positivist representations of juridical activity that many legal theorists offer. Given the elasticity of texts, which can be entirely ambiguous or, at best, contradictory, the process of declaration or judgement entails considerable latitude. Legal and judicial personnel are able to exploit the ambiguity of legal formulas by appealing to such devices as narrowing, a procedure necessary to avoid applying a law that, literally understood, ought to be applied; or broadening, which allows the application of law to situations where it ought not to be applied; as well as a range of other techniques, such as analogy and the distinction of letter and spirit, which tend to maximize the elasticity of the law. However, not all legal participants have the same capacity or technical skill to use such legal resources effectively in order to have their view of law prevail or to win their case.

The transformation of irreconcilable conflicts of personal interest into rule-bound exchanges of rational arguments between equal individuals (that is, lawyers) is constitutive of the very existence of a specialized body (that is, a court) independent of the social groups in conflict. Courts are responsible for organizing the public representation of social conflicts according to established forms, and for finding solutions socially recognized as impartial. The juridical field becomes a social space oriented to the conversion of direct conflict between actors into a juridically regulated debate between professionals acting by proxy. Participating in this field indicates an acceptance of resolving conflicts in terms of the rules and conventions of the field; conflicts can only be resolved juridically. It is salutary to contemplate that:

> Nothing is less 'natural' than the 'need for the law' or, to put it differently, than the impression of an injustice which leads someone to appeal to the services of a professional. ... The professionals create the need for their own services by redefining problems expressed in ordinary language as *legal* problems, translating them into the language of the law. (Bourdieu, 1987: 833–4, emphasis in original)

Law and discipline: Foucault

Law *per se* was not a central concept for Foucault, who dealt with various related phenomena, including discipline, power, punishment, regulation, government and governmentality. While he examined such legal or judicial institutions as the courts and the prison, by looking at discipline, regulation and governmentality, Foucault emphasized social control as diffused throughout society and not just located exclusively in the domain of the state and its legal institutions. He urged: 'We must construct an analysis of power that no longer takes law as a model and a code' (Foucault, 1981: 90; also 92–102). Foucault established his perspective on punishment as a set of power/knowledge techniques located in a field of political forces and a set of resources for administering the bodies of individuals and through them the body politic. Foucault viewed punishment as a set of disciplinary mechanisms, with discipline being a type of power that may be taken over by such specialized institutions as penitentiaries or by other authorities that use it to reinforce or reorganize their internal mechanisms of power. He developed the notion of the increasing subtlety and pervasiveness of social control in *Discipline and Punish* (Foucault,

1979), where he described the disappearance of torture as a public spectacle and the emergence of the disciplinary society. He offered two extreme images of discipline:

1   *The discipline-blockade:* characterized by the enclosed institution, established on the edges of society, turned inwards towards negative functions, namely arresting evil, breaking communications and suspending time. Bentham's Panopticon is the architectural manifestation that ensures the continual visibility of the prisoner, who is the object of information and never a subject in communication. The major effect of the Panopticon is to induce in the inmates a consciousness of their permanent visibility that assures the automatic functioning of power; surveillance is permanent in its effects even if it is discontinuous in its action. The perfection of power should render its actual exercise unnecessary: 'The inmate must never know whether he [*sic*] is being looked at any one moment; but he [*sic*] must be sure that he [*sic*] may always be so' (Foucault, 1979: 201). The actual presence or absence of the supervisor is unverifiable and clear divisions persist between prisoners/nonprisoners and, in other contexts, between the mad/sane, the dangerous/harmless and the normal/abnormal. This form of discipline has been applied in factories, schools, hospitals and military barracks as well as prisons.

2   *The discipline-mechanism:* a functional mechanism that must improve the exercise of power by making it lighter, more rapid, more effective; a design of subtle coercion for a disciplinary society. The mechanisms of power become deinstitutionalized to emerge from the closed fortresses in which they once functioned to circulate freely. The disciplines are broken down into flexible methods of control exercised in everyday life (Foucault, 1979: 209–11).

The movement from a regime of exceptional discipline to one of generalized surveillance and, ultimately, the disciplinary society rests on an historical transformation. The disciplinary practices, once concentrated in the prison and the asylum, diffuse throughout society and the power to punish becomes fragmented and less easily identifiable. Punishment entails the segregation and continuous surveillance of 'problematic populations', combined with an emphasis on discipline and correction. The punitive and juridical functions of the sovereign are visibly obvious, unlike those of the psychiatrist, the probation officer, the psychologist, the teacher, the social worker, the doctor and the counsellor. This results in punishment becoming the most hidden part of the penal process. Disciplinary mechanisms tend to become deinstitutionalized and broken down into flexible methods of control exercised by the human sciences adopting a therapeutic model. Notably educationalists, and then the medical, psychiatric, psychological, social work and counselling professions, have made the family the privileged locus for the disciplinary problem of the normal and the abnormal (Foucault, 1979: 215–6).

Generally, disciplinary practices are techniques for assuring the ordering of human multiplicities, of achieving normalization, according to three criteria:

(a) to obtain the exercise of power at the lowest possible cost, economically and politically;

(b) to bring the effects of this social power to their maximum intensity and to extend them as far as possible without failure or interval; and

(c) to link this economic growth of power with the output of the apparatuses (educational, military, industrial and medical) within which it is exercised and thus to increase both the docility and the utility of all elements of the system (Foucault, 1979: 218).

The operation of these new disciplinary mechanisms of power is ensured not by law, but rather by normalization (Foucault, 1980: 106; 1981: 144). Discipline is characteristically associated with 'norms' – that is, with 'standards' of proper conduct – rather than with offences. Interventions as components of a mode of regulation aim to secure compliance and conformity with standards of behaviour. Normalization, then, is counterpoised to Foucault's prohibition/punishment model of law (Hunt and Wickham, 1994: 49). Formally juridical frameworks are more egalitarian than processes of normalization, as they acknowledge legal rights and due process, and provide various protections for the person defending criminal charges. In contrast, the disciplines – as knowledge and occupational practices – are non-egalitarian and asymmetrical (Foucault, 1981: 83–5).

Foucault often seems to suggest that discipline supplants law as the dominant form of social control. He says:

> And if it is true that the juridical system was useful for representing, albeit in a nonexhaustive way, a power that was centered primarily around deduction *(prélèvement)* and death, it is utterly incongruous with the new methods of power whose operation is not by punishment but by control, methods that are employed on all levels and in forms that go beyond the state and its apparatus. (Foucault, 1981: 89)

Even though Foucault mostly contrasts discipline and law, he does not suggest that the institutions of justice tend to disappear or that the disciplines supplant judicial authority, but, increasingly, the judicial institution becomes incorporated into a continuum of apparatuses (medical, administrative and so on), whose functions are for the most part regulatory (Foucault, 1981: 144). Nonetheless, Foucault under-estimates the power of law, which in many jurisdictions seeks, with success, to curtail the role and authority of some professional occupations. Informed consent requirements, legislation regulating some medical practices and judicial decisions on negligence, for example, have evoked open conflict between law and medicine.

The marginalization of law is one of the most distinctive aspects of Foucault's account of the historical emergence of modernity (Hunt, 1992: 2). He describes law as the primary form of power in classical or premodern times, but it is overshadowed (although not totally incapacitated) by discipline as the distinctive form of modern power. This underemphasis on law in modernity stems from

Foucault's conceptualization of law in terms of state power (the command of the sovereign) and as repression (Hunt, 1992: 2; Hunt and Wickham, 1994: 50–1, 59–71). His focus on power in its capillary manifestations, exercised by medicine, psychiatry and other human services personnel, detracts from the continuing concentration of power in state law, legal institutions and legal actors. This presents the difficulty of attending to localized (nonlegal) power without losing sight of the significance of the state and other forms of institutionalized power (Hunt and Wickham, 1994: 17–24, 56).

The state and legal forms of power continually interact with other types of power; sometimes state power is pre-eminent and the final arbiter of social control, but this is by no means guaranteed. 'State law is always involved with, if not preoccupied with, the task of either exercising control over or exempting from control the different forms of disciplinary regulation' (Hunt, 1992: 22). Governmentality, another concept deriving from Foucault's writings, usefully captures this notion of regulatory contestation and continual interaction between legal and other forms of power. It describes the dramatic expansion in the scope of government, facilitated by the emergence of the human sciences that provide new mechanisms of calculation, especially statistics, enabling particular kinds of knowledge about populations and, in turn, becoming the basis for regulation, intervention and administration (Ewald, 1991: 96; Hunt and Wickham, 1994: 76–7). Governments attempt to unify and centralize various forms of regulation in their quest to manage populations and subpopulations. The availability of criminal statistics, for example, was an important historical predecessor of contemporary criminal justice strategies in many nations (Deflem, 1997: 157–68).

Foucault refers to a sovereignty–discipline–government trilogy, which has as its primary target the population and as its essential mechanism the apparatuses of security (and minimization of risk). He specifies three aspects of governmentality:

1 The ensemble formed by the institutions, procedures, analyses and reflections, calculations and tactics that allow the exercise of this very specific, albeit complex, form of power. Its target is the population, its principal form of knowledge is political economy, and its essential technical means are apparatuses of security.
2 The pre-eminence of government over sovereignty and discipline has resulted in the formation of a whole series of specific governmental apparatuses and the development of a whole complex of *savoirs* (knowledges).
3 The process, or rather the result of the process, through which the state of justice of the Middle Ages transformed into the administrative state during the fifteenth and sixteenth centuries, gradually becomes governmentalized (Foucault, 1991: 102–3).

Following on from this, Hunt and Wickham propose a sociology of 'law as governance', by which all operations of law are seen as instances of governance (Hunt and Wickham, 1994: 99). They modify Weber's conception of law along Foucaultian and Durkheimian lines to define it thus:

An operation is called law where it involves a calculation by some actor or other (individual or collective), using a definite means of calculation, towards conformity with an historically received norm or the avengement of a violation of such a norm, where a staff holding themselves specially ready for directing the conformity and/or conducting the avengement is involved. (Hunt and Wickham, 1994: 100)

They identify four principles of law as governance:

1 All instances of law as governance contain elements of attempt and elements of incompleteness, which at times may be viewed as failure.
2 It involves power, politics and resistance.
3 Law as governance always involves knowledge. Increasingly this knowledge is statistical, which becomes important for all types of modern governance (Feeley and Simon, 1992: 452–9).
4 Law as governance is always social and always works to bind societies together, although this also may entail social division (Hunt and Wickham, 1994: 102–16). The extension of government entails an expansion of new areas of law, including industrial, family, social security, child protection, discrimination, environmental, company and international law.

Some comment that the image of governance that Hunt and Wickham propose – namely their exhortations to detail, concern to expound principles, and their idea of governance as a machine whose features are technical and mundane – does not sufficiently capture the complexity of political life (Baxter, 1996: 470–1). Nevertheless, they address and synthesize contemporary legal theory, develop the relevance of Foucault's comments on law, discipline and governance, and rely on the sociology of law tradition. In doing so, they straddle the divide between legal theory and the sociology of law, a divide that is sometimes impossible to cross.

Neo-Marxist theories

Neo-Marxist theories show how law and legal institutions are linked with economic structures and class interests. The precise nature of the links is a source of disagreement and even individual theorists will shift their positions (Chambliss, 1964; 1974; 1979; Quinney, 1970; 1977). Neo-Marxists frequently rely on the concept of ideology to examine the connection between legal ideas and values, on one side, and economic and political interests on the other (Hunt, 1985: 13). Poulantzas, for example, concludes that in capitalist societies law fulfils 'the key function of every dominant ideology: namely, that of cementing together the social formation under the aegis of the dominant class' (Poulantzas, 1978: 88).

Some theorists extrapolate from Marx and Engels' statement that 'the executive of the modern state is but a committee for managing the common affairs of the whole bourgeoisie' (Marx and Engels, 1948: 5) to argue that law is a tool manipulated by members of the bourgeoisie to further their own interests. This instrumentalist conception is most developed in analyses of the criminal law. Quinney argues that the legal system provides the mechanism for the forceful and violent control of the rest of the community and states, somewhat rhetorically: 'In the course of battle, the agents of the law (police, prosecutors, judges, and so on) serve as the military force for the protection of domestic order. Hence, the State and its accompanying legal system reflect and serve the needs of the ruling class' (1975: 193). In contrast to such economic reductionism, other neo-Marxists recognize that, as bourgeois interests are not always protected by the law, it cannot simply be an instrument of that class. Specific laws and legal doctrines often have an affinity with capitalism in its various stages while simultaneously retaining relative autonomy from direct economic and political intervention.

Pashukanis – a Soviet legal theorist writing in the 1920s and 1930s – made an early attempt to move away from instrumentalism. He proposed a commodity exchange theory of law to argue that it is possible to understand law as a social relationship in the same way that Marx viewed capital (Beirne and Sharlet, 1980: 55). If law has its real origin in commodity exchange, and if socialism requires the abolition of commodity exchange and the construction of production for use, then proletarian or socialist law is a conceptual and a practical absurdity (Beirne and Sharlet, 1980: 12–13). Pashukanis's prediction that private law and the legal state would wither away on the elimination of private property became increasingly incompatible with the political realities of the Soviet state, where law became central to economic planning and social transformation. This conflict led to the demise of the commodity exchange school of law and to Pashukanis's disappearance in 1937.

The commodity exchange theory of law has been revived among some contemporary neo-Marxist theorists (Balbus, 1977: 573–6; Hunt, 1981: 67; O'Malley, 1983: 34–50). The central argument is that the logic of the commodity form parallels the logic of the legal form, with both forms being historically specific (Beirne and Sharlet, 1980: 3–5). As the commodity form equalizes different products and the labour that produces them, thus allowing the exchange of the substantively unequal, the legal form equalizes different people by treating them all as citizens and the holders of generic rights, thus allowing exchange relationships between formally equal but substantively unequal legal subjects. Balbus writes:

> The homology between the legal form and the commodity form guarantees both that the legal form, like the commodity form, functions and develops autonomously from the preferences of social actors [especially those of the capitalist class] *and* that it does *not* function and develop autonomously from the system in which these social actors participate. (Balbus, 1977: 585, emphasis in original)

Unequal individuals with incommensurable interests enter into formally equal relationships with one another, the prototype being contractual relations. The parties appear to be what they are not: equal. Renner – an Austrian neo-Marxist – pointed out that the 'right of choice' distinguishes contractual from feudal relations; however, the lawyer ignores the question of the extent to which economic conditions permit the employee to exercise this right (Renner, 1969: 37 fn 3). Like Pashukanis, Renner concentrated on Marx's conception of capitalist society in which socially unequal members are united in exchange and investigated how legal institutions facilitate essential economic functions.

The formal equality established and protected by the legal form ignores and thereby reproduces substantive inequalities. The notion that property laws apply equally has more resonance with people who actually own property than with those who do not. Laws dealing with vagrancy and homelessness, which apply to everyone, only affect specific segments of the population. Thus the legal form produces and reinforces illusory rather than genuine forms of equality, individuality and community. Legal equality masks class differences and social inequalities, contributing to a 'declassification' of politics that militates against the formation of the class consciousness necessary for creating a substantively more equal society. It legitimates the capitalist state, because as long as citizens perceive formality, generality and equality before the law as genuine and collective, then even gross and systematic departures from these norms will not serve to delegitimate the legal order. At most, such deviations will delegitimate specific laws and specific incumbents of political office who are responsible for these laws (Balbus, 1977: 581).

The content of legislation may not always be in the immediate interests of entrepreneurs and industry, but facilitates ongoing economic relations of production (Beirne, 1979: 379–80). Chambliss proposes a dialectical paradigm that conceptualizes law creation as a process aimed at the resolution of contradictions, conflicts and dilemmas that inevitably emerge from the prevailing social structure. Under capitalism, the basic contradiction between labour and capital generates conflicts surrounding wages and employment conditions, including discrimination and occupational health and safety. Legislation passed to manage these disputes itself creates the potential for further conflicts, which may be resolved by court decisions and/or legislative amendment. The underlying contradiction remains largely untouched by the legal process, but legal change can be interpreted as a continuing reaction to auxiliary conflicts and dilemmas (Chambliss, 1979: 7–8). A corollary is that the amelioration or management of social problems comes to be seen by social activists and policy makers as requiring more or different kinds of substantive law. The form and ideology of law and legal institutions remain unquestioned. Contemporary Marxian historians demonstrate the importance of the ideology of the 'rule of law', which has enabled draconian laws to be passed because government officials were not seen as acting capriciously but as constrained by law. In order to retain the ideology of justice and equity, on occasion laws actually had to be just and limit the powers of ruling elites (Hay, 1975: 33; Thompson, 1975: 263).

Critical legal theory

The critical legal studies movement emerged in the late 1970s, although its intellectual antecedents lie within legal realism. The Conference on Critical Legal Studies (CLS), founded in Madison, Wisconsin in 1977, comprises law teachers, social scientists, students and legal workers committed to the exploration of the relationship between legal theory and practice and the struggle for the creation of a more humane and just society. Counterparts exist in France *(Critique de Droit)* and in the UK (Critical Legal Conference). While critical legal theorists draw heavily on the Marxist tradition, they focus on legal education and scholarship as a significant source of social change. The fact that many CLS writers (and certainly the founders) are white, male academics employed in high status law schools has resulted in some scepticism about their revolutionary credentials and their capacity to assess other people's experiences and expectations of legal institutions (Williams, 1987: 410).

CLS is not a single coherent theory but a movement whose proponents reject conventional analyses of judicial decision making and legal doctrine as conservative and artificial. They express dissatisfaction with the existing state of scholarship and practice in law, reacting against prevailing orthodoxies in legal writing. These scholars despise the conservatism of law schools and criticize many features of the role of law and legal institutions in contemporary society. CLS writers are concerned to uncover or deconstruct and thereby to delegitimate the ideological mantle of law. They disagree that law can be distinguished from politics, arguing that judicial decisions and legal doctrine merely rationalize political decisions and are not the rational application of pre-existing rules (Brigham, 1996: 61–71; Davies, 2008: 183–212; Hunt, 1987: 5). CLS writers adopt the tools developed in the interpretive disciplines of anthropology, social history and literary criticism to examine the power relationships embedded in legal discourse.

CLS seeks to debunk the positivist or formalist conception of law as the application of unambiguous rules discoverable via legal reasoning to facts ascertained through evidence. Like the legal realists earlier in the twentieth century, critical legal theorists do not argue that the courts deviate from legal reasoning, but assert that there is no legal methodology or rational process for reaching judicial decisions. One theorist declares: 'we reject the idealized model and the notion that a distinctly legal mode of reasoning or analysis determines legal results or characterizes the legal process' (Kairys, 1990: 3). Legal reasoning is a distinct and elaborate system of discourse and a body of knowledge with its own language, conventions of argumentation and logic. However, as a method or process for decision making – that is, for determining correct rules, facts or results – the law provides only a wide and conflicting variety of stylized justifications that legitimate decisions. Judicial decisions are predicated on a complex mixture of social, political, institutional, experiential and personal factors, even though they are expressed, justified and largely perceived by judges themselves in terms of rules that have been objectively and rationally found and applied to unequivocal facts (Kairys, 1990: 4). For many critical legal theorists, legal reasoning is a process of reification in which the complex circumstances of individuals are either classified into legally relevant facts or excluded from consideration. Gabel argues that legal reasoning is the application of the scientific method to human interaction, providing an appearance of objectivity: 'Each situation appears as a "set of facts" which can be compared with analogical interchangeability to any other set of facts in order to determine whether the same two situations reveal the same abstract legal features' (Gabel, 1980: 30).

A further site of critique is the concept of rights formulated by liberal discourse as objective, concrete characteristics that can be claimed and judicially recognized. Critical legal scholars argue that rights are contingent on socio-political contexts and are therefore unstable or unreliable as a basis on which to make claims. Secondly, the language of rights is indeterminate, so it cannot differentiate between competing interests. For example, both opponents and proponents of legal abortion make claims to political rights to establish their cases. Thirdly, to argue that conflict or political expression is about rights reifies the complexity of real experience. Rights are abstract diversions from real situations and actual or substantive political needs. Tushnet maintains that: 'the language of rights should be abandoned to the very great extent that it takes as a goal the realization of the reified abstraction "rights" rather than the experiences of solidarity and individuality' (Tushnet, 1984: 1382–3). Situations and experiences should be viewed as directly relevant to political action and not refracted through the language of rights (Tushnet, 1984: 1384). Fourthly, the granting of rights does not necessarily translate into substantive justice or social amelioration.

Marxist influences in CLS are most evident in its proponents' concern with the ideology of liberal legalism and the claim that the legitimation function of law is crucial to understanding its doctrines, rationalizations, results and social role. Notions of the law as neutral, objective and quasi-scientific and the view of legal personnel as disinterestedly exercising technical expertise lend legitimacy to the judicial process. This, in turn, legitimates broader social and power relations that have alienating, oppressive dimensions and remain obscured by liberal legal ideology which emphasizes equality before the law and the impartiality of the justice system (Davies, 1994: 153–85; 2008: 183–212; Kairys, 1990: 4–7).

While critical legal theorists are committed to social change, they disagree about how to achieve it. Some argue that the critique or demystification of legal doctrine is sufficient to expose the limits of the system and to explore the possibility of alternatives (Feinman and Gabel, 1990: 385). Others point to the opportunities for transformation within the courts, suggesting that 'the very public and political character of the legal arena gives lawyers, acting together with clients and fellow legal workers, an important opportunity to reshape the way that people understand the existing social order and their place within it' (Gabel, 1982–83: 370). Nonetheless, CLS has not developed an active agenda of political involvement and much of the writing remains obscure and removed from the lives and experiences of disadvantaged and marginalized segments of society (Davies, 2008: 194–5; Williams, 1987: 401–2).

The principal advance of critical legal studies is its demonstration of the importance of integrating legal theory with social theory and its reassessment of the links between law and politics. In contrast to much conventional legal theorizing, CLS writers are primarily concerned with identifying the intimate relationship between law and legal reasoning and the reproduction of social and economic inequalities, at the same time as making the social order appear natural and inevitable. By demonstrating that legal doctrine is much less structured, impartial, coherent and rational than legal ideology alleges, it is hoped that the interests served by legal doctrine and the ideals of liberalism will surface and initiate political (and legal) transformation (Davies, 2008: 203–6; Lloyd and Freeman, 1985). This critique of the formal legal system and liberal legal theory has also been important in the development of informalism and alternative dispute resolution (see Chapter 5).

Despite grand claims, many CLS writers did not go beyond criticism or 'trashing' to develop a coherent theoretical position and are further hamstrung by disagreements about the efficacy or desirability of abstract theorization (Hunt, 1987: 5). This ambivalence is informed by recent debates on deconstruction, postmodernism, poststructuralism, phenomenology and the anti-foundationalist critique of the Enlightenment project. Some CLS writers express concern that generality equals abstraction, which is insensitive to the political realities of social life, thus rejecting the label 'theorist' and denying an engagement with theory (Gabel and Kennedy, 1984). Additionally, critical legal scholars often express hostility towards empirical evidence, which they equate with empiricism, inevitably allied with determinism and positivism (Hunt, 1987: 15; Trubek, 1984: 579–81).

In the USA, minority group scholars and others doubt the political sense of jettisoning rights discourse. Williams suggests that describing 'needs' – which critical legal theorists advocate – has been a dismal failure as a political strategy for Afro-American people, and writes:

> The argument that rights are disutile, even harmful, trivializes this aspect of black experience specifically, as well as that of any person or group whose vulnerability has been truly protected by rights. ... This country's [the USA's] worst historical moments have not been attributable to rights *assertion* but to a failure of rights commitment. (Williams, 1991: 159, emphasis in original)

While rights may not have been ends in themselves, rights rhetoric has been and continues to be an effective form of discourse for civil rights and other social movements (see Chapters 7 and 8). Advocating a rights strategy is not synonymous with a total reliance on litigation and success can be measured in many ways, not just in terms of a favourable judicial decision (Bartholomew and Hunt, 1991: 18, 34–9; Hunt, 1990: 317). The ways in which, and circumstances where, various social movements and individuals will utilize rights discourses as a component of their political strategies are subjects of empirical inquiry, whose importance would be lost in the simple denigration of the language of rights. Social actors deploy different rights discourses – for example property rights, social rights, moral rights and civil rights – to manage everyday disputes, thus they are not just relied on in the judicial process. Sometimes rights claims will succeed; at other times they will fail, suggesting that rights discourses in themselves are neither good nor bad.

Feminist legal theories

Feminist theories demonstrate the ways in which legal doctrine and practices discriminate against women and reinforce gender inequalities. The law gives an appearance of neutrality when in fact it is deeply biased. Despite some changes, the law remains a male-dominated profession and legal institutions and discourse reflect male concerns and priorities. A pervasive theme in feminist legal theory is that western jurisprudence and legal doctrine based on liberal notions of individual rights, freedom and reasonableness, while purporting to be value neutral and objective, actually favour men's interests and reinforce male domination. They ignore or marginalize women's experiences and approaches that value social relations and empathy (Fineman, 1991: xiii–xiv).

As with feminist theories in general, feminist legal theories have several key strands: liberal, radical and postmodern. Liberal approaches anticipate law's capacity to incorporate women's experiences and perspectives and thus become a truly general and neutral system; radical theories emphasize the masculine foundation of law, which suggests that it can never incorporate women's experiences; while postmodern approaches examine the ways in which law constitutes and is constituted by gender. These strands are not neat classifications, as Davies observes: 'Whereas it was once possible to divide feminist theory into a few fairly clear categories, this is no longer the case: it is much more likely that scholars will draw on a variety of theoretical tools and traditions' (Davies, 2008: 223). Nonetheless, it remains valuable to set out the main tenets of the different strands of feminist legal theories.

Liberal theories

Liberal feminists identify the law as sexist or biased and advocate reform as a remedy. They argue that the law can incorporate women's experiences and suggest that discriminatory legal practices (for example, excluding women from the legal profession or not allowing married women to own property) can be changed so that laws apply equally to men and women, or reflect both men's and women's experiences and social locations. Some feminists have argued that the entry of women into the legal profession and the recognition of women's experiences will make the law more relevant to the whole population, more cognizant of the wider social consequences of legal judgements and more just.

Some liberal approaches rely on Carol Gilligan's work to argue that women have a different morality or 'voice' than men. Traditionally, western legal systems reflect male values and morality and this imbalance needs to be corrected. Gilligan argues that women's identities are defined in a context of relationships and that female values are characterized by responsibility, intimacy, connection, and an ethic of care and nurturance, while male values emphasize autonomy, individualism and abstract rights and duties. Women's morality arises from the experience of connection conceived as a problem of inclusion, whereas men value individual achievement, independence, separation and competition (Gilligan, 1982: 30; West, 1988: 2–3; 1991: 130–1). The latter values underpin liberal legal theory and contemporary, adversarial legal systems. The feminist project, then, is to ensure that legal practice and knowledge incorporate male and female values equally; they are complementary rather than sequential or opposed.

Some feminists argue that such male-dominated or male-created values as victory, predictability, objectivity, deductive reasoning and universalism override so-called female values of mediation, caring, empathy and the maintenance of social relationships. They speculate that an ethic of care and a heightened sense of empathy in women indicate that women lawyers may be particularly interested in alternative dispute resolution and mediation rather than litigation (Bartlett, 1990: 863–7; Cahn, 1991: 4–5; Menkel-Meadow, 1987: 44; 1989a: 313; 1989b: 231–3). The implication is that such an approach would be more just, more sensitive and more appropriate, indeed superior to adversarial court procedures. Menkel-Meadow, for example, writes:

> The growing strength of women's voice in the legal profession may change the adversarial system into a more co-operative, less war-like system of communication between disputants in which solutions are mutually agreed upon rather than dictated by an outsider, won by the victor and imposed upon the loser. (Menkel-Meadow, 1987: 54–5)

Arguments that women have different qualities and values to men and that their increasing entry into the legal profession will transform its organization and practices tend to reinforce binary thinking: that male and female are polar opposites. Ironically, the qualities associated with women are those that have traditionally been used to justify their subordination and relegation to the so-called private sphere (Roach Anleu, 1992a: 426–7).

Radical approaches

Other feminist legal theorists disagree that the maleness of the law can be changed by increasing women's participation or by placing more value on so-called female qualities. Law is seen as 'maintaining male domination' (Polan, 1982: 294); 'a powerful conduit for the reproduction and transmission of the dominant ideology' (Thornton, 1986: 5); 'a paradigm of maleness' (Rifkin, 1980: 84); and as 'a particularly potent source and badge of legitimacy, and site and cloak of force, (MacKinnon, 1989: 238). Relying on litigation or legislation to alter women's status is misguided; the law is not, and neither can it be, a source of social change, as it reproduces rather than erodes patriarchal power relations (Thornton, 1991). Statutes and judicial decisions have restricted women's entry into the public sphere, including their access to high-paying professional occupations. For example, courts in the early part of the twentieth century often interpreted the word 'persons' to mean men and adopted the notion of 'separate spheres' to justify women's exclusion from the practice of law and other professions. Where legislation referred to persons practising as doctors or lawyers, judges decided that women were excluded because, if the legislature's intention had been to include women, then that would have been explicitly articulated (Mossman, 1990: 80–8)! Moreover, law has largely been absent from the private sphere, thereby contributing to male dominance and female subservience (Taub and Schneider, 1982: 118).

Rejecting the notion of 'different voices', MacKinnon suggests that inequality comes first – the most central inequality being gender – and differences follow. She argues that focusing on differences serves as an ideology that neutralizes and rationalizes power inequalities. Gender is a question of power, of male supremacy and female subordination (MacKinnon, 1987: 8). To re-evaluate empathy, care, mediation, concern for relationships and an orientation to others inevitably reproduces gender inequality and reinforces male dominance. MacKinnon maintains that the liberal state coercively and authoritatively constitutes the social order in the interest of men as a gender through its legitimizing norms, relation to society and substantive policies (MacKinnon, 1983: 644). It embodies and ensures male control over women's sexuality at every level, occasionally cushioning, qualifying or *de jure* curbing its excesses to maintain legitimacy. As 'male' is the implicit reference for human, maleness will be the measure of equality in sex-discrimination law. The essential features of the male perspective are rationality, objectivity, equality, liberty, privacy and freedom of speech. The adoption of these values in law reproduces gender inequalities under the guise of neutrality and justice. Law, then, not only reflects a society in which men rule women; it also rules in a 'male' way. The state, in part through law, institutionalizes male power.

MacKinnon's concern is not just to identify male dominance and propose a feminist theory, but also to engage in practical action and the transformation of power relations through a feminist method. She suggests that consciousness raising enables women to view the shared reality of their condition from within the perspective of their own experience. This methodology enables an evaluation of the purported generality, disinterestedness and universality of prior accounts. The collective speaking of women's experience uncovers and analyses male dominance (MacKinnon, 1982: 519). This assumes that women's experiences and accounts will be complementary, not conflicting, and is unclear about how consciousness raising can cast off the male point of view, which has been imposed and is metaphysically nearly perfect (Roach Anleu, 1992a: 430). MacKinnon is ambivalent about the relationship between legal change and social change. On one side, the notion of the maleness of law and its incorporation of values that reflect men's but not women's experiences helps explain why legal reform in the areas of abortion, child custody, property, equal opportunity and rape has not sufficiently changed the status of women. On the other, she appears to be very optimistic for the role of law in prohibiting sexual harassment and pornography, having actively engaged in law reform on these issues.

Both liberal and radical feminist approaches to legal theory tend to treat women and men, or male and female, as mutually exclusive, internally homogeneous categories, thereby downplaying complex class, cultural, ethnic, national, regional and other differences. The view that women constitute a category possessing distinct attributes or perspectives can lead to an essentialist position whereby 'real' women are denied other characteristics. Describing society and the law as patriarchal or male dominated often renders women passive victims and devalues their historical achievements and active resistance. Postmodernist approaches question the unity of the human subject and the transcendent quality of law.

Postmodern feminism

As with postmodernist approaches in general, postmodern feminists question the homogeneity and stability of social and legal categories, including those used by other feminists. In particular, the category of woman is criticized as reflecting the experiences of white, middle-class and well-educated women, and thereby silencing the voices of others (Harris, 1990: 585). Suggesting that women have similar experiences of inequality and oppression that unite them and provide a single set of political goals ignores differences in race, class and sexuality among women (Cornell, 1991: 2248–51; Naffine and Owens, 1997; Spelman, 1988: 133–42). Postmodernists seek to recognize sites of oppression and identify different and shifting identities that do not collapse into the list of binary opposites that has been relied on by previous legal theories (both feminist and non-feminist) to dissociate women from law and public life (Davies, 2008: 274–81).

The postmodernist standpoint is not content with proliferating categories but questions the very validity of categorization: the boundaries of the categories and the identities of the members are not fixed (Davies, 2008: 279). It also rejects a view of law as either neutral *vis-à-vis* women or as inherently male, so it does not make sense to argue that the law is sexist or male or that it affects all women in the same ways. Postmodern theorists shift attention to the ways in which law constitutes gender, especially gender differences, and the converse. They move away from general explanations to the examination of more localized and specific discourses in particular contexts. This involves a primary focus on how legal discourses and practices constitute subject positions. Law becomes a site in which gendered positions and identities are articulated; it is neither essentially neutral nor male. For example, rather than looking at the effect of domestic violence or rape laws on women as a category, postmodernists examine the ways in which these laws affect different kinds of women.

Pursuing Foucault's interest in such concepts as truth, power and knowledge, Carol Smart argues that the reform of law and legal institutions will inevitably be limited because law is not the only location of discipline and power (Smart, 1989: 6–17). Feminist reform efforts are inevitably coopted by legal knowledge and legal victories, so that no matter how radical they appear, such reforms actually extend the power of law. Ironically, using law to undercut dimensions of oppression serves to reinforce the dominance of law. Yet, despite the proliferation of non-juridical disciplines and modes of regulation, law remains one of the most powerful discourses. It invalidates other kinds of knowledge, especially feminism, or selectively incorporates those which most easily fit into its pre-defined categories (Smart, 1990: 196). Use of the term 'the law' is deceptive, as it is constituted by a myriad of often contradictory legal principles, statutes, judgements and practices; thus reform in one dimension can be easily counteracted.

Law exercises power via judgements but also through its ability to disqualify other knowledges and experiences that must be translated into legal issues before they can be processed by the legal system. Specifically, everyday conflicts must be translated into a discourse of rights to enable law to exercise its power (Smart, 1989: 11–20). Relying on rights discourse has limitations for feminists (and other progressive social movements): it extends the power of law which, as a mode of social regulation, is often antithetical to the arguments and claims of women's movements. Davies argues that a difficulty in appropriating existing legal concepts to feminist ends derives from the interrelatedness between law and property (Davies, 1994: 366–7). Specifically, conventional conceptions of sexuality resonate with juristic conceptions of property that limit possible ideas about social relationships. The notion of ownership, even self-ownership, presupposes alien-ation and the formulation of identity as the possession of certain attributes suggests objectification and commodification. A conceptual framework that allows us to say that we own our bodies and our sexuality also allows them to be given away, sold or taken (Davies, 1994: 379). The conception of women's bodies as property, mostly to be owned by men, has a long legal and social history.

The body as a site of social regulation is currently a topic of widespread interest among postmodern theorists. Feminists describe the ways in which law privileges male bodies and constitutes them as the norm while marginalizing and pathologizing women's bodies (Grbich, 1991: 67–70). Foucault's (1979) writings have placed the question of the discipline of the body at the core of social theory. Regulation of bodies becomes critical for social control, with the most efficient, effective, invisible and normal site of enforcement being self-control and self-discipline. Normative feminin-ity is centred on women's bodies, and a woman concerned about her feminine appear-ance has become 'just as surely as the inmate of the Panopticon, a self-policing subject, a self committed to a relentless self-surveillance' (Bartky, 1988: 81). Disciplines of diet, exercise and beauty that reproduce dominant cultural practices train the female body in docility and obedience to cultural requirements, while at the same time being personally experienced as control and empowerment (Bordo, 1993). Feminists describe the pervasiveness of the legal regulation of women's bodies in relation to marriage, sexuality, motherhood and employment, and the regulation of women's bodies and sexuality has been central to criminal and civil laws (Naffine, 1997: 77–80; Smart, 1991). Accordingly, such issues as abortion, reproduction, sexual harass-ment, pornography, rape and domestic violence are focal points for feminist activism (see Chapter 7).

Legal pluralism

Rather than presuming that societies have a single legal system or that legal institutions are synonymous with the scope or nature of law in society, a renewed interest in legal pluralism seeks to identify the variety of legal systems coexisting in the same social field (Fitzpatrick, 1983: 46–7; Hunt, 1993: 308; Merry, 1988: 870). In discussing legal pluralism, authors distinguish between state law, referring to legislation, the legal system, judicial pronouncements and the legal profession, and nonstate law, which might include customary law, local law and traditional law (Merry, 1988: 875–6; Santos, 1987: 287). In contrasting two forms of law, colonial administrators, researchers and political activists have tended to romanticize, construct and reinterpret customary law and local institutions (Merry, 1988: 875–6; Zerner, 1994: 111–7). Anthropologists studying indigenous societies observed that, despite the imposition of colonial law, prior forms persist. This led to research on the relationships between the different legal spheres: the imposed law and local law (Burman and Harrell-Bond, 1979; Merry, 1991). Several kinds of situations are identified.

Imposed law

Imposed law dominates, especially where law is perceived as a strategy for achieving political or social goals that conflict with the traditional society and its law. This kind of legal pluralism is embedded in relations of unequal power, even though there is evidence of resistance and the manipulation of imposed laws. There are also unanticipated consequences of using law to advance colonization or modernization. Massell examines the Soviet use of legal rules and institutions in relation to personal status, family relations and sexual equality as components of the strategy to implement a full-scale revolution in traditional Islamic societies in Central Asia in the late 1920s (Massell, 1968: 180). One aim was to politicize and emancipate women as individuals by undermining the prevailing patterns of traditional authority based on kinship and religion. Such a naive programme did not anticipate the consequences of a greater female participation in public life, which included evasion of the new rules and an explosion of hostility and violence on the part of Muslim men toward women. The imposed regime's inability to provide opportunities to support women's new rights resulted in their disillusionment, destitution, fear and shame (Massell, 1968: 206–11, 222).

Interestingly, law is again being used to facilitate the transformation of the former eastern European socialist states into democratic polities with market economies. Constitutional legal systems, often following the advice of lawyers from other constitutional democracies, are being introduced into the formerly socialist states. New legal frameworks are being imposed or transplanted onto legal systems established to advocate socialism, where judges and courts acted as bureaucrats and were expected to advance the state-determined public interest and lawyers played a subservient role. Unlike the socialist legal systems that were expected to promote government activities and policies, the new constitutionalism aims to protect citizens from the incursions of government, especially regarding economic activities (Sajo, 1990: 330–3). In postcommunist east Germany, the legal profession has been purged while, simultaneously, the political and legal transformations have created new demands and opportunities for west German lawyers who are dealing with the complex and profitable cases of compensation and property claims (Blankenburg, 1995: 235–43; see Chapter 8).

Convergence

This occurs where different legal systems and cultures are fused, which may be the result of explicit policy. The British in Malaya, Ceylon and India enacted laws that were enforced by the state supreme courts, but religious and customary laws could be recognized as relevant to the formulation of case law. In civil cases, courts made decisions on the bases of custom and usage established as having the force of law (Mastura, 1994: 475). In Thailand, with the emergence of a constitutional monarchy in the 1930s, traditional Buddhist concepts of cosmic law and religion became fused with new concepts of political administration and legal authority. While Thailand was not a colony, it experienced considerable western political, economic and religious influence and the 1932 *coup d'état,* ending absolute monarchical rule, was staged by western-trained military officers and civilians. Constitutional provision for the king to support every religion in the realm to the extent that they were adhered to by the citizens of Thailand shaped the evolving civic religious tradition (Ishii, 1994: 456–7). This civic religion resting on the concepts of nation, religion and kingship provides a framework for the imaginative-symbolic and the more practical, action-oriented discourses of modern Thai legal culture. It also engages several religious traditions, especially Buddhism but also Islam and others (Reynolds, 1994).

Local political elites may selectively introduce Euro-American legal systems and courts, adapting them to local conditions. During the nineteenth century, legal reforms in Egypt modelled after the French system, while preserving and codifying Islamic law, served to pre-empt imperialism (Brown, 1995: 106, 115). The establishment of the rule of law, courts, legal doctrines and procedures that Europeans could recognize undermined imperialist ideologies regarding the civilizing effects and rational dimensions of western law.

Parallel

Where two or more legal systems and cultures coexist results in different laws applying to different subpopulations. This might occur where a dominant secular legal system is applicable to most areas of social life, while a religious law, for example the Shari'a, will regulate the marriage and family status of Muslim citizens. In 1977 the Philippine government enacted a Code of Muslim Personal Laws that exists alongside the Philippines' Family Code and Civil Code. This indicates a tendency to make legal exceptions by acknowledging and accepting the existence of customary laws that may have a controlling force in certain circumstances (Mastura, 1994: 474–5). In Australia there has been some recognition of the validity of Aboriginal customary law in limited circumstances.

Research and theorization about legal pluralism are not only useful for examining the imposition of legal regimes in colonial or postcolonial situations. Plural normative orders also exist to varying degrees in virtually all societies. Nevertheless, it is often unclear as to whether authors mean legal pluralism or normative pluralism, as they use such terms as plural normative orders (Merry, 1988: 873), different legal orders (Santos, 1987: 200), and different forms of law (Santos, 1987: 200). These new theoretical developments are also reminiscent of approaches that compare formal and informal social control (see Chapter 6).

The concept of legal pluralism enables the documentation of how other forms of social regulation draw on the symbols of law and, while operating outside the law, actually consolidate, extend or perhaps even limit legal regulation. Nonlegal institutions and social movements rely on legal discourse that affects strategies and tactics in both legal and other arenas (Brigham, 1987: 306–7). The concern with legal language, discourse and culture, especially such concepts as rights, duties, entitlements and property, unties the discussion of law from formal legal systems and doctrine. The language of law is important, because language is the process whereby cultural understandings are enacted, created and transformed in interaction with the social structure (Mertz, 1992: 423). The idea of legal pluralism also directs attention towards everyday practices rather than towards the formal structures of a legal system. Concern is with the ways that 'the law' is actually interpreted and applied by actors in daily life; it is not a bounded set of easily identifiable rules and systems. This allows for the investigation of different forms of law in different social contexts without defining some as 'real' law and others as not law at all, as Geertz observes:

> Law may not be a brooding omnipresence in the sky, as Holmes insisted rather too vehemently, but it is not, as the down-home rhetoric of legal realism would have it, a collection of ingenious devices to avoid disputes, advance interests, and adjust trouble-cases either. An *Anschauung* [view] in the marketplace would be more like it. And: other marketplaces, other *Anschauung*. (1983: 175)

Here, law is a system of meanings, a cultural code for interpreting the world. It cannot be abstracted from cultural meanings, everyday experiences or language. It is 'local knowledge', not abstract principles in its intermingled forms and varieties. Legal facts are not self-evident and must be identified, or more accurately constructed from the maze of information that everyday life presents, and moulded or translated into a legally interpretable form. Law is 'not a bounded set of norms, rules, principles, values, or whatever from which jural responses to distilled events can be drawn, but part of a distinctive manner of imagining the real' (Geertz, 1983: 173). Ewick and Silbey examine the way in which law – or what they call legality – is infused within everyday life as people intentionally interpret law's language, authority and procedures in the course of their social relationships without necessarily engaging with formal legal institutions or personnel (1998: 20). They discern three ways in which citizens view the law: first, legality is imagined as distant and removed from the personal lives of individuals, operating primarily within formal legal structures; second, it is presented as a strategy or game whereby people attempt to achieve their goals; and third, law is viewed as arbitrary and capricious and neither objective nor disinterested (Ewick and Silbey, 1998: 28).

Santos develops a notion of law as imagination by comparing it with maps: both are concerned with scale, projection and symbolization. Local law is large-scale legality, meaning that the legal norms are specific and detail relationships between individuals; they are sensitive to particular contexts and situations, for example law regulating industrial conflict, family relations, crime and contract. Nation-state law is medium-scale legality and world law is small-scale legality, for example international law contains legal norms that are broad and non-specific, that provides less detail but represents the relative positions of its constituents. The different legal orders operate on different scales and translate the same social objects into different legal objects. For example, a factory is subject to local legality that regulates relations between employees and management; nation-state law is part of a wider network of social, political and economic forces, including the relative power among unions, business and government; and world or global law deals with such issues as international franchising or sub-contracting. In the context of world law, a workplace dispute would have little recognition but would be finely regulated by local law (Santos, 1987: 287–8).

The conception of pluralism, then, is not that of separately bounded systems that interrelate and coexist with one another while retaining their distinct parameters, but an interaction and intersection of different legal spaces operating simultaneously. Santos argues that one cannot properly refer to law and legality but to inter-law and interlegality. The sociology of law must change its priorities from engaging exclusively in the critique of the existing state legality to uncovering the latent or suppressed forms of legality in which more insidious and damaging forms of social and personal oppression frequently occur (Santos, 1987: 288, 298–99). Later, Santos uses three metaphors (which he terms *topoi* to make the comparison with maps) – the frontier, the baroque and the South – to contemplate new subjectivities, including new forms of legality (Santos, 1995: 574). These metaphors all point to subjectivities and identities outside the dominant political, economic and legal traditions of western capitalist and colonizing societies. As the rule of law is implicated in the modern paradigm, the crisis of modernity, where emancipation has collapsed into regulation, entails the crisis of modern law (Santos, 1995: 570–1). It is characteristic of modern regulatory law that attempts at emancipation paradoxically result in greater regulation: legal protection or a legal recognition of rights leads to more governmental structures, enforcement procedures and personnel (Constable, 1995: 594). Emancipation, defined as freedom from regulation, incurs more regulation under modern legality. The aim of new oppositional legal subjectivities is to explore the emancipatory potentialities of the paradigmatic shift away from modernity.

Hunt (1993) retains the insights of legal pluralism with the focus on dispersed and localized power, but appreciates the significance of state law and its centralizing tendencies, involving continuous attempts, with varying success, to consolidate and control regulatory forms. He articulates an account of law as part of a system of 'modes of regulation' that retains the focus on the proximity of law and state, while facilitating the identification of a plurality of ways in which law is implicated in the processes of governance and social regulation. He maintains that any adequate treatment of legal pluralism must address the specific articulation between state law and nonstate law (Hunt, 1993: 311–33; and see pp. 58–9). This approach takes regulation as its starting point and inquires into the extent to which social regulations exhibit legal, political or other dimensions. It rejects approaches that ground a theory of law in the assumption of legal autonomy or separate legal systems and thus disagrees with current theories of autopoiesis or self-referentiality (Hunt, 1993: 320, 329).

Globalization

Globalization has become the dominant concept for understanding contemporary social change. Though meanings and definitions of globalization are often abstract and vague, the concept is used to describe changes in the pace, volume and magnitude of global or international movements of finance, information, commodities, people and ideas (Waters, 1995). Globalization also means a heightened interdependence between nation states, international public and private organizations, and individuals, as dense networks exist between these entities (Holton, 2008: 17–47). Globalization occurs on many levels: political, technical, economic, cultural, social and individual, though economic or financial globalization has received the most attention (Brady et al., 2007). While the changes attributed to globalization are extensions of industrialization, modernization and colonization, the new term is deployed to more accurately capture the qualitative difference in the scale and rapidity of social change.

Although coined in 1980, it was not until the late 1980s that the term globalization was taken as 'master trend of a new era' (Arjomand, 2004: 341; Robertson, 1992). A number of key events, or crises, defined as having far-reaching, worldwide ramifications rather than being local, national or regional problems, spurred on the utility of the term and its derivatives: global, globality, globalism, glocal, glocalization. Such events included the US stock market crash in 1987 and the demise of communism in eastern Europe symbolized by the collapse of the Berlin Wall in 1989, which signalled a new level of global interdependence, especially in finance markets. The vulnerability of individual nation states to events beyond their borders and jurisdiction, has been shown most recently in the global financial crisis of 2008.

One axis of the debate about globalization relates to questions about the integrity of the nation state and consequences for national economies, the welfare state and inequality (Brady et al., 2007). The establishment of international conventions, and the promulgation of norms and guidelines, may oblige or influence national legislatures to pass statutes which will then constrain the activities of citizens and involve local processes of 'adjustment, articulation, ambivalence, or resistance' (Fourcade and Savelsberg, 2006: 514). While not predicting or arguing for the disappearance of the nation state, the world society thesis proposes that contemporary national societies are becoming more similar in structures and policies in domains of business, politics, education, medicine, science, the family and religion, such that: 'Many features of the contemporary nation-state derive from worldwide models constructed and propagated through global cultural and associational processes' (Meyer et al.,

1997: 144–5; emphasis deleted). Examples of isomorphic developments include mass schooling systems, centralized economic and demographic data collection, a commitment to economic development, and indeed in recent years the widespread adoption of economic rationalist and free trade policies, a recognition of human rights, and a state concern with citizens' rights, health, welfare and so on. The operation of this world society relies on its statelessness but depends on nation states for implementation. The concept of cosmopolitanism has also gained new currency as a way of understanding some of the consequences of increased social interactions across cultural and political boundaries (Skrbis et al., 2004). There is talk of the 'cosmopolitan citizen'; however, this notion must be juxtaposed with the sometimes limited access that refugee populations have to citizenship.

As well as being a historical trend measurable by the flow of capital or people, globalization is a way of interpreting various changes; it is a way of framing or making sense of events in the world. A study of US newspaper reports and press releases between 1984 and 1998 identifies three periods that are marked by the way in which the term 'globalization' is used:

1 1984–87: The emergence of a discourse of globalization occurred first in economic/ financial contexts, especially international securities markets, to suggest tight connections between international economies and markets.
2 1988–94: Use of the term is broadened and applied to other industrial sectors, including airlines, chemical, food, and telecommunications.
3 1995–98: Globalization is applied to non-economic contexts ranging from citizenship, crime, and disease, to culture and consumption (Fiss and Hirsch, 2005: 42).

Depending on the sector, context or issue, the framing of globalization shifts: in some, especially business contexts, globalization is viewed as beneficial, as opening up new markets and new opportunities. For some individuals globalization presents opportunities for greater mobility and an increasing connectedness to information and access to resources. However, for other individuals globalization has meant restricted mobility and has reduced their capacity to cross national borders. Increasingly, a negative interpretation of the effects of globalization emphasizes the ecological damage due to pollution resulting from climate change, a deterioration of workers' rights, increasing poverty, increasing insecurity and the homogenization of culture. Elliott and Lemert graphically describe the 'dark side' of globalization for our individual well-being and sense of identity, in developed as well as developing nations (2006: 84–9). Bauman notes that the global economy's demand for flexible labour markets translates into uncertainty and a lack of flexibility for the suppliers of labour, namely those seeking work (Bauman, 1998: 105). Mobility, the freedom to move, becomes a new marker of inequality (Bauman, 1998: 2).

While much is made of the international and global changes and flows, growing research points to the process of localization, the local experiences or manifestations of globalization and the local as a site of translation of, or resistance to, global imperatives. Globalization can thus be defined as 'the intensification of worldwide social relations which link distant localities in such a way that local happenings are shaped by events occurring many miles away and vice versa' (Giddens, 1990: 64). Local nationalisms emerge in response to globalizing tendencies weakening identity connections to nation states (Giddens, 1999: 13).

Globalization and/of law

Many contemporary discussions of globalization both as a phenomenon and a concept pay scant attention to law, even though law and legal norms and institutions are heavily implicated in globalization processes (Halliday and Osinsky, 2006: 447). Global business regulation involves a plethora of regulatory standards; intellectual property rights are important for cultural globalization; international criminal and humanitarian laws and international tribunals are important for redressing the atrocities of war or authoritarian regimes (Braithwaite and Drahos, 2000). A raft of multilateral conventions and bilateral agreements, which take a legal form, increasingly shape the policies and activities of states, organizations and individuals. Such agreements rely on domestic law and local legal personnel and institutions for their implementation and application. What Halliday and Osinsky (2006: 449) call 'norm-formulating organizations' include legislatures and courts within nations and at a transnational level, including the United Nations; international financial institutions, such as the International Monetary Fund (IMF) and the World Bank; supra-national courts such as the International Court of Justice, the European Court of Human Rights; regulatory bodies such as the World Heath Organization; and multilateral agreements and conventions.

Following on from the world society thesis, some suggest that 'modern legal norms demonstrate a remarkable tendency toward global convergence' (Halliday and Osinsky, 2006: 452). Diverse societies adopt common legal norms, standards, and institutional scripts further increasing the integration of nation states, organizations and individuals (Meyer, 2000). Goodale remarks on 'the speed and means with which universal human rights has become the key disciplinary logic within empires of law' (2005: 571–2). There are many examples of the export of Anglo-American legal principles and structures i.e. 'legal transplants,' including constitutional democracy, the rule of law, a constitutional court, judicial independence, and the separation of powers (Halliday and Osinsky, 2006: 458). For example, new democracies in Spain, Portugal and Greece established constitutional courts as a device to prevent the abuse of human rights (Arjomand, 2004: 11–12). While the impetus for the development of global legal norms regarding bankruptcy was the Asian financial crisis in the late 1990s the solution, including the establishment of commercial courts, was based on US bankruptcy law.

Key development institutions actively promote legal and judicial reform. '[A] central idea is that law, lawyers, and legal institutions should be far more important in the economy and in political governance than they are in most countries of the world' (Garth, 2003: 306). Judicial reform initiatives have typically contained three elements: judicial independence, efficiency and access to justice (Sieder, 2007: 215). Reforms to extend judicial independence sometimes involved the creation or strengthening of constitutional chambers or courts, for example in 1989 a constitutional chamber of the Supreme Court was created in Costa Rica and in Colombia the 1991 Constitution created a new Constitutional court. Judicial councils have been established in Argentina and Bolivia with the aim of increasing the independence of the judicial branch.

Transnational law

In this global context, individual nation states now find they are unable to control what come to be defined as transborder problems – whether this entails the flow of people (including children, asylum seekers and refugees), commodities (licit and illicit), finance, information or greenhouse gas emissions. Multi- and bilateral agreements and conventions both define and aim to regulate what become defined as transnational problems. States then become agencies for the implementation of rules that have an extra-state origin, though states may refuse to be a signatory of an international convention or sign a convention but delay or refuse to legislate.

The clearest example of transnational law and the formal assignment of elements of national sovereignty to a supranational organization, or international judicial persons whose decisions can be practically enforced, is the law of the European Union (EU) which was created in 1993 by the Treaty of Maastricht (Glenn, 2003: 845). The European Court of Justice, as a source of EU law, takes precedence over national law including national constitutions in circumstances falling within the scope of the Community competence (Shaw, 2003: 341). These developments have led to questions about whether the changes in political and legal institutions bring about changes in local identities. A study of residents in Edinburgh suggests that being European remains emotionally insignificant and far from global citizenship; the dominant identity is as Scottish (Grundy and Jamieson, 2007). Local nationalisms seem to arise and strengthen as a response to globalizing tendencies, including the weakening of nation states (Giddens, 1999: 13).

The interconnections between law and social change are complex and dynamic as both law and social change operate on different levels and social spaces and entail various institutions, organizations and individuals. Like all law, global norms are general and abstract and require translation or transplantation into national law and local practice (Merry, 2006). The development of global norms in business, trade regulation, environment, corruption and trade regulation, for example, must be negotiated with local gatekeepers who hold key positions in domestic legal systems, governments, administration and personal networks (Holton, 2008: 145–65).

A detailed analysis of the globalization of bankruptcy law in three countries – China, Indonesia and South Korea – demonstrates the complex negotiation processes whereby these global norms are enacted and translated into national laws (Carruthers and Halliday, 2006; Halliday and Carruthers, 2007; Halliday and Osinsky, 2006). Efforts to develop global insolvency norms are one way of preventing, or cushioning, the effects of financial crisis, though it could be argued that these efforts were of limited success in 2008. Understanding the emergence of global bankruptcy reforms requires paying attention to the world's dominant economic nations, the Organization for Economic Cooperation and Development (OECD) and international financial institutions – the IMF, the World Bank, the Asian Development Bank, the European Bank for Reconstruction, and the global prescriptive standard drafted by the United Nations Commission on International Trade Law (UNCITRAL) in 2004 – as well as pressuring or persuading transitional and developing nations to structure their laws and legal systems in line with global norms and expectations (Carruthers and Halliday, 2006: 525).

Professional experts, including lawyers and accountants, play essential roles as intermediaries between a global institution such as the World Bank and local actors. 'Perhaps the most important capacity of the intermediary is an ability to bridge the ideological or cultural divide between the global and local. This requires translation of global scripts into frames that are legitimate, recognizable, and appealing to national and local parties to reform and implementation' (Carruthers and Halliday, 2006: 530).

Carruthers and Halliday investigate 'how the emergence of global normative scripts constrains and empowers local actors', proposing a dynamic understanding of law and social change (2006: 523). Global scripts are the documents that formalize global norms, including statements of overarching principles, lists of best practices, model laws or international conventions. This is an example of convergence in law as the global scripts limit possible local variations. By 2005 all countries in the southeast Asian region had a single standard legitimated by the United Nations to which they were pressed to conform. The movement to 'globalize the local' can occur in at least three ways: many elites in developing countries obtained a professional education in western universities providing access to networks and an exposure to ideas on western legal traditions; contacts by government agencies; and the use of global discourse by locals to strengthen their own positions domestically (Carruthers and Halliday, 2006: 546–55). However, the demands of international agencies, multilateral banks and donors involved in post-conflict peace implementation or post-crisis financial reforms can affect the reforms of nation states despite opposition from local elites (Sieder, 2007).

Theorizing interconnections between global norms, the role of intermediaries and the emergence of national law aligned to global expectations, Halliday and Carruthers propose that: 'legal change in the context of globalization can be conceived as a process of recursivity' (Halliday and Carruthers, 2007: 1142; see also Halliday and Osinsky, 2006: 460). A socio-legal theory of recursivity emphasizes the influences of legal actors – for example lawyers' ability to creatively interpret law, perhaps applying it to new or unanticipated purposes, and judges' capacity to interpret and apply laws to resolve new problems – and the constitutive power of law which means that the law's subjects come to see their problems as legal problems requiring a legal solution. Change also depends on the power of legal institutions – regulatory agencies, enforcement authorities, the legal professions and courts – in shaping the law and the influence of the form of law itself – codes, regulations, cases – on the ways in which change is implemented or initiated (Halliday and Carruthers, 2007: 1142–3).

The idea of recursivity implies the dynamics of four mechanisms which exist in a dynamic interplay:

1   the *indeterminacy of law*: all legal forms – case law, statute, regulation – contain ambiguity and uncertainty which can result in unexpected or uneven consequences;
2   *contradictions* might emerge between national laws and international norms due to underlying and conflicting worldviews or values;
3   *diagnostic struggles* among actors, including lawyers and policy makers, who have different orientations and work with different assumptions and traditions. Such differences will affect the extent to which external participants can alter national or local practices and the struggles become played out between professionals; and
4   *actor mismatch*: typically the law makers are separate from the administrators of the law, and those subject to the law and their activities can undermine or transform the reforms anticipated by particular laws (Halliday and Carruthers, 2007: 1149–52).

The distances between international norms, national legislation and practical implementation can be great and mediated by organizational and professional constraints which often leads to further legislation or legal interpretation to solve some of the practical problems, producing perpetual motion, rather than a static conception of law. Local or national circumstances explain cross-national differences in the timing of adoption and in the different frameworks and practices for implementation shaping the content of corporate bankruptcy laws (Carruthers and Halliday, 2006). National experiences and local circumstances influence global law making while the existence of global norms and expectations impinges on the substance of national laws.

Adopting legal principles and institutions from one culture may not easily translate into other contexts and settings (Dezalay and Garth, 2002; Garth, 2003).

> The sanctity of the rule of law and judicial independence while touted as universal principles of justice and essential for development and modernization are culturally and nationally specific and will not necessarily ameliorate what are defined as local problems, authoritarian regimes, weak states, human rights abuses, economic inequalities or injustices. (Dezalay and Garth, 2002: 5)

Dezalay and Garth's (2002) investigation of the role of law in social transformation in the post-World War II period in Argentina, Brazil, Chile and Mexico finds that the courts were unable to manage the transition from violent military regimes in which the courts were ideologically and socially associated with the military to a society where an independent judiciary, free from the influence of political elites, could effectively apply human rights laws. Nonetheless, the extent of judicial independence can shift. For example, in Guatemala, the 1985 Constitution extended the Constitutional Court's powers of judicial review and the Court ruled as unconstitutional proposed increases in taxes and public utility fees. However, the perception of judicial independence declined when the Court agreed that the former military dictator, Rios Montt, could be a candidate in presidential elections, and it has not succeeded in defending the collective rights of indigenous peoples (Sieder, 2007).

A lack of political will, the pervasiveness of entrenched interests, the power and influence of extended family ties and widespread corruption, as well as structural barriers arising from historical interconnections between the judiciary and repressive regimes, have meant that judicial and legal reforms advocated by various nation states and funding agencies have not met the goals of reformers (Dezalay and Garth, 2002: 221).

Social change and the risk society

Another theoretical approach to understanding social change and the character of contemporary, highly industrialized societies is the notion of risk. Some social theorists point to the many ways contemporary western society is characterized by risk, uncertainty and anxiety at social (structural) and individual (agency) levels (Beck, 1992; Lupton, 1999). Environmental hazards, ecological risks, including polluted air, water and soil, and even climate change are the unintended consequences of modernization and industrial production (Giddens, 1999). Beck (1992) refers to the 'risk society' or the 'world risk society' in which risk becomes the dominant frame for understanding social change and human action. The continuous production of wealth and general consensus on the nature and meaning of progress have increasingly relied on radioactive substances, petrochemicals matched by increased environmental hazards and associated health dangers, which in turn threaten the basis of industrial society.

In pre-industrial societies danger, calamity and disaster were viewed as acts of God, an inevitable fate or natural occurrences, and not as the culmination of risks which, at least in theory, are calculable. 'Risk society is not an option which could be chosen or rejected in the course of political debate. It arises through the automatic operation of autonomous modernization processes which are blind and deaf to consequences and dangers' (Beck, 1996: 28).

Beck proposes a theory of reflexive modernization which entails the rejection of totalizing concepts of society: structures become fluid and unbounded, boundaries between categories or institutions become blurred. Even what are perceived as national problems cannot be solved nationally (Beck and Lau, 2005: 527). The language of risk also suggests that it can be calculated and managed, especially by public (welfare state) and private (individual contract) insurance. While law does not feature in the social theories of risk, it is central to insurance and the assignment or enforcement of responsibility under doctrines of negligence and due care (Roach Anleu, 2006).

However, Beck's focus on higher levels of risk, ambivalence and uncertainty seems inconsistent with recent theory 'that emphasizes the regularization and standardization of daily life in advanced societies' (Elliott, 2002: 308). A more general critique of Beck suggests that 'his work does not appreciate the full significance of interpersonal, emotional and cultural factors as these influence and shape risk-monitoring in contemporary societies' (Elliott, 2002: 312).

Research suggests that the identification of risk is contingent on local history, the everyday routines and knowledge of employees or residents and the power relations in which they are enmeshed, and perhaps the presence or absence of advocacy groups or whistleblowers that can affect the way incidents and risks are recognized and defined (Auyero and Swistun, 2008: 375; Beamish, 2000; Vaughan, 1999). An analysis of why an oil spill in California could continue for four decades without its identification as a major health risk concludes that as the spillage was incremental and not catastrophic, was denied by the company and workers accustomed themselves to the toxicity, making it no one's responsibility, the hazard had become normalized (Beamish, 2000: 491).

A study of an Argentine shanty town surrounded by an oil refinery dominated by a large multinational corporation, a hazardous waste incinerator and an unmonitored landfill concluded that the refinery's provision of social services to the community, combined with uncertainty and confusing and contradictory information about the toxic contamination, meant that 'uninterrupted routines and interactions worked smoothly as blinders to increasing environmental hazards' (Auyero and Swistun, 2008: 360). Even where citizens are aware of illness caused by exposure to toxic hazards, for example in the case of workers in nuclear weapons facilities, the institutional and organizational resources available to corporations and their clients – for example the US military – and assertions of national security give them a tactical advantage of casting these illnesses as individual and not social problems (Cable et al., 2008). In these examples, international norms around health and safety and the regulation of toxic waste, even around human rights, seem far removed from the daily life experiences of the local inhabitants, and without (or even with) active enforcement regimes, companies are able to transgress or ignore international standards, even national law.

Conclusion

This chapter has provided an overview of contemporary discussions of law. Most of these theories dispute the idea that the law is a reflection of general social norms and deny that the operation of law is restricted to legal institutions. They also disagree with the claim that the law is objective, neutral or impartial. Feminist legal theorists demonstrate the ways in which law privileges certain knowledge and information, perpetuates particular conceptions of gender and disadvantages women; legal pluralism points out the diversity of legal norms and discourses that can operate in one setting; and critical legal theorists indicate how such central legal concepts as rights are reifications of citizens' everyday experiences of life and of law.

A second main theme regards the transformative capacity of law, which is discussed from a variety of theoretical perspectives. At one extreme, Luhmann describes the law as an autonomous, closed system that engages with its environment only to the extent that it transposes it into legal language, legal concepts and legal problems. Bourdieu also indicates the ways in which the juridical field – a more fluid and flexible concept than the legal system – translates social conflict into legal debates. For Bourdieu, conflict and competition among legal actors characterize a participation in the juridical field. Habermas also attends to the increasing juridification of the lifeworld and recognizes the importance of law for regulation in highly diverse societies. Yet the law also constitutes constraints on citizens' lives. The next chapter examines one dimension of the operation of law, namely the legal profession and legal practice.

4 The Legal Profession

Law is one of the original professions; the others being medicine, the clergy (out of which grew university teaching) and, less frequently, the military. Several important cross-national differences exist between legal professions regarding their histories, organization, training, activities, status and prestige.[1] The division between barristers and solicitors is characteristic of the English legal profession and is retained by some of its former colonial counterparts. As Weber observes, the reliance on judicial decisions or case law in the English, or common-law, legal system means that barristers skilled in oral argument assume a special prominence, prestige and influence. However, the emergence of the barrister as a distinct profession of advocates 'was a slow and tentative process' occurring in sixteenth century England, in part in response to increases in litigation (Prest, 1986: 5). The Bar is also significant in common-law systems, because it is from this pool that most members of the judiciary are appointed. Practising lawyers are less important on the European continent in terms of law making, and in Germany for many years it was not even necessary for a litigant to be represented by a lawyer (Weber, 1978: 785–90). Historically, the universities were more important as educators of lawyers and the state was more important as an employer of lawyers in the continental as compared to the English legal system, where legal training was by apprenticeship and most lawyers were in private practice, that is, self-employed (Abbott, 1988: 197–205; Macdonald, 1995: 72–7, 85–7, 91–2; Prest, 1986; Weber, 1978: 784–5). Because of the relative independence and power of the legal profession in common-law countries, lawyers (as a group) enjoy greater financial rewards and higher social status than their counterparts in civil-law countries.

Despite cross-national differences, the legal professions of all advanced capitalist societies have experienced a number of critical changes since the 1960s (Abel, 1985: 19–35; 1989), and particularly over the past two decades (Faulconbridge and Muzio, 2008; Heinz et al., 2005). There has been an enormous expansion in the number of lawyers, the proportion of women lawyers is increasing, lawyers are now more likely to be employed by large, bureaucratic organizations (including law firms, some of which have international offices), aspects of legal work are becoming routinized and deskilled due to technological change, the market for legal services has become more competitive, some dimensions of professional control are waning, and the legal profession has been subject to unprecedented public scrutiny in the form of government inquiries, media attention and criticism from consumers. While these changes seem most pronounced and best researched in the USA, the pattern of change is widespread (Galanter, 1992: 2; Muzio and Ackroyd, 2005). Some commentators conclude that these developments undermine professional autonomy, question lawyers' claims to a professional status and herald deprofessionalization (Rothman, 1984). Others maintain that changes to the legal profession signal a redefinition of professionalism which becomes a hybrid of traditional professional ideals, especially collegial control, combined with the values of business and participation in a competitive market; lawyers have become 'commercialised' professionals (Hanlon, 1997; Heinz et al., 2005).

This chapter first examines theories of the professions, then investigates the considerable changes that legal professions have undergone over the past three decades and, finally, assesses some of the implications of these changes for the professional status of lawyers.

Theories of the professions

There are two broad theoretical approaches to the professions within sociology. The trait model focuses on identifying the key attributes of professional occupations, while market approaches view professions as emerging from the successful monopolization of skills, resources and clients.

Trait model

Prior to the 1960s, sociologists sought to distinguish professions from nonprofessions by identifying their core defining characteristics (Carr-Saunders and Wilson, 1933; Goode, 1957; Greenwood, 1957). They argued that professions are special and deserve their high social status, prestige and financial rewards. Despite scant agreement on the irreducible attributes of a profession, the most frequently enumerated include:

(a) formal educational and entrance requirements;
(b) a monopolization of esoteric knowledge and associated skills;
(c) autonomy over the terms and conditions of practice;
(d) collegial authority vested in a code of ethics;
(e) a professional association; and
(f) the commitment to a service ideal.

This attribute model emphasizes the special quality of professional knowledge and the professions' ethical orientation towards clients. Professional knowledge and skills should be abstract and esoteric but also applicable to the solution of practical problems (Goode, 1969: 277). For Parsons, professional authority has a peculiar sociological structure in that it is based on and limited to superior technical competence

(Parsons, 1954: 38). Because of the asymmetry of expertise, the client is not able to evaluate the advice or service of the professional and thus trusts him or her to perform the required tasks properly, especially if a failure to do so would cause harm (Goode, 1969: 296). On the distinctive professional–client relationship, Parsons writes:

> The relation of attorney and client is a relation of 'trust' not of competition for profit; the client's fee is for 'service,' not simply the best 'bargain' he [*sic*] can get in a competitive market; his [*sic*] communications to his [*sic*] attorney are protected by law and cannot be revealed in the attorney's or any other interest. (Parsons, 1954: 374–5)

As well as a special relationship with clients, members of professions have a distinctive orientation to each other, in that the social organization of professional occupations is said to be collegial (Waters, 1989: 956). Members look to each other for professional recognition, control and protection. Parsons observes that, like the businessperson, the professional is oriented towards success, but they take different paths: the professional seeks occupational recognition and reputation, while the businessperson seeks financial success. Thus, professionals are not distinguished from businesspeople by their altruistic rather than self-interested behaviour, but they are 'collectivity-oriented' rather than 'self-oriented' (Parsons, 1954: 42–5, 375 fn 2).

Members of a profession who are all formally equal and expert are responsible for regulating each other's conduct. Most professions have some kind of formal, written ethical code that prescribes obligations towards colleagues and *vis-à-vis* clients. Codes of ethics usually proscribe professionals from dealing with outsiders; for example, traditionally, lawyers were unable to form partnerships or attend court with nonlawyers. Professional codes have also prohibited intra-professional competition for clients and resources, thus rendering advertising, solicitation and price cutting unethical and unprofessional. The committee of the professional association is the location of most collegial decision making and regulation (Waters, 1989: 955–9). The council of the law society or bar association presides over complaints about members' alleged unethical behaviour. This committee also sanctions professional misbehaviour, the ultimate punishment being to revoke a member's practice licence and membership of the professional association. Ironically, while obligations toward peers predominate, sanctions for violation are not usually severe, whereas obligations to clients are few and specific but sanctions are the most radical following deviation (Abbott, 1983: 863; Carlin, 1966: 150–62). In a fascinating account of professional discipline, Daniel (1998) argues that to maintain their autonomy and a sense of collectivity and cohesion, plus some level of public accountability, the professions, every now and then, will identify and persecute scapegoats. The 'crimes' of such scapegoats may be relatively minor (not all members who are guilty of such 'crimes' will be scapegoated) or incidental; the purpose of scapegoating is not the punishment of an offender – because the sentence of banishment usually holds out no opportunity for expiation or reform – but a ritual cleansing of the profession and a reassertion of its distinctive identity. 'Overall, the scapegoat's timeless purpose is to relieve the group of its guilt' (Daniel, 1998: 17).

The attribute model of the professions seems most applicable to the solo practitioner who deals with a series of individual, relatively powerless clients. Indeed, some would argue that the structure and values of professions are antithetical to bureaucratic employment (Hall, 1968: 266; Scott, 1966). Specifically, employment in a large private or public organization ensures conflict between hierarchical and professional authority. Professional employees experience role strain as their orientation to clients and the demands of their employer inevitably collide, compromising professional values and ethics. Such concerns are misfounded theoretically and empirically. First, Weber recognized long ago that professions and bureaucracies share a number of traits and that professionalization and bureaucratization are complementary aspects of the process of rationalization (Ritzer, 1975: 632). Despite differences in internal govern-ment, collegial and bureaucratic organizations both rely on technical expertise to achieve specific goals (Waters, 1989: 969). Secondly, numerous studies point to the increasing employment of medical personnel and lawyers in large, bureaucratically organized hospitals and law firms and demonstrate that solo practice is the least powerful and prestigious segment of professional work and the most vulnerable to market influences. However, organizations that hire professionals are different from other bureaucratic organizations and professional employees differ from other staff. Professional organizations are distinctive in their structure, organization, administra-tion and orientation, and it is now impossible to discuss professions independent of their (often organizational or corporate) employers (Brewer, 1996: 23–35). Interestingly, a recent study of the Chicago Bar indicates that solo practitioners and lawyers in very large firms report the greatest capacity for client choice. Solo practi-tioners and those in small firms and in-house counsel indicate high degrees of control over the nature of their work (Heinz et al., 2005: 279).

Sociologists adopting the attribute approach may uncritically accept the official rhetoric of occupations claiming to be professions, thus becoming apologists for the power, prestige and monopolies on clients, tasks and skills of the established profes-sions (Roth, 1974: 6). This approach does not identify the cultural, economic, political, social and historical conditions under which occupations will assert claims to professional status and success (Klegon, 1978: 267–8). Freidson suggests that the failure to identify a single definition of a profession derives from attempts to treat the concept as if it were generic, rather than as a changing historic notion with particular roots in an industrial nation strongly influenced by Anglo-American institutions (Crompton, 1990: 149–50; Freidson, 1994). Nonetheless, he warns against jettisoning any definition of profession by suggesting that: 'One does not attempt to determine what profession is in an absolute sense so much as how people in a society determine who is a professional and who is not, how they "make" or "accomplish" professions by their activities, and what the consequences are for the way in which they see themselves and perform their work' (Freidson, 1983: 279). For example, in England and the USA the title 'profession' was used to establish the status of successful occupations and appeared in official occupational classification schemes; it was not just a descriptive term. In contrast, in France the state was much more active in organizing both training through the *grandes écoles* and employment, which thereby reduced the professions' autonomy (Abbott, 1988: 24–8).

Market-control approaches

Proponents of a more dynamic conception of professions will move away from talking about 'the professions' as though they are objective, immutable social categories and instead argue that professionalism is a strategy for organizing and controlling work; it is a type of occupational control, not an expression of the nature of a particular occupation (Johnson, 1972: 45; Macdonald, 1995: 17–35). Their central concern is to identify the social contexts and economic conditions that enable a particular occupational group to successfully claim and perpetuate their control over knowledge, skills or techniques, clients and themselves (Freidson, 1994: 173; Hughes, 1971: 375–7; Klegon, 1978: 270–6). The disagreement here is more about the origin and function of professional attributes than their existence: attribute theorists will view them as inherent properties of the established professions while control approaches will emphasize their attainment and importance in securing markets.

Professionalization can be viewed as an attempt to translate one type of scarce resource – special knowledge and skills – into another, namely economic rewards and social recognition. The modern reorganization of professional work and professional markets tends to be based on the claim to sole control of superior expertise and independence (at least in appearance), from the traditional and external guarantees of the social stratification order (Larson, 1977: 13). As a method of organizing the performance of work, professionalism differs from the free market and from bureaucracy in that it revolves around 'the central principle that the members of a specialized occupation control their own work' (Freidson, 1994: 173, emphasis deleted).

An important mechanism for controlling markets is placing restrictions on the numerical size of the profession through increasing educational requirements and admission standards. This achieves occupational closure and denies opportunities for practice to the noncredentialled (Macdonald, 1995: 27–9). Such closure is finalized by successfully obtaining a legislatively mandated monopoly on practice. Legal practitioner legislation defines 'legal work' (often some what differently in different jurisdictions) and reserves that work towards licensed lawyers. Once a practising certificate is obtained, the lawyer can offer services within the area reserved by legislation to licensed lawyers. The role of the state *vis-à-vis* education and its attitude to monopolies of expertise and skill are critical in the attainment of professional status (Larson, 1977: 15).

The rise of professional occupations, especially the legal profession, during the twentieth century is intertwined with the development of corporate capitalism. Observing a symbiotic relationship between business activities and the legal profession, Weber writes:

> The increased need for specialized legal knowledge created the professional lawyer. The growing demand for experience and specialized knowledge and the consequent stimulus for increasing rationalization of the law have almost always come from the increasing significance of commerce and those participating in it. (1978: 775)

This relationship is characterized by the emergence in the USA in the early part of the twentieth century of the large urban law firm, whose clients were business entrepreneurs and corporations (Smigel, 1964: 1–17). In contrast, legal professions in other countries were unprepared to take full advantage of the opportunities that capitalist development presented and accordingly their histories and structures differ. For example, English solicitors lost the preeminent position that American lawyers rapidly gained in the twentieth century (Abbott, 1988: 275). As these solicitors relied on clerkship for legal training, their numbers could not expand rapidly to respond to new areas of potential legal work. Tradition, etiquette and the fact that training neophyte lawyers could not be the sole task of solicitors, who also had clients, meant that they could take on only a few clerks. Solicitors could not respond to new opportunities in the business and governmental spheres and their staple work remained conveyancing. In comparison, the development and popularity of law schools in the USA greatly increased the supply of lawyers, especially as a law degree took two years and a clerkship five. Combined with a less interventionist government, the rapid expansion in the number of lawyers enabled the legal profession, or at least the elite segments of it, to make successful claims to new work and clients, especially in business activities, in the USA.

The obverse of control is competition. Abbott argues that 'control of knowledge and its application means dominating outsiders who attack that control. Control without competition is trivial' (Abbott, 1988: 2). He conceptualizes the professions as forming an interdependent system where each performs activities within various kinds of jurisdiction, the boundaries of which can be relatively stable or contested, and will change over time depending on a range of social, economic and cultural factors. The control of work brings the professions into conflict with each other and makes their histories interdependent, and it is these interprofessional relations that are potentially the central feature of professional development (Abbott, 1986: 189). Jurisdictional claims can be made in several possible arenas (Abbott, 1988: 59–60):

1 *The legal system*, which can confer formal control of legal work. Acts of Parliament usually provide that only licensed legal practitioners can provide legal advice. Law societies lobby governments to guarantee lawyers' monopoly on conveyancing, for example, in the face of competition from land brokers, banks and real estate agents. Other changes affect the legal division of labour, for example reforms to rights of audience allow solicitors to appear in lower courts, historically the exclusive preserve of barristers (Prest, 1986).

2 *Public opinion*, where professions build images that pressure the legal system. Lawyers and their professional associations often advocate legal change by issuing press statements, conducting interviews, and addressing public meetings and other public activities. They usually claim that their interests are aligned or are even synonymous with the public interest and the needs of potential clients. For example, plans by one Australian state government (Victoria) to allow nonlawyers to represent people in court were met by the president of the Law Institute's claims that the proposal 'represents the most significant threat to the rights of clients to quality legal representation and advocacy in many years' (Coffey, 1995).

3 *The workplace*, where successful claims blur and distort the official lines of legally and publicly established jurisdiction. Lawyers employed by government departments and business corporations will seek to demarcate their work from that of nonlawyers.

Even in law offices, work will be negotiated between lawyers, paralegals and clerical/administrative staff. In the courtroom, lawyers face competition from the police, probation officers, social workers and other professions, including medical practitioners, psychiatrists and psychologists, who provide expert evidence. One way in which barristers seek to reassert their dominance in the courtroom is to discredit other professionals' knowledge and credibility or seek to have their evidence declared inadmissible in court.[2]

Jurisdictional disputes can be settled by excluding competitors, shedding or vacating certain tasks, subordinating a competitor or increasing the division of labour:

1 The successful claim to monopolize certain areas of work and clients excludes, or reduces, the number of potential competitors. For the most part, until recently, solicitors have been successful in monopolizing conveyancing work, thereby excluding or restricting such other occupations as land brokers, sometimes termed conveyancers. In England and Wales solicitors' monopoly over conveyancing was removed in the 1980s.
2 There can be a reduction in the control or loss of a jurisdiction. Some areas of legal work are increasingly being performed by other professions and occupations, for example tax accountants will interpret tax laws and provide advice to clients; public servants will advise clients of their legal rights and obligations *vis-à-vis* the government.
3 Subordination of a competitor may be attempted. In a number of jurisdictions, lawyers employed by the Director of Public Prosecutions or District Attorney have taken over criminal prosecution work in the lower courts, which previously had been the sole domain of the police.
4 A final division of labour can be formed, either in terms of the content of the work or the nature of the client, thereby splitting the jurisdiction into two more or less independent parts. The redefinition of core tasks typically entails the delegation of less skilled, simple and uninteresting tasks to lower-status occupations (Wilensky, 1964: 144). In some law offices such routine legal work as research, document searches and initial interviews with clients is performed by paralegals, which is a relatively new occupation (Johnstone and Wenglinsky, 1985: 15–65).

Legal work

Contrary to popular perceptions and media representations, the bulk of lawyers' work does not occur in the courtroom; indeed, very little legal work entails preparing for or undertaking litigation. The tasks lawyers perform include:

(a) offering advice regarding citizens' responsibilities, entitlements and rights;
(b) representing clients' – both corporate and individual – interests in various negotiations;
(c) drawing up legal documents, including contracts, statutes and articles of association for corporations and voluntary organizations;

(d) settling or mediating disputes either in or out of courts, other tribunals, or other fora;

(e) court work, which entails the prosecution or defence of persons accused of criminal offences and representing clients' interests in civil litigation.

According to Parsons (1954: 375), the legal profession holds an 'interstitial' position in the social structure, that is, lawyers will mediate between legal rules and the practical situations that clients present. The settings where lawyers work include the following.

Solo practice: a single lawyer who is self-employed, usually located in rural, regional or suburban areas.

Law firms: are organized as partnerships; some members are partners and share in the firm's profits, whereas others are salaried associates. Promotion to partnership often involves an 'up or out' policy, where associates who do not make partner must leave the firm and those who do will have a life tenure. The large law firm became a particular institutional phenomenon during the twentieth century and is the subject of considerable socio-legal research (Galanter and Palay, 1991; Smigel, 1964). Large law firms serve mostly business clients who require ongoing legal advice and are based in major metropolitan and financial centres, especially New York City and London, and often have branches throughout the world. Divisions of labour also exist among lawyers employed by the same firm and engaged in the same substantive areas of law. Using the language of a senior partner in a large firm whom he interviewed, Nelson distinguishes between finders, minders and grinders (Nelson, 1981: 119–26). Finders are entrepreneurs who establish and govern the basic structure of the firm and have the most responsibility for recruiting clients, sometimes termed 'rainmaking'. Minders are the managing partners who seek to coordinate a large staff working in various fields of law. Grinders are the associates and newer partners who perform the day-to-day legal work.

Government offices: legal departments, for example the Attorney-General's Department, the office of the Director of Public Prosecutions, will hire lawyers whose tasks may include drafting legislation, interpreting legislation, undertaking legal research, preparing cases for litigation, undertaking legal action, and offering legal advice to government. Lawyers are also employed in a variety of other government departments and positions.

Law schools: following World War II the university-based law school has become the predominant form of legal education. Legal academics may simultaneously practise law, but this is not usually a requirement.

Business corporations: many corporations will hire their own in-house counsel to perform day-to-day legal tasks and to liaise with any outside legal firm with which it has a retainer.

Legal aid schemes and public defenders' offices: established by many governments in the 1960s and 1970s to ensure that people with few economic resources, especially those defending criminal charges, could have access to legal representation. Different models of lawyering are adopted in legal aid commissions and legal aid lawyers are often progressive social activists committed to the alleviation of social inequalities. Legal aid commissions will hire their own lawyers as well as nonlawyers and recruit volunteers. They will also brief private legal practitioners.

The judiciary: in common-law countries appointment to judicial office usually follows on from an extensive legal career. Judges of the higher courts are typically recruited from the senior ranks of the Bar, usually via a fairly informal and opaque process (Darbyshire, 2007; Mack and Roach Anleu, 2008). Depending on the jurisdiction judges in lower courts can be recruited from diverse legal and nonlegal backgrounds. For example, many magistrates in England and Wales are lay, do not have legal training and are voluntary, whereas in many other common-law countries magistrates are legally qualified judicial officers (Roach Anleu and Mack, 2007). In civil-law systems the judiciary is part of a career structure and the decision to pursue the judicial path is made much earlier on in a career.

Other settings: including various nongovernment and professional associations and social movement organizations oriented to social change through law reform. This is sometimes known as public interest or cause lawyering. Belief in a cause and a desire to advance it will drive cause lawyering actions (Hilbink, 2004: 659). Activist lawyering includes feminist law firms and practices (Epstein, 1983: 130–61) and poverty lawyers who aim to enforce welfare rights through the courts. Cause lawyering entails ethical dilemmas arising from a tension between the interests of the individual client and the broader social cause to which the lawyer is morally or politically committed (Dotan, 1999). Research on cause lawyering usually focuses on social justice or welfare activism, often downplaying the existence of right-wing cause lawyers (Heinz et al., 2003). Much of the work of the conservative movement – conservative religious organisations, libertarians, nationalists, and business interests – occurs through not for profit foundations in which lawyers will play an important role.

The actual mix of legal tasks performed depends on the work setting, the field of substantive law and the types of clients with whom the lawyer interacts. Lawyers who perform mainly corporate work will be more likely to be engaged in negotiating and drawing up contracts, and advising clients of their legal obligations, compared with criminal lawyers who will defend their clients against criminal charges or family lawyers who are concerned with settling disputes. The everyday work of lawyers is often far removed from the image of legal work as the application of technical rules to unambiguous facts and preparing for litigation. Lawyers' work entails translating clients' concerns into legal questions and remedies, managing uncertainty, diverting clients from the formal legal system and negotiating and seeking consensual outcomes with lawyers for other parties to the dispute, both in civil and criminal cases.

Clients will bring various issues, concerns and experiences to a lawyer that they will express in various everyday discourses. Rather than inevitably subordinating or controlling the client and their desired outcomes, the lawyer will then translate and reconstitute the issues in terms of a legal discourse that has trans-situational applicability. For example, a client's concern that his or her children should inherit any real estate (a concern for family relations) will be translated into legal questions about the type of tenancy and the resulting ownership potentialities and capacities. The skill of the lawyer derives from the extent to which the statements that she or he formulates in legal discourse produce a legal outcome that is congruent with the outcome that the client articulates in everyday nonlegal language (Cain, 1983: 111–8). Lawyers will accept their clients' desired outcome, especially where the clients are powerful and prestigious and where the solicitor seeks to establish an on-going relationship with the client as a source of future legal work. Nevertheless, the process of translation is not automatic and sometimes lawyers will refuse to do it, especially in cases where individuals bring one-off problems and where the solicitors are integrated with the profession and perhaps do not wish to risk being regarded as 'unreasonable' or 'unconventional' by other lawyers or actors within the justice system (Cain, 1983: 122–8).

While the solicitors Cain discusses primarily deal with middle-class clients, an Australian study of legal aid and community legal centres, which deal with disadvantaged clients, illustrates the ways in which lawyers will choose to help particular clients and turn others away (Parker, 1994: 149). In interviews with clients, the lawyer asks questions in order to fit their story into a typology based on the lawyer's previous knowledge and experience of the type of problems that such clients have. The lawyer controls the interview and seeks to mould the client's problems into the typology as a way of efficiently managing a large caseload (see also Sudnow, 1965). This also discourages clients from expecting or demanding that the lawyer become personally committed to the details of their individual case. Clients who refuse to accept the lawyer's assessment of the situation and follow his or her advice regarding the appropriate response are viewed as difficulties to be managed. For the lawyer, such clients are refusing to accept legal reality or are trying to demand the achievement of an inappropriate objective (Parker, 1994: 157). Lawyers will respond by refusing to empower the client and terminating the interview.

In the criminal courts defence lawyers – both in private practice and employed by legal aid – will often become agent-mediators who will help the accused to redefine the situation and restructure their perceptions commensurate with entering a plea of guilty (Blumberg, 1967: 20). The lawyers' relationships with prosecutors, the police and other court officials may be more important than a brief encounter with a particular client, thus the needs and interests of the latter are subordinate to those of the former, who are important for the lawyer's career and achievements in the legal system. From the point of view of the lawyer, tension will exist between the pressures to process large numbers of criminal cases and the ideological and legal requirements of the due process of law and advocacy. Lawyers will adopt such strategies as creating anxiety for the client regarding the risks of going to trial and appearing to be of help and service to their interests, which tend to lead to a guilty plea (Blumberg, 1967: 22–8; see also Chapter 6). Many lawyers, including law teachers, would agree that the success of litigators relies on their ability to manipulate people's emotions for the specific goal of winning a case in the very competitive trial environment. Pierce argues that the majority of litigators who 'do dominance' are men and this can involve intimidation to impugn a witness's credibility and strategic friendliness to win a witness over (Pierce, 1996: 1–5). This masculinized form of emotional labour relying on manipulation and pragmatism contributes to the exclusion of women lawyers from trial work or a perception among court personnel, other lawyers and the public that women are not as effective as litigators as men.

An in-depth analysis of the lawyer–client interaction in divorce cases identifies the ways in which lawyers and clients will negotiate their different views of law and the legal process and how this influences courses of action (Sarat and Felstiner, 1986: 96). The most common pattern is an exchange in which the lawyer persuades a somewhat reluctant client to try to reach a negotiated settlement. This involves three steps. First, the legal process itself is discussed and interpreted, which prepares the way ahead for a decision about settlement by providing the client with a sense of the values and operations inherent in formal adjudication. The lawyer describes the court process as involving risks stemming from the human frailties of judicial decision makers, the contradictions between appearance and reality, carelessness, incoherence, accident and built-in limitations. This creates in the client doubts about the legal process, while reassuring them of the wisdom of relying on the legal adviser. 'What the lawyer can provide is not a *corpus juris* learned in law school or available in any texts but rather a personal view of how the legal system actually works in the community in which he [*sic*] is practicing' (Sarat and Felstiner, 1986: 131). Secondly, there is a discussion on how best to dispose of the case. Lawyers will tend to construct an image that settlement is the appropriate mode of dealing with the case, which counters the conventional view that lawyers will escalate disputes by contesting every point, inducing competition and hostility and transforming noncontentious clients into adversaries. The third dimension of the discussion involves considering what the client will have to do and how they will have to behave if a settlement is to be reached. This involves the 'legal construction of the client', where lawyers will help their clients view the emotional process of dissolving an intimate relationship in instrumental terms, especially regarding a property settlement and other financial issues.

An ethnographic study of an elite corporate law firm in Chicago finds that the central role of business lawyers not engaged in litigation is managing uncertainty, both for themselves and their clients (Flood, 1991: 42–3). Three main tasks constitute the everyday work of business lawyers: advising, negotiating and drafting documents. These lawyers rarely enter a courtroom and are in constant negotiations with other lawyers and their clients to effect commercial or financial deals. The critical uncertainty is that a deal may collapse; the corporate world is fickle and changes in such external economic events as interest rates or share prices can cause potential contracts to fail. This may result in the loss of a valued corporate client and reduced income to the firm, which places great emphasis on establishing and maintaining almost avuncular relationships with clients who seek advice on a wide range of issues; the distinction between strictly legal and other advice thus disappears.

Developing such new legal practices and devices as tax shelters, arrangements for the ownership and leasing of property, new types of securities and bonds, and new forms of corporate organization are also dimensions of corporate lawyers' work (Cain, 1994: 31; McBarnett, 1994: 81–3; Powell, 1993: 424). In the mid-1980s, New York corporate lawyers created and used an innovative legal device: the shareholder rights plan, known as the 'poison pill', which is an anti-takeover measure. Its aim is to facilitate target or potential target companies in avoiding a hostile takeover and involves the issuing of new rights to shareholders (Powell, 1993: 429). The validity of the device was questioned and confirmed by the courts, which meant that case law consolidated the status of the innovation. Corporate lawyers were entrepreneurial in developing and refining this device, which they perceived as beneficial to their corporate clients, and law firms actively marketed the product through client memoranda and presentations to boards of directors (Powell, 1993: 447–8).

The actual content of legal work is also shaped by relationships between members of the profession and the organization of the legal system. In the English context, Morison and Leith (1992) describe the plethora of constraints – from solicitors on whom barristers depend for briefs, from judges and from legal procedures – that affect barristers' work. The life of the barrister is not so much concerned with abstract legal rules, but with negotiating various competing demands while simultaneously carving out a living from a sometimes hostile environment. This involves establishing and maintaining personal contacts, especially with solicitors who are the barrister's actual client and conduit for briefs, and participating in networks that will provide information and patronage (Morison and Leith, 1992: 19–59). Much of the law with which barristers deal on a day-to-day basis is routine, standardized or anecdotal in character rather than formally researched, specific or specialized. The process whereby barristers will creatively construct legal information is shaped by the nature of the information available, time limitations, a consideration of how the information will be viewed by the judge/court, policy questions, their own experience of the courtroom and trials, and the practical demands of the situation rather than general case-law principles. As one of the barristers interviewed observes: 'Cases where you have to read all the authorities and go into all the arguments are fairly few and far between' (Morison and Leith, 1992: 94). The law that barristers use is either based on memory or researched as needed – perhaps just by asking other barristers – but it is practically oriented and limited rather than technical, legalistic or overly concerned with abstract legal principles. Indeed, rather than arguing about the law in court, there is a tendency among opposing barristers to agree on common interpretations of the law and to argue about some of the facts or the evidence.

Stratification

The field of legal practice and work settings are not just descriptive differences but axes of stratification within the legal profession. Far from being a community of equals or a 'community within a community' (Goode, 1957), research reveals a widespread stratification or segmentation in terms of social background, legal education, kinds of practice, clients, income and prestige.

Smigel's study of elite Wall Street law firms in the 1950s finds that 'there is keen competition for the preferred lawyer – the personable man from one of the select eastern law schools, who graduated with honors from an Ivy League college, and was at the top of his law school class' (Smigel, 1960: 57). Similarly, Carlin's study of 800 lawyers in private practice in New York City in the early 1960s concludes:

'The metropolitan bar is ... a highly stratified professional community' (Carlin, 1966: 36). The business community is the principal consumer of lawyers' services, while individual clients are primarily in the middle to upper middle income brackets. The elite in this stratification system are the lawyers in large firms who have the highest average income, represent the most affluent and highest-status clients, and have most contact with the upper levels of both judiciary and government. Individual practitioners and small-firm lawyers have the lowest incomes, represent the least affluent and lowest-status clients, and deal largely with the lower-level courts and agencies. The principal business clients of large-firm lawyers are large, wealthy corporations in industry and finance, while small-firm and individual lawyers will generally work for small companies and individual proprietors in retail, personal services, real estate and light manufacturing industries.

A more recent study of solo-practice and small-firm lawyers in the New York metropolitan area indicates that little has changed since Carlin's research in the 1960s (Seron, 1996). Seron categorizes these lawyers as either *entrepreneurs*, who explicitly advertise and adopt innovatory practices; *experimenters*, who adopt new technology and opportunities but not to the same extent as entrepreneurs; or *traditionalists*, who shun the opportunities offered by legal reforms and technological advances. She finds that changes in the practice of law, especially the entrance of entrepreneurial and women attorneys, mostly translate into professional rather than commercial legal practices for most lawyers (Seron, 1996: 152–4).

Ethno-religious and social-class differences also exist, with large-firm lawyers having higher social-class backgrounds, being of north-west European and Protestant backgrounds and having attended a prestigious university. Research in the 1960s showed that small-firm and individual lawyers are first- or second-generation Americans of eastern European Jewish origin from less wealthy backgrounds, have attended less prestigious law schools and have clients of a similar background and social status (Ladinsky, 1963). There were very few Hispanic or Afro-American lawyers or clients. A study of Detroit lawyers found that solo practitioners more often than firm lawyers came from working-class and entrepreneurial families and were more likely to be Catholics or Jews from eastern and southern Europe than Protestants from northern Europe. Solo lawyers have quantitatively less and qualitatively inferior education when compared to firm lawyers and they are more likely to experience marginal law work, including minor criminal defence, divorce cases and negligence claims (Ladinsky, 1963: 48–9). Lawyers at the two extremes of the legal profession bar are largely isolated from professional or social contact with one another, which tends to reinforce divisions in the profession (Auerbach, 1976).

These divisions persist. Following interviews with 777 Chicago lawyers, Heinz and Laumann (1982) concluded that the two hemispheres of the legal profession still continue. They argued that one fundamental distinction within the legal profession overrides all other differences, namely the distinction between lawyers who represent large organizations – corporations, labour unions and government – and those who represent individuals. The basis of the divide is the type of client rather than substantive differences in the type of law work; however, different types of client will usually bring different legal problems. The corporate client sector is constituted by securities and antitrust laws, business tax, real estate, regulatory work, litigation and criminal prosecution, while family law, personal injury, personal tax, property and criminal defence work characterize the personal/small-business client legal sector. Only about two-fifths of the lawyers reported doing any work in both client hemispheres. Heinz and Laumann suggest that 'specialization within the legal profession is not so much a division of labor as a division of clientele. Lawyers tend to specialize in the representation of limited, identifiable types of clients and to perform as broad or narrow a range of tasks as their clientele demands' (1982: 56).

This divide also represents differentiations in origin, work, prestige and social status among Chicago lawyers. Lawyers who work in firms performing corporate work are most likely to be white and male, to be Protestant and have northern European ancestry, and to have graduated from an elite law school. At the other end of the spectrum, southern and eastern European Catholics are overrepresented at local law schools that produce predominantly solo practitioners. They conclude that 'two polar or "core" types of careers center, on the one hand, around practice in large firms serving corporate clients and, on the other, around solo practice serving individuals and small businesses' (Heinz and Laumann, 1982: 206).

The fields of law also differ in prestige. The lawyers in this Chicago sample ranked most highly 'big-business law' – securities, tax, patents and antitrust work – followed by other sorts of commercial law, then personal injury, civil rights and criminal law, with poverty law, divorce and landlord/tenant law ranking the lowest in prestige (Heinz and Laumann, 1982: 91–3). Again, the type of client is a central determinant of prestige; fields serving big-business clients are at the top and those serving individual clients, especially those from lower socioeconomic groups who engage in what Heinz and Laumann term 'unsavory litigation', are at the bottom (1982: 127).

Two decades later, the Chicago Bar was again surveyed (using face-to-face interviews) providing an opportunity to assess changes across the profession (Heinz et al., 2005). One of the striking changes observed was the increased percentage of women, up from 3.9 per cent of the sample in 1975 to 29 per cent in 1994–95. The profession remained predominantly white with a decline in the proportion of Jewish lawyers over the time span. The percentage of lawyers in firms of more than 30 lawyers had nearly doubled and the percentage of solo practitioners had declined. The corporate client fields had grown more rapidly than the personal client fields and the hemispheres had become more unequal. In the earlier survey Heinz and Laumann indicated that as a proportion of total legal effort, the corporate client sector accounted for 53 per cent and the personal/small-business client sector 40 per cent; by 1995 this ratio was 64 per cent to 29 per cent. They suggest that the profession remains divided, but not equally: the time expended on corporate legal fields and those relating to large organizations outstrips the time spent on personal client legal fields. 'The kinds of work that lawyers do, the style of their work, and the places in which they do it differ greatly' (Heinz et al., 2005: 44). The work of lawyers had become more specialized with the Chicago Bar remaining clearly stratified: women and minorities are more likely to work in lower-status practice settings and in lower-status roles within their practice settings. Jewish, African Americans, Hispanics and women are all underrepresented at partnership level.

Alternative to the emphasis on the differential prestige of fields of law, Abbott explains intra-professional status as deriving from professional purity. The highest-status professionals are those who deal with issues pre-digested and pre-defined by a number of colleagues who have removed human complexity and emotion to leave a problem professionally defined. In contrast, the lowest-status segments will deal with problems from which human complexities and interventions cannot be or have not been removed (Abbott, 1981: 823–4). It is not surprising that corporate law is the most prestigious, because the corporation itself is a legal creation; much of corporate legal practice entails interpreting complex statutes and company documents, whereas criminal cases, divorce cases and landlord-tenant disputes will often not raise questions of law but determinations of the facts and will involve intense human relationship, concerns and feelings. Where legal professions are divided into barristers and solicitors, the former will garner the most prestige and status. Barristers will receive briefs from solicitors who will interview clients and identify the main legal issues. It is the solicitor who is the barrister's client.

Using data from the Chicago Bar Survey, Sandefur (2001) finds support for both the client type thesis and the professional purity thesis in understanding the distribution of esteem among lawyers and prestige regarding areas of legal work. She argues that: 'The crucial aspect of autonomy is not autonomy from client control of lawyers' actions; it is freedom from client "dirtying" of the legal matter with nonlegal considerations' (Sandefur, 2001: 387). Client type largely determines the kinds of problems and, importantly, the way these are presented which affects the amount of diagnosis, inference, and treatment required in lawyers' work. Corporate clients present purer problems as they have the resources (legal and other) to purify them, extracting the human emotion and nonlegally relevant detail.

Stratification within the legal profession also structures professional deviance and its identification. The combination of inexperience or a lack of time in practice, resulting in fewer clients and less income, stratification within the profession, which places solo practitioners at the bottom of the hierarchy, and economic recession will help to explain professional misconduct among lawyers. Research on lawyers against whom complaints were lodged with a Canadian provincial law society indicates that the cumulative effects of inexperience, solo practice and economic recession will increase the probability of prosecution, and that inexperienced solo practitioners are prosecuted for professional misconduct at a higher rate during a recession because they experience a heightened risk of surveillance (Arnold and Hagan, 1992: 778–89, 1994; see also Daniel, 1998).

Codes of ethics, while applicable to all members of a profession, may actually reinforce inequalities. The American Bar Association Canons, which were quickly adopted by state law societies during the early twentieth century, benefited the elite and established segments of the legal profession and disadvantaged solo practitioners. The Canons, emphasizing such values as reputation, moral character, honour and propriety, were easily adopted by an homogeneous upper-class metropolitan legal constituency, where they served as an elite club against lawyers whose clients were excluded from that culture, especially the urban poor, new immigrants and blue-collar workers. The Canons particularly impeded those lawyers who worked in a highly competitive urban market with a transient clientele. These lawyers confronted problems of client procurement that established corporate practitioners would not experience (Auerbach, 1976: 41–4). A prohibition on advertising instructed lawyers that their success flowed on from their character and conduct, not from aggressive solicitation. It thereby rewarded the lawyer whose law-firm partners and social contacts made advertising unnecessary, and disadvantaged the urban, immigrant solo practitioners who lacked lucrative personal networks and relied on personal injury or criminal cases. Any form of client recruitment would be attributed to an inferior character and unethical behaviour, hence the derogatory term 'ambulance chasers' to describe lawyers who seek personal injury cases.

However, possible connections between a lawyer's self-interest, especially financial, the client's best interests and intra-professional stratification are not necessarily clear cut. A large body of research suggests, that for various reasons, ranging from institutional pressures to self-interest, criminal defence lawyers can influence defendants to plead guilty which goes against the legal principle that all guilty pleas must be voluntary and clashes with the service ethic (Mack and Roach Anleu, 1995; McConville, 1998). A recent study of criminal defence work in Scotland deploys the concept of 'ethical determinancy' to indicate that the advice lawyers give can be in the interests of both defendant and lawyer; they are not always mutually exclusive. However, where there are several courses of action equally beneficial to the client, but only one that will advance the defence lawyer's own interests, then the lawyer will be more likely to advise the client in a way that benefits his/her own interests, including financial considerations, perhaps particularly where there is legal aid funding (Tata, 2007a).

Changes to the legal profession

The legal profession in most countries has experienced numerous changes over the past three decades. The number of lawyers continues to grow; the proportion of women lawyers is increasing; lawyers are now more likely to be employed by large, bureaucratic organizations rather than being in solo practice; some legal tasks are becoming routinized and deskilled due to technological change; some dimensions of professional control are waning; and the legal profession has been subject to unprecedented public scrutiny. Some of these changes stem from the profession's response to the increased numbers and changed demographics of law school graduates and new legislation, especially administrative law and corporate regulation, which creates demands for new kinds of legal services. Other changes are the outcome of greater state intervention – including judicial pronouncements and government policies – oriented towards reducing the profession's traditional monopoly on such areas of practice as conveyancing, probate and preparing the early stages of litigation, and making it more competitive and responsive to market pressures, especially the demands of consumers.

In the USA, Supreme Court judgements reduced the absolute prohibition on advertising and outlawed bar associations' minimum fee schedules that reduced intra-professional competition (Andrews, 1981: 969; Powell, 1985: 282). In England and Wales, the Courts and Legal Services Act 1990 subjects the bar to direct legislative regulation (previously barristers' autonomy and authority derived from the common law), and provides for greater statutory intervention in the maintenance of professional standards, including the establishment of a Legal Services Ombudsman (prior to the Act, the Law Society, albeit legislatively based, had very wide powers of self-regulation). The legislation makes significant changes to the regulation of competitive practices among lawyers, and replaces barristers' monopoly on the right of audience in the higher courts by a new institutional mechanism that will determine who shall have such rights (Brazier et al., 1993: 207–8). Similarly, in Australia, the Trade Practices Commission (now the Australian Competition and Consumer Commission) made widespread recommendations that aim to increase competition, both among lawyers and between lawyers and other occupational groups, by opening up the market in legal services; allowing more flexible structures in the organization of legal work, including permitting partnerships and profit sharing with nonlawyers; abolishing fee scales and removing existing advertising restrictions (Trade Practices Commission, 1994). Interviews with Australian lawyers regarding the proposed competition and accountability reforms suggest that individual practitioners and professional associations respond positively to persuasion and dialogue when they perceive reform as inevitable, but resist change when they view it as excluding them from their own regulation and reform (Parker, 1997: 50–3).

Some authors argue that such changes herald deprofessionalization, that is, the erosion of professional autonomy and status. Others suggest that these changes signal a reorganization of the legal profession, entailing more stratification within the occupation but also new opportunities for the expansion of legal services and practice settings. The following section examines the changes and assesses the implications for the legal profession.

Growth

Exponential growth has occurred in the legal population in a number of societies since the 1960s (Galanter, 1992: 4). In the USA fewer than a quarter of a million lawyers existed in 1950; by 1980 the number had more than doubled and in 1993 there were 777 000 employed lawyers. The legal profession grew both absolutely and relatively faster than the general population (Curran et al., 1985: 4; United States Bureau of the Census, 1994: 407). In England and Wales there were 1919 barristers in private practice and 19 069 solicitors with practising certificates in 1960; these numbers had grown to 5642 and 47 830 respectively by 1987 (Zander, 1989: 5). In Australia, 6636 full-time lawyers practised in 1961 and by 1991 the number had more than quadrupled to 28 720 (Roach Anleu, 1992b: 187). This numerical expansion of lawyers stems from a variety of demand and supply factors.

Changes in legal education   The expansion of law schools and the move away from the apprenticeship model of education increase the number of students who can be trained as lawyers. The size of the legal profession is not constrained by its existing numbers and the amount of legal education available is determined by universities and governments, not by law firms and professional associations. In Australia, articles of clerkship as a method of providing practical training were formally abandoned or supplemented in most jurisdictions in the 1970s, thereby reducing law firms' 'gate-keeping' function. Where articles constitute the practical (or only) component of legal education, law firms and legal practitioners control training. In traditionally male-dominated law firms, control was maintained by recruiting socially homogeneous lawyers, emphasizing conformity and requiring diffuse and unbounded loyalty, producing a club-like atmosphere (Kanter, 1977; Smigel, 1964).

More legal regulation   There has been growth and increasing complexity in legislation in almost every aspect of social life, including business activities, family relations, employment, taxation, immigration, the environment, social welfare and insurance. The growth of government departments dealing with these areas and implementing the legislative requirements also expands administrative law. Additionally, governments will initiate Royal Commissions and other inquiries, often chaired by lawyers or retired judges, and usually lawyers will provide evidence in a quasi-courtroom environment.

More litigation   Increasing numbers of cases are being commenced in both civil and criminal courts (Galanter, 1992: 8–11). The establishment of government-funded legal aid services means that more people have access to some form of legal representation (Zander, 1989: 5). Additionally, cases are taking longer to litigate. Increasingly complex rules of evidence, the provision of expert evidence, greater numbers of class action suits (in jurisdictions where they are available, for example in the USA) and various tactical or court-ordered delays all contribute to the length of cases. Even where civil cases are settled out of court and where criminal defendants plead guilty, the participants will often have legal representatives who can accomplish the settlement and negotiate with the other side. Moreover, the establishment of tribunals, committees and mechanisms for alternative dispute resolution all increase the demand for lawyers, even though such bodies aim to reduce litigation and limit the involvement of lawyers (see Chapter 5).

The entry of women

Historically, law has been an almost exclusively male profession. Women have been either excluded from, or have obtained only limited access to, the practice of law by formal and informal law school quotas or by the absolute refusal to admit women (as was the case at Harvard University Law School until 1951), judicial decision, legislation, discrimination by potential employers and pervasive sex-role expectations.

Despite the lifting of many of the formal restrictions during the early part of the twentieth century, the number of women lawyers remained negligible until the 1970s. A pioneering study of women lawyers in the New York area in the late 1960s demonstrates how women seemed to be selectively recruited into fields, specialties and jobs that are not good conduits for mobility or prestige and how the informal organization of legal work, especially at the top echelons, mitigated against their integration and achievement within the profession. In particular, the sponsor-protégé system that determines access to the highest levels of the profession, women's exclusion from informal networks and participation in clubs and associations where job opportunities are made known and informal recommendations made, their presumed lack of commitment and motivation, plus their own perceptions of exclusion all contributed to maintaining the sexual division of labour in the legal profession (Epstein, 1968: 194–232, 237–61; 1970: 966).

Over the past few decades the numbers of women in law schools and in legal practice have grown dramatically in several common law and civil law countries (Schultz and Shaw, 2003). The rates of increase are especially impressive due to the previous dearth of women. For example, in the USA more women entered the legal profession between 1970 and 1980 than during all the previous decades of the century (Epstein, 1983: 4). In Australia before the 1950s, only two women practised at the New South Wales bar, three in Victoria and none in Queensland (Mathews, 1982: 635). Women constituted 11.4 per cent of all law students in 1960 and by 1994 approximately 50 per cent of students studying law and 35 per cent of legal academic staff were women (Australian Law Reform Commission, 1994: 136).

Despite larger numbers of women lawyers, the career prospects of men and women differ. Simply comparing the aggregate numbers of men and women law graduates and practising lawyers obscures differences in types of employment, work, opportunities for promotion and income (Sokoloff, 1992: 124–7). Women lawyers' return on their human capital – education and law school achievements – is not equivalent to that of their male counterparts (Faulconbridge and Muzio, 2008). Research in several nations demonstrates that gender segregation, albeit more complex and nuanced than previously, remains within the legal profession.

While women have achieved numerical parity with men in terms of law school students and graduates, admission to legal practice and commencing solicitors inequalities persist (Bolton and Muzio, 2007). Women solicitors tend to be employed on less favourable terms and conditions, earn lower salaries, experience less autonomy in their work, have lower chances of promotion and making partnership, and are less integrated into informal professional networks that provide essential information about careers and mentoring (Feenan, 2005, 2007; Muzio and Ackroyd, 2005; Sommerlad, 2002; Sommerlad and Sanderson, 1998). Sex discrimination and gender bias might not be overt but nonetheless inhibit women barristers' advancement (Hunter, 2002, 2005).

The persistence of gender segmentation in the legal profession arises from both the organization of legal work and the occupational culture which constrain the kinds of opportunities and choices available to both women and men. The culture of long working hours, lack of flexibility in the workplace, and the difficulty for many women of fitting work patterns into a male working paradigm which requires open-ended availability for after hours work all constrain women's careers in the legal profession (Heinz et al., 2005; Sommerlad, 2002; Webley and Duff, 2007). This is occurring in a context of increasing competition for legal services and the deterioration of working conditions stemming from longer hours and increasing workloads.

A study of small-scale private legal practice in the USA finds that women and men work expanded hours but the demand for 'unbracketed time commitment' has qualitatively different effects for men and women as women primarily retained responsibility for family needs and obligations (Seron and Ferris, 1995). 'From the standpoint of work-based opportunities, they [men] enjoyed a privilege [ie release from most private obligations] at home that translated into a resource at the office' (Seron and Ferris, 1995: 31). The Chicago Bar study shows that women are more likely than men to perceive conflicts between work and family demands and to experience stress as a result (Heinz et al., 2005: 265).

A study of lawyers in the New York City metropolitan area demonstrates how the determination of earnings varies by sex and organizational sectors that differ in sex composition and the bureaucratization of decision making (Dixon and Seron, 1995: 383). Women remain underrepresented in private firms where decision making is nonbureaucratic. In this organizational context, having children has a significant, positive effect on men's incomes while for women the opposite attains. A prestigious law degree increases earnings for men but not for women, but success in law school and work experience benefit men *and* women in this sector. In the more sex-integrated government sector where decision making is formal and bureaucratic, women with children face fewer income disadvantages; experience is important for all lawyers, while education has little impact on salaries. Sex integration is increasing in the corporate sector where decision making is mediated by a corporate culture and in this setting family factors affect earnings in complex ways. Men receive positive returns for children, while marriage benefits women (Dixon and Seron, 1995: 404–5). Women solo and small-firm practitioners have fewer opportunities to develop their practices and less time for legal work, to a large extent because of their domestic responsibilities (Seron, 1996: 33–6).

Even workplace reforms aimed at recognizing the different family obligations of men and women lawyers and removing barriers to women's advancement in the legal profession do not necessarily enhance women's career prospects. A study of corporate law firms in Australia finds that women taking up opportunities to work part time or avail themselves of flexible hours or take maternity leave are allocated work such as managing intellectual resources, documents, preparing notices, advice and settlement deeds, that does not entail high billable hours involving corporate clients (Thornton and Bagust, 2007). Taking advantage of flexible work arrangements seems to be interpreted as evidence of lower commitment and invisibility resulting in career disadvantage (Webley and Duff, 2007).

A number of characteristics of law firms can disadvantage women, albeit not overtly. Criteria for hiring or promotion can at face value be gender neutral but have unequal consequences for women lawyers. Hiring in large law firms – namely more than 30 lawyers – involves the development of categories and schemas, or profiles of what firms are looking for in candidates. An examination of the hiring criteria listed in the 1995 National Association for Law Placement (NALP) Directory measures the extent to which a law firm's descriptions and prescriptions about people who perform successfully in a position include stereotypically masculine – ambition, assertion, energy and objectivity – or feminine – cooperativeness, friendliness – attributes. When selection criteria include more stereotypically masculine characteristics, women constitute a smaller proportion of new hires, and when criteria include more stereotypically feminine traits, women are better represented among new hires. This finding confirms that organizational decision makers evaluate male and female candidates through the lens of gender stereotypes and compare these perceptions with the role-incumbent schemas operating within their organizations (Gorman, 2005: 721–2).

Canadian data confirm the persistent gap between the earnings of men and women, even after accounting for differences in credentials, positions and employing organizations. Men obtain more reward for the acquisition of human capital and the earnings differential widens as women ascend the mobility ladder. Approximately two-fifths of the earnings differential results from the fact that men and women lawyers work in different positions, different fields of law and different firms and organizations. The remaining differential is attributed to different rates of returns to men and women for their education, work, specialization and experience (Kay and Hagan, 1995: 304–6). Women's poorer prospects for partnership cannot be explained entirely in terms of tangible factors, including skills and training plus labour-market segmentation; cultural variables are also important. To improve their chances for partnership, women must exhibit an extraordinary work commitment, assessed by their bringing in of new clients, maintaining a large network of corporate clients, returning promptly from maternity leave and expressing practice-oriented career goals (Kay and Hagan, 1998: 741).

Uncertainty in a law firm's work also negatively affects the promotion of women. Decision makers consider both performance and gender to assess ability and the capacity to perform work at a higher level. As the male gender carries a presumption of general competence and the female gender carries a corresponding presumption of a lack of competence, women must perform better than men to neutralize such presumptions (Gorman, 2006: 879). This finding coincides with Kanter's (1977) notion of 'homosocial reproduction' whereby social similarity is seen as essential for trust.

Faulconbridge and Muzio (2008) identify a number of internal processes which lead to distinct career patterns for female solicitors in private legal practice:

(a) *Stratification*: women lawyers are unable to access senior positions, including partnership, and become concentrated in salaried positions. This can result from apparently gender neutral processes, including the way commitment is operationalised as visible long hours. Taking maternity leave and working part-time become defined as fragmented, and thus deviant, career paths (Sommerlad, 2002; Sommerlad and Sanderson, 1998).

(b) *Segmentation*: women are clustered in low prestige, lower income areas of legal practice, such as family, employment, and personal injury law.

(c) *Sedimentation*: women mobilize typically feminine skills such as compassion, good communication and empathy as resources and find a special niche which in turn reinforces segmentation and stratification (Faulconbridge and Muzio, 2008: 50). A study of women law professors in UK universities finds that women undertake more mentoring than their male colleagues and take on more pastoral work and are perceived to be better at it (Wells, 2002). Formal mentoring and nurturing work are not the skills widely identified with the high-paying, prestigious areas of legal practice or with successful academic research careers.

The extent to which men and women stay in or leave the practice of law is an important indicator of their integration and success within the profession. Women depart from law to a greater extent than do men, which partly explains their marked underrepresentation in partnerships and other top legal positions. Motives for departing relate to difficulties in combining family life and legal practice, the lack of flexibility in work arrangements, the additional work-related hours required and experiences of discrimination in the workplace. In England and Wales a Law Society commissioned project sought to identify the reasons as to why women solicitors had a break from practice or chose to leave the profession entirely (Sommerlad, 2002; Sommerlad and Sanderson, 1998). It finds that women solicitors do work long hours, enjoy the intellectual challenge and the variety of work, appreciate the interaction with clients and teamwork and are very satisfied with salaries which tempers the negatives of working as a solicitor (Sommerlad and Sanderson, 1998). These women solicitors disliked the less favourable promotion prospects, poor management practices, inflexible workplaces and the dehumanization of the individual by the firm (Webley and Duff, 2007).

Canadian research also indicates that particular aspects of the workplace and available opportunities cause women more dissatisfaction than men but these effects are often neutralised by high levels of satisfaction with the nature of the work, the associated tasks and responsibilities and the financial advantages from legal practice, even when they involved gendered disparities (Hagan and Kay, 2007: 70). Women are more likely than men to express and experience concerns about the consequences of having children for their careers. Some US research reports that women lawyers experience less job satisfaction than their male counterparts due to a relative dissatisfaction with insufficient influence, fewer promotion opportunities, and less pay rather than wanting a less demanding career (Chiu, 1998; Chiu and Leicht, 1999). Job satisfaction and commitment are important for reducing the likelihood that early-career lawyers will leave firms to work in government or exit from practice altogether. A national survey of US law graduates also found that a higher percent of women compared with men indicated that they intend to change jobs within the next two years (Dinovitzer et al., 2004).

Women's experiences of legal practice are also qualitatively different to those of men. A study of lawyers in Arizona finds that women are more likely to report receiving compliments unrelated to their professional achievements, experiencing less credibility in professional settings, hearing sexist jokes and remarks from judges and other lawyers, being patronized, being referred to by their first names and asked whether they are lawyers (MacCorquodale and Jensen, 1993: 590). Another investigation of the occupational experiences of women lawyers indicates that one-quarter reported being sexually harassed, most specifying that it occurred more than once in the previous year, and the primary perpetrators were other lawyers, followed by clients, judges and other legal personnel (Rosenberg et al., 1993: 423).

During the late 1980s, several North American and other jurisdictions commissioned special task forces to investigate the treatment and experience of women in the courts, which generally found that a pervasive gender bias persists against women lawyers, litigants, witnesses and court employees. These reports detail the tendency of judges to accord less credibility to women's claims and show that court officials provide women lawyers with less respect and dignity than their male counterparts: women are more likely to be addressed in familiar terms, be subjected to comments about personal appearance and to experience verbal or physical sexual advances. These reports indicate the general acceptance of aggressive behaviour by men but not by women. They recommend reforms to legal education, the legal profession, the judiciary and court administration to ensure that the various participants are aware of and can attempt to eradicate gender bias in the legal system (Australian Law Reform Commission, 1994; Law Society of British Columbia, 1992; Schneider, 1988: 87–8; Tannen, 1990: 917–26).

Another area of law which has traditionally been completely closed to women is the judiciary. There is growing socio-legal research on the ways in which women are excluded from judicial office, and recognition that simple demographic change in the legal profession is not sufficient to change predominantly male judiciaries (Feenan, 2005; Schultz and Shaw, 2003). Aside from overt discrimination, other more subtle mechanisms seem to be at work, including a lack of transparency in the appointments process, women's ignorance of opportunities and men's ignorance of women's experiences (Feenan, 2007). Two key events make the appointment of women to judicial officer more likely now than in the past: first, in common-law countries, women have entered the pools from which members of the judiciary are typically drawn, notably the senior bar. Second, the parameters of the judicial labour market also have shifted (slightly). Changes in appointment processes include widening the recruitment pool, making more explicit and transparent the qualifications and skills required, and formalizing the selection criteria for judicial office (Feenan, 2007: 523; Malleson, 2006: 131). Such reforms have created opportunities for the appointment of solicitors, lawyers with law reform experience, and those with careers as legal academics, all areas of legal practice and work where there are relatively more women, compared with some other legal settings (Rackley, 2006; Thornton, 2007). There is considerable discussion and research on the difference to judicial office and judicial decision making that the appointment of women judges might make (Malleson, 2003; Martin et al., 2002; Roach Anleu and Mack, 2009; Schultz and Shaw, 2003, 2008; Thornton, 2007).

Salaried employment

Increasingly, the dominant form of legal practice is not solo practice but employment in law firms, government departments and business corporations. Although firm practice is frequently equated with employment in a large firm, most lawyers who practise in firms are in small to medium firms (Curran et al., 1985: 14). At the end of World War II, two-thirds of all US lawyers in private practice were solo practitioners, but by 1970 the proportion had declined to half, where it has more or less remained. This reduction in solo practice has been offset by an increase in the proportion of lawyers employed in firms. There is evidence in other societies of a shift from solo to firm practice, although it is not as marked or as well documented as in the USA (Lee, 1992; Roach Anleu, 1992b: 190).

Not only do more lawyers work in firms, but law firms are also increasing in size through mergers and expansions and the establishment of multinational law firms. The globalization of the market in legal services has accompanied and facilitated the internationalization of financial markets. Corporate law firms have become more widespread and national differences in legal systems, professions and cultures may be on the decline in some respects (Dezalay, 1990: 281–5; Faulconbridge and Muzio, 2008). Dezalay suggests that this globalization is for the most part an Americanization, as large North American firms have been the most entrepreneurial and well positioned to respond to the new opportunities (1990: 281). Nevertheless, it is not clear the extent to which the rule of law and western models of law will dominate international economic relations, which still rely on personal relations and connections, especially in Asia and Latin America (Dezalay and Garth, 1997: 111).

While large law firms have been in existence in the USA throughout the twentieth century, they have not been as evident in other jurisdictions. In England and Wales, large law firms could not develop because partnerships of any kind were prohibited from exceeding 20 members until the passing of the Companies Act in 1967 (Flood, 1989: 569–70). The restructuring of the British economy in the 1980s, the considerable inward investment into Europe, especially from the USA and Japan, and the growth of the European Union have boosted the market for legal services, to which law firms in the City of London have responded. The removal of the partnership limit and new demands for corporate legal services have enabled London law firms to increase in size and become more corporatized (Flood, 1989: 584; Lee, 1992: 34–9). Galanter identifies a distinctive style of legal practice – mega-lawyering – which is associated, but not synonymous, with large law firms (Galanter, 1983a: 153–4). In contrast to ordinary law practice, mega-law firms are organized on a national or international basis; are divided into departments and their lawyers tend to specialize; legal services are viewed as a product to be sold; clients – usually corporate actors – are served by several lawyers; and litigation tends to be complex, labour intensive, time consuming and expensive.

The shift to larger firms and the hiring of more entry-level lawyers reduce opportunities for promotion and career development. An investigation of four large Chicago law firms finds that associates currently entering law firms confront an increasingly bureaucratic organizational setting characterized by higher levels of turnover, earlier and more intensive specialization, decreased levels of client responsibility and more frequent assignment to large-scale litigation (Nelson, 1981: 110–8; 1983: 123–7). Partnership policies may become more restrictive for newer, larger cohorts of associates, either by limiting the proportion of those who make partner or by increasing the number of years with the firm required for admission to full partnership. As associates and solicitors are a critical source of revenue for the law firm, the ratio of equity partners (i.e. those who share in the firm's profits) to associates is a central aspect of firm economics (Lee, 1992: 36; Nelson, 1981: 126). The salaries paid to nonpartners, while considerable compared to other employees' incomes, are only a fraction of the income and profit that the lawyer generates for the firm, as their fees tend to be high and they bill by the hour or part thereof. Some firms will alter their career hierarchies by creating positions for salaried partners and permanent associates. Salaried partners may attend but not vote at partners' meetings, they do not share in the profits but may be liable for the firm's debts. Salaried partners will expect to become equity partners; however, delaying the process preserves firm profits (Lee, 1992: 35). Permanent associates will remain salaried employees but are ineligible for partnership (Spangler, 1986: 55–6, 68–9).

The establishment and growth of in-house legal departments further increase the scope of salaried employment within the legal profession. In the late 1970s this was one of the fastest-growing segments of the profession and the largest employer of lawyers after private practice (Spangler, 1986: 70–106). The rapid expansion of in-house legal departments was a response to significant changes in legal and economic environments. Environmental protection, occupational safety, equal opportunity and product safety laws and regulations expanded the volume of legal work that corporations have to perform to stay in compliance. Increased litigation followed these regulatory changes. Yet for the corporation the sheer cost of hiring outside counsel represents a large, unfixed overhead with no guarantee of success or profit. In light of these regulatory changes and soaring litigation costs, it became economical to employ in-house counsel, thereby reducing legal costs by an estimated 35 to 50 per cent (Lancaster, 1982). By 1982 approximately eight in every ten in-house legal departments performed at least one-half to three-quarters of their corporation's legal work. Even so, many companies still retain outside law firms for their special expertise, major litigation, or for very large, infrequent cases.

At the other end of the spectrum, salaried employment has increased as a result of new kinds of legal services for individual clients with personal problems. Since the late 1970s, legal aid offices funded by central governments have become an important sector of the legal profession and aim to provide legal advice and, where appropriate, legal representation, mostly in criminal law cases. In part, the impetus for the establishment of such legal services came from radical lawyers seeking to expand access to legal resources and advice to individuals unable to afford private legal counsel. Legal aid offices will hire salaried lawyers to provide legal work but will also contract out cases to private practitioners (Tomsen, 1992: 309–12, 321–2).

Another form of salaried legal work that aims to provide advice to a large client base is the franchise law firm, which has developed in the USA over the past two decades. These firms, often consisting of a network of law offices, will adapt mass-marketing and mass-production techniques to the delivery of such legal services as uncontested divorce, simple wills, name changes, some tenancy problems and personal bankruptcy (Van Hoy, 1995: 703–5). They are located in shopfronts and shopping malls, will aggressively advertise on television, seek a high volume of clients in each office, and employ both lawyers and legal secretaries to perform the legal tasks. Clients' problems are handled by standardized procedures and 'boilerplate forms', and there is little scope for either individualized attention to clients' needs or creative legal solutions based on research and a fine attention to detail. Firms will impose strict production requirements on branch offices, which standardize and limit the legal issues that can be dealt with, the kind of advice to be offered to clients and the organization of work. Employment in franchise law firms is relatively lowly paid, staff tend to be recent graduates who have been unsuccessful in obtaining other kinds of legal employment, there is high turnover of staff, the work is relatively unskilled, lawyers experience their work as repetitive and uninteresting and they tend to view their work as processing, rather than practising, law (Van Hoy, 1995: 707, 715–25).

Specialization

Unlike the medical profession, the legal profession has been loath to formally recognize specialization or to offer certification. Yet occupational expansion combined with new demands for legal services has meant a decline in general practice work and increasing specialization and subspecialization. In Heinz and Laumann's (1982) study of the Chicago Bar 70 per cent of their respondents considered themselves specialists in one or more legal subfield. The authors added that fewer than three-quarters of the self-assigned specialists devoted as much as half of their practice time to a single field of law. Only criminal prosecution commanded the exclusive attention of as many as half of its practitioners and only patents came close to their measure of specialization of effort, that is, 50 per cent or more of time spent (Heinz and Laumann, 1982: 43–4). Two decades later Heinz and colleagues report that specialization in the legal profession had increased since the mid-1970s, with one third of practising lawyers indicating that they only worked in one legal field (Heinz et al., 2005: 37). In Australia, it also seems that specialization has become a major feature of all segments of the profession and of all types of lawyers, with government, corporation and city lawyers most likely to designate themselves as specialists, and suburban and country lawyers least likely to do so (Tomasic and Bullard, 1978). Barristers will also acquire reputations for specializing or concentrating on certain kinds of cases (Morison and Leith, 1992: 59–63).

Despite these trends, ethical codes will generally forbid lawyers from representing themselves as specialists, except in such specific areas as patent, trademarks and admiralty law. Some jurisdictions have begun to certify legal specialists in a few fields, but these developments have been tentative, opposed and experimental. Since 1973, a specialist certification scheme for lawyers covering criminal law, workers' compensation, taxation and family law has operated in California, yet there is widespread opposition to this (New South Wales Law Reform Commission, 1982: 35–6). Formal accreditation of specialist practitioners has been introduced in some Australian states (Trade Practices Commission, 1994: 109). Nevertheless, decisions relating to specialization are firmly in the hands of the various law societies, which promulgate guidelines to control the scope and type of specialization.

Professional control

Restrictions on advertising and the setting of fee scales – traditionally embedded in the professional ethics of bar associations and law societies – constitute a hallmark of the professions. They form an important aspect of self-regulation and collegial control as well as preserving the market for legal services. Bans on advertising and the setting of fee scales enable the control of competition among lawyers and from other occupational groups. Opponents argue that advertising would result in lawyers adopting a business rather than a service orientation, that is, they would be concerned primarily with recruiting large numbers of clients and increasing profit margins rather than with providing a quality service to their clientele. Professional associations traditionally regard advertising as an unacceptable mode of client recruitment.

Nevertheless, bans on advertising have become less absolute. In 1977, the US Supreme Court held that lawyers have a constitutional right to advertise their prices for routine legal services in print (Andrews, 1981: 969). The court agreed that the ban on advertising inhibited the flow of information about legal services. The judgement strengthened the position of more marginal segments within the legal profession, specifically solo practitioners, small unknown firms and legal clinics, by providing them with access to important channels for recruiting clients, especially those on moderate incomes and ineligible for government legal assistance (Powell, 1985: 298–302). It has also been an impetus for the establishment and expansion of franchise law firms, which rely on mass advertising to recruit clients.

In Australia, both statutory and nonstatutory professional rules prohibited solicitors from advertising until the 1980s. These rules permitted solicitors to make limited public statements providing information on address changes, the opening or resumption of practice and to advertise for new staff, as long as such notifications were not aimed at attracting clients. Prohibitions on advertising have been lifted in most Australian jurisdictions. Even so, solicitors must advertise in accordance with guidelines established by their respective law societies and with general consumer protection legislation relating to false or misleading advertising (Roach Anleu, 1992b: 192–3; Trade Practices Commission, 1994: 171–8). Similarly, in England and Wales, while some forms of institutional advertising had been permitted since the 1960s, in 1984 the Council of the Law Society announced that solicitors could advertise the range of services they offered to the public together with their charges. Radio and newspaper, but not television, advertising was allowed in accordance with Law Society guidelines (Zander, 1989: 11–14).

Fee scales – that is, lists of specified legal services with an attached charge – establish minimum or maximum fees to be charged and can be administered by the courts, statutory bodies or the legal profession itself. While it may be permissible to charge fees below those specified in the scales, restrictions on advertising meant that potential clients had little information on price differences. Fee scales have come under judicial and governmental scrutiny as anticompetitive and as violating trade practices' legislation. In 1975, the US Supreme Court ruled against bar associations' minimum fee schedules that reduced intra-professional competition. The court established that the legal profession is not outside the terms 'trade or commerce', and therefore minimum fee scales represent price fixing and restrict free trade (Powell, 1985: 285). This decision effectively ended the legal profession's immunity from competitive market forces and its exemption from the provisions of antitrust legislation. The abolition of fee scales facilitated the establishment of legal clinics that provide low-cost legal advice on issues such as probate, divorce, separation, custody and child support, consumer and bankruptcy law. Similarly, the Australian Trade Practices Commission's study of the legal profession concludes that:

> The existing fee scales for legal services have serious weaknesses as indicators of market prices or reasonable charges for legal services and can also have adverse effects on competition and efficiency. ... All professional rules which prohibit discounting below fee scales, set fees and retainers according to fee scales or are variants on the two-thirds rule for charging by QCs [Queen's Counsels] and junior barristers should be eliminated. (Trade Practices Commission, 1994: 9–10)

These changes – growth in the number of lawyers and firm size, increased specialization, expansion of salaried employment and reduced opportunities for partnership, and law firms' heightened sensitivity to market forces and orientation to business strategies – have been occurring for some time, however, they seem to have become more acute during the twenty-first century. The business context of the legal profession has become more competitive, in part due to economic changes, commercial realities, and national and international market forces, as well as more public and consumer criticism of professional practices, claims, arrangements and services (Faulconbridge and Muzio, 2008; Hanlon, 1997, 1998). New pressures for entrepreneurship, competitive edge, consumer focus, and managerial efficiency impinge on legal practice.

In 1989 the administration of the legal aid scheme in England and Wales was removed from the Law Society and placed with a government agency, the Legal Services Commission. This had the effect of loosening the solicitors' control on the scheme and introduced nonlawyer providers of legal services into the scheme. The market for publicly funded legal assistance – historically the preserve of solicitors in private practice – became a contested market. A comparison between nonlawyer and solicitor organizations in civil areas (not family and not involving litigation of debt, welfare benefits, housing or employment) finds that taken as a group nonlawyers perform to higher standards than lawyers: 'non-lawyers can successfully challenge the monopolies of lawyers without diminishing quality,' at least in this specific market for legal services (Moorhead et al., 2003: 96).

At the large firm end, law professionals no longer have control of the professional–client relationship and do not view their work in altruistic or general social service terms. Clients are accepted based on their capacity to pay and not need, and then there is a strong identification with the client's needs and interests. The values of business and market engagement – recruiting clients, creating profits, pressures for entrepreneurship – seem to overwhelm traditional professional values (Hanlon, 1997: 820). In this context, law firms, like many other business firms, have undergone significant restructuring.

In England and Wales there have been dramatic increases in the ratio of salaried solicitors – associates, assistants and junior partners – to profit sharing partners, thus extending professional hierarchies. This is paralleled with a decline in the numbers of non-fee earning – managerial, clerical and administrative – staff. The expanding cohort of salaried legal staff confront work intensification, more direct supervision and less autonomy, more economic exploitation and decreased job security (Muzio, 2004; Muzio and Ackroyd, 2005). Principles of quality assurance – service delivery, performance measurement – are being increasingly applied to professional settings (Travers, 2007).

These changes are not necessarily the inevitable consequence of directive market forces but are actively instigated by professional elites in defence of their traditional status, privileges and rewards (Muzio and Ackroyd, 2005). Law firms should be seen as 'strategic actors' capable of responding to external market imperatives in innovative ways and in turn can potentially reshape the market in terms of their own professional self-interests (Heinz et al., 2005: 137).

Interpreting the changes

Recent market, bureaucratic, judicial, legislative and membership demands are eroding some aspects of the self-regulatory authority and autonomy of the legal profession. These changes also appear to be accompanied by a decline in the average income for lawyers (Sander and Williams, 1989: 447–8; Stager and Foot, 1988: 80). Some observers interpret these changes as evidence of deprofessionalization, that is, an erosion of the profession's unique qualities, specifically the monopoly over knowledge, a public belief in the service ethos and occupational autonomy *vis-à-vis* the performance of tasks and the client (Haug, 1973: 197; Rothman, 1984: 189).

Others regard professional employment in bureaucratic organizations and incorporation into the wage-labour system as proletarianization, that is, the increasing division of labour and specialization that widens the gap between what the professional employee does and the end product (Oppenheimer, 1973). Derber (1983: 318–25) suggests that professional employees experience ideological rather than technical proletarianization. They are unable to select their own projects or clients or to make budgetary or policy decisions; nevertheless, they maintain their skill and discretion over specialized technical procedures.

More specifically, it is argued that the decline in lawyers' professional status stems from:

(a) the profession's inability to control the supply and social composition of its membership;
(b) employment in large firms that fragments relations with clients who may actually be more powerful than the lawyers, who in turn may be placed under pressure to compromise their professional judgements;
(c) employment in bureaucratic organizations that will ensure conflict between managerial and professional imperatives;
(d) employment in government offices and business corporations, which means that lawyers depend on one client who controls the employment relationship;

(e) specialization, which leads to routinization as professionals will be expected to perform the same tasks repeatedly without any knowledge or control of either the whole case or the client;

(f) the fact that many legal procedures have become so standardized that 'do-it-yourself' manuals and 'boilerplate' contracts suggest that much legal knowledge is neither esoteric nor accessible only by lawyers;

(g) the relaxation of prohibitions on advertising and deregulated salaries, which expands opportunities for intra-professional competition, thereby reducing collegiality and professional status;

(h) encroachment from other occupations, which threatens the legal profession's monopoly, or at least its claims to superior expertise, on such tasks as conveyancing and taxation advice.

Arguments that the legal profession is deprofessionalizing ignore a number of critical considerations. First, to suggest that salaried employment reduces lawyers' autonomy assumes that solo practitioners have more control over their work. However, self-employment without effective control of one's position in the labour market does not ensure the capacity for regulation and control of the types of legal work and clients with which a lawyer must deal, even though the pace of work and the hours can be controlled to some extent. Lawyers in solo practice have always been vulnerable to market controls that will determine their ability to locate and retain clients, and clients will frequently exercise some control over these lawyers (Carlin, 1962; 1966; Heinz and Laumann, 1982). In contrast, Freidson maintains that the central issue is market dependence, because 'if a particular kind of work is scarce and valued, it is still possible to "write one's own ticket", whether one is employed or self-employed' (Freidson, 1983: 284).

Moreover, large firms tend to provide a wide range of legal specialties, thus offering the lawyer more scope for choice and control over areas of practice. In contrast, small legal firms offer less variety; they will either be generalist or highly specialized practices. Lawyers in traditionally organized general service firms report that the firm dictated their choice of work more often than did those in bureaucratically organized speciality firms. Lawyers in large bureaucratic firms deal with the most complex legal issues, the most controversial kinds of litigation, the most creative forms of financial transactions, and the most rapidly changing bodies of law (Nelson, 1981: 137; 1983).

Secondly, even though employment in such nonlegal bureaucratic organizations as business corporations and government offices involves the loss of some autonomy, as these organizations attempt to ensure professional employees' loyalty and commitment to their goals, it enhances autonomy and influence in other areas. Business-people and government officials are more likely to consult with in-house counsel than with outside law firms to obtain preventive advice and suggestions early on in the development of a project. This represents an increase in the parameters of legal expertise. The legal profession's association with large bureaucracies consolidates its position by controlling the flow of clients, provides practitioners with a legitimate mandate to monopolize certain activities, and enables them to exercise discretion within those boundaries. An analysis of legal aid policy in Australia illustrates that despite hostility from law societies who lost control of legal aid, the establishment of publicly funded legal aid schemes subsidized and benefited the private legal market. Rather than competing with and encroaching on the work of private practitioners, extensive engagement in the legal aid sphere has been of long-term benefit for the whole occupation, resulting in new legal markets and career paths, and has expanded lawyers' influence over areas of public policy (Tomsen, 1992: 321–5, see also Tata and Stephen, 2006).

Thirdly, professional employees maintain jurisdiction over their own knowledge base, which preserves their autonomy and reduces managerial encroachments (Freidson, 1983; Powell, 1985). The legal profession retains tight control over the credentialling process, specifically certification, accreditation and registration that determine the knowledge and skills necessary for legal practice, and thereby its members. Specialization does not necessarily lead to deskilling and routinization. Freidson (1983: 285) distinguishes specialization that is generated by the professions themselves from detailed specialization among industrial workers. In the former, professionals refine and advance their knowledge and skill into new applications, whereas in the latter, specialization is imposed by managers and their agents in order to increase worker productivity. While lawyers will delegate such nontechnical and routine tasks as legal research and title searches to paralegals and legal secretaries, they will guard the new specialist and more esoteric areas for themselves.

Fourthly, many law firm and employed practice contexts combine bureaucratic and collegial forms of control. Hierarchical management structures do not necessarily outlaw democratic governance, even in the largest firms (Heinz et al., 2005: 138). Despite increasing internal stratification – firm and occupational – professionalism remains resilient and distinct. Faulconbridge and Muzio argue that 'defensive professionalism' (2008: 641) has enhanced the income and status of senior members of the profession and enabled the expansion of the legal profession. Senior partners, even in large commercial firms, retain control over the definition, organization and evaluation of legal work attesting to the continuance of legal professional autonomy, even if salaried legal practitioners experience less control over everyday work. Management principles and imperatives remain subservient to professional control. Faulconbridge and Muzio (2008: 8) describe a new form of professionalism – 'organizational professionalism' – even existing within large, global law firms, where managerial concerns about efficiency and profit coexist with professional values, autonomy, service quality and technical expertise: 'decisions regarding strategy and strategic overview [are] administered by professionals themselves in a consensual (professional) rather than directive (managerial/bureaucratic) manner' (Faulconbridge and Muzio, 2008: 15). Hanlon describes this redefinition of professionalism as 'commercialized professionalism' (1998: 50), emphasizing the need for managerial and entrepreneurial as well as technical legal skills.

Finally, legislative and judicial controls may diminish professional self-regulation and autonomy in some respects; however they may benefit and strengthen other segments or aspects of the profession. The abolition of absolute bans on advertising and minimum fee schedules increases competition and enabled the emergence of legal services clinics in the USA, which are unlikely to undermine the centrality within the profession of private practitioners, especially those in large law firms. Statutory removal of the ceiling on the size of partnerships in England facilitated the expansion of large law firms that specialize. While the 1990 English legal reforms eroded the solicitor's monopoly on conveyancing – a staple of small-firm or solo practice – they removed the ban on multinational partnerships, thus allowing big firms to expand internationally, and perhaps paved the way for prohibitions on multidisciplinary partnerships, for example between lawyers and such adjacent occupations as account-ants, to be dropped (Brazier et al., 1993: 210). Emergent segments of the profession seeking to redefine the nature and reach of professional ethics or to create their own niche in the market for legal services facilitate, and in some cases initiate, changes in the regulatory mechanisms of the legal profession (Powell, 1985: 283).

These changes affect the legal profession's opportunity structure, the terms and loci of employment and salaries. Types of legal employment that vary in bureaucra-tization, opportunities, types of work, remuneration and clientele have increased. The legal profession has become more complex, stratified and rationalized. This is not synonymous with deprofessionalization or with the absolute loss of autonomy and self-regulatory authority. Developments in the regulation of lawyers suggest a more complex process of reprofessionalization, whereby the parameters of profes-sional self-regulation are redefined. Nonetheless, empirical research unequivocally demonstrates that such changes have vastly different implications for men's and women's careers within the profession. The legal labour market remains segmented and different opportunities exist for men and women, with the latter remaining subject to discriminatory work practices and unequal expectations regarding perform-ance and commitment.

Conclusion

This chapter discusses law as a profession that has undergone considerable change during the past three decades. Overall, it has become larger and more heterogeneous and has been active in creating new markets for legal services. It could be asked whether the move from solo practice to salaried employment has lowered the profes-sional status of, or deprofessionalized, lawyers. Considering the professional attributes outlined earlier in the chapter, legal practitioners still possess the most: credentials, esoteric knowledge and skills, which in some circumstances are not their exclusive remit, a high degree of autonomy, though this varies in practice settings, collegial authority, which is more infused with, but not necessarily neutralized by, bureau-cratic imperatives, a professional association, codes of ethics, and a commitment to a service ideal. However, these characteristics seem to be redefined in terms of the specific service needs of clients and the law firm's or legal practitioner's financial advancement. While there has been and continues to be considerable change, lawyers remain professionals but work in diverse settings and experience different lawyer-client relationships.

Despite recent discussions regarding the internationalization of law and the globalization of legal professions, it remains important to investigate and assess national differences in terms of the structure, organization and constitution of the legal profession. Law remains a highly stratified occupation with very different career trajectories and work experiences for different types of lawyers. Most legal work entails negotiation with clients and dealing with their uncertainties, and is not necessarily oriented to litigation or courtroom work. The very high cost of legal services means that the formal institutions of law are not a source of dispute resolution for many citizens. The cost of legal advice and the inappropriateness of legal resolutions to many social issues and disputes have been important considerations in the development of Alternative Dispute Resolution (ADR) mechanisms that aim to reduce the role and input of legal actors. The ways in which law and other mechanisms are invoked to resolve various disputes are the subject of the following chapter.

Notes

1   It is impossible to take into account all the various differences between diverse national legal systems. The discussion here focuses primarily on legal professions in the English-speaking common-law world, particularly the English, North American and Australian professions. The most comprehensive source of comparative information on lawyers across a large number of societies is the three-volume collection *Lawyers in Society* (Abel and Lewis, 1988a, b, c).
2   In the adversarial legal system, barristers aim to delegitimate the input of other professions, for example forensic scientists, psychiatrists and other experts, while barristers for the opposing side will use the expertise and knowledge of those same professions to bolster their own legal arguments. Thus the history of the legal profession may not be one only of direct competition but may encompass the ways in which some lawyers use nonlegal professionals and their knowledge to further their legal goals without necessarily seeking to appropriate that knowledge as their own. I am grateful to Margaret Cameron for suggesting this point.

5 Dispute Resolution

Social life is replete with disagreements, grievances, troubles, problems and conflicts. Not all of these become defined as disputes and extremely few become defined as legal disputes. This chapter addresses the social practices involved in the emergence, identification and processing of disputes. Processes and associated social arrangements oriented to the settlement of disputes include adjudication, mediation, conciliation and negotiation. Dispute resolution arrangements vary in their level of formality and prevalence, and in terms of the kinds of disputes and disputants with which they deal. This chapter examines the concept of dispute, and then examines litigation and such alternative dispute-resolution measures as neighbourhood justice centres, family mediation services and administrative tribunals. The settling or management of particular disputes may also have wider ramifications for social change, for example litigation may establish important precedents or policy decisions that will affect future social practices. Recent reforms in dispute processing have been heralded as providing greater access to justice, an increased range of remedies for disputants and a significant shift away from the adversarial legal system.

Disputes

A dispute can be defined as a particular stage of a social relationship in which conflict between two parties (individuals or groups) is asserted before a third party, who may be a family member, neighbour, the police, a community organization, or an administrative tribunal or a court (Mather and Yngvesson, 1980: 776). Third parties will vary in their level of independence from the claims being asserted by either disputant, their role in the management of the dispute and the level of formality or public accountability that they provide. The third party will usually define the nature of the dispute and specify how it should be resolved or settled. While litigation is the ultimate and most visible form of dispute resolution in contemporary societies, it is not the most prevalent.

Most disputes are settled or managed without recourse to formal mechanisms like courts. For disputes to emerge and remedial action to be taken, an injury or harm must be perceived, identified and named. Secondly, a person must attribute the injury to the fault of another individual or entity; and thirdly, they must voice the grievance to the person or entity believed to be responsible and claim some remedy or resolution. A claim becomes a dispute when it is rejected and the complainant seeks a remedy outside the relationship. A dispute becomes a civil legal dispute when it entails rights, resources or remedies that could be granted or denied by a court (Felstiner et al., 1980–81: 633–6; Miller and Sarat, 1980–81: 327–9).

Most grievances never become disputes, and most disputes are never litigated, but are managed or processed by ignoring the problem, successfully negotiating directly with the protagonist or withdrawing from or limiting the dispute-producing relationship. Alternatively, disputes may be mediated informally, whereby a third party facilitates an agreement or compromise between the disputants. Mediation depends on some shared cultural values, common experiences and a sense of collectivity or community among the participants in a dispute, including the mediator, who may bring to the processing of disputes an intimate and detailed knowledge of the perspectives of the disputants and the context in which the dispute emerged. Ideally, the mediator negotiates an outcome in light of the social and cultural context of the dispute.

Adjudication is a mode of dispute resolution often relied on where mediation fails or is inappropriate because of the lack of common ground among disputants. In adjudication, the third party – for example a court – has the authority to determine the outcome of the dispute. This determination is binding and typically the process is adversarial, where the adjudicator rules in favour of one of the disputants and orders the other to pay damages, provide restitution, undergo punishment or alter their behaviour. The third party evaluates the behaviour of disputants by referring to generalized rules of conduct, rather than to the socio-cultural context or the relations between the disputants (Felstiner, 1974: 69–74). Of the disputes reaching a court, a vast majority will be abandoned, withdrawn or settled without judicial adjudication (Galanter, 1983b: 26).[1] The threat of initiating court action or the formal filing of a complaint may itself influence the resolution process. For some disputants litigation represents the first step in dealing with conflict; for some it is a continuation of that process; and for others it is the accumulation of it. Many law suits will be filed that the plaintiff will have no intention of pursuing or that will not be pursued because of the availability of alternative remedies or the lack of funds. Case attrition is more likely when the defendant has greater experience than the plaintiff in using the court and when only the former has legal representation (Sarat, 1976: 369–70). Indeed, judges may actively encourage resolution to occur outside the court by referring cases to mediation or to an arbiter. The elaborate formal procedures and the expense of legal counsel involved in the formal resolution of disputes also make settlement or alternative forms of resolution more time and cost efficient.

Given this pyramidal structure where unarticulated grievances are more frequent than disputes that in turn are less frequent than litigation, it is important to consider the processes whereby disputes are ignored, settled, resolved or transformed into new kinds of disputes. Third parties will often play a critical role in dispute transformation; they will be able to define the categories in which a particular dispute is framed, especially if they have more power or authority than the disputants (Sarat and Grossman, 1975: 1208–9; Yngvesson, 1984: 237). For example, a police officer may define or categorize a complaint as a personal, family or private matter, therefore deciding that it does not present any legal or public issue, or may view it as a breach of the criminal law warranting arrest and prosecution. Such decisions are based on a wide range of factors: the police officer's experience of similar situations, assessments of the likelihood of successful prosecution, their perceptions of the blameworthiness of the victim, the relationship between the disputants, and the relative credibility and dangerousness of the apparent aggressor (Stalans and Finn, 1995: 302–12).

Similarly, lawyers will evaluate a client's dispute in terms of whether it raises legal issues or violates legal rules and will advise seeking a compromise or initiating litigation on that basis. Defence lawyers will assess a criminal case in terms of the quality of the evidence and whether they think the prosecution can prove its case beyond a reasonable doubt, before they advise their client to plead guilty or suggest entering into negotiations with the prosecution in the hope of having the charges reduced. Such assessments may be unrelated to the client's own view of the matter or preferred course of action.

Three important variables shape the transformation of disputes: *language* – how a relationship or dispute is phrased has significant implications for the power of competing individuals or factions with vested interests; *participants* – their relative power to shape the dispute and influence its outcome; and the *audience* – who will usually determine the outcome of the dispute (Mather and Yngvesson, 1980: 780–2). Merry (1990: 14) identifies the ways in which mediators and court officials transform interpersonal disputes into nonlegal problems. While a plaintiff may initially frame the issue as one of legal rights and entitlements, legal officials may eventually reframe the dispute as one of how people relate to each other and as inappropriate for legal consideration or remedy. She examines the ways in which the process of naming in mediation sessions and in the lower courts exerts a form of cultural domination over the people who bring to these fora their interpersonal problems with neighbours, spouses, partners and children. Individuals present images of themselves and events in ways designed to justify and convince. The mediation sessions become a contest over interpretations of ambiguous events, with most of the arguments being about their meaning and interpretation. In the mediation of disputes three distinct discourses are identifiable: *morality* – where there is a focus on relationships and obligations to family and neighbourhood; *legality* – which emphasizes a language of rights and property and truth; and *therapy* – actions are explained in terms of environmental factors or illness rather than as a result of rational planning or malice. While most complainants will initially frame their grievances as questions of property or legal rights and entitlements, mediators and court officials will tend to reframe them as moral issues, a question of how people relate to each other, thereby encouraging them to view their problems as not raising legal issues and therefore as unworthy of court attention (Merry, 1990: 2–9, 14).

Disputes can be narrowed, where third parties use established categories to organize the events and issues in dispute. This entails determining the real issues in dispute or identifying the legal issues. Lawyers play an important part in the transformation of disputes. It is often claimed that they amplify disputes perhaps to satisfy their own rather than their clients' interests or because they treat disputes through the adversarial forms prescribed by the formal legal order (Miller and Sarat, 1980–81: 526). However, lawyers can often diffuse disputes and direct them away from litigation (see Chapter 4). Macaulay shows that even though lawyers were unfamiliar with recent consumer protection legislation that created individual rights, most had nonadversarial techniques for dealing with clients who were dissatisfied with the quality of products or services that they had purchased. Some avoided clients with consumer protection claims altogether, or sought to persuade them that they could not afford to pursue the matter; others acted as their therapist or knowledgeable friend, leading the client to redefine the situation so that she or he could accept it (Macaulay, 1979: 152–66). A dispute can also be expanded beyond the two protagonists to reflect wider social problems and then becomes linked centrally with the prospect of social change (Mather and Yngvesson, 1980–81: 797, 817; see also discussion below).

Courts and dispute processing

One arena where disputes are heard by a third party is the court. In theory each party to the dispute argues their case and an impartial, neutral judge adjudicates. This judge's decision is binding on all parties to the dispute, but the extent to which it resolves the underlying dispute is an empirical question. Much empirical research examines the process of judging across the range of judges' everyday work, regardless of the substantive legal issue or particular outcome (see for example Cowan et al., 2006). This includes analysis of the way judges understand or approach their role, the kinds of factors they take into account when decision making, their orientation towards participants and perhaps their overall philosophy or consciousness of the purpose of the courts in dispute resolution and justice.

Drawing on Becker's (1978) elaboration of craftwork, Kritzer (2007) proposes the notion of judgecraft to analyse judging from the point of view of the judges making decisions, managing the cases, and interacting with diverse audiences, in criminal or noncriminal law contexts. Elements of craftwork as applied to judging are: consistency (treating like cases alike, especially when sentencing, is a mantra), utility (the important legal and social role of courts), a clientele (litigants, the legal profession, and the public, including the media), skills and techniques (such as legal reasoning, judgement), problem solving (can emerge when routine, ordinary proceedings are disrupted, for example by litigants in person [Moorhead, 2007]), as well as an aesthetic (creativity and effective communication) (Kritzer, 2007).

How judges perform their work and communicate with participants is important for legitimacy, not only in terms of the immediate decision/outcome, but also in terms of the legitimacy of the justice/legal system (Moorhead et al., 2008). Tyler (1990) and his associates have shown that people are more likely to accept an adverse decision (from their point of view) if they feel that the authority (whether the judge or another decision maker) has taken the time to listen to their arguments and has treated them in a fair manner. The decision to comply with rules and regulations or an acceptance of the outcome of legal proceedings can derive more from the parties' experience of the process and procedures followed by the decision maker than the actual result or determination. Procedural justice is evident in both civil and criminal law settings. A study of tax evasion showed that tax payers who had been punished by the Australian Tax Office (ATO) were more likely to make negative judgements about the ATO's legitimacy when they felt it had treated them in a procedurally unfair way. The measures of neutrality used included assessments of the ATO's honesty, impartiality, and the use of fact and not personal opinion in decision making. The most disgruntled taxpayers were engaging in tax evasion behaviour to neutralize the effects of their tax debts (Murphy, 2005: 584–5). Tax payers' perceptions of their treatment by the ATO appeared to be more important in explaining their views about the ATO's legitimacy than their judgements about their own financial gain or loss. Such judgements of legitimacy can go on to influence views about compliance, i.e. the degree of resistance towards paying tax and the ATO. The policy implication is that applying excessive financial penalties for tax avoidance may not act as a specific deterrent in the long run.

Litigation and dispute resolution

A central question underpinning the discussion of disputing is why some social actors use the courts more frequently than others to settle disputes. Cross-culturally the question becomes: why are some societies more litigious than others? Research seeks to specify the conditions under which some members or segments of a society turn to the courts to resolve their disputes or, alternatively, use other strategies to manage conflict and disagreement. It identifies the ways in which the institutionalization of negotiation, mediation or adjudication is linked with other aspects of social organization (Felstiner, 1974: 76–85).

Put simply, it appears that disputants initiate court (or other formal) proceedings when informal mechanisms are either unavailable, have been exhausted, or will jeopardize the continuation of a valued relationship. Despite carefully planned contracts, disputes among business people are usually settled without reference to the contract or potential legal sanctions (Macaulay, 1963: 61–5). Business people hesitate to speak of legal rights and obligations and are often reticent to threaten to sue when confronting disagreements. Even where contracts are detailed, law suits for breach of contract appear to be rare, reflecting a preference for finding other solutions. Business people often deem contract and contract law as unnecessary for dispute resolution because of the salience of nonlegal norms, especially the expectation that commitments are to be honoured in almost all situations, and the importance of maintaining exchange relationships that litigation would jeopardize. The threat of using legal sanctions to settle disputes occurs when other strategies fail and when the business considers that the gains will outweigh the long-term costs. The absence of sizeable numbers of legal actions in which individuals or firms of substantial financial means appear on both sides of law suits stems from their capacity to use legal expertise to structure their affairs so as to prevent trouble. They pursue nonlitigious avenues for dispute resolution but, more importantly, their own interests are enmeshed in continuing relations with potential opponents (Hurst, 1980: 422).

Nevertheless, individuals may threaten to or actually use courts as part of an arsenal for managing disputes, without necessarily expecting that the courts will be the forum for settling the dispute. Merry finds that for many of the economically marginal, poorly educated residents of a multiethnic neighbourhood in a US city, the court serves as a way of harassing an opponent, often as an alternative to violence, rather than constituting a direct mechanism for dispute resolution (Merry, 1979: 892). Appealing to the court occurs mainly where the disputants' interpersonal relationship has a limited future, even if it is of long duration. Ultimately, however, the resolution of these disputes occurs primarily through avoidance when one or more of the protagonists moves away from the neighbourhood. She observes that:

> the heterogeneity and complexity of the city undermine informal social sanctions and allow disputants to jettison hostile or disapproving relationships if necessary. Thus, the costs of using formal mechanisms for resolving disputes are less than in isolated, small-scale societies where one must continue to confront the consequences of disruptive actions long into the future. (Merry, 1979: 908)

Inequalities affect citizens' inclination and capacity to access the law to resolve disputes. People of higher socio-economic status are more likely to take some action in response to problems and to take action involving the law than are poorer or other lower status people (Genn et al., 1999; Sandefur, 2008: 346). Class differences in how people respond to problems are important not only because they reveal class inequality, but also because they may reproduce it. Three main kinds of mechanisms emerge through civil justice experiences that may reflect or affect inequality (Sandefur, 2008: 352):

1 balance of resources – finances, information, social connections and social capital affect individuals' capacities to initiate legal action that they can afford in order to protect stakes of value to them;
2 subjective orientations – beliefs about law's legitimacy, efficacy, fairness and so on; and
3 differential institutionalization – some kinds of problems have been institutionalized and are more amenable to legal solutions.

There has been considerable interest in the question of why some societies seem more litigious than others and cultural differences are often invoked as explanations. Commonsense views and media reports based on high-profile legal cases or on information about large court-ordered damages payments in some tort cases conclude that the USA is a highly litigious society. Explanations focus on the salience of rights consciousness and an overly individualistic orientation, which translates into a proclivity to sue in order to remedy individual disputes and social problems. Evidence of the so-called litigation explosion or *hyperlexis* – too much law, too many lawyers, overburdened courts and citizens' alacrity to utilize the legal system for all kinds of disputes and harms – consists of the growth in filings in federal courts; the expansion in the size of the legal profession; reports on huge, time-consuming and resource-intensive cases; atrocity stories about cases that seem trivial and ridiculous; and accounts of how litigation impairs business efficiency, absorbs public and private resources and is generally dysfunctional (Burger, 1982: 274–6; Galanter, 1983a: 6–11; McHugh, 1995: 42–5). Other societies with lower litigation rates, in particular Japan, are depicted as based on a greater sense of collectivity, community, consensus and harmony, and therefore as less reliant on the courts to manage disputes.

Japanese legal consciousness is often portrayed as nonlitigious due to cultural norms and values (Miyazawa, 1987: 220). Kawashima explains the relative lack of litigation in Japan as deriving from a traditional preference for extra-judicial, informal means of settling a controversy, in particular reconcilement and conciliation. He suggests that the relatively small number of lawyers and lack of litigation in Japan relative to its population and level of industrialization confirm that there is less demand for legal services, as people do not go to court as frequently as in western nations (Kawashima, 1963: 42–3). The hierarchical nature of Japanese society and the cultural emphasis on harmony result in 'a strong expectation that a dispute should not and will not arise; even when one does occur, it is to be solved by mutual understanding' (Kawashima, 1963: 44). Apology forms an essential aspect in the resolution of any conflict, thereby reflecting and reinforcing the cultural emphasis on social harmony and interdependence. Japanese courts may require disputants to participate in conciliation and compromise where the offer of an apology is a crucial step. In contrast, the values of autonomy, independence and individual rights in the USA mean that a person convicted of wrongdoing 'is likely to consider that paying the damages or accepting punishment ends further responsibility and that there is no need for personal contrition to the injured individual' (Wagatsuma and Rosett, 1986: 462).

Others do not agree that lower litigation rates in Japan stem from cultural differences or that relative use of the courts is a valid indicator of legal consciousness. They identify institutional barriers that restrict access to the courts, thus making litigation unattractive or impossible and impeding the development of a more individualistic consciousness of rights. Haley suggests that the passage of numerous laws establishing formal conciliation proceedings between the first and second world wars was not a response to popular demand for alternatives to litigation, but instead reflected a conservative response to an increase in law suits and judicial activism from about 1905 to the mid-1930s and the view of the governing elite (not the population in general) that litigation destroys the hierarchical social structure based on personal relationships (Haley, 1978: 373–5). Insufficient judges, resulting in acute time delays in the court processing of cases, further restrict a resort to litigation. Control of the supply of lawyers and judges is a direct outcome of governmental policy rather than of the absence of citizen demand. Moreover, the absence of effective formal legal sanctions or remedies for violations of legal norms, especially as court orders are rarely reinforced by contempt powers, tends to buttress community cohesion and encourages the use of private mediators in dispute settlement (Haley, 1978: 381–5; 1982: 273–8). Other barriers to litigation in the regulatory area include the wide discretion allowed to administrative organizations in their enabling legislation, thus rendering many decisions unchallengeable; onerous standing requirements restricting the kinds of people who can bring complaints; few opportunities for class action suits; and difficulties for plaintiffs in acquiring the relevant documents and information on which to build their case (Hamilton and Sanders, 1992: 36).

Even where Japanese plaintiffs do initiate litigation, it appears that their orientation towards and expectation of the process are distinctive. An analysis of four large pollution cases in the 1970s demonstrates that the most striking characteristic is the communal and anti-individualistic attitudes of the participants; respect for the community – rather than assertion of individual rights and responsibility – was at the heart of most of the decisions. The victims, poor people from fishing and farming communities whose health and economic livelihood had been damaged by the pollution, utilized the legal system to satisfy demands for moral vindication and community accountability. Initially, many were reticent to litigate because of economic insecurity, a desire to reduce any disruption, a wish to avoid singling themselves out from their peer group as well as a deep-seated fatalism and willingness to endure hardship (Upham, 1976: 589–91, 616–18). Moreover, differences existed between the plaintiffs in the different cases, suggesting regional variations in the likelihood of resorting to litigation. In one case, litigation was not initiated until some years after the discovery of the harm resulting from the activities of a large chemical company, whereas in another town, victims filed suit much earlier. In the first case, victims and their communities depended on the chemical company for employment and the social services it provided; in the other region, the victims lived further downstream and there were no substantial ties between the community and the factory (Kidder, 1983: 46, 50–1, 77).

In the debate about the extent to which differences in disputing stem from cultural variations, there is an assumption that the identification of institutional or structural factors *per se* replaces cultural explanations. However, it is difficult to explain the emphasis on mediation and the importance of apology and confession without referring to the attitudinal and cultural differences that affect legal consciousness. Hamilton and Sanders seek to recombine structural and cultural factors in their comparison of justice in the USA and Japan, and argue that 'the concept of the responsible actor is a bridge between general cultural values (such as view of the self) and specific attitudes towards litigation' (1992: 195). They conceptualize responsibility as a relationship between people, not as an abstract ideal or psychological attribute. Their analysis rejects cultural-determinism and links actors' perceptions of wrongdoers as responsible with structural and cultural differences, finding that:

> In the United States a person tends to be perceived by self and others as an *individual* actor whose identity and sense of self stand apart from the community, while in Japan a person is perceived by self and others as a *contextual* actor whose identity is, in substantial part, defined by social relationships. ... [T]he response to responsibility – the possible punishment – that is consistent with a contextual view is to restore the role relations. The response to responsibility that is consistent with the individualistic view is to isolate the perpetrator. (Hamilton and Sanders, 1992: 19; emphases in original)

Treating people as connected rather than as separate, and with the emphasis on minimizing conflict, suggest that Japanese people are less likely to use law to settle disputes than their US counterparts. Importantly, observed differences stem from structural factors rather than cultural values or personal preferences; citizens in strong networks will be likely to perceive resolving disputes through adjudication as potentially destroying those valued networks.

Comparing national litigation rates to determine litigiousness is fraught with difficulty, stemming from differences in legal systems and court organization, differences in legal rules and entitlements and different recording practices. Litigation rates are not good indicators of the amount of disputing that occurs in a society or of the preferred mode of dispute settlement. Nevertheless, examining litigation rates is preferable to commonsense or stereotypical conclusions about legal consciousness and can also reveal other important differences in disputing practices. Comparing the rate of per capita use of regular civil courts reveals that the USA falls in the same range as England, Canada, Australia, Denmark and New Zealand, but is higher than Germany, Sweden, Japan, Spain or Italy (Galanter, 1983b: 51–5). More importantly, the nature of litigation has changed; it has become more complex and refined, but most cases are settled via bargaining, negotiation or mediation. The cases that do end in a court judgement have become bigger and more visible. Rather than an overall expansion of litigation, the fourfold increase in the number of civil filings in the US federal district courts between 1960 and 1986 resulted from increases in court action in six types of cases (in descending order): civil rights, social security, recovery of government overpayments and loans, prisoner petitions, other contract cases and tort cases (Galanter, 1988: 92–8). Even though federal court filings have risen dramatically, the percentage of cases reaching trial declined, suggesting a reduced reliance on litigation that may reflect courts' increasing role in encouraging alternative dispute resolution (Galanter, 1983b: 43; 1988: 951).

Comparisons of litigation frequencies point to the importance of national dispute-processing structures, the size and organization of legal professions and the politico-economic environment to explain differences. For example, despite similar legal systems, (the former) West Germany and the Netherlands had vastly different litigation frequencies. This pattern did not stem from differences in legal consciousness, but in the Netherlands various institutional developments created an infrastructure for avoiding litigation. Lawyers did not monopolize the provision of legal advice or representation in lower courts. Access to wider sources of legal advice diffuses a resort to the courts, as nonlawyers are more likely to advise against litigation, especially as there were more alternatives to courts and more pre-court conflict-resolution institutions in the Netherlands as compared with the former West Germany. In contrast, Germany tended to draw conflicts into the courts by discouraging alternative legal services, and the court system was very efficient and inexpensive (Blankenburg, 1994: 790, 805–6).

Comparatively less frequent litigation in Australia does not seem to be due to greater harmony or fewer disputes. Australian lawyers have practices less oriented to litigation than do their US counterparts and there are fewer lawyers per capita (FitzGerald, 1983: 30, 42). The USA has many more lawyers than any other country – more than twice as many per capita as its closest rival – and lawyers play a central role in the transformation of disputes (Galanter, 1983b: 55). Since the late

1970s, the dramatic changes in the size and organization of the legal profession and styles of lawyering have revealed the tendency of the US legal system to combine an entrepreneurial responsiveness to changing business and social conditions with massively unequal access to legal representation.

National styles of administrative regulation also affect litigation rates. The USA resorts to detailed rules, deterrence-oriented enforcement patterns, intensely adversarial procedures and frequent judicial review and reversal of administrative policies (Kagan, 1988: 726). Research on environmental policy indicates that British regulation is based on an ethic of cooperation between business and government officials, in part because of the relatively high status of the civil service, which is linked closely with the class structure. In the USA the pursuit of wealth through economic gain characterized the upper classes and the civil service was never viewed as superior to business elites, thus fostering an increasingly adversarial and legalistic regulatory system (Vogel, 1986: 242–5). Striking features of the American tort system include the heavy deterrence-oriented sanctions reflected in the enormous sums awarded in some jury verdicts and settlements; the contentiousness and costliness of the adversarial process where lawyers may receive more than plaintiffs; and the amount of political controversy that the system engenders, with a plurality of interests attempting to change liability rules (Kagan, 1988: 727). This approach has its origins in the political environment, particularly the advent in the late 1960s of well-funded, highly visible environmental and consumer-advocacy groups, and their success in making strongly worded federal laws and judicial rulings enforceable through public-interest litigation, a principal goal of political action. Media-oriented entrepreneurial politics became more important as political party control of legislative agendas declined, and public advocacy of the rights of consumers, minorities, the poor and the natural environment became important routes to political success (Kagan, 1988: 735).

A litigation crisis?

Often claims of a litigation crisis are not well grounded empirically (Roach Anleu and Prest, 2004). An examination of publicly available data on litigation rates measured by annual filings (cases commenced) provided by New South Wales courts of civil (excluding family) law concludes that 'the belief that litigation is increasing cannot be sustained, and in fact the very opposite may be true' (Wright and Melville, 2004: 97). The study finds 'no evidence of a general litigation explosion. Further, filing rates in the various courts demonstrate significant fluctuations over comparatively short periods of time' (Wright and Melville, 2004: 109). A range of micro processes affect court filings including jurisdictional changes and other factors affecting choice of court, changes creating, abolishing or affecting legal rights, and litigant behaviour, as well as the way court administrators collect data and decide what to include. Similarly, an examination of the Australian federal civil justice system found no crisis in litigation rates (Weisbrot and Davis, 2004: 125).

Longitudinal historical analyses of litigation in England from the thirteenth century onwards shows that the use of litigation to resolve disputes is not an exclusively contemporary phenomenon (Brooks, 2004). The civil law and the courts were not the sole domain of the aristocracy and other elites, as all kinds of English people from across the occupational and class strata used legal instruments, including marriage contracts, property deeds, trusts, agreements and orders. 'The use of courts of all kinds as a means of collecting debts, settling disputes between landlords and tenants, defending reputations through actions of slander, or indeed challenging the authority of local officials, took place on an astonishingly large scale' (Brooks, 2004: 28). Round about the turn of the sixteenth into the seventeenth century, court usage per 100 000 of population was the outstanding high-water mark of litigation, higher than it ever had been before or has been since in England (also see Churches, 2004). Since the twelfth century, five phases of increased civil litigation have been identified, four of which have been followed by no less significant decreases. The pattern seems to be one of periodic fluctuation rather than simple linear escalation, with key variables such as costs playing an important role in the nature of the experience of litigation. The legal historian Christopher Brooks concludes, perhaps counter-intuitively that 'medieval and early-modern communities were as often litigious as they were harmonious' (2004: 41).

One highly significant qualitative difference between litigation crises in contemporary compared with medieval societies is the existence today of a 'juridico-entertainment complex' (Haltom and McCann, 2004: 28). Aside from the question of whether there is a litigation explosion, the idea of a litigation crisis has significant cultural dimensions. Consideration of the 'litigation crisis' also entails looking at the ways in which legal knowledge and the law itself are constructed, and how legal narratives develop and become accepted as descriptions of reality in the context of modern mass-mediated culture (Haltom and McCann, 2004: ix). 'How did it come about that prominent elites – politicians, media pundits, news reporters, celebrities, comedians, cartoonists, film makers, novelists, and other producers of mass culture – routinely blame a myriad of social ills on an epidemic of litigiousness among American citizens and their lawyers?' (Haltom and McCann, 2004: ix–x).

Stories of proliferating litigation often assume a hegemonic status projecting a recurring image of greedy, rights-obsessed plaintiffs and lawyers extorting innocent business corporations and undermining communal norms of civility. The most famous story has become emblematic of crisis claims, namely the 79 year old woman who sued McDonalds in 1994 for burns caused by spilled hot coffee. The media, almost single-handedly 'made this story into a mass cultural symbol of the lawsuit crisis' (Haltom and McCann, 2004: 184).

The prevailing news coverage, popular narratives, and policy debates provide a highly inadequate knowledge base for understanding tort law institutional arrangements and practices but academic studies on litigation are: 'by standards of ordinary discourse, unfamiliar and difficult, and, by standards of opinion leaders, esoteric and tedious. Such sophisticated forms of knowledge simply do not translate into modern mass communication' (Haltom and McCann, 2004: 109).

Litigation and social change

Even though courts are used infrequently for settling disputes, litigation can be a strategy to affect public policy or initiate social change, particularly in regard to economic inequalities and civil rights. Tocqueville (1969: 270) regarded the transformation of political issues into legal questions and litigation as distinctive of the USA. Social movements may adopt lawsuits as part of a campaign to use the courts as a route to reform and change (Felstiner et al., 1980–81: 639). This entails the transformation of disputes about individual harms into mechanisms to remedy social problems and to implement social change (Mather and Yngevsson, 1980: 817). Using the courts in this way means that arguments, issues and grievances must be couched in legal language, and most frequently the language of rights. Indeed, court decisions infuse and inform social movements themselves by becoming an essential part of their thought, identity and social boundaries. Movements are constituted in legal terms when they view the world in those terms and organize themselves accordingly; law plays a key role in constituting the language and strategies of social movements (Brigham, 1987: 306–7; 1996: 29–50).

Social activists conceptualize social change and approach law in different ways and may continue to use legal strategies in a quest for social change in the face of a general belief in law's limited capacity to facilitate social change (Kostiner, 2003). Interviews with 25 social justice (educational justice) activists identify their understanding of law and change in terms of three distinct cultural schemes:

1 *Instrumental*: emphasizes the needs of marginalized people to access collective resources, including health care, employment, and education;
2 *Political*: emphasizes the importance of empowering marginalized groups; and
3 *Cultural*: entails a broader, educative agenda to transform widespread taken for granted assumptions or worldviews.

Social movements can benefit from the use of legal tactics regardless of any actual success in the courts due to the empowering effects of participation in legal campaigns (Kostiner, 2003; McCann, 1994).

Social activists' engagement with law and the meanings they give to legal tactics are complex and situational, highlighting the extent to which law and social change remain dynamic and multi-layered. Various social movements strategically and selectively formulate rights discourse to further their arguments and claims in various (not just legal) arenas. For example, both proponents and opponents of abortion and reproductive technologies, for example *in vitro* fertilization, use the language of rights in such public arenas as the media, government inquiries and conferences, and seek to have certain rights (but not others) recognized in law (Eisenstein, 1988; Roach Anleu, 1996). In debates about mental health policy in the USA, both the National Alliance for the Mentally Ill – a consumer-oriented movement – and the American Psychiatric Association use rights discourse to build their respective communities and social movements and to make claims to be appropriate advocates for the interests and well-being of those using mental-health services (Milner, 1989:

656–62). However, other social movements and litigants may decide against using rights discourse. In a case dealing with family benefits initiated by two gay litigants under the Canadian Charter, the New Christian Right, which intervened in the litigation, consistently maintained that the case was about the definition of the family not about rights; presumably considering it strategically unwise to seek to deny or erode gay rights (Herman, 1993: 37–9).

In the USA, the apparent successes in civil rights litigation during the 1950s and 1960s and the receptivity of the Supreme Court encouraged other groups and organizations to adopt a law-reform strategy that focused on the courts (Handler, 1978). The National Association for the Advancement of Colored People (NAACP) relied on litigation as the principal means to erode the doctrine of separate but equal, which legitimated race segregation, especially in the areas of housing and education. The spreading and consolidation of civil rights in the 1960s were achieved through the judicial process rather than through the legislature (Parsons, 1967: 719–20). This was paralleled by a rise in lawyer organizations interested in law reform, especially public-interest law firms. A pervasive view among these law reformers was that benefits would be obtained through court representation of groups and interests that were traditionally underrepresented. Expanding access to the courts and providing legal advocacy would increase the power and status of such marginalized segments as welfare recipients and tenants, especially in public housing. Since the 1950s, US Supreme Court decisions have moved from desegregation to integration in schools, banned organized prayer in public schools, transformed the criminal justice process by imposing strict due-process requirements on law-enforcement officials, and struck down state laws prohibiting abortion (Lasser, 1988: 2).

The features of the US politico-legal system that provide courts with a larger role in public policy than in comparable other societies include the following:

1 The process of judicial appointment is explicitly political, which provides opportunities for various interest groups to lobby for the rejection of a proposed appointment and to influence the kinds of people, in terms of philosophical or political orientation, who are on the bench. Nominees for the Supreme Court must be supported by the Senate and during the confirmation process individuals and groups can make representations about candidates' suitability for appointment. In other countries there are few opportunities for public input or discussion into judicial appointments; they are simply announced by the government. Moreover, as many formal rights in the USA depend on judicial interpretation, a nominee's views on such topics as affirmative action or abortion and their past personal actions can play a significant role in the process of judicial appointment (Abadinsky, 1991: 172–84).

2 The Bill of Rights, enshrined in the Constitution, means that a course of action that aims to protect personal liberties or individual rights can be brought to the constitutional court. Constitutionally guaranteeing freedom of speech and of the press, the capacity to bear arms, protection from unreasonable searches or seizures, due process and equal protection of the law provide many opportunities to seek to realize such rights and to demonstrate that some groups or individuals are being

denied their constitutional rights. Many important and controversial cases in the USA are brought under the Bill of Rights.

3 From the 1950s to the 1980s the Supreme Court was very activist, but recent appointees have adopted a more formalist approach and view their role in public policy as limited by strict and legalistic construction of the laws.

4 The availability of amicus briefs (arguments by interested parties who are not directly engaged in the court action) and Brandeis briefs (providing the court with historical, political and economic, not just legal, arguments and considerations) gives interest groups and social movements opportunities to present their views and to submit various arguments to the court that it may take into consideration during its deliberations.

5 Relatively liberal rules of standing provide a wide scope for plaintiffs to bring law suits. Strict rules of standing mean that test cases and class-action suits may not be available in many countries; however, they are an important social-reform strategy in the USA. For example, in 1978 Vietnam veterans sued a number of chemical manufacturers, blaming them for various diseases and traumas that they and their families had allegedly suffered following exposure to Agent Orange, the herbicide that the US Army used to defoliate the Vietnamese jungle. This action was a mass toxic tort; the case actually consolidated into one class action – more than 600 separate actions originally filed by more than 15 000 named individuals throughout the USA. In a mass tort the number of victims is large and its scale inevitably creates qualitative as well as quantitative changes in the character of the case and the ways in which it must be litigated (Schuck, 1987: 6).

The propensity to use courts to affect public policy can change and is not limited to the USA. In the past few decades, the High Court of Australia has facilitated a change in the balance of power between the central and state governments and has recognized, albeit to a limited extent, certain implied constitutional rights. As a result of High Court decisions, the Commonwealth (Federal) government has prevented the flooding of wilderness areas in Tasmania, adopted race- and sex-discrimination legislation and recognized some indigenous land rights. Social movements have played a central role in placing such issues on the political agenda in Australia and during the 1980s the Commonwealth government was prepared to legislate on these issues. Litigation arose not via social movements directly seeking test cases or acting as plaintiffs in the courts, but as a result of state governments contesting Commonwealth legislation. However, the more conservative political climate from the mid-1990s resulted in the winding back of some of these reforms and led to unprecedented debate about the role of the High Court in the political process (Gale, 2005: 37–72). The financial dominance of the Commonwealth government has also been supported by the High Court, which has adopted broader conceptions of taxation. Several decisions extended the definition of excise tax: manufacture and production came to include distribution and then sale, and possibly any consumption tax could be classified as an excise tax which has reduced the states' financial resources as they cannot levy this tax (Solomon, 1992: 85). The Court's decisions are not always compatible with extending central government power and it has rejected the

Commonwealth's attempt to gain complete control over company legislation. Similarly, the Israeli High Court of Justice supports and legitimates state-sponsored policies in general, but by overruling government policy in landmark cases concerning the occupied territories it is able simultaneously to retain an image of judicial impartiality and independence (Shamir, 1990: 781–3).

A new discourse of rights has emerged recently in the Australian High Court and it has found, or more accurately constructed, implied guarantees protecting the freedom of political speech, although the Constitution does not explicitly mention any such right. In the first case, the court rejected a Commonwealth law purporting to limit political advertising before an election as unacceptable political censorship, which 'severely impairs the freedoms previously enjoyed by citizens to discuss public and political affairs and to criticize federal institutions' (*ACTV* v *Commonwealth* 1992: 587). Later, it decided that a national daily newspaper that had criticized the Industrial Relations Commission had not commited the offence of defamation, and argued that 'there is to be discerned in the doctrine of representative government which the Constitution incorporates an implication of freedom of communication of information and opinions about matters relating to the government of the Commonwealth' (*Nationwide News* v *Wills* 1992: 723–4). Subsequently, the court narrowly decided that the Constitution's protection of the implied freedom of political communication includes a discussion of the conduct, policies or fitness for office of government, political parties, public bodies, public officers and those seeking public office, thereby denying a member of the then Labour government's claim that comments published in a newspaper regarding immigration policy were defamatory (*Theophanaus* v *Herald & Weekly Times* 1994: 1–8).

Lawsuits in local or lower courts can also be political resources that affect public policy, especially given the growth of administrative law and the increasing number of governmental or official decisions that can be subject to judicial review. Administrative decisions where government ministers or their delegates act beyond their power, abuse their power, fail to exercise discretion, make errors of law or fail to adhere to the principles of natural justice can be quashed through judicial review (Allars, 1990: 161–276). Organized interests, social movements, firms and individuals employ litigation as a political resource more regularly in cases before lower courts than in the occasional cases that reach the appellate courts.

Correcting the view that 'appellate courts make policy and trial courts generally do not', Mather points out that judges in lower courts often construct local norms through pretrial and trial proceedings, and participate in changing policy by defining entirely new legal norms (1995: 188). Judges in lower courts that process large numbers of private disputes and criminal matters will often depart from the prototype of the neutral adjudicator bound by legal rules. Mather suggests that 'judges who are doctrinally innovative (not bound by precedent), assertive toward other political actors (not deferential), or managerial (not the passive umpire) are more likely to shape cases before them in dynamic and political ways' (Mather, 1995: 189). The ways in which judges frame issues, define problems and mould cases both in courts and in interactions with lawyers in case negotiation can initiate social change. An analysis of anti-smoking litigation from 1994–98 shows that trial court decisions significantly influenced national policy making on tobacco in the United

States (Mather, 1998). This litigation resulted in new conceptions of liability regarding tobacco and generated new ways of thinking about responsibility for smoking. The problem moved from a private problem of individual assumption of risk to become a public concern over collective health and health care costs. Courts rather than legislatures became important locations for this transition and development of new policies (Mather, 1998: 934).

Research on magistrates and their (lower) courts in Australia suggests that they do have some capacity and inclination to effect social change in a 'local, personal, and incremental, and perhaps enduring' way by directly engaging with court users in a more positive vein than the traditional model of the judge as neutral arbiter suggests (Popovic, 2002; Roach Anleu and Mack, 2007: 203). Some magistrates are oriented towards attempting to facilitate change in the lives of some court participants, especially in the criminal courts where defendants often experience complex social and personal problems. However, these courts' scope to contribute to social change is shaped by institutional limitations. 'The court, as a structure, simultaneously constrains magistrates' autonomy and offers opportunities for them to work in creative or innovative ways' (Roach Anleu and Mack, 2007: 203).

Following interviews with district judges and court observations of housing possession proceedings for rent arrears in the United Kingdom, Cowan et al. (2006) identify three styles of judging, each with different implications for social change:

1 *Liberal* – active role, informal approach, concerned with systemic failure as the cause of social problems, empathetic to the defendant and adopts a social welfare orientation;
2 *Patrician* – passive and legalistic, the problems are seen as stemming from contractual debt and the defendant's failure to comply with certain standards; and
3 *Formalist* – follows procedure and law and appears neutral but is procedurally active, albeit legalistic. This type of judge recognizes systemic problems but feels constrained by the contractual debt issue at hand (Cowan et al., 2006: 555). Plus, the authors identify a fourth, idiosyncratic approach in which the judges adopted an individual approach that was sometimes expressly different from other judges.

Judicial activism and numerous progressive court decisions do not necessarily translate into the desired social change, sparking considerable debate about the appropriateness of litigation as a strategy and the utility of legal arguments based on rights discourse. The value or effect of a court decision may be symbolic by affirming a norm or value, thereby legitimating the public worth and power of one subculture or viewpoint over others, regardless of the actual effects of the decision (Gusfield, 1967: 176–8). Such considerations present larger questions of how to define, assess and measure the success or failure of litigation. What does a favourable court decision really mean? For example, the 1954 US Supreme Court decision of *Brown v Board of Education* removed official legal barriers to the equal participation of blacks with whites in education, public housing and voting, yet considerable inequalities and race discrimination remain and have even widened (Schmid, 1988: 68–70; Tomaskovic-Devey and Roscigno, 1996: 567–70).

In a discussion of the capacity of the US Supreme Court to initiate significant social reform, Rosenberg (2008: 10–21) describes two conceptions of courts:

1 The Constrained Court view maintains that courts will not effectively produce significant social reform because of the limited nature of constitutional rights; the lack of judicial independence, especially in relation to the appointment process; the judiciary's inability to develop appropriate policies; and its lack of powers of implementation.

2 The Dynamic Court view proposes that the constraints are not as far reaching as the constrained view suggests, but in some cases courts can be more effective than other government institutions in bringing about reforms. Security of tenure means judges are free from electoral accountability, thus enabling them to decide cases which might counter public opinion or frustrate government policies. Moreover, courts are formally accessible to all citizens in a way that other institutions of government are not.

Following a detailed discussion of key areas of significant social reform litigation – in civil rights and women's rights, same sex marriage – and their leading symbolic cases Rosenberg (2008) argues for a model of the law court as constrained rather than dynamic. He concludes that US courts can never be effective agents of significant social reform because of the limited nature of constitutional rights. Not all social reform goals can be plausibly presented in the name of constitutional rights and courts may be unwilling to expand the scope or existence of rights, and the political appointment process explains why Supreme Court decisions rarely deviate from what is politically acceptable. The hope that US courts can bring about social reform is 'hollow'.

However, it is naive to expect that judicial pronouncements will automatically and unproblematically translate into anticipated social changes. One element of the disjunction between a court decision and social change is enforcement. For example, ensuring that a bureaucratic organization will obey a court order is difficult; many agencies are large and decentralized, and a great deal of discretion exists. Conversely, unfavourable court decisions may actually mobilize social activism, resulting in successful legal, even social, change. Highly publicized court cases where individuals convicted of serious offences have received what some perceive as lenient sentences have become an impetus to victims of crime movements, which, in turn, have successfully lobbied for reform in the criminal justice process. Judicial commentary in sexual assault and domestic violence cases has also mobilized women's groups and feminist activists to pressure governments to reform the judiciary via gender and cultural awareness training and increasing the appointment of women.

Court decisions that extend rights are not necessarily determinative or definitive; they can be very unstable and have unanticipated consequences. Indeed, if judicial interpretation ultimately acknowledges the existence of rights, then future interpretations can extend, limit or alter them. For example, the US Supreme Court decision legalizing abortion *(Roe v Wade 1973)* mobilized right-to-life activists, whose primary aim is to have that decision reversed. Subsequently, an increasingly formalist and legalistic Supreme Court has narrowed but not actually overturned *Roe v Wade* by recognizing the right of states to impose restrictions on the availability of abortions and to demand conformity with additional organizational requirements, including mandatory counselling on the negative consequences of abortion and then waiting 24 hours before the procedure (Farr, 1984: 172–7).

The basic architecture of the legal system creates and limits its potential to bring about redistributive change. Those who use the courts more frequently will have advantages in terms of knowledge and experience *vis-à-vis* those who rarely resort to legal action. Galanter distinguishes between 'one-shotters' – claimants who have only occasional recourse to the courts, including partners in a divorce case, road accident victims and most people accused of a criminal offence – and 'repeat players' – who are engaged in many similar court cases and include insurance and finance companies as well as prosecutors. Repeat players have low stakes in the outcome of any particular case, anticipate repeated litigation, and have the resources to pursue long-term interests. Their familiarity with the process, accumulated expertise and informal relations with actors in the justice system provide them with an advantage over 'one-shotters'. This position of advantage is one of the ways in which a legal system formally neutral between 'haves' and 'have-nots' may perpetuate and augment the advantages of the former (Galanter, 1974: 103–4).

Some would suggest that law or legal doctrine does not have an independent and external impact on social change, but is itself changed by broader social forces, and that the social context is essential for understanding changes in legal doctrine and court decisions. The argument that legal doctrine reflects the nature of the social system and does not initiate substantial change in that system explains the growing empirical evidence of law's inability to contribute to the alleviation of social problems. The view that legal thought operates as a mirror of the social order rather than as an important influence on it is supported by the fact that decisions of the US Supreme Court are usually congruent with American public opinion (Barnett, 1993: 17, 37 fn 15). For example, shifts in the status of women, their increased participation in higher education and an increase in egalitarian values since the 1960s are more important for understanding changes in the legal doctrine banning discriminatory practices than is viewing judicial decisions as enhancing gender equality. Thus, the decisions reflect or symbolize rather than increase gender equality (Barnett, 1993: 50–5). Indeed, public confidence in the US Supreme Court was at its lowest when it was at its most individual rights oriented, from the mid-1960s to the early 1980s (Milner, 1989: 645).

Disillusionment with the courts as a source of social change also incorporates strong criticisms of strategies that entail rights claims. Adopting legal frames of reference and relying on lawyers' activism and litigation reflect an oversimplified approach to complex social issues. Scheingold regards the direct linking of litigation, rights and remedies with social change as the myth of rights (1974: 5). There is considerable ambivalence regarding the use of rights and rights discourse: on the one side, they are denigrated, viewed as contingent and as legal categories unable to encapsulate everyday experiences; on the other, they are important in legal ideology and remain a critical resource (Milner, 1989: 631). Scheingold argues that rights are simply political resources that may or may not be successful in pursuing broader goals (1974: 6–7). A rights strategy does not necessarily imply the espousal of litigation; rather, it can be one tactic within a broader political, and not just legal, strategy (Hunt, 1990: 317). The notion of rights is continually contested and the concept is deployed in various settings in an attempt to achieve hegemonic influence for a preferred set of meanings (Bartholomew and Hunt, 1991: 6). The questions then become: under what conditions will a rights strategy be pursued? When are rights strategies successful and is success short/long term; substantive/symbolic; or direct/indirect? Which social movements, or segments, employ rights discourses in combination with which other strategies and in what kinds of arenas? Rights do not have any essence and one cannot make universal statements regarding their inherent goodness or badness. Legal rights claims can be both a resource and a constraint for collective efforts to transform or reconstitute social relationships. As law-reform activity is newsworthy, legal rights advocacy potentially increases public awareness about social relations and can be an important means of generating publicity for social movements; it can contribute to the development of citizens' expectations about possible remedies and reforms and can help forge a common identity of experienced victimization and aspiration among diversely marginalized citizens, thereby enhancing collective organization (McCann, 1991: 228, 234).

Since the 1970s, critics and reformers in many contemporary western legal systems have argued that reliance on the courts is inappropriate for many kinds of cases: courts are too slow, crowded, cumbersome and too expensive, plus adversarial litigation – where one party wins and the other loses – is neither conducive to the long-term settlement of many disputes nor sensitive to the needs and interests (as distinct from the legal rights) of disputants. The court experience is alienating, inflexible and dissatisfying for many complainants and defendants and cannot adequately resolve disputes involving continuing interpersonal relationships. The involvement of lawyers, court procedures and evidentiary rules mean that individuals do not control their own disputes, the way in which their experiences are presented or the types of information a court receives. This perceived crisis in the courts constituted a significant impetus for the development of Alternative Dispute Resolution (ADR) or informalism in the legal process (Astor and Chinkin, 2002; Buck, 2005; Harrington, 1985). Other reforms include greater and more explicit roles for judicial officers in case management, including the promotion of settlement, departing from the traditional view of the judge as passive arbiter, and various procedural changes aimed at diverting matters from adversarial contest (Bamford, 2004).

Alternative dispute resolution (ADR)

While ADR can be described as a movement, diverse programmes, interests and motivations fall within its parameters (Roberts and Palmer, 2005). Proponents tend to present ADR as the antithesis of the formal legal system (Danzig, 1973; Sander, 1985: 3; Tomasic, 1982: 221–2; *Yale Law Journal*, 1979). As Abel observes:

> Informal justice is said to be unofficial (dissociated from state power), non-coercive (dependent on rhetoric rather than force), nonbureaucratic, decentralized, relatively undifferentiated, and non-professional; its substantive and procedural rules are imprecise, unwritten, democratic, flexible, ad hoc, and particularistic. (Abel, 1982b: 2)

The overall aim of ADR is to provide alternatives to litigation and the courts, that emphasize informality, voluntary participation, opportunities for direct communication between disputants and outcomes based on consensus. The prototype of ADR is mediation, in which a neutral mediator facilitates a resolution process but should not intervene, coerce or impose a particular outcome or remedy. Proponents of ADR argue that mediation will enhance satisfaction with the dispute-settlement process and increase compliance with any settlement. More importantly, as ADR does not require legal representation or advice, judicial determinations or engagement with a court, it provides affordable and accessible options for dispute management. Accordingly, ADR may facilitate access to justice for groups and individuals unable to afford legal representation or who are denied legal remedies because of restrictive legal procedures. Outcomes will be more just, due to increased participation by disputants, greater flexibility and informality than adversarial legal procedures (Cappelletti, 1993: 291–6).

Examples of successful nonadjudicatory dispute processing from anthropological research have been central in the initial promotion of ADR. Popular tribunals in socialist societies dealing with petty crimes, torts and interpersonal conflicts that aim to involve and educate the community in the day-to-day laws of their society, especially the new laws promulgated following a revolution as well as labour and commercial arbitration, also inspire proponents (Berman, 1969: 1318–22; Merry, 1982: 173). In an early influential paper, Richard Danzig (1973) looks to the tribal moot found among the Kpelle of Liberia (Africa) as a model of informal dispute resolution. This forum involves community members and is presided over by a mediator, who expresses the consensus of the group and deals primarily with matrimonial disputes. The moot allows the full airing of grievances – unlike courtroom hearings that are subject to procedural and evidentiary rules it takes place in familiar surroundings, and the outcome is more consensual, and thus more durable, than a decision imposed by an adjudicator (Gibbs, 1963: 3–5). Indeed, Gibbs goes so far as to claim that the moot is not only conciliatory but therapeutic suggesting its resonance with psychotherapy.

Danzig asks: 'Despite the differences between a tribal culture and our own, isn't there a place for a community moot in our judicial system?' (1973: 43). He proposes that such a moot might handle family disputes, some marital matters, including paternity, support or separation, juvenile delinquency, and disputes between property owners and tenants, as well as small torts, breaches of contract and misdemeanours involving community members only. Compared with the courts, this forum would be conveniently located, considerate, much faster in dealing with cases, and may enhance community integration by providing opportunities for local discussion (Danzig, 1973: 47–8; Danzig and Lowy, 1975: 686). Danzig envisages such reforms as complementing rather than displacing the formal court structure and suggests that the existing system does some things well, for example the criminal trial protects the rights of the accused through due process (Danzig, 1973: 7–9, 41). Diverting interpersonal disputes and minor criminal issues from the formal courts would allow the latter to deal with more serious issues and complex, large cases more efficiently.

Contemporary developments in ADR commenced in the USA, culminating in the opening of the first neighbourhood justice centres in 1978. Since then, the number and variety of new dispute processing fora have expanded and extended to other societies, including Australia and the UK. Nonetheless, examples of informalism predate the ADR movement and the fact that most disputes are settled without relying on courts even where litigation is initiated indicates that informal mechanisms of dispute settlement occur frequently. What is new, however, is the expansion and diversity of noncourt locations and arrangements for the resolution of disputes, including neighbourhood or community justice centres, mediation or conciliation services and administrative tribunals.

Neighbourhood justice or community legal centres

These handle both civil and criminal grievances, rely on the disputants' voluntary participation, and employ techniques of mediation and compromise. Proponents argue that these features and the community base facilitate the exploration of the root causes of disputes, thereby increasing the chances of an effective settlement (Tomasic and Feeley, 1982: x). The centres provide for the mediation of disputes by a third party who is a member of the community, has some training in mediation and is supposed to be impartial (Faulkes, 1990: 62). The mediator assists the disputants in reaching a consensual settlement; she or he does not decide the outcome but may offer or evaluate options (Astor and Chinkin, 2002: 149–57). If a consensual agreement is not reached through direct negotiation, the dispute may be arbitrated by the mediator (Harrington, 1985: 126). Community justice centres are not entirely distinct and separate from the formal court system. In the USA, neighbourhood justice centres are created by the Department of Justice and, in Australia, community legal centres receive a large number of referrals from magistrates or local courts.

The Neighbourhood Justice Centre established in a Melbourne suburb in 2007, is the first community justice initiative of its kind in Australia (NJC Project Team, 2007; see also www.justice.vic.gov.au). It provides a multi-jurisdictional court, on-site support services for victims, witnesses, defendants and local residents, mediation services available to residents, government departments, agencies and local community organizations and crime prevention programmes. The overall aim is to address the causes of offending by undertaking crime prevention and increasing the community's involvement in justice administration. The mediation service delivery model includes the use of local and locally trained mediators, the use of mediation processes to assist in the resolution of 'community problems' and 'an ability to contribute to local anti-social behaviour issues, without recourse to court processes' (NJC Project Team, 2007: 21).

Family conciliation or mediation centres

These offer a range of services to families for resolving conflicts and provide an alternative to formal courts and legal methods. It is often argued that family disputes, because of the usually high level of emotion, are more appropriately mediated and that a negotiated settlement is better than pursuing the conflict through the courts (Fineman, 1988: 727–34). The emphasis is on a multidisciplinary approach to service provision; trained community mediators conduct the proceedings with the goal of empowering individuals, families and communities, enabling them to take responsibility for their own disputes. The centres aim to provide an environment that is conducive to constructive negotiation and to improve the conflict-resolution skills of families in order to reduce the reliance on litigation (Astor and Chinkin, 2002: 336–9).

Since the late 1970s a large number of marital conciliation services have been established in Britain. Some are 'out-of-court' schemes run by social workers and take clients who may not have yet initiated legal proceedings; 'in-court' schemes are organized by court welfare officers and take cases following legal action (Bottomley, 1985: 166). This marks a shift from a concern with reconciliation – that is, reuniting the spouses – to a concern with the consequences of marital dissolution. Conciliation came to mean assisting parties in reaching agreement regarding custody and child support, financial arrangements, the division of marital property and reducing conflict. Some suggest that the popularity of conciliation reflects a focus on saving the children rather than saving the marriage (Bottomley, 1985: 170–1; Eekelaar and Dingwall, 1988: 11–14). Conciliation schemes vary in the extent to which they are associated with the formal court system; specialized family courts established during the 1970s emphasize conciliation and mediation and attempt to be less adversarial and formal than other courts.

Administrative tribunals

Established by governments, these tribunals review administrative decisions in such areas as taxation, immigration and social security, and aim to resolve grievances against the state and to deal with some specific disputes between individuals, for example industrial commissions seek to resolve disputes between employers and employees. Proceedings vary in the degree of informality, the grounds of complaint are wide, rules of evidence are relaxed and legal representation on behalf of applicants is unusual. Tribunals are often presided over by an expert from the field, and sometimes a combination of expert and laypeople, who will have more scope for asking questions and directing the proceedings than a judge does (Genn, 1993: 394–5). The Australian Administrative Appeals Tribunal Act 1984, for example, specifies that one of its objectives is to 'establish an independent Tribunal to review administrative decisions ... in an informal and expeditious manner; and permit a broad range of persons whose interests are affected by a decision to participate in a proceeding' (s4). A second type of legislatively established tribunal enables minor disputes to be settled without going to court. Examples include residential tenancy tribunals for disputes between landowners and tenants and small claims courts that deal with consumer complaints against businesses. While such tribunals often pre-date the current ADR movement, they exhibit various levels of informalism, making them comparable with other nonadversarial mechanisms of dispute resolution. In addition, their number and variety have expanded considerably since the 1970s (Allars, 1990: 56–8). There may be scope for lawyer involvement at tribunal hearings. A study of cases before a public housing eviction board shows that those tenants with legal representation can avoid eviction, as they are more able to secure delays allowing them the time needed to resolve their problems. They are also more likely to attend the hearing because of their lawyer's insistence on the importance of so doing (Monsma and Lempert, 1992).

Arbitration

Arbitration has elements of informalism: it can be entered into by an agreement between the parties or court ordered; parties may select the arbitrator(s); hearings are private rather than public; it is considered to be less expensive and more efficient than litigation; and arbitrators are not judicial personnel (although they may be legally trained and have been judges previously), but are often nonlawyers with specific expertise in a field, for example engineering or architecture. However, arbitration also resembles adjudication, as lawyers are usually involved as advisers and a third party hears the evidence of the disputants and makes a binding award to which the parties normally have to agree (Astor and Chinkin, 2002: 89–90, 297–311; Flood and Caiger, 1993: 425–36). In the dispute between France and New Zealand arising out of the sinking of the *Rainbow Warrior* in 1985 the parties agreed to arbitration by the UN Secretary General (Astor and Chinkin, 2002: 416).

International commercial arbitration has become the paramount mechanism for the resolution of transnational commercial disputes over contracts dealing with the sale of goods, joint ventures, construction projects and international incidents. The International Chamber of Commerce (ICC), founded in 1919 and based in Paris, is the leading institution, but there are others such as the American Arbitration Association and the London Court of International Arbitration.

Arbitration solves difficulties arising from the fact that there is no international court where private or legal individuals will have standing and the parties are not forced to submit to the courts of the other disputant (Dezalay and Garth, 1995: 30–1). Arbitration under the rules of the ICC is on the increase. Since 1999, the court has received new cases at a rate of more than 500 per year (www.iccwbo.org/id93/index. html; Dezalay and Garth, 1996a: 5). The ICC is an organization of private businesses without formal ties to nation states. For example, the contract dealing with the English Channel tunnel construction project provided that any disputes be heard initially by a specially convened panel of five experts presided over by a law professor; if that was unsuccessful then the aggrieved party could take the dispute to arbitration in Brussels under the rules of the ICC (Flood and Caiger, 1993: 412–3, fn 6). International commercial arbitration has become 'a key institution in the structuring of international markets', and itself has been transformed somewhat over the past few decades (Dezalay and Garth, 1996a: 7). For example, The iCC offers suggested ADR clauses for commercial contracts (http://iccwbo.org/court/dr/id5346/index.html).

Following almost 300 interviews in 11 countries with most of the leading members of the international arbitration community and the representatives of leading institutions in the field of international commercial arbitration Dezalay and Garth conclude that international commercial arbitration has evolved into a relatively adversarial, formalized and legalized variety of offshore litigation. It has shifted from informal, compromise-oriented outcomes to advance the interests of business dominated by European academics to a form of offshore litigation (1996b: 295). Litigators in large US law firms servicing corporate elites insisted that the arbitrators should adopt more adversarial behaviour in the interests of their clients and pay more attention to the facts. They promoted the idea that only if it became a (US) court-like substitute could arbitration legitimately serve international business transactions (Dezalay and Garth, 1996b: 298). In the context of transnational business disputes, arbitration has become one kind of forum, among others, for litigation (Dezalay and Garth, 1996a: 55).

> The legitimacy of international commercial arbitration is no longer built on the fact that arbitration is informal and close to the needs of business. Rather legitimacy now comes more from recognition that arbitration is *formal* and close to the kind of resolution that would be produced through litigation – more precisely through the negotiation that takes place in the context of US-style litigation. (Dezalay and Garth, 1996b: 299, emphasis in original)

Other developments in informalism

These include the establishment of ombudspeople, options for counselling, mediation, centres for the resolution of commercial disputes and statutory provision for conciliation in family disputes and discrimination complaints. These developments result from government policy and legislation, which in some instances require mediation or conciliation before the courts can be accessed. For example, the Family Law Act (Commonwealth) in Australia emphasizes alternative methods of dispute resolution: it provides for property disputes to be referred to conferences held by a registrar and allows for counselling with a view to reconciliation between disputants and regarding their children. Divorce laws in other jurisdictions provide for voluntary or mandatory mediation regarding various aspects of the divorce process and child custody (McEwen et al., 1994: 152–6). The process of mediation may become an early step in the settlement of a dispute rather than an alternative to court procedures. Additionally, some courts have adopted elements of informalism, further blurring the distinctions between different forms of dispute processing. In some small claims courts in the USA, mediation was introduced in the 1970s (Wissler, 1995: 323–7). Judicially mandated pre-trial and settlement conferences, which may involve the judge directly, increase the incentives for negotiated settlements rather than litigation, in both civil and criminal law (Galanter, 1985: 4; Glasser and Roberts, 1993: 277; Roberts, 1993: 459). Statutes and/or rules of court enable most Australian courts to refer disputes to ADR without party consent (Mack, 2003).

The development of ADR is not just restricted to civil disputes; in the criminal law new reforms emphasize the role of the family, neighbourhood and community in the management and sanctioning of criminal offences (see Chapter 6). Reformers refer to diversionary programmes, deinstitutionalization, decriminalization and restorative justice to signify reduced citizen contact with the criminal justice system. A unifying theme is that substantive justice is often unobtainable in conventional courts due to the plethora of procedural (legalistic and technical) rules governing the disposition of a case.

ADR provides new opportunities for redefining the market for dispute-resolution services on the part of various interests, including members of the 'helping' professions. Social workers, counsellors, therapists, psychologists and others will attempt to advance their own professional claims as appropriate providers of mediation services and settlement techniques *vis-à-vis* interpersonal disputes. This has also led to the development of training courses and issues regarding appropriate credentials, accreditation, ethics and confidentiality (Astor and Chinkin, 2002: 204–6, 211–19). However, the development of ADR has not excluded the legal profession, nor provided alternatives to lawyers in all situations, as many legal practitioners claim to possess mediation as well as advocacy skills and both the courts and the legal profession support the development of and their involvement in ADR (Astor and Chinkin, 2002: 206–10; Roberts, 1992: 261; Silbey and Sarat, 1989: 446). The rapid growth of mediation courses within law schools and continuing legal education attest to lawyers' interest in ADR (Twining, 1993: 392).

In England, lawyers are rapidly showing an active and proprietary interest in ADR. While initially cautious, both the Bar and Law Society sponsored major reports heralding ADR as something new and important and identifying central roles for lawyers. IDR (Europe) is a company established in 1989 that offers private mediation and whose mediators are solicitors drawn from a network of law firms and given mediation training by the company. Nevertheless, an involvement in mediation presents a new role orientation for lawyers from common-law countries, who now must act as neutral mediators, in contrast to their more traditional adversarial approach as the advocate for a particular client in a dispute (Roberts, 1992: 258–9; 1993: 456, 464–5 Roberts and Palmer, 2005). Research in Maine (USA) shows that divorce lawyers have embraced mandatory, court-sponsored divorce mediation that encourages a focus on settlement; they view mediation as providing new options and resources for them, they are likely to represent parties in mediation and regularly attend mediation sessions (McEwen et al., 1994: 155–9). However, this involvement presents numerous tensions, including how to pursue both negotiation and trial preparation; how to encourage client participation in case preparation while retaining professional authority; how to provide clients with legal advice while addressing such nonlegal issues as organizing access visits or dividing personal property; and how to manage cases so that they can be finalized predictably and expeditiously (McEwen et al., 1994: 150).

The critique of ADR

Despite proponents' enthusiasm, the development of ADR has spawned enormous theoretical commentary and evaluation research that casts doubts on its efficacy and possibilities for realization. The terms *alternative dispute resolution* and *informalism* are criticized as misnomers, as many of the reforms are neither alternatives to conventional courts nor devoid of formality. Moreover, ADR is not a recent phenomenon, as the current reform strategies have historical parallels, including the juvenile court movement and the institutionalization of conciliation and arbitration in industrial relations (Faulkes, 1990: 62–3; Harrington, 1982: 39–50). Critics question the transferability of anthropological research dealing with tribal societies to inform the ADR movement. They argue that the reforms are not separate from or alternative to the formal legal system, and find that the operation of mediation deviates significantly from the idealized models of reformers. The following discussion examines each of these issues in turn.

Anthropological research

An examination of dispute processing in tribal societies suggests that reformers' reliance on anthropological research has been misplaced and their conclusions misapplied to contemporary, urban, western societies, resulting in a somewhat naive enthusiasm for ADR. Proponents tend to idealize the process of mediation, emphasizing its consensual and conciliatory aspects but ignoring issues of power and coercion (Merry, 1982: 20). In small-scale, politically unorganized societies, mediation will essentially be compulsory, as individuals will risk vengeance from the adversary for refusing to participate. Mediators are neither neutral nor disinterested but respected, influential and authoritative community members who will exert considerable moral suasion to achieve a settlement. Mediators will advocate a settlement that accords with generally accepted notions of justice and to flout it defies the moral order of the community (Merry, 1982: 30). Noncompliance with a mediated settlement may have further negative consequences for political, economic and kinship relations, thus the community itself exerts a pressure to settle. The meaning and significance of mediation in tribal societies are vastly different from the model of mediation that contemporary advocates propose.

Urban neighbourhoods obviously differ markedly from tribal societies and social organization will affect mediation processes and outcomes (Felstiner, 1974: 86). The level of heterogeneity and geographical mobility is higher and consensus about appropriate behaviour is lower in urban settings. As a result, few incentives exist for mediation and, where it does occur, the consequences for noncompliance are probably trivial. Disputants are rarely embedded in an intimate, cohesive social system where they depend on cooperative relationships. Avoidance may be the most frequent strategy for managing disputes in complex societies, while it would be untenable in tribal villages. Where pockets of community prevail within highly urbanized settings, for example in workplaces or local organizations, the equation of community with geographical neighbourhood is problematic. Where the social structure is fragmented and the population mobile, the need to settle may be slight and the incentive to mediate and compromise correspondingly low. The corollary of this is that some conditions will exist where mediation might be appropriate in contemporary societies, namely where it can be built on existent community structures, rather than appended to the legal system, or where it is restricted to disputes between relative equals, or between those who perceive a need to settle (Merry, 1982: 34–40).

The extension of state control

Some critics argue that the 'picture of the state withdrawing its authority over minor dispute management, and a proactive community mediation process providing a therapeutic context for dispute resolution' is ideological (Harrington, 1985: 35). It is part of the imagery and rhetoric of the ADR movement contradicted by the continuing actual links with the formal legal system. Legal concepts, legal rules and legal actors tend to move into or take over nonlegal institutions, but not replace them with the most formalized model of courts and litigation (Harrington and Merry, 1988: 712–14). The idealized conception of ADR as nonadversarial, community based, informal, flexible and just, downplays the dependence on state support and conventional courts. As governments sponsor the expansion of informal dispute processing in a number of ways, then, their development actually extends the scope of the state and further legitimates the formal judicial system (Abel, 1982a: 304; Hofrichter, 1987: 96). To varying degrees, proponents of this thesis will focus more on social control than on dispute processing, the former being what is actually occurring, while the latter is central to the ideology. Abel maintains that because informal state institutions reduce or disguise coercion, they can seek to review behaviour that presently remains outside the system. Unlike courts, there are no jurisdictional or evidentiary constraints and fewer procedural and constitutional protections are afforded by informal institutions, which would rarely dismiss a case. As informal measures are less expensive than litigation, more state intervention is possible within the same budget (Abel, 1982a: 270–3).

Rather than undermining or replacing judicial authority, the diversion of minor disputes into mediation increases the capacity of courts to deal exclusively with major cases (Abel, 1981: 249; 1982a: 274). ADR may herald a bifurcated justice system, as the clients of neighbourhood justice centres and other forms of mediation are economically and politically disadvantaged segments of society. Informal justice removes poorer and less powerful litigants – or the 'junk' cases – from the courts to enable them to serve the needs of wealthy, powerful and business interests better (Hofrichter, 1982: 195). From this perspective, mediation provides second-class justice for those lacking in resources, and in fact may weaken their access to the courts by extending the time involved in the dispute process.

Instead of providing greater access to justice and more control over disputing, state-supported informalism expropriates conflict from the parties and reduces citizen participation by instituting trained arbitrators and mediators. Informal processes moderate the antagonistic adversarial posture of the parties (Abel, 1982b: 277, 283; Hofrichter, 1982: 195). Abel suggests that both formal courts and their informal alternatives tend to mollify conflict as their processes support the structures of domination characteristic of contemporary capitalist society (Abel, 1981: 250). More vehemently, Hofrichter (1982: 197) argues that neighbourhood justice centres are new modes of social control by local elites for disapproved conduct or violations of social norms; they represent an alternative to politics and community organizing. He announces that 'neighborhood dispute resolution activities are institutions of crisis management and social control within the capitalist state' (Hofrichter, 1987: 3). From this viewpoint, informal dispute resolution is a way of incorporating citizens into the social order through a decentralized state institution embedded in everyday life. Urban decay and unemployment threaten the stability of capitalism and neighbourhood justice siphons the tension into mediated settlements, which remain at the level of the community.

Within this critique of informalism, some commentators rely on simplistic functionalist assumptions about capitalism's 'need' for ADR and present capital and the state as having an easily defined, unitary set of interests (FitzGerald, 1984: 641–3). While Abel indicates that informalism has an ambiguous effect and informal legal institutions have a contradictory relationship with their formal counterparts, he focuses on the negative and conservative elements rather than on the opportunities for transformation. He envisages little scope for change resulting from the ADR movement: informalism is disguised formalism. The argument that institutional change is illusory because it simply reproduces existing inequalities is reductionist. A further problem relates to the conception of the court system as subsumed within the state apparatus. It is difficult to see how court reform and the attempt to provide new arenas for disputing translate so rapidly and directly into enhanced state control and more subtle coercion. Rather than arguing either that the ADR movement represents a complete shift away from the formal legal system or that it is nothing more than a diluted or diffuse form of it, it is more productive to attempt to specify theoretically and empirically the relationships between informal and formal disputing, between mediators and the legal profession and between new structures for dispute processing and the courts.

Evaluation research

A number of case studies examine neighbourhood justice and mediation centres regarding the origins or recruitment of cases and their outcomes, the satisfaction of disputants, the role of the mediator and the voluntariness of participation. Research identifies problems stemming from the lack of sanctions and difficulties in enforcing agreements, and the assumptions that the parties to a dispute are equal and that any settlement reflects a consensus. There are difficulties in assessing whether an ADR programme is successful, as definitions of success might differ from the viewpoints of the disputants or the court referring the dispute. Notions of success in evaluation research are often defined in terms of settlement rates and/or participant satisfaction.

The idea of predicting factors that will be general indicators of ADR success seems highly difficult if not impossible (Mack, 2003).

Participants   It appears that most of the participants in neighbourhood justice centres (NJCs) are referred by the criminal justice system. In one US study, only 12 per cent of the cases were 'walk-ins' and the remainder came from private attorneys, legal aid and various other agencies (Harrington, 1985: 111–15). The centre established three eligibility criteria for referring cases to mediation:

(a) the disputants should have a continuing relationship;
(b) disputes should be of a minor civil or criminal nature; and
(c) cases should show a potential for successful mediation.

Disputes involving people in domestic and neighbourhood relationships constituted the largest group of criminal justice referrals to the centres. Harassment and assaults were the most frequent; other common complaints related to neighbours' dogs, children and property. Women, unemployed people and those on low incomes were the majority of those referred. It was found that disputants were more likely to participate in neighbourhood justice mediation when there were strong ties to the official remedy system, most importantly referral by a criminal justice agent or when an arrest charge was involved. The coercion and authority of police, prosecutors and judges are essential to the institutional existence of neighbourhood justice centres (Harrington, 1984: 216–20; 1985: 170). Incentives and sanctions to participate in mediation are not solely within the disputants' relationship but are structured by the referral source. The delegalization of minor dispute processing operates within a broader context of social reform, namely an administrative-technocratic rationalization of judicial work and the management of order in urban poor and working-class communities. Harrington concludes that:

> The Neighborhood Justice Center is a shadow of conventional adjudication practices. The dependency of these centers on courts for their place and meaning in the legal process and, through the use of official coercion, to provide cases contribute to the proposition that the justice in the neighborhood justice centers is a shadow justice. (1985: 170)

Satisfaction   Overall, research suggests that people who participate in mediation programmes are satisfied with the outcomes. Complainants tend to perceive the mediation process more positively than adjudication, which also enhances their perceptions of their relationships with defendants (Davis, 1982: 159; Roehl and Cook, 1982: 101). An investigation into the implementation and impact of three experimental NJCs in the US finds in follow-up interviews six months after a mediated settlement that a substantial majority of disputants (84 per cent of complainants and 89 per cent of respondents) were satisfied with the mediation process and were holding to the terms of their agreements (79 per cent of complainants and 87 per cent of respondents). Mediation can be more satisfactory to disputants and at least as effective as courts in resolving disputes in the long term, and NJCs can resolve disputes much faster and at a lower cost than courts (Roehl and Cook, 1982: 97–103). Over a third of the cases reached a mediation hearing and 82 per cent of these resulted in a mutual agreement. Of all referred cases, 17 per cent were resolved without a hearing, primarily due to the respondent's refusal to participate. The cases were fairly evenly divided between interpersonal criminal disputes (45 per cent) involving family or other personal relationships and civil disputes (55 per cent) between tenants and landowners, consumers and vendors, and employees and employers. However, an important difference was that courts tended to refer interpersonal criminal disputes while civil cases were self-initiated. The former were more likely to reach a hearing than were consumer complaints, probably due to a perception that referrals from the criminal justice system entail coercion. Apparently, corporate respondents – business owners and employers – and landowners feel little need for a compromise and will refuse to participate (Roehl and Cook, 1982: 97–103).

A comparison between mediation and adjudication in the small claims divisions of four district courts in Boston over a five-month period indicates that disputants viewed mediation as permitting a longer, more thorough and less hurried discussion of a broader range of solutions and issues, allowing them more control over the process and outcome than with adjudication. The mediator was more likely than the judge to be seen as neutral and was perceived as interested in and understanding of the dispute. Mediated agreements were more likely than trial awards to contain nonmonetary terms and payment arrangements. Disputants in mediation were also more likely to say that the process was fair and that they were satisfied with it compared to those in adjudication. Parties who had an on-going relationship and who resolved their dispute via mediation indicated that the process had had a less negative effect on their relationship (Wissler, 1995: 351).

Voluntariness   When compared to the populations that mediation programmes serve, citizens with interpersonal problems do not appear to consider them a useful resource unless they have been shunted in that direction by the justice system (Felstiner and Williams, 1982: 149). Disputants are reluctant to participate in mediation and there are very low levels of self-referral. A comparison of three neighbourhood justice centres in different US cities shows that referrals largely derive from the criminal justice system, mostly from judges, court clerks or prosecutors and police. Such centres seem to be exit points from the justice system rather than providing greater access (Tomasic, 1982: 219). In a number of jurisdictions, mediation has been suggested as mandatory for certain types of cases, thus deviating from reformers' expectations that participation would be voluntary (Grillo, 1991: 1549–55; Harrington and Merry, 1988: 721). An examination of court-sponsored mediation in the Family Court, the Federal Court and a Small Claims Court in Australia finds that each departed from the model of mediation as a voluntary and non-adjudicative dispute-resolution process (Ingleby, 1993: 446). Each of the settings was established by statute, with the impetus for mediation originating from the court. The Family Court does not permit a contested hearing in relation to property unless the parties have attended a conference and endeavoured to reach an agreement; the Federal Court allows parties to request mediation or the judge might suggest it; and the Small Claims Court has a duty to attempt to bring the parties to a settlement. Voluntariness is constrained because mediators promote the benefits of settlement as a way of maintaining control of events against the disadvantages of litigation, where the outcome is unpredictable and cross-examination emotionally traumatic. Secondly, mediators are not neutral; they comment on the merits of each disputant's claims, attempt to adjudicate the outcomes and tend to control the content and structure of the discussion by making judgements about what statements are relevant. Additionally, conciliators concerned primarily to safeguard the interests of children reflect values about the welfare of children and thus they are not objective or neutral (Bottomley, 1985: 174–7). Where mediators or conciliators enjoy the authority of the court and are accorded expertise as settlement professionals, they exercise a quasi-adjudication function that is far removed from the ideal type of mediation (Ingleby, 1993: 446–8). The notion of consensus is redefined from a voluntary decision to participate in a noncourt setting to a consensual decision-making process where participation is required (Harrington and Merry, 1988: 721).

Mediators Another concern regarding the divergence between the ideal of mediation and actual practices revolves around the role of the mediator and the extent to which she or he has strong links to the community, is able to contextualize the dispute and be familiar with disputants. Among the mediators in three different local mediation programmes (in New England, US), an elite emerged with disproportionate input into defining good practice, hiring, training, evaluating other mediators and the handling of cases (Harrington and Merry, 1988). These mediators tended to have more education, to have professional backgrounds in law or social work and be viewed as possessing more ability or skill than the others; their personal and residential links with the community were tenuous or nonexistent. The 'elite' mediators define neutrality as the central symbol of their practice, by which they mean detachment and 'objectivity'. Interestingly, despite the commitment to involve community members, mediators with strong local ties were often viewed as less effective and used less often because of their tendency to evaluate participants morally and to express value judgements, thus failing to adopt the preferred neutral stance (Harrington and Merry, 1988: 724–30).

A study of community mediation in disputes between neighbours in London shows that while remaining an aspiration 'the adoption of a neutral stance serves to exacerbate existing inequalities between disputing parties and promotes injustice' (Mulcahy, 2001: 506). Mediators sought to recognize rather than deny the possibility of bias while attempting to minimize its impact on outcomes. They feel constrained by the expectation of neutrality and seek to adopt a reflexive approach to their role in mediation, openly discussing the ways their personal assessment of the issues at stake in the dispute and the behaviour of the parties impact on the construction of options and management of the process (Mulcahy, 2001: 506).

Community mediators in housing disputes were selected because of their identification with local residents, capacity to make connections, and membership of the community, but what rendered mediators partial was their willingness to promote the interests of groups within the community thus placing themselves on the side of local people against the state authorities (Mulcahy, 2001: 517). Mediators tended to consider the immediate source of the dispute – noise, rubbish, poor housing conditions – resulting in the identification of behaviour as anti-social as more properly located in a wider political context, often casting themselves as advocates exerting pressure on housing or welfare officers. Issues of public housing are often the site of disputes and in the UK there is a growing expectation that social landlords will provide mediation services that can regulate the relations and interactions between residents rather than the behaviour of individuals (Flint, 2006b: 226).

Criticisms of neutrality – in practice it is unattainable, it is impossible for mediators to disavow their own values and interpretations, mediators do influence mediation outcomes, it does paper over power imbalances – have not dislodged its centrality as a value in mediation (Astor, 2007: 228–9). Astor argues that 'neutrality is even more important for mediation than adjudication' (2007: 228–9). As mediation occurs in private its legitimacy relies not on the law but on consensual decision making by the parties to the dispute and mediator neutrality. Neutrality, a much debated and contested term, can have several meanings: the mediator does not influence the decision produced by the mediation; the mediator is impartial and treats all sides equally; mediators should not be influenced by personal or financial relationships with the disputants; and there is freedom from governmental influence (Astor, 2007: 222). For most disputants, especially in court-ordered mediation or statutory mediation schemes, the mediator is a stranger and their promise of neutrality is relied on to ensure a fair process.

Consensus   ADR assumes that disputants will have equal bargaining power or negotiating skills. In many disputes this will not be the case and the absence of legal force may reproduce inequalities and injustice. In the area of consumer protection, the establishment of nonjudicial tribunals and complaint bureaux is likely to be inadequate, because of their inability to compensate for the ineffective bargaining position of the individual who confronts large corporations (Astor, 2007: 223).

There is also a concern that the areas of law where women are most likely to be complainants or victims, including family and equal opportunity laws, are precisely those where ADR is the most developed. This tends to privatize disputes and divert public attention and policy from the wider causes of the problems (Nader, 1979: 1020). The use of ADR in family disputes and divorce has been especially criticized because of inequalities in economic resources, information and credibility between the disputants. Economic, social and psychological vulnerability counteracts the ideal image of the equal negotiating situation presumed to exist in mediation (Bottomley, 1985: 179–80; Scutt, 1988: 503). Many women who may well have benefited in the courts by being granted custody may now be subtly coerced into accepting a joint custody order through a process of conciliation that further weakens their bargaining position. The present presumption that a mother will take preference in custody has been the strongest bargaining factor that a woman will have in relation to property. Women's interests may be better protected in a court setting because while formal justice gives substantive, albeit fragile, protections it offers procedural safeguards, and it involves lawyers who can mitigate the power imbalance between the parties (Mack, 1995: 126–32).

There is also a general acceptance that cases where violence or the threat of violence exists are inappropriate for mediation (Bottomley, 1985: 184). The weakness of mediation as a remedy for abused women is reflected in agreements that commonly fail to address the issue of violence or do so only euphemistically, and this suggests that diverting cases from prosecution to mediation amounts to the decriminalization of wife abuse (Astor, 1990: 143–6). Structural problems include mediation programmes accepting cases that are often serious enough for formal legal action; mediation hearings are held in private so that there is little public accountability; the sessions are short; in some programmes both parties are present throughout, which may make it impossible for the victim of violence to discuss the abuse while the abuser is there; the parties normally do not have advocates, which could otherwise alleviate power imbalances; and some programmes require victims to forgo the pursuit of formal legal remedies before participating in mediation (Lerman, 1984: 92–4).

Conclusion

Rather than conceptualizing developments in dispute processing as alternatives to the courts and litigation and as somehow more appropriate, just and accommodating of the diverse interests and resources of disputants, it is important to investigate empirically the extent to which different fora for resolving disputes are informal, voluntary, facilitate communication, are nonadversarial and nonlegalistic. It is incorrect to assume that all courts possess the same characteristics and that community justice centres or tribunals, by definition, must be more informal and more concerned with mediation. It is important to investigate the relationships between different fora for resolving disputes and to identify the conditions under which certain kinds of dispute-settlement mechanisms will emerge, the kinds of problems and disputants with which they deal and the extent to which they can facilitate dispute settlement. The movement towards informalism and discontent with courts as a mechanism for the management of disputes is also occurring in the criminal justice sphere. In some respects there seems to be a blurring of distinctions between dispute resolution and social control and between civil- and criminal-law institutions and remedies. Nevertheless, these two dimensions of law are distinguishable and it is useful to consider their relationship in different social settings and the associated tensions between dispute resolution and social control in the legal arena. The next chapter examines forms of social control and investigates recent changes within various aspects of the criminal justice system.

Note

1 The focus on disputes, disputing, dispute processing and dispute resolution loosens legal scholars' monopoly on the discussion of law and opens up opportunities for social scientists to develop the concept of disputes. Anthropologists have been especially significant in developing the concept of dispute as a new way of contemplating law in society (Silbey and Sarat, 1989: 440; Snyder, 1981: 145–9).

6 Social Control

While the topics of dispute resolution and social control are divided into separate chapters, increasingly mechanisms of dispute resolution and social control converge. Several authors point to qualitative differences in concerns about social control and crime from the late twentieth century, including a focus on crime prevention, partnerships between individuals, neighbourhoods, communities and the state, and the control and management of crime being nested in public housing, education, welfare, and transport sectors, not just the criminal justice system.

Contemporary crime control policies often emphasize risk, security and individual responsibility for both the choice to engage in criminal offending and the choice to minimize risk (Garland, 2001). 'In criminal justice, this has meant less focus on the identification, prosecution and rehabilitation of guilty individuals, and more on identifying, preventing or reducing potential crime risks' (Mazerolle and Ransley, 2005: 65). Security and harm minimization are not only the concern of the conventional criminal justice agencies.

Policing and surveillance have been uncoupled from the police, governance uncoupled from the government, and crime control uncoupled from the criminal justice system (Roach Anleu, 2006: Chapter 3). There are new participants in the social control edifice – police partnerships and networks among businesses community organizations extend the networks charged with crime prevention and blur civil and criminal categories and methods (Mazerolle and Ransley, 2005: 71). New techniques of social control have become embedded in everyday life, for example Closed Circuit Television (CCTV), speed cameras, bar codes, pin numbers, and so on (Lianos and Douglas, 2000).

This chapter examines the relationship between legal and nonlegal social control and focuses primarily on the criminal justice system in contemporary societies. The criminal justice system is often a site of social engineering and attempts to effect social change by altering the behaviour and opportunities of law breakers and by redefining criminal laws in order to prohibit certain activities and encourage, or at least allow, others. The kinds of criminal laws that exist in a society, the range and types of punishment that are prevalent and the organization and ideology of the criminal justice system can be barometers of wider social trends. For sociologists in the functionalist tradition, social control, of which one type is law, is intimately linked with social integration and the maintenance of social life.

Social control entails efforts to obtain a conformity to or a compliance with norms, that is, rules and expectations about how to behave or act. Not all social control takes a legal form, nor are all norms legal. According to Black: 'Social control is found wherever and whenever people hold each other to standards, explicitly or implicitly, consciously or not: on the street, in prison, at home, at a party' (1976: 105). Laws are norms that involve an evaluation of behaviour in terms of what it ought to be, an expectation as to what behaviour will be and particular reactions to behaviour, including attempts to apply sanctions or induce a particular kind of conduct (Gibbs, 1965: 589; 1982). Extra-legal norms, for example morals, etiquette and customs, involve collective evaluation (law may or may not have popular or consensual support) and there is not a high probability that someone in a special status will seek to secure conformity (Gibbs, 1966: 322; Weber, 1947: 127).

Formal sanctions are associated with legal control and may be:

(a) repressive/punitive, for example the deprivation of life or liberty;
(b) restitutive, including damages, compensation and an apology, which aim to restore the status quo; or
(c) regulatory, which aim to achieve compliance with a legal-administrative regime via such sanctions as the denial or forfeiture of licences, orders to cease or desist from acting in a proscribed manner or, in the case of immigration law, deportation.

From a structural functionalist viewpoint, law is an integrative mechanism; it aims to control illegal activity, including crime, thereby restoring social equilibrium (Parsons, 1962: 58). There is a sense that laws reflect some level of social consensus that is important for social order. Until recently, sociologists concerned with social control were less interested with the formal means of social control than with its informal norms and processes of socialization, thus paying less attention to the phenomenon of law (Coser, 1982: 14; Ross, 1896: 518–22). Social control theorists concentrated on classifying the forms of social control, recognizing law as one of these forms but identifying distinctions between them. Law was of interest as a manifestation of larger social processes, rather than a topic of inquiry *per se*. This approach presents all forms of social control as constituting a continuum from informal to institutionalized forms, with law the most formal or specialized. It also tends to stress the normative character of law and emphasize the relationship between societal values and legal rules, which embody the most widely diffused and shared social values (Hunt, 1978: 145–7). In this paradigm, law is the key to achieving order and stability in complex societies where there are few shared interests (Hunt, 1978: 19–22).

However, law has coercive elements and is applied despite the absence of consensus. Weber's emphasis on the relationship between law and domination enables an exploration of the coercive dimensions of law without ignoring its normative character (Hunt, 1993: 42–3; see Chapter 2). More critical theorists argue that law is oppressive, reflects or reinforces the interests of dominant segments of society and is used to control those whose interests and activities are defined as contrary to those of law makers. It is important not to reduce law to coercion but to examine the relationship between coercion and legitimacy (Hunt, 1978: 147).

Approaches to law deriving inspiration from Foucault move away from the notion of law as social control to conceptualize law as governance. Law is viewed as constituted by historically specific regulatory devices – which entail power/knowledge, and derive especially from the social sciences – that mediate between the state and civil society and between the state and the individual (Hunt, 1993: 292; Hunt and Wickham, 1994: 99–116). From this perspective, law seeks to regulate (sometimes unsuccessfully) problem populations under the banner of crime control and crime prevention, and empirical questions can be asked about the relationship between legal regulation and such other forms of regulation as social welfare and psychiatry. New legal sanctions are deployed that are less visible and more diffuse than the prison and may be applied to individuals who have not been found guilty of a criminal offence in a court of law. Indeed, much of the operation of the criminal justice system occurs outside of formal trial processes. In both criminal and civil spheres, alternative dispute-resolution mechanisms that aim to divert certain kinds of cases from the formal system are gaining in popularity. The distinction between repressive (criminal) and restitutive (civil) sanctions is becoming less precise with the development of community-based sanctions, which may involve the payment of compensation, an apology, or a restoration of the status quo.

Legal and nonlegal control

Considerable research, especially anthropological, has been devoted to distinguishing legal from nonlegal social control, specifying the relationships between the two and identifying those social conditions where one form of control predominates. Informal sanctions are adequate where little individualism or privacy exists, strong primary relationships prevail and the community or extended family retains primary authority. A comparison of two Mexican communities finds that the one where marital conflicts were settled in courts had experienced rapid population growth through migration, thus increasing heterogeneity. The family of origin's ability to an influence their married children was weakened by the fact that their share of an inheritance had already been distributed at the time of marriage and married children formed their own households. In the other community, conflicts between spouses and censuring of their actions were usually mediated by senior family members and rarely in the town courts. It was smaller, with a more stable population, inheritance began at marriage and continued intermittently until the death of the parents, and the majority of couples lived near, if not within, the house of the husband's father (Nader and Metzger, 1963: 589–91).

Black (1976, 1993) seeks to articulate the relationship between legal and nonlegal social control without reference to individual motivations, values, intentions or perceptions. He defines law as governmental social control, or 'the normative life of a state and its citizens, such as legislation, litigation and adjudication' (Black, 1976: 2; 1993: 3) and formulates propositions that seek to explain the quantity and style of law in every setting. According to Black, many societies have been anarchic (that is, without law), which does not mean that they were disorganized or lacked social control, but that the type of social control was not 'legal'.

His central proposition is that 'law varies inversely with other social control' (Black, 1976: 107); law is stronger where other forms of social control, including etiquette, custom, ethics, bureaucracy and medicine, are weaker. Where other types of social control operate, recourse to law is unlikely; indeed, legal sanctions often do not exist. Law also varies inversely with stratification, morphology (the division of labour and social interaction), culture and organization. According to Black, the amount of law is quantifiable, for example:

> A complaint to a legal official ... is more law than no complaint, whether it is a call to the police, a visit to a regulatory agency, or a lawsuit. ... In criminal matters, an arrest is more law than no arrest, and so is a search or an interrogation. An indictment is more law than none, as is a prosecution, and a serious charge is more than a minor charge. (Black, 1976: 3)

The style of law – namely penal, compensatory, therapeutic or conciliatory – also varies; each style has its own way of defining deviant behaviour, each responds in its own way and has its own language and logic. Regarding the fundamental proposition, the question emerges: why do some situations have more law than others? The only response is that they have relatively less nonlegal social control, a tautology that explains nothing. Black avoids formulating any causal relationships and only asserts connections between variables (Greenberg, 1983: 338–48; Sciulli, 1995: 823–8). The theory conflates correlation with causation, rendering it 'nothing more and nothing less than the attempt to systematize "commonsense"' (Hunt, 1983: 20).

Empirical assessment of Black's propositions is mixed. Generally, research regarding victims' and others' mobilization of law is not supportive (Doyle and Luckenbill, 1991; Gottfredson and Hindelang, 1979b; Lessan and Sheley, 1992; Mooney, 1986). A study of the mobilization of officials in dealing with various neighbourhood problems (including crime) found a weak or insignificant relationship between the quantity of law and stratification, morphology, culture and organization (Doyle and Luckenbill, 1991: 112). Alternative forms of social control and dispute resolution – talking with the person involved or getting together with neighbours – are positively not inversely related to the mobilization of law. Instead, the seriousness of an offence is an important dimension affecting a victim's decision to inform the police and thereby to invoke a legal response. An adequate theory of the behaviour of criminal law must incorporate a proposition stating that the quantity of criminal law varies directly with the seriousness of the infraction as indicated by harm to the victim, which involves a subjective assessment, but this is explicitly excluded by Black's framework, which does not consider individuals' motivation or conduct (Gottfredson and Hindelang, 1979a: 16–17). In support of Black's propositions, Kruttschnitt indicates that for most of the offences she examined involving female defendants, the legal system exerts less control over women who rely on others for day-to-day existence compared with those who are financially independent. Economic dependence entails a concomitant quantity of social control that is inversely related to the probability of more severe penal sanctions for women offenders (1982: 497–8). Nevertheless, it is not clear the extent to which Black's propositions are gender specific, and he certainly would not claim that they are.

In contemporary societies, law as social control is often equated with the criminal justice system and the management of crime. 'Law and order' campaigns initiated by governments, the mass media, interest groups or concerned citizens advocate more criminal law with tougher sanctions. They also seek increased police numbers and resources to enable the identification of crime and surveillance of potential offenders, especially in 'hot-spot' locations, for example parks, shopping malls and central business districts after shopping hours, where it is feared that crime is most likely to occur. This crime-control model is based on the premise that the control of criminal activities via the punishment of offenders is the most important function of the criminal justice system. It assumes that officials in the criminal justice process make decisions based on their investigations and the evidence amassed; those who are not guilty will be screened out of the system, those who are at fault will be moved on to the next stage (Packer, 1969: 158–63). Others concerned with the rights of people coming into contact with the criminal justice system will focus on due process. Here, the preoccupation is with procedure, rather than with the question of whether a person actually engaged in the conduct that is charged as the offence. Given that police and other criminal justice officials have enormous power, ultimately to subject citizens to criminal punishment, their actions need to be clearly specified, curtailed and controlled by law. To accommodate doubts about the accuracy and impartiality of police investigations, procedural safeguards for suspects and those arrested are put in place, especially regarding searches, the use of force, interrogations, the use of weapons and the right to legal advice. This is an attempt to address the power imbalance between the person accused of a crime and the official accusers, and to assure that the agents of social control act within their legally defined powers (Packer, 1969: 163–6).

The criminal justice system

The police are the primary gatekeepers of the criminal justice system. Their role is to investigate crime and, in some jurisdictions, to prosecute criminal cases. Police deal with most so-called ordinary or common crimes, including driving offences, theft, drug offences, assault, robbery, homicide and rape. Most police work is reactive rather than proactive, with police relying heavily on citizens to initiate complaints and to report suspected crime (Black, 1970: 735). Other statutory agencies will investigate and often prosecute such corporate crimes as tax fraud and securities violations, as well as organized crime, including drug importation and trafficking, corruption and money laundering. These agencies tend to be more proactive in their investigatory functions.

The criminal justice system comprises a number of crime-processing stages; the number of people receiving criminal sanctions is far fewer than the number coming into contact with the police. While each jurisdiction varies in the procedures adopted, Figure 6.1 provides a general overview of the kinds of processing stages involved.

At the outset, a suspected, alleged or actual crime is reported or becomes known to the police: they decide whether to ignore the complaint or initiate an investigation. An investigation may identify any suspected offender(s), whom the police may arrest and charge. If suspects are juveniles, they are ordinarily referred to the juvenile justice system. After charges are laid, a defendant appears before the first instance

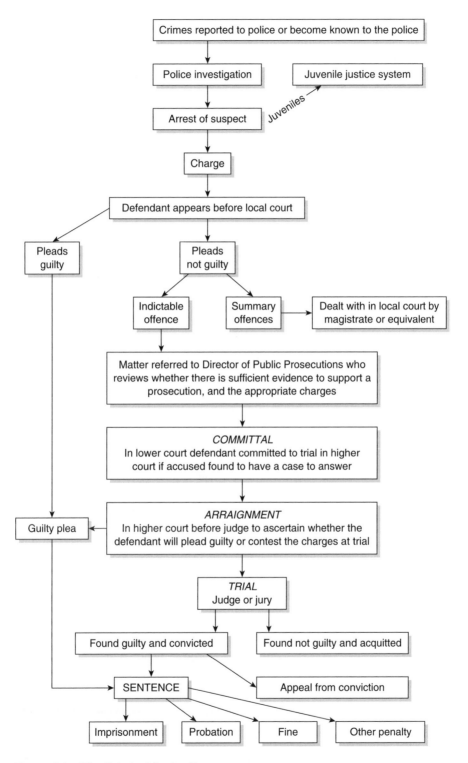

Figure 6.1   The Criminal Justice System

(local, magistrates or other lower) court where he or she enters a plea of guilty or not guilty. If the defendant pleads guilty, there is no trial and the defendant might be sentenced immediately or a date for sentencing will be fixed. A plea of not guilty to summary (less serious or minor) offences will be dealt with by the lower court, but if the offences are indictable (more serious or major) then these are typically referred on to the Director of Public Prosecutions (DPP). The next stage involves the committal (though not all jurisdictions have this stage), where in Australia a magistrate determines whether or not the accused has a case to answer; if so, then they will be arraigned in a higher court and required to decide whether to plead guilty or to contest the charges at trial, which might be by judge alone or by jury. At the conclusion of a trial, the accused is found guilty and sentenced or is found not guilty and acquitted.

The criminal trial

A criminal trial aims to determine whether someone charged with any offence(s) is guilty beyond a reasonable doubt. In common-law systems, the trial is an adversarial process where the prosecution and defence counsel will present their competing evidence, witnesses and arguments. Unlike civil-law legal systems, there is little scope for the judge to make independent inquiry or to test the evidence directly by interrogating witnesses or their lawyers. Less serious offences are usually tried in lower courts, sometimes called local or magistrates courts, by the judge alone. Such offences as murder, rape and armed robbery are normally tried by juries in higher courts, which means that the determination of guilt or otherwise is made by 12 members of the community. Recurrent debates focus on the capacity of jury members to assess legal argument and evidence impartially, especially where sophisticated expert evidence is tendered, and on the time involved in jury selection and deliberations (Mungham and Bankowski, 1976: 210–17). In jury trials, the role of the judge is adjudicatory: to ensure that the conduct of the case accords with the law and that any legal ambiguities are clarified for the jury. However, the judge sums up the trial for the jury by providing directions that can influence the jury's actual decision regarding the guilt or innocence of the accused person.

After trial, if the defendant is found guilty, the judge determines the sentence in light of any statutory guidelines, including mandatory sentences, or with regard to judicially established sentencing tariffs or guidelines. While the assessment of guilt, or otherwise, by a public trial is held out as the pinnacle of criminal justice systems derived from English legal institutions, it is in fact more unusual than usual. Most criminal defendants will plead guilty and there will be no trial. In the USA, around nine out of ten felony convictions are obtained through guilty pleas rather than by trial (Padgett, 1985: 753). In England, around 90 per cent of cases in the magistrates' courts and more than 60 per cent of cases in the crown court do not go to trial because a guilty plea has been entered (Zander, 1989: 188). The same pattern exists in Australia (Mack and Roach Anleu, 1995: 4). This discrepancy between the institutional framework emphasizing jury trials and the conditions under which most defendants plead guilty, especially if they initially plead not guilty but change their plea just before their trial, is a topic of widespread research and commentary.

Some defendants will plead guilty immediately because they recognize and accept their guilt, are remorseful, cannot afford a lawyer or are denied legal aid, or they fear the experience and uncertainties of a trial. Others will plead guilty – often to reduced or different charges – after their lawyer and the prosecution have held 'out-of-court' discussions regarding the facts of the case, the charges to be laid and the likelihood that the defendant will be found guilty. In this sense, the guilty plea results from negotiation, which in some jurisdictions is the outcome of explicit exchanges or informal bargaining between legal personnel. Plea bargaining has been defined as occurring where 'the defendant relinquishes his [*sic*] right to go to trial in exchange for a reduction in charge and/or sentence' (Heumann, 1975: 515) or, more vehemently, as consisting 'of the exchange of official concessions for the act of self-conviction' (Alschuler, 1979: 213). The defendant will expect some benefit to accrue from entering a guilty plea and not contesting the charges at trial, and the articulation of those benefits may come after discussions between defence and prosecution counsel, or even in some US jurisdictions with the sentencing judge. In such an informal process there are no guarantees or legally binding promises: agreements with the prosecution do not necessarily reduce sentences and, even if the judge is involved, he or she is not legally obliged to comply with any out-of-court agreement. Thus the defendant must weigh up competing risks: the risk of contesting the charges, being convicted and sentenced versus relinquishing the chance of an acquittal, but increasing the chance of a lesser penalty because the prosecution agrees to reduce or alter the original charges. In addition to cost and time considerations and the desire to reduce uncertainty, many defendants would not plead guilty unless they believe that they have a good chance of receiving a lighter sentence, and it does seem that defendants often perceive that going to trial is punished by harsher sentences (Brereton and Casper, 1981: 64–5).

Plea bargaining and negotiations are the subject of enormous academic controversy, research and policy debate, with considerable ambiguity about what is being discussed. The term plea bargaining conjures up images that critics view as antithetical to the justice system. On the one side, there are concerns that the defendant is enticed, or coerced, by their lawyer into pleading guilty, thus deviating from a central legal principle that guilty pleas must be free and voluntary (Alschuler, 1975: 1313). The incentives offered combined with the uncertainties of a trial create unacceptable inducements for innocent defendants to plead guilty. Defendants with few financial or cultural resources may be subject to stronger coercion, thereby reproducing social inequalities. Schulhofer suggests that the conscription of unwilling lawyers, low remuneration and heavy caseloads within public defender or legal aid offices place lawyers for the indigent under powerful pressure to resolve cases quickly without going to trial, whether or not such a disposition is in the best interests of their clients (Schulhofer, 1984: 138). Other critics maintain that guilty individuals avoid appropriate punishment because they are able to strike a deal with the prosecution or the sentencing judge, leaving the victims of crime and law-and-order advocates cynical about the justice process. They presume that any sentence will be more lenient than one following a trial and the fact that discussions are informally conducted in private jeopardizes wider public interest and accountability (McCoy, 1993: xiv–xv, 67, 190–1).

Four principal types of plea bargain or exchange are identifiable (Padgett, 1985: 75–8):

1 *Implicit plea bargaining*, where the defendant pleads guilty to the original charge and expects a sentence discount for not taking up the court's time. There is no actual bargaining or negotiation, but defendants perceive that they will be better off if they plead guilty (Friedman, 1979: 253; Heumann, 1975: 52–7). Defendants plead guilty both because they anticipate a lower sentence and because trial outcomes can be unpredictable and involve a greater risk of high or even maximum statutory penalties (Padgett, 1985: 761). In some jurisdictions the existence of sentence discounts is formalized in appellate judgements or by statute and thus these are not the creation of individual sentencing judges (Zdenkowski, 1994: 171–3).
2 *Charge reduction,* where the prosecutor reduces the number or alters the type of charges to which a defendant agrees to plead guilty. It is assumed that reduced charges will translate into a reduced penalty.
3 *Sentence recommendation* involves the prosecution recommending a particular disposition to the judge, who usually imposes the recommended sentence following the plea of guilty.
4 *Judicial plea bargaining* occurs where a judge, after consulting with the defence and prosecution lawyers, offers the defendant a specific sentence if he or she agrees to plead guilty. Such consultations can occur informally in the judge's chambers or formally, for example in the Sentence Indication Schemes trialed in some jurisdictions (Zdenkowski, 1994: 175–6).

At least some of these practices appear to be commonplace, even though the inevitability or necessity of plea bargaining is often questioned (Schulhofer, 1985: 570–91). In the USA, plea bargaining emerged as a significant practice after the Civil War, thereby reversing the common law's discouragement of confessions and guilty pleas. Only 15 per cent of all felony convictions in Manhattan and Brooklyn were by guilty plea in 1839; in 1926 this figure had increased to 90 per cent, where it has remained, more or less (Alschuler, 1979: 223). By the end of the nineteenth century, plea bargaining had become the dominant way of resolving criminal cases, although it was only given US Supreme Court validity in 1970.

Until the late 1970s in England there was little interest in the subject of guilty plea negotiation, reflecting an assumption that the scope for plea bargaining had all but been eliminated, especially in the light of official and explicit condemnation (*R* v *Turner* 1970). Nevertheless, research into late guilty pleas and situations where defendants appeared to change their minds abruptly and decided to plead guilty reveals widespread informal plea negotiation, with most defendants experiencing pressures calculated to induce them to plead guilty (Baldwin and McConville, 1979: 27). Many of the 121 defendants interviewed in Birmingham said that in return for pleading guilty, their barrister had been able to obtain an undertaking from the judge or the prosecution and as a direct result an offer was made that they then accepted (Baldwin and McConville, 1977: 27). Such undertakings include explicit indications from the judge regarding the sentence. This contravenes case-law guidelines that permit the defence and prosecution counsel to discuss a case with the judge, who 'should never indicate the sentence which he [*sic*] is minded to impose. ... This could be taken to be undue pressure on the accused, thus depriving him [*sic*] of that complete freedom of choice which is essential' (*R* v *Turner* 1970: 327). Defendants often felt coerced into pleading guilty or were presented with no alternative by their barristers (Baldwin and McConville, 1977: 46–56; 1979: 296).

In Australia, informal discussions between defence and prosecution lawyers dealing with the charges to be laid and the facts of the case occur every day. The negotiations are informal, relying on the trust and reciprocity of participants, and rarely involve discussions with a judge in chambers (Mack and Roach Anleu, 1995: 17–42). While participants will often use the language of bargaining or striking a deal, there is a strong belief that there is no plea bargaining as is understood to exist in the USA. There is a perception that because the judge is not involved, and as defence lawyers always maintain that they are acting on their client's instructions, the potential for coercion and corruption is not common in Australia. Participants view these negotiations as a process of identifying the correct outcome and circumventing the need for a trial. They view the system as self-regulating, or self-correcting. There is a widespread belief that the police opt for more serious charges, not necessarily intentionally or out of *mala fides,* but because of a lack of legal training, police culture and ambit claims. Thus, discussions between defence and prosecution lawyers will correct the charges to be laid. They also suggest that, once a defendant has reached this point in the criminal justice system, they are guilty of something; the task of the prosecution and defence discussions is to identify exactly what offence this is (Mack and Roach Anleu, 1995: 44–9).

Why do plea discussions/bargains occur?

Much research is preoccupied with identifying the causes of plea discussions and specifying the conditions under which different forms of discussion prevail. Central themes include administrative capacity; substantive justice; the strength of the prosecution case; the organization of work and occupational relationships in the criminal justice system; and reducing uncertainty.

Administrative capacity Plea bargaining emerges in response to large caseloads that make it impossible for courts to deal with all cases. The most trenchant criticism of plea bargaining is that justice is being compromised or even substituted by organizational and managerial imperatives. Nevertheless, the relationship between caseloads and plea discussions is ambiguous (Nardulli, 1979: 89–91). Padgett (1990: 444) found that the massive criminal caseload during Prohibition in the USA increased federal plea bargaining in those districts with high caseload pressures. Judges responded by intensifying sentence discounting within a preexisting implicit plea-bargaining framework, rather than by altering the form of plea bargaining by becoming directly involved.

Meeker and Pontell (1985) note that a statutory change in California permitting less serious felonies to be dealt with in the lower courts suggests a relationship between caseloads and plea bargaining. The consequent reduction in superior court caseloads was accompanied by a change in rates and types of plea bargaining. The proportion of original or fast guilty pleas representing the least adversarial proceedings declined, while the proportion of changed or slow guilty pleas increased (Meeker and Pontell, 1985: 138). Even where there is a low caseload, trial rates are not necessarily increased and nor are plea discussions absent (Church, 1976: 399–400; Heumann, 1975: 524; Mack and Roach Anleu, 1995). Accordingly, some commentators would suggest that plea bargaining in some form is inevitable: the criminal justice system is self-regulating or 'hydraulic', with changes in one facet of it translating into unintended consequences in another. Policies to reduce discretion in one aspect of the criminal justice system will often create pressures for the exercise of discretion to achieve guilty pleas at another point. What varies is the type, the participants and the situations where negotiations will take place (Feeley, 1979: 204).

Attempts to eradicate plea bargaining may increase court caseloads and place pressure on the judiciary to participate in negotiations, both to ease the caseload burden and to provide a more appropriate outcome for the defendant. A strict prosecutorial policy in a Midwest US community forbidding charge reduction plea bargaining in drug-sale cases increased contested trials and the backlog of criminal cases. Many judges responded by encouraging pleas through personal participation in sentence-bargaining procedures. They did this via a pre-plea sentence commitment regarding a hypothetical situation, rather than an explicit granting of a sentence in the individual circumstances, thus retaining the fiction that judges were not part of explicit plea bargains in those cases in which the prosecutor's policy did not allow charge reductions following plea negotiations (Church, 1976: 386–7). It appears that when a prosecutor cannot make concessions and the judge will not, then defendants are less likely to plead guilty (Church, 1976: 399). Similarly, in the Texas district courts, a 1975 prosecutorial ban on explicit plea bargaining in felony cases caused an immediate increase in the level of jury trials and a gradual decline in the disposition rate. Although most felony cases still involved guilty pleas, the ban affected the courts' ability to move the felony docket efficiently, suggesting that explicit prosecutorial plea bargaining helps the administration of justice (Holmes et al., 1992: 1534). In Michigan, a prosecutorial prohibition on plea bargaining in cases where the law warranted a mandatory sentence, namely an additional two-year prison term if the defendant possessed a firearm while committing a felony, did not alter sentencing patterns significantly. In many serious cases, judges reduced the sentence for the primary offence to accommodate the additional two-year mandatory penalty. Following the bans on plea bargaining, sentence bargaining became common and replaced charge bargaining (Heumann and Loftin, 1979: 416–25). In contrast, the 1975 Alaska ban on charge and sentence negotiations in all crimes seems to have reduced explicit plea bargaining substantially without increasing implicit bargaining or the number of contested trials (Rubinstein and White, 1979: 369–74).

McCoy demonstrates how a 1982 Californian law restricting plea bargaining in serious felony cases actually shifted bargaining to the lower courts but did not ban it (1993: 37–8). Legislators presented this legislation – the *Victims' Bill of Rights* – to the public as a ban on plea bargaining, which would thereby incorporate victims' interests and concerns, given that a major criticism of plea bargaining is the exclusion of victims from the criminal justice process. Nonetheless, the bulk of the bill did not relate to victim participation and dealt with the right to be assured safe schools, the use of evidence that had previously been excluded for constitutional reasons and changes in the substantive rules of sentencing (McCoy, 1993: 28–9). The legislation contained major loopholes, including exceptions to the prohibition, which allowed plea bargaining to persist. It only limited plea bargaining in the superior court, leaving it unrestricted in the municipal court where almost every felony initially appeared and which became the primary forum for plea bargaining in serious cases. This loophole allowed court professionals to continue plea bargaining despite the restrictions. Consequently, more serious felony cases were concluded through guilty pleas prior to proper investigation or full evidentiary review and, paradoxically, by encouraging guilty pleas at earlier stages of the prosecution process, the new law actually strengthened rather than eliminated plea bargaining (McCoy, 1993: 37–8, 79–82, 178–84).

The increasing length of trials and complex rules of evidence also expand the volume of court work (Padgett, 1985: 762). Before the middle of the eighteenth century, the jury trial was a summary proceeding and it seems that between 12 and 20 felony cases could be tried every day. Trials were expeditious because neither prosecution nor defence were represented by lawyers in ordinary criminal trials, the defendant had fewer legal rights or privileges, the common law of evidence was virtually nonexistent, and there were few appeals (Langbein, 1979: 262–5). Now, criminal trials can take several days or even months, especially in corporate crime cases (Aronson, 1992).

Substantive justice

Plea discussions attempt to achieve the correct outcome as defence and prosecution lawyers, unfettered by formal court procedures, are able to discuss issues freely. One aim is to substitute flexible sentencing standards that remain sensitive to the individual defendant (in terms of background and perceived criminality), for the harsher provisions of criminal codes, especially for offences where there are mandatory penalties or narrow sentencing guidelines that restrict judicial discretion. Legal practitioners will often justify their participation in plea negotiation as enabling the best and fairest outcome for everyone. Discussions facilitate the identification of the correct or appropriate offence; the defendant avoids a trial; the victim will not have to provide oral evidence or be subject to cross-examination; and the court time is saved (Mack, 1995: 42–9; Mulcahy, 1994: 421–3).

Negotiated pleas provide a degree of certainty that is absent in cases that go to trial. From the point of view of the defendant, the greatest uncertainty (perhaps even greater than conviction) relates to the type of penalty. While in most types of plea negotiation there is no guarantee of actual sentence, it is expected that a change or reduction in the original charges will result in a lesser penalty. For the prosecutor, uncertainty arises especially where there is a reliance on oral testimony and questions about how the witnesses will perform, particularly under cross-examination, or even about whether they will appear (Mulcahy, 1994: 420).

Strength of the prosecution case   Plea discussions and negotiations are mechanisms whereby the prosecution can secure at least some punishment where it considers that the defendant is factually guilty but conviction is unlikely, perhaps because of evidentiary problems. Concessions that prosecutors are willing to entertain for a guilty plea will depend on their estimate of the probability of conviction at trial. The influence of evidentiary considerations on the prosecutor's decisions varies by the type of offence and seems to be more important for property crimes. Prosecutors will selectively use their discretion to offer better plea concessions when the evidence is weaker (Adams, 1983: 536; Finkelstein, 1975: 309). Some participants in the criminal justice system argue that by this stage the accused person must be guilty of something, as prior filters – the investigatory process and the decision to arrest and charge someone – would have directed her or him away from the criminal justice process earlier (Mack and Roach Anleu, 1995: 44–8).

Organizational relationships   Organizational relationships and norms are shared by frequent users of the courts, especially such professional personnel as police officers and lawyers. At trial the defence and prosecution lawyers will represent opposing sides, yet they will regularly interact and work with each other on a daily basis. They are 'repeat players', unlike the defendant who is usually a 'one-shotter' (Galanter, 1974). They will get to know one another, work out exchange relationships and rely on each other for the performance of their own tasks. The defendant becomes a secondary figure in the court system, which is a complex organization whose task is to coordinate the activities of a variety of actors who are both competitive and interdependent (Blumberg, 1967: 19–24; Cole, 1970; Farr, 1984: 295). Over the course of their interaction and repeated bargaining discussions, prosecutors and public defenders (defence attorneys provided by the state) will develop a set of unstated recipes for reducing original charges to lesser offences in exchange for a guilty plea (Sudnow, 1965: 262). Emergent local legal work cultures may emphasize plea negotiation, regardless of the probability that most defendants do not want a trial (Lynch, 1994: 118–25). An examination of local legal culture – defined as the practitioner norms governing case handling and participant behaviour in a criminal court – in four courts found that two emerged as plea-bargain oriented and two trial oriented (Church, 1985: 506). However, in every court and across all cases, defence lawyers tended to view negotiation as appropriate, while prosecutors supported nonnegotiated dispositions. Not surprisingly, only where the prosecution case is weak did the prosecutor seek a plea bargain more readily than did the defence. Such organizational reforms as pre-trial conferences will create opportunities and incentives for agreements to be reached between defence and prosecution counsel (McConville and Mirsky, 1993: 181).

Some researchers suggest that the rise of specialization, professionalism and managerialism on the part of occupational groups participating in the criminal justice system increase the likelihood of negotiated agreements about pleas. Improved police investigation and the emergence of forensic science can enhance the quality of evidence making it less contestable; the involvement of legally trained prosecutors who are independent from the police enables the earlier identification of legal issues and sources of disagreement, thus circumventing the need for a trial to reach adjudication on the facts of a case (Feeley, 1979: 201). Padgett argues that judges' professional stakes were central in understanding the development of implicit plea bargaining during Prohibition, while enabling them to chastise lower courts that used more explicit plea bargaining (Padgett, 1990: 444–9). Implicit plea bargaining emerged as a result of elite lawyers' struggle to professionalize the courts, as it was judges from elite law schools who pioneered the federal courts' development of implicit plea bargaining. The employment of court administrators also increases the emphasis on calendar administration and case-flow management (Brown, 1994: 702–3).

McConville and Mirsky (1995) question that the increasing reliance on guilty pleas during the nineteenth century stems from more professional police and lawyers. Their data from New York City's Court of General Sessions, the major criminal court at the time, suggest that changes within the wider political economy provide a more adequate explanation than focusing on the criminal justice system as a self-regulating independent organization. First, they identify the politicization of crime as central: by mid-century, public policy emphasized confining the 'dangerous' classes, who were identified as outsiders and immigrants, by maximizing the rate of conviction through a reliance on guilty pleas to lesser offences. Second, the rise in the importance of the District Attorney's (DA's) office, as distinct from private prosecutions, increased the rate of guilty pleas. The DA and some judges became elected officials and openly aligned with the political interests of the state. Third, the reorganization of the police meant that law-enforcement officers rather than individual complainants or victims became identified with the case for the prosecution; and finally, juries became more marginal, as a result of the abolition of property qualifications for jury service, and less willing to convict defendants of the most serious offence (McConville and Mirsky, 1995: 460–4).

Sentence discounts   Many jurisdictions provide for courts to take into account the timing of guilty pleas when exercising their sentencing discretion to reduce the amount of the sentence. The general principle is that earlier pleas attract greater discounts, though the extent to which judges may or must take into account the guilty plea varies. For example, the New South Wales Crimes (Sentencing Procedure) Act 1992 provides that the court must take into account the timing of the guilty plea and 'may accordingly impose a lesser penalty than it would otherwise have imposed' (§22(b)). England, Wales, Scotland and New Zealand have similar legislation.

Guidelines regarding sentence discounts tend to be suggestive rather than prescriptive and binding and there is considerable academic and judicial discussion on the efficacy of sentence discounts and their effects on the production of guilty pleas, the rights of defendants, the voluntariness of the plea and on sentencing practice (Mack and Roach Anleu, 1997; McConville, 1998; *Cameron v R. 2002; R. v Thomson, R. v Houlton 2000*). An investigation of the English Crown Court finds that only half (53 per cent) of the 310 judges in the study explicitly articulated that they were giving the defendant a sentence discount in recognition of the guilty plea and only one third of these judges explained that it was the timing of the plea that had brought about the benefit (Henham, 2002: 378–9). Nonetheless, advice about a sentence discount is perhaps the most direct or active strategy a judge can adopt to increase the likelihood of an early guilty plea. This judicial offer of a lesser sentence in exchange for a prompt plea of guilty has been characterized as 'a plea bargain in its crudest form' (Mack and Roach Anleu, 1997).

Sentencing

When a person pleads guilty or is found guilty by a jury or single judge, then he or she is sentenced. Usually, legislation establishes the maximum penalties for specific offences and, within those maxima, the sentencing judge decides on the specific criminal sanction. The aims of criminal sanctions, their availability and the amount of discretion that the sentencing judge has in determining the sentence are topics of widespread discussion and research (Ashworth, 1992a: 311–28; Australian Law Reform Commission, 2005: 93–106; Tata and Hutton, 2002).

The formal goal of the criminal justice system is crime control and prevention through deterrence, rehabilitation, incapacitation, punishment and, most recently, reintegration and restoration. These values are not necessarily compatible and criminal justice officials and policy makers emphasize some of them over others, depending on prevailing concerns about the existence of crime, the philosophical and moral bases of punishment and predominant theories about the causes of crime. The extent to which criminal sanctions focus, or should focus, on the offence and its legal seriousness or on the offender and her/his specific needs and welfare is a recurring theme. This also translates into a tension between the rule of law (or formal rationality), where all offence types are dealt with in the same way, versus flexibility (substantive rationality), where accommodations are made for the particular characteristics or circumstances of an offender (Ashworth, 1992a: 55–69). The following sections address the various philosophical goals or justifications underlying different sentencing options.

Deterrence   This refers to individual and collective sanctions that seek to alter behaviour, on the basis that the individual or others in the society should be prevented from committing subsequent criminal acts. The individual learns by the unpleasant experience of the criminal sanction; others in society learn by the publicized example of penalties that have been administered. Advocates of deterrence would argue that sanctions, or the threat of them, must be sufficiently burdensome or painful to prevent future law violation, either by the individual convicted or potential offenders in the general population. The assumption is that actors are rational and that before contemplating criminal activities they will assess the associated risks. However, crime is often impulsive, unplanned and hedonistic rather than following on from an assessment of the relative costs and benefits (Cohen, 1955; Katz, 1988). There is little conclusive evidence of the 'success' of deterrence in reducing crime; however, sanctions are more likely to have a deterrent effect under certain kinds of conditions. Where commitment to crime is low and the act is instrumental such as occasional shoplifting, white-collar crime or traffic law violations, both general and specific deterrence are effective. Conversely, where a high commitment to crime as a way of life exists, for example with drug addiction, or where the act is expressive, such as homicide, the threat of punishment, including capital punishment, seems to have little deterrent effect (Chambliss, 1967: 713).

Rehabilitation   Like deterrence, rehabilitation is oriented towards modifying future actions by changing the behaviour, attitudes or character of the convicted offender with the aim of reducing the probability of reoffending. The idea is to treat or reform the convicted offender via retraining, counselling and learning programmes rather than to sanction him or her for having committed the particular offences. Within the rehabilitative ideal, the notion of individualized sentences is important; the sentencing court will have a wide latitude to select the sanctions and thereby tailor the sentence to the individual's needs rather than only punishing the offender for breaking the law. By the 1960s, courts had increasingly come to consider the offender as an individual whose needs, rather than guilt, would form the basis of the sentence passed (Thomas, 1970: 3). The sentencing judge specifies the maximum prison sentence and a parole board has a wide discretion to determine the actual release date. During the parole period, a parole (or probation) officer determines the actual measure of counselling or guidance required. This orientation created scope for social workers, psychologists, educationalists, probation officers and counsellors to make recommendations to the sentencing judge about the sentence that would most suit the assessed needs of the offender. The rehabilitative ideal was an important rationale for the separation of juveniles from adult justice systems and has been most developed in the latter (Roach Anleu, 2006: 321–3).

Until the 1970s, rehabilitation was a dominant concept in sentencing ideology, but became less popular because rehabilitation programmes in prisons generally did not reduce reoffending and individualized sentences are seen as unfair, often resulting in unjustified inconsistencies in penalty (Ashworth, 1992b: 184–92; Brody, 1976: 37; Martinson, 1974: 25). The decisions of parole boards can be unpredictable and uncertain, thereby creating considerable anxiety on the part of prisoners regarding their actual release dates. A sentence is indeterminate; at the point of sentencing, neither the court nor the convicted offender will know the actual length of the prison term. A prisoner will become eligible for parole after about one-third of the sentence, but there will be no guarantee of release. The parole board's decision takes into account prison reports, parole officers' and perhaps psychiatrists' or social workers' assessments and recommendations. These reports may have little bearing on the particular offence, but will be more concerned with the offender's employment opportunities, family life, attitudes and potential for reform. Release on parole is conditional and imprisonment can be reactivated if the parolee reoffends, violates one of the conditions of the parole agreement or ignores a parole officer's requests. Decision making becomes divided among psychiatric or psychological experts, social workers and correctional services officers, thereby extending punitive powers beyond the court. In many jurisdictions, the role of parole boards has been curtailed in an attempt to make sentencing more determinate and to reduce prison populations.

Incapacitation   This refers to punishments that aim to protect the community by making convicted offenders incapable of offending for substantial periods of time. Imprisonment, disqualification, some forms of torture and capital punishment are examples of sanctions that incapacitate in some way. 'Protective' sentencing is often deemed appropriate for dangerous offenders, persistent career criminals and the perpetrators of sexual and violent offences. The main problems with this approach include difficulties in defining dangerousness, which often becomes blurred with the seriousness of the offence committed, and in reliably predicting future behaviour; those making predictions are more likely to be incorrect than accurate in their assessments (Cocozza and Steadman, 1978: 339–40; Nash, 1992).

Punishment   This focuses on past activities: the punishment is for the offence committed. There is also a notion that any punishment should be proportional to the seriousness of the offence. If someone makes a 'rational choice' to engage in criminal offending, then she or he deserves punishment; moreover, the punishment should 'fit the crime', that is, it should reflect the amount of criminality and the resulting harm. Beccaria, an early proponent of the 'just deserts' model of justice, maintains that a penalty must be commensurate with the crime and formal sanctions must be proportional to the extent of damage that the law-breaking activities have caused (Monachesi, 1960: 43). Punishments should be carefully graded to correspond with the gravity of the offences. If sanctions contain other aims, such as reformation or general deterrence, then the individual's rights are encroached, signifying injustice and an abuse of power.

In the latter part of the twentieth century there was renewed support for this model of corrections (von Hirsch, 1976: 66–76). The American Friends, a Quaker organization, maintain that justice and equity require that punishments are deserved and that they correspond with the gravity of the offences. They support sentencing standards that specify the penalties attached to different crimes. The central idea of the 'back to justice' movement is that punishment constitutes a 'just desert'. Andrew von Hirsch argues that the principle of commensurate deserts is a requirement of justice and any social benefits of punishment, for example general deterrence or rehabilitation, do not justify depriving convicted offenders of their rights. Punishment must be deserved and the principle that penalties should be proportionate in their severity to the gravity of the defendant's criminal conduct is a fundamental requirement of fairness (von Hirsch, 1976: 69–70). Policy makers have adopted this 'just deserts' model in many jurisdictions and have attempted to institutionalize proportionate sentencing via sentencing commissions and guidelines.

Restoration and reparation   A significant development in criminal justice systems since the late 1980s is the increasing recognition of the rights and needs of victims of crime. This is part of a wider movement within criminal justice ideology and policy to incorporate the community into the prevention and management of crime (Lacey and Zedner, 1995: 302). Legislative reforms seek to incorporate victims in the formal criminal justice process, as well as establish new noncourt and often community-based forums for the processing of crimes. An aim of such developments is to reintegrate the offender into the community and to provide an opportunity for offender/victim mediation and some form of restitution. Braithwaite develops a model of reintegrative shaming where expressions of disapproval, ranging from a subtle informal reprimand to a judicial or other official pronouncement, are followed by gestures of reacceptance into the community (1989: 55–9; Braithwaite and Petit, 1994: 767–8). The aim of shaming is not isolation or stigmatization – which may lead to a rejection of social norms, further offending and the development of criminal subcultures – but social disapproval – by victims, family members, or members of a specific community – which seeks to induce guilt and remorse while simultaneously reinforcing membership of a collectivity and the value of conformity.

Traditionally, victims will have a minimal role in the criminal justice process. Prosecutors are not obliged to consult with victims when filing charges or preparing cases. Where a defendant pleads guilty there is no trial, victims are not called as witnesses and do not have the opportunity to present their point of view, and sentencing courts are not automatically made aware of the harm caused by a particular crime. Among the concerns expressed by victims are a lack of information regarding 'their' crime, a desire for restitution from the perpetrator or compensation from the state, the ability to confront offenders to make them aware of the consequences of their actions for the victim(s) and their families/communities, an opportunity for offenders to apologize and for victims to have some input into the outcome of the case. Legislation recognizing victims' concerns modifies the traditional view that crimes are against the state; there is now a re-emphasis on crime as offences against victims who have specific interests and needs that may diverge from those of the state as represented by the prosecuting authority.

The United Nations' *Declaration of Basic Principles of Justice for Victims of Crime and Abuse of Power* provides that:

> The responsiveness of judicial and administrative processes to the needs of victims should be facilitated by: (a) Informing victims of their role and the scope, timing and progress of the proceedings and of the disposition of their cases, especially where serious crimes are involved and where they have requested such information; (b) Allowing the views and concerns of victims to be presented and considered at appropriate stages of the proceedings where their personal interests are affected, without prejudice to the accused and consistent with the relevant national criminal justice system. (www2.ohchr.org/English/law/pdf/victims)

A number of jurisdictions have institutionalized victim-impact statements, which inform sentencing courts of the impact of the crime on the victim, and some require the sentencing judge to take into account the victim's views about the appropriate sentence (Ashworth, 1993: 499–501).

At a general level, restorative justice (RJ) seeks to reintegrate an offender (i.e. someone who has pleaded guilty to criminal charges) within the community and restore relationships between crime victims, offenders and others affected by the criminal offending (Daly and Immarigeon, 1998). Concepts of restorative justice are subject to considerable attention from law reformers, criminal justice administrators, criminologists and policy analysts (McEvoy et al., 2002). It is allied with John Braithwaite's (1989) theoretical elaboration of 'reintegrative shaming' which allows for social control without stigmatizing or ostracizing the offender from the community. Disapproval and shame are followed by reintegration rather than punishment and isolation. Practical reforms in criminal justice which seek to incorporate RJ principles include diversionary conferences, mostly established in juvenile justice, which will divert young people from prosecution and court adjudication. While there is considerable variation in the organization, the personnel involved, and the statutory framework, the general expectation is that when the young offender confronts the victim and learns of the harm caused by the criminal behaviour then he/she will experience remorse, shame and empathy which is also educative. The conference provides the opportunity to apologize, compensate the victim or repair any damage, and ultimately the young person will desist from further criminal offending (Daly and Hayes, 2002; Roach Anleu, 2006: 310–12).

Reforms that address some of the concerns of victims by institutionalizing victim/offender mediation are most developed in juvenile justice systems. In New Zealand, the Children, Young Persons and Their Families Act 1989 established Family Group Conferences (FGCs), the first of their kind, which allow for the integration of western and indigenous approaches to juvenile offending, the involvement of families in decision-making processes, victim/offender mediation and victims' participation in negotiations over possible penalties. An evaluation of this innovation finds that the goal of diverting young people from both courts and institutions has been achieved, and most juveniles will agree to perform tasks that appear to make them accountable for their actions. Some research suggests that the scheme has not succeeded in engaging young people in decision-making processes; only around a half of the FGCs in the study had victims or victims' representatives present and around one-third of young offenders said that they felt worse as a result of their involvement. Victims also felt inadequately prepared regarding what to expect from the FGCs (Morris and Maxwell, 1993: 84–9).

The extent to which RJ achieves a range of goals including diversion from court, reducing the likelihood and severity of subsequent offending, victim satisfaction, perceptions of procedural justice and cost is the subject of evaluation research (Daly and Hayes, 2002). A recent evaluation of three restorative justice schemes for adult offenders in England, some convicted of very serious offences, finds evidence that those offenders who participated in the RJ scheme committed significantly fewer offences subsequently. Interestingly, demographic variables – age, ethnicity, gender – and offence type did not affect the findings (Shapland et al., 2008: iii). Where offenders perceived the conference as useful, realized the harm done following their offending behaviour and their active involvement in the conference all these decreased the likelihood of reconviction (Shapland et al., 2008: iv).

Critics of victims' direct involvement in the criminal process (often legal scholars and professionals) argue that it will inject a level of subjectivity and punitiveness unwarranted by the type of offence. It may also increase sentencing disparity because, depending on the impact on the victim and their perceptions of their losses, those convicted of the same offence may receive very different penalties (Ashworth, 1993: 506). This is a counter-trend to the movement for greater sentencing consistency, as victim-impact statements (potentially) will be significant only where the sentencing judge has wide discretion.

Research suggests that the involvement of victims has not had some of the feared effects regarding increased sentences. An evaluation of the South Australian scheme finds that victim-impact statements rarely include inflammatory, exaggerated, prejudicial or other objectionable statements; only defence counsel (not prosecutors or judges) express concern about the accuracy of victim input regarding psychological and mental harm, yet they were not prepared to cross-examine the victim for fear that this would have an adverse (from their viewpoint) effect on the jury/judge and, ultimately, the sentence; and victim-impact statements did not increase the severity of sentences. Overall, the legal professionals involved consider that victim-impact statements offer a symbolic recognition and voice to victims' needs and that victims view their involvement as relevant and essential for justice. While there is agreement about the importance of victim input into the sentencing decision, there is little consensus regarding its nature (Erez et al., 1994: 70–3). Some suggest that victim-impact statements have not significantly affected sentencing patterns because the legislation does not specify the weight to be accorded such a statement within the sentencing decision, thereby leaving it within judicial discretion, and judges remain unchanged in their method of determining sentences (Hinton, 1995: 85, 91–3).

An examination of 500 felony cases prosecuted in Ohio in the 1980s, where victims could submit an impact statement, indicates that many are neither vengeful nor punitive. Filing a victim-impact statement has some effect on determining whether the sentence will be probation or incarceration, although offence and offender characteristics are primary factors and victims' requests for a particular sentence do not affect the actual penalty. The victims who do exercise their participatory rights are those whose victimization is personal and involves a high degree of suffering and pain. The victim-participation variable that did affect prison-sentence length was the presence of the victim in the court, thus providing a reminder of the severity of the crime and the pain incurred (Erez and Tontodonato, 1990: 467–70).

While policy makers assume that involving victims will increase an offender's reintegration, accountability and sense of responsibility, this may depend on the nature of the crime and the relationship between the victim and the offender. The Community Protection Act passed in 1989 in Washington state is an effort to control sexual violence by increasing penalties, requiring offenders on release from imprisonment to register with the police, and allowing civil actions that may result in the preventive detention of those deemed as sexually violent predators. Victim-advocacy groups played a prominent role in the formulation and passage of this act, but rather than advocating reintegrative measures, they were instead primarily concerned with prevention and punishment, and policy makers responded more to their punitive impulses (Scheingold et al., 1994: 729–31). Commentators on this reform suggest that it is unrealistic to expect victims and their supporters to pioneer the movement towards reintegrative shaming, because of their perception that those who commit crimes of sexual violence are predators destined to reoffend and that the public fear generated by brutal and well-publicized incidents of sexual violence mitigates against reintegrative policies (Scheingold et al., 1994: 759). It is perhaps more reasonable to expect that victim participation may have a reintegrative effect in the juvenile justice context and where most of the offences are relatively nonserious.

Depending on the emphasis in criminal justice policies or judicial ideology, similar acts may incur very different legal sanctions. Since the 1970s, numerous investigations into sentencing and reform proposals have been conducted (Ashworth, 1992a; 1992b; Zdenkowski, 1994). Two central themes have emerged:

1 A concern that the punishment should fit the crime and the sanction should be clear and predictable. Much attention focuses on the role of the judge in determining sentences, with many critics decrying wide judicial discretion because it allows opportunities for judges to take into account irrelevant variables, especially class, race and gender, and to exercise their own prejudices. Given the wide scope of discretion, sentences can be uncertain, unpredictable and unequal, which many see as unfair and unjust.
2 The use of imprisonment as a last resort. There is a demand for increased sentencing options to allow a greater fit between the penalty and the crime for which someone is convicted. Imprisonment is an appropriate sanction for dangerous offenders and those convicted of serious crimes.

Sentencing and the role of the judge

Considerable literature documents widespread disparities in sentencing practice in relation to similar cases, and the general concern is that equity and fairness demand that the criminal justice system administer a similar punishment to similar cases. According to the Australian Law Reform Commission: 'Consistency in sentencing is fundamental to maintaining a just and equitable criminal justice system' (Australian Law Reform Commission, 2005: 111). Discrimination or unequal outcomes might be institutionalized, as members of minority groups are less likely to be able to afford good lawyers, more likely to be scrutinized in any law violation, more likely to be arrested, more likely to be on remand, more likely to be found guilty, and more likely to receive harsher treatments than other people (Chambliss, 1969: 86). Some analyses finding that minorities receive harsher penalties than nonminorities interpret this as evidence that sentencing processes reflect political oppression or discrimination. Others suggest that racial differentials in sentencing result from legal attributes correlated with race, particularly a prior record, the offence seriousness, the number of charges, the harm inflicted and weapon use (Dixon, 1995: 1158). A study of the sentences imposed on over 2000 black and white defendants in one of the largest US cities finds that black males did receive harsher sentences than their white counterparts, primarily due to the fact that they were charged with more serious offences and had more serious prior criminal records. Afro-American males are slightly more likely to be incarcerated than white males, who are more likely to receive probation. While the researchers found little evidence of direct racial discrimination, they did observe that those defendants unable to afford private legal counsel (more likely to be black defendants) received harsher penalties (Spohn et al., 1981). Similarly, research on sentencing in Leeds magistrates' courts finds that Afro-Caribbean defendants in three subgroups – the 26–30 years age group, females, and those charged with theft – are more likely to receive custodial sentences than are their white counterparts. This variation in sentencing is explained by the defendant's criminal record. No difference was identified regarding noncustodial sentences, but more Afro-Caribbean than white defendants were committed for trial in a higher court (Brown and Hullin, 1992: 47–50). Judges may attempt to manage uncertainty by developing patterned responses that are the product of an attribution process involving assessments of the offender's likelihood of committing future crime. Racial stereotypes increase uncertainty in achieving a successful outcome, resulting in an increase in sanction severity. When judges attribute stable, enduring causes of crime to black offenders, the defendant's race affects the exercise of discretion. An attribution link between race, the disposition to commit future criminal behaviour and uncertainty can explain the observed race effect on sentence severity (Albonetti, 1991: 261). Such attributions are still forms of discrimination, albeit not necessarily direct or intentional.

Research on the links between gender and sentence severity yields a complex picture. Early analyses explained that women are less likely to receive harsh penalties than men as evidence of chivalry or paternalism, but noted that paternalism translates into more severe penalties for girls found guilty of status offences (Chesney-Lind, 1973, 1978). Some studies demonstrate that sentencing disparities are not informed by gender *per se,* but by economic relationships and family obligations. Sentencing disparities within offence categories can be predicted from the degree to which a woman is economically dependent on someone else; the greater the dependence, the less severe the criminal sanction (Kruttschnitt, 1982: 508–10). Daly shows that defendants' familial circumstances explain gender differences in court outcomes, with such differences being greatest for black defendants (Daly, 1989a: 151–2). She also suggests that protecting children and families characterizes the type of paternalism that judges might practise. Depending on the nature of the offence and the defendant's prior record, judges may rationalize family-based sentencing disparities for both men and women as necessary for keeping families together. They view the care of children as primary and economic support as secondary for maintaining families; it is the care of children that is critical, not the gender of the carer (Daly, 1989b: 27). Sentencing data from Pennsylvania also demonstrate that gender has a minor effect on the likelihood of imprisonment towards less frequent jailing of women. Quantitative and interview data identify sentencing judges as being primarily concerned about blameworthiness, indicated by prior record, type of involvement and remorse, and practicality, as indicated by childcare responsibility, pregnancy, emotional or physical problems and the availability of jail space. Where men and women appear in criminal court in similar circumstances regarding background and status, and charged with similar offences, they will receive similar criminal sanctions (Steffensmeier et al., 1993: 435–9).

The converse of the argument that marginalized groups fare badly in the criminal justice system is that elite offenders are able to avoid criminal punishment. Again, research findings are inconclusive and contradictory. An examination of securities violations in Canada suggests that employers located in positions of power that allow them to use organizational resources to commit white-collar crimes do not receive sanctions commensurate with these crimes, in large part because they are less likely than others to be charged under the criminal law and more likely to be charged under corporation laws that carry less stigma and sentence exposure. However, the prosecution of managers increased and they were more likely to be subjected to criminal proceedings and sanctions (Hagan and Parker, 1985: 312–13). A different analysis of the sentencing of white-collar offenders suggests that social class has a strong and significant influence on the length of the prison term imposed; employers and managers are punished more harshly, while employees, workers and the petty bourgeoisie receive relatively more lenient sanctions. This finding may be explained by judges viewing higher status as an indicator of greater culpability and responsibility (Weisburd et al., 1990: 234, 237). Other researchers have found that socio-economic status is not related to sanction severity or length (Benson and Walker, 1988: 299).

The discussion of sentencing disparities and calls for reform usually focus on the judge as decision maker and dwell on the question of judicial discretion. However, judicial work depends on other participants, including prosecutors, defence lawyers, experts, including pre-sentence report writers, and defendants. Decision making is a collaborative process, even though the judge will have the ultimate authority to manage the court proceedings and make rulings. In busy criminal lists in lower courts, judicial officers must manage time pressures and unpredictability which might entail their 'active intervention in the process, direct engagement with other participants, communication (listening and speaking), use of legal knowledge, and practical problem solving, (Mack and Roach Anleu, 2007: 342). In the context of sentencing, Tata (2007b) argues that a distinction between legal rules and judicial discretion is unstable as in actual practice judges (and other discretionary actors) will define the limits and roles of both concepts for particular purposes. This argument emphasizes the agency of decision makers, even when they may claim they have no choice or little discretion in arriving at a decision or are constrained by relevant statute and precedent. '[C]onceiving of sentencing as craftwork leads us to consider the social production of sentencing accounts as a purposive and pragmatic enterprise, rather than as an individual intellectual exercise problem to be solved' (Tata, 2007b: 434).

Discretion is more fluid and amenable to judicial interpretation – expansion and contraction – than a conception of discretion as rule bound, shifting only when legislative change allows (Tata, 2002). The accounts of sentencing that judges provide are socially produced and 'are necessarily mediated, constructed and reconstructed according to the audience and requirements of the ability to account for the decision' (Tata, 2002: 419). Judges can give a different account of sentencing practice to different audiences: other judges, the appeal court, academic researchers, the defendant, the legal profession, the appeal court. This also suggests the performative dimension of sentencing (Tait, 2002). Sentencers' narrative accounts of the decision process are not simple factual presentations of a linear decision process, but are necessarily socially constructed and reconstructed by situations, and are mediated by the expectations of different audiences. Similarly, Tombs and Jagger (2006) describe the ways in which sentencers in Scotland neutralised their decisions to incarcerate convicted offenders by denying responsibility for that outcome by detailing the constraints – statutory or deriving from the case at hand – on their discretion to make any other decision than one of imprisonment. Sentencers can present themselves as the passive conduit of inevitable sentencing decisions or as more active participants in the process as was the case in the juvenile court that Travers (2007a) observed.

A number of studies have investigated the process of sentencing and decision making from the point of view of the judicial officer and thus represent a break from scholarship that either looks at sentencing patterns or undertakes doctrinal/ jurisprudential research on judicial pronouncements in both decided cases or extra-judicial statements. One author concludes: 'What judges think about sentencing and how they approach this task are largely missing links in sentencing research' (Mackenzie, 2005: 2). Following interviews with 31 judges she concludes that judges view the 'sentencing task in fairly practical and procedural terms, as opposed to a process based more on theoretical rationales or justifications for punishment' (Mackenzie, 2005: 20). Judges tend to see sentencing as a process which entails the balancing of competing considerations and one in which they are the key players. Many of the judges also experience sentencing as a difficult and stressful decision, one of the hardest things that judicial work involves (Mackenzie, 2005: 39).

A study of the exercise of judicial discretion in rent cases (noncriminal) finds that judges recognize a diverse range of factors as influencing their exercise of discretion. The question for the judge in these cases is whether to evict a tenant of a social landlord (i.e. a local authority or housing association) from their home for rent arrears (Cowan and Hitchings, 2007; Hunter et al., 2005: 1). The approach of judges to decision making in these cases ranged from *legalism*, which conveys a reliance on the framework of contract law and a recognition of the role of the judiciary in debt management, to *pragmatism*, which evinces a concern with social welfare issues and the primacy of the home (Hunter et al., 2005: v).

An ethnographic study of a children's court highlights the practical activities, including the organizational and administrative tasks, involved in judicial work. The judge engaged in direct interaction with the defendant and took time to explain procedures rather than viewing the sentencing process as only about punishment for law violation. The judicial officers in this study considered detention as a sentence of the last resort that had little rehabilitative value (Travers, 2007a).

Despite inconclusive research findings regarding the impact of extra-legal factors on sentencing decisions, numerous proposals are advanced as ways of decreasing unjustified disparities in sentencing and remedying inconsistencies in the treatment of like cases. Developments include the promulgation of sentencing guidelines, the establishment of sentencing commissions, and legislatively mandating the types and lengths of sentences.

Sentencing guidelines and sentencing commissions

Guidelines can be voluntarily created, adopted and applied by judges. Most evaluators would conclude that voluntary guidelines are usually ignored and have little impact on sentencing patterns (Tonry, 1991: 310). Alternatively, presumptive sentencing guidelines can require judges either to impose a sentence from within a range of sentences specified in legislation, or to provide reasons that the presumption should be rebutted and a different sentence imposed. Usually sentencing commissions will promulgate such guidelines, as well as general sentencing principles, which are then incorporated into legislation and will have a binding effect on the courts. Numerous US jurisdictions have adopted this approach with mixed success; some sentencing commissions failed to reach consensus on the need for guidelines, and some legislatures refused to adopt the sentencing commission's recommended guidelines (Tonry, 1991: 314–17). Other jurisdictions rejected a determinate sentencing approach because of the difficulties in structuring discretion, practical problems in constructing guidelines, debate over the width of sentence ranges in a guidelines grid and the extent of judicial latitude to depart from guidelines, and implications for plea negotiations (Griset, 1994: 538–44; Savelsberg, 1992: 1364–71).

Minnesota was the first US state to establish a sentencing commission, in 1978. The commission submitted guidelines in 1980 intended to establish a set of consistent standards for sentencing that would increase the uniformity in sentencing decisions, thus reflecting a modified 'deserts' standard (Dixon, 1995: 1170–1). The system works on a two-dimensional grid: criminal offences are divided into a number of categories according to offence severity, and defendants are split into several groups on the basis of criminal history scores, determined primarily by the number of prior felony convictions. The grid shows the applicable sentence for every combination of offence severity and criminal history. The sentence indicated by the grid is not mandatory but presumptive, that is, the sentencer may impose any lawful sentence after indicating that the circumstances overcome the presumption (Tonry, 1987: 27–30). The Minnesota guidelines provide an elaborate policy for departure, specifying that such considerations as race, sex, employment and socio-economic status are excluded, while mitigating or aggravating factors related to the number of prior convictions and the seriousness of the offence can be considered in the sentencing decision. Guidelines that establish presumptive sentences do not remove judicial discretion, but instead structure it and allow judges to depart from the guideline on giving reasons (Ashworth, 1992b: 215–17).

Overall, the Minnesota system has been relatively successful in achieving its goal of eliminating unwarranted sentencing disparity while not increasing prison populations (D'Alessio and Stolzenberg, 1995: 285; Tonry, 1991: 317–26). First, the 'hydraulic effect' thesis, that the apparent success of reforms is undermined by abuses of discretion elsewhere in the system, is not borne out by research findings. It does not appear that prosecutors adjust their practices and increasingly take account of extra-legal factors when deciding charges and participating in plea bargains (Miethe, 1987: 171–6). Even so, some unintended consequences include an increase in the use of county jail sentences, partly due to judicial attempts to constrain the growth of the prison population (D'Alessio and Stolzenberg, 1995: 298; Stolzenberg and D'Alessio, 1994: 307). Second, policy makers were unable to guarantee an exact implementation according to the guidelines, as the judges did not always accept the association of offences to the seriousness scale (Savelsberg, 1992: 1375). In contrast to the relative success of the Minnesota model, the US federal sentencing commission guidelines that took effect in 1987 have been criticized widely because they are rigid, harsh, complex and difficult to apply; they unduly limit judicial discretion while shifting discretion onto prosecutors; and they are unfair because they take into account only offence elements and prior convictions, thus requiring that very different defendants will receive the same sentence (Tonry, 1993: 131–2).

Outside the USA there have been various legislative attempts (albeit less precise and directive) to increase sentencing consistency, structure judicial discretion and establish determinate sentences. Some legislation specifies the factors that a court must take into account when deciding on a particular sentence; to ignore these directions would constitute an appealable error. In England and Wales, the primary location for achieving sentencing principles and sentencing consistency has traditionally been the Court of Appeal Criminal Division (Thomas, 1970). In the 1980s, particular judgements became important in specifying guidelines in certain types of cases to assist the lower courts in determining the balance between various considerations. This involves the selection of key distinctions of degree within a certain offence category, for example the quantity of a prohibited substance imported, the amount of money defrauded, and the presence of such aggravating factors as the seriousness of the physical and mental effects on the victim in rape cases. These judgements also indicate factors that may or may not mitigate, such as gender or race (Ashworth, 1992b: 218–19; Henham, 1995: 220–1). The Criminal Justice Act 1991 (England and Wales) established the criteria for sentencing decisions regarding offences that are moderate or low in terms of seriousness, and specified proportionality as the leading principle, but left the courts to work out its applications to the different kinds of offences. The courts have remained unfettered in their decisions regarding the most serious offences (Ashworth, 1992a: 69–72). In Victoria (Australia), the Sentencing Advisory Council was established in 2004 to provide statistical information on sentencing, including current sentencing practices, undertake research and gauge public opinion on sentencing, provide advice to government and provide the Court of Appeal with views on guideline judgements (www.sentencingcouncil.vic.gov.au).

Mandatory or mandatory minimum sentences   In some jurisdictions, legislation provides that where a person is convicted of a particular crime the court must pass a particular sentence, or may pass a greater but not a lesser penalty. This option is increasingly popular on the part of policy makers and has been adopted for such crimes as murder, people smuggling, drunk driving, some juvenile offences and for particular types of offenders. For example, the Western Australian government passed the Crime (Serious and Repeat Offenders) Sentencing Act 1992 in response to public concern over a series of deaths arising from high-speed police chases of juveniles who had stolen cars. The legislation specified that for repeat violent offenders – juveniles and adults – a sentence of detention or imprisonment is mandatory; the sentencing court only has discretion regarding the length of the sentence (Broadhurst and Loh, 1993: 253). While this provision is no longer in operation Western Australia still has mandatory penalties for burglary (Australian Law Reform Commission, 2005: 441).

Another example of mandatory sentences is the so-called three strikes initiative, implemented for example in California in 1994, whereby legislation mandated a life sentence for any person convicted of three felonies (Tyler and Boeckmann, 1997: 238). Mandatory sentencing has been criticized for its inflexibility, constraint on judicial discretion, perceived injustice, discriminatory impact on certain groups, and the way it escalates sentence severity and contravenes international human rights (Australian Law Reform Commission, 2005: 442–3). Critics of mandatory sentences argue that discretion taken from the judge may shift to other aspects of the criminal justice system, particularly the prosecuting authority. Prosecutors may make strenuous efforts not to charge offences that would result in a mandatory minimum sentence that they consider unduly harsh; alternatively, they may charge the offence with the mandatory penalty as leverage to effect a guilty plea (Ashworth, 1992b: 214).

Following a series of changes to the state's sentencing guidelines, Engen and Steen (2000) examined trends in the conviction and sentencing of drug offenders in Western Australia from 1986–95. In the new determinate sentencing model the specific charge for which an offender is convicted and his/her criminal history largely determined the sentence, thereby enhancing the impact of prosecutors on sentencing outcomes. In this period there were more severe sentencing outcomes for defendants who pleaded guilty and for those convicted at trial, but the impact was greater for the latter group. This finding supports the hydraulic displacement conception of discretion and identifies different sentences for similar offenders thus undermining the goal of uniformity in sentencing. The research concludes: 'It appears that a principal effect of sentencing reforms is to structure the ways in which courtroom workgroups use their discretion in charging and plea bargaining to encourage guilty pleas and thereby maintain organizational efficiency' (Engen and Steen, 2000: 1387).

Truth in sentencing   The movement for 'truth in sentencing' stems from a concern that the sentence specified by the court, especially if it is a period of imprisonment, is usually not the actual sentence that the offender receives. This discrepancy arises because the sentencing court will specify a maximum prison term (the head sentence) and a minimum term of imprisonment, the nonparole period. Prisoners will rarely spend the maximum period incarcerated and a parole board will determine the actual release date. More recently, systems of remission for good behaviour can reduce the nonparole period; while they have to be earned, in effect they are often automatic. The establishment of remissions systems via legislation does reduce judicial sentencing discretion and, to offset their perceived effects, some judges will increase minimum nonparole periods (Weatherburn, 1985: 280). The Australian Law Reform Commission's inquiry into sentencing found widespread community concern about the discrepancy between the stated maximum prison term and the actual time that a person spends in jail, which has led to perceptions that the punishment ordered by the court as appropriate to the offence is not actually served (Australian Law Reform Commission, 1988: 37). The impetus for truth in sentencing refers to a system whereby the sentence announced by the court is clearly understood by the community and reflects the sentence actually served by the offender (Zdenkowski, 1994: 204). The New South Wales Sentencing Act 1989 abolished all remissions and states as its primary purpose: 'To promote truth in sentencing by requiring convicted offenders to serve in prison (without reduction) the minimum or fixed term of imprisonment set by the Court' (s3(a)).

Each of these sentencing reforms fetters judges' decision-making power to different degrees and, accordingly, generates considerable discussion among the judiciary. Judges are protective of judicial independence and will seek to maintain the separation of judicial and legislative powers (Ashworth, 1992a: 38–54). They would claim that the judicial function requires wide discretion to enable flexibility in decision making, whereas specific legislative requirements regarding sentencing will curtail that function. Judges will also usually maintain that formulating strategies for achieving consistency in sentencing is a judicial matter. They prefer judicial conferences, seminars, consultation and some forms of judicial education rather than legislation, sentencing guidelines or mandatory penalties to promote sentencing consistency (Australian Law Reform Commission, 1980: Appendix B; Sallmann, 1991: 129–31). Judges will often view sentencing as involving a complex consideration of individual cases and circumstances that do not lend themselves to formula judgements without causing injustice (Corns, 1990: 145–6). According to the Victorian Supreme Court: 'ultimately every sentence imposed represents the sentencing judge's instinctive synthesis of all the various aspects involved in the punitive process' *(R* v *Williscroft* 1975: 300). Yet this plea for judicial autonomy points to the subjective dimensions of sentencing, which can result in unwarranted disparities.

Current sentencing reforms illustrate the irreconcilable tensions between the search for uniformity and fairness in sentencing while allowing judicial flexibility, and over whether the focus of the criminal sanction should be on the offence or the offender. These reforms also represent efforts to further formalize the law; to supplant substantive rationality (allowing economic, sociological and ethical criteria to intrude in decision making) by formal-rational reasoning (Weber, 1978: 657, 880–95). Savelsberg argues that reforms to cure the dilemmas of substantivization – the lack of due process, sentencing disparities and discrimination – face serious cultural and structural impediments in contemporary societies (1992: 1346–7). Organized interest groups and the acknowledgement of diversity encourage substantive rationality, resulting in demands for interventionist, purposive and often welfare-oriented types of law that aim to adjust legal decisions to individual cases (Savelsberg, 1992: 1357, 1374).

Other sentencing reforms aimed at increasing consistency but that do not impact on judicial discretion in the same direct way as sentencing guidelines or mandatory sentences include sentencing legislation which explicitly sets out sentencing principles. Guideline judgements delivered by an appellate court can extend beyond the particular case to suggest a sentencing scale or appropriate starting point for a category of offence or type of offender, or elaborate general sentencing principles or considerations. Such judgements are not binding but do aim to assist in the exercise of sentencing discretion. Other reforms include sentencing databases, which provide information on the range and type of penalties for similar offences over a period of time which may become normative, and judicial education which can take various forms from dedicated sessions on sentencing to more general conferences (Berman and Feinblatt, 2001; Freiberg, 2001).

Another recent development in the criminal justice system includes the expansion of specialist or problem-oriented courts (Australian Law Reform Commission, 2005: 429–41; Mackenzie, 2005: 166).

Specialist courts

While specialized courts are not new (for example, specific children's courts have existed for some time in many jurisdictions), the number and variety of new courts, sometimes also termed specialist, problem-solving or problem-oriented courts, signal a change in the administration of justice and the role of the judicial officer. This development is also an example of the way in which the courts have responded to significant changes in their social environments (Burns and Peyrot, 2003; Plotnikoff and Woolfson, 2005; Roach Anleu and Mack, 2007). Examples include drug courts, mental health courts, community courts, and domestic or family violence courts which have been established under various legal regimes – not all have statutory backing – to deal with specific groups or people or problems. The first drug court was established in Florida in 1989 (though there were forerunner diversion programmes) and their subsequent adoption has been widespread and subject to considerable evaluation research and academic commentary (Burns and Peyrot, 2003; Matrix Justice Group, 2008). The general philosophy of such courts is that certain law breaking behaviour is symptomatic of deeper social, economic and personal problems and unless these are dealt with, then the offending behaviour will continue.

Some judicial officers will adopt a stance known as therapeutic jurisprudence (TJ), which first emerged in the mental health context. TJ stresses the importance of the nature of the interaction between the bench and the defendant. The judicial officer is more active, engaged in direct communication with the defendant, and is more aware of the personal circumstances of individuals than the model of the judge as a passive, neutral arbiter requires (King, 2003; Popovic, 2002).

Problem-oriented courts are a site where there is emphasis on treatment rather than punishment and a reliance on the input from human services personnel. Legal and therapeutic especially 'psy disciplines, actors, knowledges and practices' intersect and blend in such courts (Moore, 2007: 43). The judicial officer is part of a team, albeit the primary decision maker, constituted by health and welfare personnel each contributing advice, assessment and recommendation, but these distinctions blur. A study of two drug treatment courts in Canada found that the involvement of treatment personnel was not as an expert witness or assistant to the court, but they did share in the legal decision-making processes (Moore, 2007). Judges also engaged in clinical-medical assessments and took up psychological treatment knowledges in their interactions with clients. The blurring of therapeutic and punitive goals 're-imagines justice' as: 'Detention translates into therapy; a warrant is now an incentive and appearance in a criminal court a chance to process a drug-use relapse' (Moore, 2007: 57).

This crossover between judicial/legal and psy knowledges and personnel also occurs in juvenile justice (McCallum and Laurence, 2008). Nonetheless, the interplay between welfare versus legal models in juvenile justice is not static. A study of juvenile courts in California documents the way that an increased emphasis on punishment rather than assessing rehabilitation prospects within the juvenile justice system is altering the juvenile court (Harris, 2007). Statutory changes that enable young people to be prosecuted in adult courts and ideological shifts toward punishment and the 'war on crime' serve to expand prosecutors' capacity to influence the decision-making process and marginalize judicial officers who espouse the former rehabilitative ideals (Harris, 2007: 43).

Problem-oriented courts can combine a focus on social change and substantive justice with social control functions and can operate within a court administration (Mirchandani, 2005). One study looks at the capacity of a domestic violence court to bring about social change and retain the substantive goals and values of the battered women's movement at the same time as responding to administrative concerns with case flows, speed, effectiveness and efficiency. It finds little evidence of conflict between technocratic justice imperatives and social movement values because the judge is able to moblize the discourse of the battered women's movement, reiterate the anti-violence values, and challenge patriarchal attitudes, thus aiming to facilitate individual and social change (Mirchandani, 2005: 405–9).

Indigenous sentencing courts have been set up in many parts of Australia and overseas jurisdictions to allow for more indigenous input and participation in sentencing and to provide an environment that is less alienating and more cultur-ally relevant for indigenous participants than conventional courts. These courts rely on therapeutic jurisprudence and restorative justice principles to some degree but the most important aim is the involvement of a wide range of indigenous partici-pants and the establishment of trust between them (Marchetti and Daly, 2007). Indeed, one evaluation study concludes, after documenting that 'circle sentencing [the New South Wales Indigenous sentencing court] has no effect on the frequency, timing or seriousness of offending', that this should not be taken as indicating that the process has little value because 'reducing recidivism is just one of several objec-tives of the process' (Fitzgerald, 2008: 7).

Nonetheless, there has been caution regarding these developments. Such specialist courts are not public, the role of the judge entails more intervention than the model of neutral arbiter allows and some of the procedural rights of the defendant may be compromised, especially the right to trial. Referral to these courts also usually requires a plea of guilty, which may jeopardize the voluntariness of the plea (Ashworth, 2002; Burns and Peyrot, 2003).

Criminal punishment

Durkheim (1973), Black (1976) and Foucault (1979) all predicted that the dominant form of punishment in contemporary societies will change from repressive to restitu-tive; from deprivation of life to deprivation of liberty. The prison emerged in the nineteenth century as the central form of legal penalty and was observed by many to be a more humane form of punishment than exile, torture or the death penalty. Despite globalization or general trends in punishment, national/societal differences remain.

A survey of 52 nations indicates that Russia and the USA have incarceration rates five to eight times higher than those of most industrialized nations, with Indonesia, India, the Philippines and Cyprus having the lowest rates of incarceration (Mauer, 1995: 115). Changing crime rates or a differential use of other criminal sanctions do not explain the pattern. Rates of incarceration dramatically increased in the USA in the latter part of the twentieth century but have remained stable in Germany (Savelsberg, 1994: 911). While both countries are western and industrialized, with capitalist economies and democratic governments, they differ in terms of the institutionalization of domination and knowledge production in the public, political and academic spheres. The predominantly privately owned news media and the steady monitoring of public opinion create more, and often volatile, public pressure in the USA as compared with greater state and neocorporate involvement in German news media and less information about public opinion. In Germany, institutions are more strongly bureaucratized, interrelationships between private and public spheres neocorporate and status groups are more secure, in comparison with the greater pluralism and diversity of interests in the USA. In the latter, most judges and prosecutors are elected or nominated and confirmed through political processes, whereas in Germany they are appointed as civil servants with tenured positions; the former are more sensitive and vulnerable to public opinion and approval, whereas the latter are more independent (Savelsberg, 1994).

In the 1970s, imprisonment received widespread criticism. Some argued that the use of prison was inappropriate for most convicted offenders: it is too harsh, inhumane and disruptive and does not facilitate a reintegration into social life; it does not deter crime, indeed many would argue that imprisonment has criminogenic effects; and it represents a huge drain on public resources. Many societies have adopted an official policy of using imprisonment as the criminal sanction of the last resort, and particularly for violent and dangerous offenders, those involved in large-scale drug trafficking and other organized crime. However, some researchers also identify the phenomenon of 'mass imprisonment' whereby incarceration has become a new stage in the life course for recent birth cohorts of black men of low skill (Pettit and Western, 2004: 164). Imprisonment is now a common experience for many black noncollege men in the USA and rivals or overshadows the frequency of military service and college graduation for these young African-American men, constituting a key social division.

To complement this policy of relying on imprisonment as a last resort, there has been a proliferation of community-based sanctions, including community service orders, work orders, attendance centre orders, home detention and periodic detention. These measures all curtail liberty to some extent, but to a lesser extent than full-time imprisonment. The frequently cited benefits of these reforms include cost savings, opportunities for rehabilitation, preservation of a convicted offender's self-esteem, less disruption to employment and family obligations, avoidance of the stigma of imprisonment and no contact with the prison population (Australian Law Reform Commission, 1988: 63; 2005: 155–97). At first, community-based measures were proposed as alternatives to prison; however, these have now emerged as sanctions in their own right. Ironically, and despite the proliferation of criminal sanctions, prison populations are generally not in decline. Indeed, the emphasis on community and informality may mask the expansion of a discretionary power that further compromises liberty. Critics suggest that rather than reducing social control, the community corrections movement represents an expansion of control and surveillance, albeit one that is more invisible, blurred, subtle and diffused than within the prison (Cohen, 1979: 346–50; 1985: 40–4, 57; Foucault, 1979: 22–3). Increasing numbers of professions and individual experts administer the criminal justice system and make decisions, thus dispersing surveillance and disguising social control under the veneer of welfare and assistance (Carrington, 1993: 104–10; Chan and Zdenkowksi, 1986: 141).

Crime prevention and management

Some recent discussions of crime prevention have focused on the ways in which policy makers and criminal justice officials use civil law to achieve criminal justice goals, namely the reduction of crime and social control (Roach Anleu, 1998). While the use of civil remedies to control criminal or antisocial behaviour has had a long history, the expansion in the kinds of responses to deviance and the explicit admixture of civil and criminal sanctions as a crime-control policy are distinctive (Cheh, 1991). Such civil remedies as compensation, restitution, forfeiture and apology are being directly incorporated into criminal laws.

New administrative or regulatory laws also attempt to regulate the behaviour of various subpopulations in order to stem the opportunities for criminal offending. This is especially true in situational crime-prevention strategies (Clarke, 1992; National Crime Prevention Council, 1996). Local government regulations and ordinances, licensing procedures, orders to cease and desist from certain behaviours, and the statutory establishment of specialized crime investigation and prosecution agencies all seek to curb antisocial, harmful and criminal activities, but emerge outside, or in the shadow of, the criminal justice system. Administrative law and civil remedies are also used to control corporate crime where establishing individual culpability may be difficult or impossible.

One area where civil law and criminal law converge is in the regulation of behaviour defined as anti-social. In a context of new developments in social control which emphasize the identification and management of risks, security and crime prevention, there is increasing use of the contractual form to regulate behaviour and advance personal responsibility (Crawford, 2003; Donoghue, 2008; Flint, 2006b; Roach Anleu, 2006). Statutory and policy changes in a number of jurisdictions provide for an increasing range of agents – neighbourhood wardens, housing officers, community support officers, private security personnel – who will extend state powers to regulate the behaviour of individuals and groups in public and private settings (Atkinson, 2006: 103; Crawford, 2006: 222–4). There is particular attention paid to public housing as a site of social control, the attendant changing nature of the landlord-tenant relationship and the extending panoply of sanctions oriented towards managing the behaviour of tenants and others.

The emergence of Anti-Social Behaviour Orders (ASBOs), has attracted considerable discussion in the United Kingdom, and the discourse of anti-social behaviour is now widespread (Arthurson and Jacobs, 2006: 261). ASBOs were first introduced by the 1998 Crime and Disorder Act and then elaborated in the Anti-social Behaviour Act 2003, covering a raft of activities and areas including premises where drugs were used unlawfully, housing and social landlords, parental responsibilities, dispersal of groups, firearms, noise, and graffiti, the environment, waste and litter. The Crime and Disorder Act 1998 (England and Wales) defines anti-social behaviour as occurring where a person aged 10 or above has acted in 'a manner that caused or was likely to cause harassment, alarm or distress to one or more persons not of the same household' as the person subject to the application for an ASBO (section 1(1)(a)). Applications are to be made by complaint to the magistrates court of the local area. Thus an ASBO is 'a civil order directed towards the prevention of future anti-social behaviour through the deterrent effect of criminal sanction on breach' (Cobb, 2007: 344). An ASBO is a written court order for an individual to behave or desist from behaving in a particular way, and can restrict their presence in a particular location or neighbourhood; breaching this can result in criminal sanctions, including imprisonment (Flint, 2006a: 3; Lister, 2006: 122).

The concept of anti-social behaviour is notoriously wide and can mean different things and encompass different activities in different contexts. The imprecision of the concept has allowed it to cover a wide range of circumstances and people, including young people, sex workers and those begging, and has led to concerns that individuals might receive custodial sentences (for a breach) where the initial behaviour would not amount to an imprisonable offence (Macdonald, 2006: 199–201).

Initially, only the police or local authorities could apply for ASBOs but this was extended and now potential applicants include registered social landlords (i.e. property owners providing social or public housing) who have the power to evict a tenant for the anti-social behaviour of nontenants and to seek an injunction in relation to nuisance or annoying behaviour which affects the social landlords' housing management activities (Hunter, 2006: 143). There is also provision for 'good neighbour agreements' in relation to noise, children, pets, and the conditions of gardens, which are oriented to the prevention and management of behaviour defined as anti-social.

From the point of view of some local residents ASBOs can be sources of empowerment and engagement and affect the implementation of the policy as well as the capacity to promote intolerance and marginalization. These 'consumers', 'service-users' and 'citizens' can also be instrumental in shaping the strategies or interventions of the local authorities or police, by exerting pressure on these agencies to intervene in certain ways and by expecting that any action taken will reduce the anti-social behaviour (Donoghue, 2008: 349–50). Similarly, empirical research in Australia identified the experiences of tenants who felt powerless as victims of anti-social behaviour who confronted the dilemma of whether to report the incidents, and then face retributive acts – threats, harassment, property damage – or not to report and still experience the unwanted behaviour (Arthurson and Jacobs, 2006: 266). The research found that housing managers and other professionals generally eschewed more stringent, legally-based punitive measures and supported more community based responses, including mediation in some circumstances, where both parties are willing to accept responsibility for their actions and other interventions that seek to address the causes of anti-social behaviour (Arthurson and Jacobs, 2006: 269–73).

Reducing the opportunities for criminal activity can involve regulating the activities of individuals (third parties) who are not engaged directly in criminal activity but, because of their relations with potential offenders, can actually (albeit inadvertently) enhance criminal opportunities. Administrative laws and regulatory codes initially established to achieve other noncrime-related goals – for example protecting the rights of tenants *vis-à-vis* property owners, enhancing public health and safety, and protecting employees from dangerous or unhealthy workplaces – can be used to require property owners to maintain their premises in order to reduce the likelihood that they will become crime sites. The Specialized Multi-Agency Response Team (SMART) programme in California entails administering civil codes to ensure that property owners take responsibility for properties that show evidence of drug and disorder problems, as a strategy for reducing the likelihood that related offences will occur. Officials from housing, fire and public works departments will control and inspect drug-nuisance locations and enforce the relevant codes. The programme extends the responsibility for crime will control into the realm of nonoffending third parties (Buerger and Green Mazerolle, 1996: 12–17; Green, 1996: 5–6, 83–104).

Third party policing involves various willing and unwilling partners who will come together with the aim of solving a crime problem (Mazerolle and Ransley, 2005: 2). Third party policing initiatives have escalated for two main reasons: first, in response to the 'blurring' of civil and criminal laws; and second, as part of the move from state monopolies on social control to decentred networks of governance and crime control agents, albeit with explicit roles for the police. Third party policing relies on the police to persuade or coerce nonoffending persons or organizations, such as public housing agencies, property owners, parents, health and safety inspectors, building inspectors and business owners, to take some responsibility for preventing crime or reducing the opportunities for crime problems to emerge. Key here is the use of a range of civil, criminal and regulatory rules and laws to influence or require third parties to adopt crime control responsibility (Mazerolle and Ransley, 2005: 2–3).

A comprehensive overview of evaluation research concludes that successful drug law enforcement depends on the ability of the police to establish productive partnerships with third parties rather than simply increasing the police presence or making more arrests at drug hotspots (Mazerolle et al., 2006: 409). Partnerships with nonpolice agencies and community and local organizations and levering additional resources to deal with drug problems are more effective than a direct police intervention involving drug raids, search and seizures, crackdowns, undercover operations, and intensive policing (Mazerolle et al., 2007).

The growing reliance on opportunity reduction and loss prevention suggests a movement towards an insurance or actuarial model of social control. Such a model tends to treat crime as a fortuitous event, the effects of which can be spread across categories of risk takers (Ewald, 1991: 201–5; Reichman, 1986: 152). Property insurance operates to manage the consequences of criminal activities by allocating the risks across potential victims, that is, property owners. The classifications of risk groups that insurers develop are not moral communities constituted by a shared identity among members, but are instead artificial actuarial groupings compared and ranked according to a series of attributes correlated with assessments of risk (Ewald, 1991: 203; Simon, 1987: 63–4; 1988: 772). Increasingly, the onus is falling on individuals to minimize their chances of becoming a crime victim. Police and insurance companies require home and business owners to install appropriate and adequate security and not to act negligently. The responsibility for the management of relatively minor property crime thereby largely shifts from the police to insurance companies; attention is diverted from suspected offenders to victims, both actual and potential. As victims of burglaries receive little satisfaction from the criminal justice system because of the negligible clearance rate for these crime reports, insurance policies (for those who can afford them) are essential for security and compensation in the event of victimization. This means that insurance regulations and the law become important resources for regulating the behaviour of potential victims, placing an onus on individuals to reduce their chances of victimization and *ipso facto* the amount of criminal activity.

Conclusion

This chapter demonstrates the ways in which different forms of law are incorporated into the quest for social control, both in everyday life and as part of the institutions of the criminal justice system. Two predominant models of law have emerged: law as punishment and prohibition, with the adversarial trial being paramount; and law as regulation, entailing mediation and compensation. Various legal practices and organizations contain elements of both. The discussion also examined the operation of the criminal justice system and its links with other forms of social control in managing criminal deviance. While the formal organs of the criminal justice system are held out as the pinnacle of the social control of crime, much processing of criminal justice issues occurs outside, or in the shadow of, legal institutions. Most criminal cases, especially in the lower courts, are resolved via plea discussions that will result in a defendant agreeing to plead guilty. In common-law legal systems, considerable faith is placed in the role of the judge, and sentencing practices and ideologies are the subject of continuing debate. Currently, there are attempts to formalize the sentencing process, to make it more predictable and rational (in the Weberian sense) and less open to claims of discrimination and bias between types of offenders. This trend is countered by increasing demands from victims' groups and others for judges to take greater cognizance of the substantive, contextual or nonlegal elements of a case, for example the degree of harm experienced by the victim or the nature of the relationship between defendant and victim.

7 Feminism and Legal Reform

Law is an important arena where women's movements and feminist activists (including lawyers) seek to change women's status and achieve equality. Early efforts extended property rights, education, training for the professions and the right to vote to women. Since the 1960s, feminism has concentrated on law reform in areas of employment, family and crime, especially regarding rape and domestic violence. This chapter examines activism oriented towards promoting awareness that employment discrimination, rape, domestic violence, pornography and reproductive autonomy require attitudinal changes, new government policies, structural renovations and the revision of laws that actively perpetuate gender inequality. Not all feminist organizations agree on the ways towards achieve gender equality and the strategies actually adopted depend on, and are shaped by, specific institutional structures and legal cultures. In the USA, a primary focus of women's groups (and other civil rights activists) has been the courts. Much women's rights litigation uses test cases and *amicus curiae* briefs to present broader perspectives and to ensure that women's voices are heard in court. In Britain, Canada and Australia, political lobbying aims to encourage parliaments to implement legislation furthering equality or entrenching women's rights. There is also feminist engagement with and within state instrumentalities, involving attempts to change the formulation and implementation of government policy.

While there is no single, discrete organizational movement, feminism is a political force that even within a single country can encompass a broad ideological variety and range of organizational expressions (Katzenstein, 1987: 5). The term feminism covers a multitude of movements including efforts for reproductive rights, employment and pay equity, the political representation of women and a rejection of violence perpetrated against women (Ferree and Martin, 1995: 4–5). Feminist organizations vary in the extent to which they are organized on local, national or global levels, the kinds of strategies and discourses they adopt, their membership, resources, leadership, the nature of their successes and their longevity.

Scholarship on social movements distinguishes identity or status-based politics from class politics, and seeks to understand relationships between experience, culture, identity, politics and power (Bernstein, 2005). It also identifies 'the strategic dilemmas movement organizers face when the identities around which a movement is organized are also the basis for oppression' (Bernstein, 2005: 48). Bernstein (1997) argues that the concept of identity in the context of social movement analyis has at least three dimensions: (i) a shared collective identity which might be the outcome of debate, division and negotiation regarding group membership; (ii) collective expressions of identity can be deployed as political strategies aimed at bringing about social, legal, political or other institutional change; and (iii) identity can be a goal and outcome of activism either gaining acceptance of a previously stigmatized status or deconstructing status categories by highlighting their internal heterogeneity and ambiguity. For example, many have argued that social movements organized around the category 'women' or 'feminist' often overlook or sideline other differences in equality stemming from race, income, sexual orientation and so on (Watson and Heath, 2004).

Social movement organizations are also shaped by the governmental and legal institutions of the societies in which they operate, their links with the political process (including political parties and trade unions), and the ideological nature of the political environment, all of which affect opportunities for action (Gelb, 1987: 270–8; Martin, 1990: 190–1; Staggenborg, 1989: 234–6; 1995: 339–42). Indeed, sometimes a social movement's identity is externally imposed which in turn can form part of the basis for grievances (Bernstein, 2005: 48). Law, legal institutions and legal concepts and symbols will often shape and constrain the way grievances, social movement identities and objectives are framed or articulated (Pedriana, 2006). Looking at transformations in the US Women's Movement in the 1960s, Pedriana concludes: 'Legal frames and legal framing processes offer a unique analytic framework for exploring the link between social movements and social change because *law is simultaneously a collective action frame and a collective action goal*' (Pedriana, 2006: 1754, emphasis in original).

A central aim of various feminist organizations is to achieve the reform of laws to reflect women's experiences more accurately and to ensure that laws are applied in the private or domestic domain. Nevertheless, considerable ambivalence exists about the role or the capacity of law to ameliorate diverse women's situations and to effect enduring social change. Legislation prohibiting or criminalizing sex discrimination, differential pay structures, rape, domestic violence and sexual harassment has had little deterrent effect and such reforms do not seem to have empowered significant numbers of women or provided greater access to justice. Law enforcement and judicial personnel often dilute the promises held out by progressive legislative change. Some feminist critics maintain that a focus on law as a route to social change is self-defeating from the outset. A reliance on law merely reproduces gender inequalities because law is so infused with patriarchal or masculine values. Resorting to law may in fact make conditions worse for the groups supposed to benefit as the resolution of problems is usually formulated as requiring more law, thereby extending the power and reach of law and further marginalizing nonlegal discourses, especially feminist perspectives (Smart, 1989: 161–2; Thornton, 1991: 454).

Claims for women's rights have increasingly been used to articulate political demands for equality and for changes in gender roles. Feminist ambivalence towards law centres on the meaning of equality and the utility of rights discourse. Claims for greater equality beg the question of equal *vis-à-vis* whom or what? Demands for equal employment opportunities have been criticized for taking as their standard the unencumbered male worker. Arguments for equal pay have been thwarted by endemic job segregation, where very few jobs and occupations are equally held by men and women. Some feminists argue that while it might have been appropriate for early feminists to demand legal rights, because they had so few formal legal rights, the rhetoric of rights has lost its utility and may even be detrimental (Smart, 1989: 138–9). The problems with rights discourse include the following:

1   Many women will not be able to realize their formal rights because of substantive and pervasive gender inequality.
2   The notion of rights means that different rights are equivalent and conflicts in the legal arena become contests over whose rights will predominate. For example, contemporary abortion debates are often couched in terms of the woman's rights versus those of the fetus, or even the embryo.
3   The legal recognition of rights requires an individual, or sometimes a group, to actively lodge a complaint and to initiate legal proceedings.
4   Rights discourses are easily appropriated by opposing groups. For example, in 1982 the *Charter of Rights and Freedoms,* which guarantees equal rights, was entrenched in the Canadian Constitution and heralded as a political victory both by and for the women's movement. However, some of the first equality cases to come before the courts consisted of attempts by male defendants to invoke the guarantees of sex equality in order to invalidate statutory rape provisions of the criminal law (Fudge, 1989: 450–1).

Nevertheless, rights claims can give women an important sense of collective identity, actively shape public discourse and be a source of empowerment. The public nature of rights assertion is especially significant because of the often private nature of discrimination against women (Schneider, 1986: 624–6). Moreover, women do adopt a rights discourse in everyday life, and not just in legal arenas, in their attempts to effect social change on local and personal levels (Villmoare, 1991: 401–7).

Employment discrimination

Equal pay and work discrimination have been central issues for feminists seeking change through legal or industrial relations systems. Historically, women have been paid less than men for identical work, reflecting an assumption that women's income supplements the male wage; women have been explicitly excluded from employment after marriage or child bearing or relegated to jobs with fewer opportunities and less pay. In addition, women's commitment to their careers, jobs and employers is often viewed as lower than that of men (Hakim, 1995: 432–5). Women have lobbied in the legal arena to reduce wage gaps between men and women and to achieve equal employment opportunities (Burstein, 1991: 1203–5). Debate continues regarding the relative importance of women's choices and the structural constraints that impinge unequally on women's opportunities to combine employment with family responsibilities (Crompton and LeFeuvre, 1996: 436–42; Ginn et al., 1996: 169–70).

Wage gaps

The construction of women as economically dependent on men has had a long history and has resulted in the development of such concepts as the 'family wage', that is, the amount that an average (male) worker is considered to need in order to support himself, his wife and an average of three children (Graycar and Morgan, 2002: 139–70). In Australia, the minimum rate for adult women was defined in terms of the needs of an average female employee who has to support herself. Thus, the family wage concept perpetuated the notion of differential needs between men and women workers and reflected assumptions about the respective responsibilities of men and women, both in the labour market and at home (Cass, 1985: 70; Hunter, 1988: 148–9; Land, 1980: 74). The notion of the family wage assumes that male earners will equitably distribute their income among family members/dependants (Zelizer, 1989: 353). Even where women worked in male-dominated occupations, special female classifications attracted lower wage rates (Hunter, 1988).

Most western industrial nations have implemented equal pay laws to close the gap in earnings between men and women. Intentional and direct pay discrimination is easy to identify and to remedy (so long as the political will and adequate resources exist). The fact that most men and women work in different kinds of occupations has led to claims for equal pay for work of equal or comparable value as an attempt to achieve pay equity.

In 1963, the US Congress made it an illegal sex discrimination for most employers to pay women less than men for equal work in jobs that require equal skill, effort and responsibility and that are performed under similar working conditions. This was interpreted as requiring the jobs being compared to be very similar in work content (Treiman and Hartmann, 1981: 3–4). The UK's Equal Pay Act 1970 provided equal pay for like work, not work of equal value, and abolished male and female rates for the same job. Equal pay for work of equal value was limited to jobs that had been evaluated by the employers (Atkins and Hoggett, 1984: 21). Because of job segregation, many women found themselves unable to find a suitable comparison and, even where this was possible, the assessment of equal value depended on the employer's consent. In 1983, the European Court ruled that the Act be extended to fully embrace the concept of equal pay for work of equal value (Byrne, 1984: 247–8). In Australia in 1969, the Arbitration Commission granted equal pay for equal work, that is, equal pay for women working in predominantly male occupations. However, four-fifths of women workers were engaged in disproportionately female occupations (Hunter, 1988: 157–60). In the national wage and equal pay cases in 1972, the Australian Council of Trade Unions (ACTU), the peak union organization (which had been confronted by women unionists demanding that it attend to the special needs of working women), successfully argued for the adoption of the principle of equal pay for work of equal value. In 1974, the Arbitration Commission, after a long history of activism by the National Council of Women, the Union of Australian Women and the Women's Electoral Lobby, removed the consideration of family needs from the calculation of minimum wages (Cass, 1985: 75–6).

The notion that there is equal pay for work of equal value implies that comparisons can be easily made between jobs held predominantly by men and women. But when men and women are largely segregated into different types of employment, then comparisons are difficult. The pay gap deriving from pay discrimination is small compared to the pay gap resulting from devaluing women's jobs. Women's and men's segregation into different jobs is the mainstay of the pay gap (Reskin and Padavic, 1994: 117). Jobs that are traditionally women's jobs, for example nursing and secretarial work, are systematically remunerated less than jobs that are held predominantly by men, for example a motor mechanic, even though they possess similar skill and responsibility levels. In many instances, the jobs held mainly by women and minorities are paid less, at least in part, because they are held mainly by women and minorities (Treiman and Hartmann, 1981: 93).

The doctrine of comparable worth is one strategy to overcome this problem. Comparable worth emphasizes formal job-evaluation plans to help establish equitable wages. The content of jobs is described (as distinct from descriptions of their usual incumbents) and jobs are compared and scores assigned in terms of such criteria as knowledge, skill, complexity, responsibility, effort and working conditions (Acker, 1990: 148). Jobs having the same number of points – that is, they are similarly situated in the overall work organization – should be compensated similarly. Nevertheless, practices of assessing the worth of jobs and assigning relative pay rates do incorporate discriminatory elements. For example, skills in managing money, more often found in men's jobs, receive more points than those dealing with clients or human relations skills, more often found in women's jobs (Acker, 1990: 150).

Comparable worth arguments have been used in Australia, but with little success. In 1985, a union of nurses lodged an application via the ACTU before the Australian Conciliation and Arbitration Commission as part of a broad strategy to reduce structural inequality between men and women in the labour market by addressing the traditional undervaluation of women's work. The nurses argued that pay increases were justified in accordance with the principle of equal pay for work of equal value and incorporated in the notion of comparable worth. The Commission, pointing out that comparable worth meant different things in different countries and that it was inappropriate to adopt the US model, rejected the use of the term, maintaining that it would be confusing and inappropriate to equate it with the 1972 principle of equal pay for work of equal value (Hunter, 1988: 167–9).

Sex discrimination laws

Sex discrimination legislation renders discrimination on the grounds of sex (and usually pregnancy, marital status and sometimes sexuality) unlawful in specific circumstances. In the USA, Title VII of the 1964 Civil Rights Act prohibits discrimination on the basis of an individual's sex (as well as race, colour, religion or national origin). In 1975, Britain and, in 1984, the Australian Federal government passed specific sex discrimination legislation. Often related to this antidiscrimination legislation are affirmative action policies, which mean different things in different countries. In the USA, executive orders require that firms entering into contracts with the federal government modify their employment practices to ensure that minorities and women have equal job access with white men, which includes timetables and numerical goals for integrating minorities and women into their workplace. Courts can also order affirmative action plans to reduce discrimination (Bergmann, 1986: 161–72; Reskin and Padavic, 1994: 70). The economic power of government is used to increase compliance with affirmative action programmes; however, enforcement has been uneven. In Australia, the Affirmative Action (Equal Opportunity for Women) Act 1986 required employers with more than 100 employees to develop and implement measures to secure the advancement of women within their organization. The usual sanction was being named in parliament; however the government also required compliance by large employers before eligibility for government contracts and some forms of industry assistance (Australian Law Reform Commission, 1994: 34–5). This legislation was updated by the Equal Opportunity for Women in the Workplace Act 1999 which requires a range of larger (more than 100 people) organizations including private companies, community organizations and unions to implement programmes to remove barriers to women's entry and mobility (www.eowa.gov.au/About_EOWA/Overview_of_the Act.asp).

Two forms of discrimination can be identified. Direct discrimination (disparate treatment in the USA) occurs where a policy or practice treats one person less favourably than another solely on the ground of sex. Direct comparison of one woman with one man, or a hypothetical man, is the mode of analysis of direct discrimination. Indirect discrimination (or disparate impact) exists when an ostensibly neutral job requirement, for example height and weight restrictions that may not necessarily be essential for task performance, has differential effects on a segment of the population (O'Donovan and Szyszczak, 1988: 53, 97; Thornton, 1990: 187–93). In the USA, disparate treatment looks for evidence of discrimination against an individual, while disparate impact looks for statistical evidence of discrimination against a class of persons, with no need to demonstrate an employer's intent to discriminate (Zevnick and Davis, 1993: 89). Direct and indirect discrimination may not be easy to disentangle in practice.

The difficulty in demonstrating indirect discrimination is exemplified by the Sears Roebuck litigation in the USA. The US Equal Employment Opportunity Commission (EEOC) filed a discrimination suit against the nation's largest retailer and private-sector employer of women, which came to trial in 1984. The case involved three main claims, namely that Sears:

(a) failed to hire female applicants for commission sales positions (which involve selling expensive items netting high commissions and better pay than ordinary wages) on the same basis as male applicants;
(b) did not promote female noncommission salespersons to commission sales positions on the same basis as males; and
(c) paid women in certain management and administrative jobs less than similarly situated men (Milkman, 1986: 379–80).

The EEOC relied on statistical evidence (which controlled for age, education and job experience) of widespread and continuing disparities in the kinds of jobs that men and women held at Sears to demonstrate patterns of discrimination against women. Between 1973 and 1980, women constituted around two-thirds of sales applicants at Sears, yet they were only 27 per cent of full-time and 35 per cent of part-time commission sales hires. The Commission also presented evidence that Sears' hiring practices were biased in favour of men as the company's profile of the commission salesperson was unmistakably masculine (Milkman, 1986: 381–2). In defence, Sears maintained that statistical evidence did not prove that it intentionally discriminated against women and criticized the EEOC for not introducing testimony from alleged victims of discrimination. It argued that despite its affirmative action programme, women generally were not interested in commission sales jobs but preferred to work in departments selling familiar and traditionally 'feminine' items.

A controversial aspect of this case was the deployment of historians as expert witnesses for both sides. For Sears, Rosalind Rosenberg testified that historically men and women have different relationships and orientations to paid work. She suggested that 'many workers, especially women, have goals and values other than realizing maximum economic gain' (United States District Court, 1986: 758). Specifically, women predominantly choose jobs that complement their primary family obligations. Differences between men and women in the workplace are not evidence of discrimination by Sears. In contrast, Alice Kessler-Harris argued that women's choices are constrained by available economic opportunities that, in turn, are shaped by employers' actions, preferences and assumptions about women's roles. Where opportunities have existed, women have moved into a wide variety of occupations. The judge was not convinced by the EEOC case and decided that the underrepresentation of women in the better jobs was not due to sex discrimination on the part of Sears. This case also occurred against a backdrop of increasing conservatism in the political arena; Sears was able to devote USD $20 million to defending the case, while the EEOC spent USD $2.5 million; and the head of the EEOC – Clarence Thomas – had proclaimed publicly his dislike of statistical evidence (Milkman, 1986: 394).

What does equality mean in the workplace? This question poses particular difficulties regarding pregnancy and maternity or parenting-leave policies. Should all workers be treated the same for equality to be attained – that is, formal equality is the goal – or should some be treated differently in order to overcome existent inequalities – that is, substantive equality? Should pregnancy be viewed as comparable to other physical conditions or as unique and special? On the one hand, treating all workers the same denies the reality of pregnancy and motherhood but, on the other, feminists are very wary of special treatment arguments because, in the past, they have been used to exclude women from some occupations and industries (Vogel, 1990: 9; Williams, 1984–5: 326). The intensity of the equality/difference debate in the USA – which is not paralleled in Australia or Britain – arises from the fact that, in general, there has been no guaranteed maternity leave, paid or unpaid, in that country. In Britain, maternity leave is covered, if only minimally, by national insurance, and in Australia, industrial awards formally guarantee paid and unpaid leave (Bacchi, 1990: 111).

In the 1970s, the US Supreme Court did not consider that the exclusion of pregnant women from disability insurance schemes violated sex discrimination legislation. It disagreed that discrimination based on pregnancy is sex discrimination reasoning that exclusion from the insurance provision was based on a physical condition (pregnancy) and not sex. It reached this conclusion reasoning that only some, and not all, women would be excluded, therefore the insurance programme did not discriminate against any definable group or class; both men and nonpregnant women were included in the disability scheme (Williams, 1984–5: 336–9). Eisenstein observes: 'The engendered nature of the law privileges non-pregnant persons. It is this category – which includes *all* men and *some* women – that is used to deny the sex-class status of pregnancy – which applies to no men but a majority of women' (1988: 67, emphasis in original). Thus the Court asserted that pregnancy is unrelated to sex/gender; it is something special, with no comparable disability.

A number of court decisions resulted in a polarization between equal treatment and special treatment advocates. Equal treatment proponents argue that pregnancy is just one of the physical conditions that affect workplace participation; pregnancy does not create special needs, it is one human condition among others that may affect an employee's activities (Finley, 1986: 1145). In contrast, special treatment advocates emphasize substantive equality and support laws requiring employers to provide maternity leave to those who want or need it. In both instances, the norm for determining whether treatment is the same or different is the unencumbered male worker. Thus the issue becomes whether women (and which kinds of women) are like men and, if they act like male workers, whether they should receive the same benefits and rewards (Finley, 1986: 1155). While this norm is a stereotype itself, arguably more women than men will find conformity to it difficult (Naffine, 1990: 146).

A coalition of feminist, labour, civil rights, church and even antiabortion groups mobilized to support the passage of the Pregnancy Discrimination Act in the USA, a 1978 Amendment to Title VII, which rendered discrimination based on pregnancy (or other physical characteristics unique to one sex) as sex discrimination and therefore illegal. This law requires that employers treat pregnant workers in the same way as others who are comparably able or unable to work and assess their capacity to work. An examination of appellate court decisions indicates how judges undermined the economic justifications for a range of practices, including forced leave, discharge, loss of promotion opportunities, and exclusion from health insurance and sick-leave benefits, that had previously rendered pregnancy incompatible with paid work. Pregnant workers' mobilization of equal employment law achieved success, albeit limited by the continuing absence of paid maternity leave, in shifting the responsibility for accommodation on to employers (Edwards, 1996: 254–65). Nevertheless, unease remains regarding the provision of special benefits to pregnant workers and the achievement of equality in the workplace (Vogel, 1990: 14–19).

Interestingly, in the United States many employers had created maternity leave programmes in the 1970s and 1980s well before the Family and Medical Leave

Act 1993. A neoinstitutional analysis argues that these programmes were not the voluntary actions of employers in an environment absent from government requirements but occurred instead in a legal context where not offering maternity leave provisions was difficult. For example, in 1972 the Equal Employment Opportunity Commission (EEOC) ruled that employers providing leave for disabling health conditions must also provide maternity leave to avoid breaching sex discrimination laws. As the 1972 ruling was contested in court it attracted public attention and popularized maternity leave policies, their absence became an issue of sex discrimination (Kelly and Dobbin, 1999).

Sexual harassment

Catharine MacKinnon's book *Sexual Harassment of Working Women* (1979) was especially influential in the early publicizing of sexual harassment and its framing as an issue of sex discrimination. She argues that 'sexual harassment of women at work is sex discrimination in employment' (MacKinnon, 1979: 4). The emergence of sexual harassment as a public issue followed the activities of such organizations in the USA as Working Women United and the Alliance Against Sexual Attention, as well as other groups providing support and assistance. These interest groups organized public rallies and counselling services for the victims of sexual harassment, promoted links with the legal profession and monitored legal developments, sought media attention, and attempted to institute legislative change through research and lobbying. Although these specialist interest groups did not engage in litigation as a central strategy, the courts were critical in redefining sexual harassment as sex discrimination remediable under Title VII of the Civil Rights Act of 1964. Activist lawyers involved in the landmark cases of the mid-1970s constituted an informal network of information exchange and contributed to the huge increase in media publicity during the late 1970s and early 1980s (Weeks et al., 1986: 435–41).

Most definitions of sexual harassment focus on the unwelcome or unwanted nature of sexual advances from the viewpoint of the recipient (Dine and Watt, 1995: 355–77; *Meritor Savings Bank* v *Vinson* 1986: 60). The Australian Commonwealth Sex Discrimination Act 1984 (as amended) provides that:

> a person sexually harasses another person if: (a) the person makes an unwelcome sexual advance, or an unwelcome request for sexual favours, to the person harassed; or (b) engages in other unwelcome conduct of a sexual nature in relation to the person harassed; in circumstances in which a reasonable person, having regard to all the circumstances, would have anticipated that the person harassed would be offended, humiliated or intimidated. (s 28A(I))

It defines 'conduct of a sexual nature' to include an oral or written statement of a sexual nature to a person or in the presence of a person (s 28A(2)). Sexual harassment can result from a prerequisite to hiring or promotional decisions or be part of the general work environment. The US EEOC's guidelines[1] reflect this distinction between two forms of illegal sexual harassment, namely:

1   *Quid pro quo* practices where there are specific retaliatory consequences for the victim who refuses to comply with sexual advances; that is, the harassment is directed at specific individuals.
2   *A hostile or offensive work environment* where a person or an employee may not be able to demonstrate that they were not hired or promoted because of sexual harassment, but their capacity to perform their work is impeded by general work practices or values. In this case, the harassment is not necessarily directed at specific individuals. The Commission maintains that employees have a right to work in an environment free from discriminatory intimidation, ridicule and insult. The US Supreme Court affirmed this distinction, deciding that 'the language of Title VII is not limited to "economic" or "tangible" discrimination ... Nothing in Title VII suggests that a hostile environment based on discriminatory sexual harassment should not be likewise prohibited' *(Meritor Savings Bank* v *Vinson* 1986: 58–9).

Given the development of the notion of a hostile work environment, where both male and female employees may be impeded in their capacity to work by sexual harassment, some would suggest that it is therefore not an issue of sex discrimination. Some law academics argue that sexual harassment does not necessarily involve any disparate treatment of the sexes, but concerns an inappropriate use of sexuality regardless of the gender of the victim. They reject the view that only women are subjected to harassment by heterosexual men (Dine and Watt, 1995: 343). Nevertheless, sexual harassment appears to be a problem that more women than men confront (Coles, 1986: 89). A study of federal employees in the USA showed that two-fifths of women and just under one-fifth of men had experienced some form of harassment (Collins and Blodgett, 1981: 79). A 1980 survey of 360 workers in a heavy manufacturing firm, a nonmanufacturing service firm and a public agency suggests that women working in 'male' jobs or challenging male authority in other ways are most likely to experience discrimination and sexual harassment (Di Tomaso, 1989: 88–9). Others claim that it is women in such traditionally female jobs as nursing and secretarial work who are most likely to be harassed, because they are in subordinate positions performing service work, and that harassment is an institutionalized part of their occupations (Fain and Anderton, 1987: 292).

Ordinarily, complaints regarding sexual harassment are initially dealt with by administrative tribunals, for example Employment Tribunals in the UK and, in Australia, the Human Rights and Equal Opportunity Commission. Under these arrangements, there is a commitment to resolve complaints via alternative dispute resolution mechanisms, rather than adversarial court proceedings (see Chapter 5). In Australia, the Commission may seek to resolve a complaint by conciliation and attempt to effect 'an amicable settlement of a complaint the subject of an inquiry and for this purpose may adjourn an inquiry at any stage to enable the parties to negotiate with a view to settlement of the complaint by amicable arrangements' (Sex Discrimination Act 1984, s 73(b)). The Commission can dismiss complaints, declare that the respondent has engaged in unlawful behaviour, order him or her to pursue a course of conduct (for example an apology), or pay damages as compensation for any loss or harm to the complainant (including injury to feelings, mental or physical health problems and loss of wages), or initiate proceedings in the Federal Court. The Commission is not a judicial forum, that is, it does not adjudicate in adversarial proceedings and sanctions are civil or restitutive, not criminal (Graycar and Morgan, 2002: 381–403).

Despite legal provisions, sexual harassment is an area where victims are often reticent to file a complaint (Schneider, 1991: 538–43). This is because most sexual harassment occurs where there are no other witnesses besides the victim and the alleged perpetrator, and the former is usually in a much less powerful position within the organization than the latter. The victim fears that their story will be disbelieved or trivialized, that they will be blamed for the incident(s), and that the consequences of filing a complaint will be highly detrimental to their workplace relations and employment (Cossins, 1995: 538–9; Ross, 1992: 1451). An investigation of workplace assaults shows that the most usual response from victims was to remain in their jobs, but to adopt informal ways of managing and minimizing contact with the perpetrator. Only one in five complained through formal workplace channels and one in five quit their jobs; moreover, complaining and quitting were mutually exclusive responses – very few victims did both (Schneider, 1991: 543).

One of the most controversial and high-profile sexual harassment claims was Anita Hill's accusations in 1991 that President Bush's Supreme Court nominee – Clarence Thomas – had engaged in inappropriate sexual conduct at work. This incident was particularly complex because Hill and Thomas are both Afro-American. Some Afro-American groups supported Thomas, yet others opposed him on grounds that he worked against policies that most Afro-Americans supported (Scheppele, 1995: 999–1000). The Senate Judiciary Committee hearings that investigated Hill's allegations were transformed from a forum in which the Senate could determine Thomas's suitability to serve on the Supreme Court, into a criminal trial in which Thomas was portrayed as the defendant (Curtis, 1992). Virtually all of the participants were lawyers or at least trained in the law; witnesses were called and subject to examination and cross-examination; the burden of proving the allegations was placed on Anita Hill and the central issue revolved around her credibility. Hill's evidence was discredited during the hearings via the standard tactics of lawyers in a criminal trial, namely a focus on the lack of physical evidence and the creation of an appearance of contradictory testimony. Republican senators emphasized the fact that her allegations had emerged ten years after the events took place, which reinforced the idea that delayed stories are thereby less believable and more prone to inconsistencies and conflicting details; because the story is unstable, it must also be untrue (Scheppele, 1992: 128–37; 1995: 1000–1). At the same time, Thomas's use of racial imagery – especially the powerful and persistent stereotypes about black men's sexuality – transformed him from sexual harasser to racial victim, perhaps the single most important element leading to his confirmation (Jordan, 1992: 19). This confirmation process demonstrates an intricate balancing act, as those senators who sought to discredit Hill's account had to appear worried about the problem of sexual harassment in general, while simultaneously saying that this particular case was not an example of it. This is prototypical legal reasoning: the law is adhered to and supported while the individual case is distinguished on its facts and therefore deemed as not coming within the prohibitions.

Rape and domestic violence

In the 1960s and 1970s, feminist organizations lobbied for a substantial revision of rape laws and changes to traditional attitudes about rape, especially among police, the medical profession and the courts (Martin and Powell, 1995: 856–9; Rose, 1977: 75). The ensuing changes in rape laws did not necessarily incorporate all of the demands made by feminist antirape movements. Indeed, the passage of law usually depended on political coalitions with 'law-and-order' groups and other nonfeminist legal reformers concerned about rising crime rates and lenient criminal laws, and on offering a reform agenda palatable to legislators holding traditional rather than feminist ideologies (Berger et al., 1988: 336). While there is great diversity in rape laws, the two main areas of reform relate to the definition of the offence and to evidential and procedural rules. There have also been changes in penalty structures.

Definition of the offence

Traditionally, the common-law crime of rape was defined as 'the carnal knowledge of any woman above the age of ten years against her will, and of a woman-child under the age of ten years with or against her will' (Hale, 1971: 628). In effect, the insertion by a man of his penis into the vagina of a woman without her consent, where he knew or believed she was not consenting but went ahead regardless, constituted the common-law crime of rape (Law Reform Commission of Victoria, 1986: 6–7). This definition means that only men could rape and only women could be raped. Moreover, where the woman and the man were married to one another, rape law did not apply. Rape in marriage was not always recognized by the law and occurred in 1991 in Australia, for example (Waller and Williams, 1993: 85). Many jurisdictions have reformed their rape laws through legislation that has either:

(a) amended the criminal law, rendering the crime of rape nongender, nonorifice and noninstrument specific; or
(b) abolished the crime of rape, replacing it with categories of sexual assault based on the harm done to the victim.

As well as amending the substantive definition of the crime, notions of consent or the lack of it have been reformed, as have evidential and procedural rules pertaining to the trial and the role of the victim.

Evidential and procedural rules

Legal rules that primarily pertained to rape trials highlighted concerns about women's credibility, in particular the supposed ease with which allegations of rape can be made and the difficulty in defending oneself against them (Mack, 1993: 329–38; 1994: 186–7; 1998: 60–3; Scheppele, 1992: 161–6). At common law the trial judge was required to warn the jury of the dangers of convicting a person accused of sexual assault on the uncorroborated evidence of the complainant; the law allowed a cross-examination of the complainant about her previous sexual history in order to establish credibility and the likelihood of consent. Corroboration rules pertaining to women alleging rape contrast sharply with the usual common-law rule that the jury is entitled to convict on the unsupported testimony of one witness (Mack, 1993: 332). The specific application of these rules to rape charges has been modified. The defence counsel can no longer cross-examine the victim about her/his previous sexual relations in an attempt to demonstrate a lack of credibility, but the court may allow such cross-examination if it is of sufficient relevance (Ligertwood, 1993: 139–41). Feminists consistently question the common-law view that the sexual past of a victim is relevant to the issue of consent (Naffine, 1992: 745 fn 24). In Australia, where a corroboration warning has not been given (as part of the trial judge's discretion) and a conviction results, appeal courts have reversed some decisions, holding that the trial judge did not sufficiently advise the jury of special circumstances, for example a lapse of time before the complaint was made, which they suggest raises doubts about the credibility of the female victim (Mack, 1994: 189).

The rape reform movement also established rape-crisis centres and shelters (or refuges), telephone 'hot-lines' to provide information, new hospital and police practices via training, more sensitive protocols to the needs of the victim, and special sexual assault units within police departments. These reforms aim to facilitate the bringing of allegations and the prosecution of rape cases, to remove some of the difficulties in securing convictions in the courts and generally to empower victims.

Impact studies indicate that many of the goals of rape reform have not been realized due to persistent assumptions about the crime of rape and its victims and because the judicial interpretation of statutes has tended to dilute their effects. For many women who have been sexually assaulted, a rape trial, even the pre-trial discussions and procedures, remains traumatic and humiliating (MacKinnon, 1983: 651; Smart, 1989: 34). Sexist assumptions about the nature of women that were previously enshrined in the law sometimes persist in judicial statements and media portrayals of rape trials. This highlights the limitations of relying on statutes that must be interpreted and applied by various actors in the criminal justice process, who may hold biased and stereotypical views of women in general, and of rape victims in particular. The main findings of this research include the following:

1 Many police, prosecutors, defence lawyers and judges continue to operate on the basis of traditional assumptions and do not always comply with the statutes (Berger et al., 1988: 334). As many of the legal changes seek to reform the trial process, discretion exercised earlier on in the criminal justice system may not be affected by such changes. An examination of rape-processing organizations and

actors – the police, hospital emergency rooms, rape-crisis centres, prosecutors, judges and defence lawyers – finds that various internal characteristics as well as external relations with other agencies prompt their staff to subordinate victims' needs and interests to their own (Martin and Powell, 1995: 858). The authors suggest that the legal system's framing of rape victims as primarily witnesses to rape crimes rather than as traumatized victims of rape subordinates the latter's needs to those of the former. While rape-crisis centres place a high priority on victims' needs, legal organizations and hospitals minimize their contact with the centres unless they provide valuable and acceptable assistance, as defined by the legal and medical personnel who often view these centres as unpredictable, mysterious and of questionable trustworthiness. This situation inhibits the ability of rape-crisis centres to respond to victims (Martin and Powell, 1995: 869–72, 888).

2   Victims are routinely not believed or made to feel responsible for the incident. In deciding to file a sexual assault complaint, prosecutors rely on a repertoire of knowledge about how particular kinds of rape are committed, postincident interaction between the parties in an acquaintance situation, victims' emotional and psychological reactions to rape, and their impact on victims' subsequent behaviour. The typification of rape-relevant behaviour is a resource for discrediting the victim's account (Frohmann, 1991: 217; 1997: 541–52). To the extent that the incident deviates from the 'classic' rape situation (that is, where the victim and perpetrator are strangers, the rape occurs in a public place, violence is involved, there is evidence of the victim's resistance, immediate reporting and cooperation with the police), the victim's allegations and the denial of consent may be perceived as less credible (Williams, 1984: 460).

3   Courts continue to use woman-unfriendly habits of evaluating what counts as legal evidence. The ways in which facts are constructed in legal argument often work to the disadvantage of women. Women may not be viewed as credible if they delay in reporting or if their stories present inconsistencies (Scheppele, 1992: 123–7). Judicial commentary often reinforces assumptions about rape and rape victims, in particular that victims are responsible for rape, that they are not credible witnesses and that most allegations are false (Soothill et al., 1990: 218–27). Although the corroboration warning is no longer mandatory, judges may still retain discretion to give the warning as part of their general power to comment on evidence. They continue to exercise this discretionary power, thus demonstrating on-going judicial scepticism towards female complainants in rape cases (Mack, 1993: 339–45). As one commentator suggests: 'There is no reason to think that women are both especially prone to lie, and so terrifically good at concealing their falsehood that special warnings are needed to a jury, which is otherwise likely to be misled by these especially effective female liars' (Mack, 1994: 188). Judges and others may also assume that certain types of women are more credible and more harmed by rape. Judges have suggested that the harm and trauma to the victim are lessened if she is sexually experienced, works as a prostitute, or is unconscious at the time of the attack. Some judicial comments have received widespread media attention and public discussion, followed by suggestions for reforming and re-educating the judiciary (Senate Standing Committee on Legal and Constitutional Affairs, 1994; Sullivan, 1994: 1–2).

4 Conviction rates remain relatively low. South Australian research indicates that legal reforms have been followed by an expansion in reports of rape and sexual offences to police and increasing numbers of people are being charged with rape and indecent assault. But such increases are not reflected in convictions; a high and increasing percentage of rape charges are withdrawn, dismissed or result in a *nolle prosequi* (a formal statement to the court by the prosecution that it does not wish to proceed further with the charges). Chances of acquittal are relatively good, perhaps because of the persistence of traditional attitudes about rape on the part of juries, and defendants are more likely to plead, or to be found, not guilty of such offences (Edwards and Heenan, 1994: 219; Heath and Naffine, 1994: 45–50).

Similar assumptions are also evident in some media portrayals. Not all rape cases receive widespread media attention. There is a tendency towards immense coverage of a few high-profile or spectacular cases, either due to the social status of the accused or where the incident involves multiple offenders, multiple victims or high levels of violence. News reports have a central role in constructing or perpetuating an image of the 'normal' rape situation so that other incidents are presented as trivial, unworthy of legal or public attention, and perhaps imagined by the complainant or accuser (Bumiller, 1990: 125). A comparison of legal discourse and media portrayals of rape during the trial of six defendants (four of whom were ultimately convicted) accused of raping a woman on a pool table in a New Bedford (Massachusetts) bar shows how the victim was redefined in line with suppositions about the 'normal' victim. Initially, this incident was depicted as an inconceivably brutal gang rape cheered on by pitiless bystanders. As the facts became public knowledge, however, the unnamed complainant was portrayed as a confused young woman of unreliable character (Bumiller, 1990: 140). Negative feelings developed around the victim because of the defendants' Portuguese ethnicity and the perception that the rape accusations were an attack on the entire Portuguese community in New Bedford (Chancer, 1987: 248–52).

Similarly, the Mike Tyson and William Kennedy Smith trials in 1992 demonstrate the representation of rape as something that only certain 'types' of men do to certain 'types' of women (Freeman, 1993: 527). News reports described Tyson as aggressive, unintelligent, brutal and rapacious, thus reflecting enduring stereotypes about black men. They portrayed the victim – Desirée Washington – as an innocent, sexually inexperienced, naive and trusting 'all-American girl' and therefore as credible and rapable. This enabled her to overcome the stereotype of black women as always being sexual and consenting (Dalrymple, 1994). This contrasts with Patty Bowman – the accuser in the Kennedy Smith trial – whose age, single-motherhood status, extroverted social behaviour and presence in a bar late at night made her appear promiscuous, unreliable, desperate and a 'social climber'. Kennedy Smith's family background, education, social class and race militate against conclusions that he is the kind of man who commits rape.

A close analysis of the Kennedy Smith trial demonstrates the ways in which information about the victim's sexual history and related character evidence can be put to the jury by the defence as a strategy for impeaching credibility or proving consent, without coming within the legal prohibitions on introducing evidence about past sexual relationships. The defence lawyer's use of language, their manner of posing questions and presenting details generated scepticism about Bowman's version of events. For example, asking about the father of her child indicated to the jury that she had not been married but had previously engaged in premarital sexual relations. The defence lawyer portrayed her wish to visit the Kennedy house as a desire to see Smith and suggested that this interest, late at night after conversations in a bar, could only be inferred as sexual interest, thereby raising doubts about the absence of consent. Bowman was presented as deviating from cultural prescriptions about appropriate gender behaviour and from expectations about how a 'normal' victim of rape should behave; she phoned an acquaintance (not a close friend or the police) after the alleged crime and several times expressed concern about the where-abouts of her shoes (interpreted as a trivial matter) (Matoesian, 1995: 678–83).

Despite law reforms aimed at reducing the trauma of the trial for the victim and thereby increasing rates of reporting and convictions in rape cases, the organization of the trial process and the presentation of evidence can create an environment where sexual history inferences can emerge that do not infringe legal prohibitions. The reforms only apply to the presentation of evidence during a trial and do not prohibit issues of sexual history or character from being taken into account in police decisions to arrest a suspect or in prosecutors' decisions to take the charges to trial rather than drop them, or to seek to obtain a guilty plea to fewer or lesser charges (Frohmann, 1991: 217).

Domestic violence

As with rape-law reform, the development of legal and social consciousness around domestic violence is inextricably linked with the activities of the women's movement. Since the 1990s outlawing domestic violence has become a major international human rights issue (Hajjar, 2004: 12). As with all law reform, the nature of the pressures and initiatives for change depend on different national, socio-legal and cultural contexts. A comparison of the battered women's movements in the USA and Spain finds that, in the USA, grass-roots action was joined by professionals – social workers, psychologists and lawyers – and feminist organizations mobilized to combat domestic violence in the 1970s. Over time, the movement has undergone great changes, with strong feminist or political principles and practices being engulfed by a more social service-oriented framework. In contrast, at the beginning of the 1980s in Spain, a group of 15 women professionals – mostly lawyers, social workers and psychologists – worked on consciousness raising about the problem of battered women and immediately sought legitimation from the state in the form of legislation, institutionalization of the problem and the creation and funding of services (Miller and Barberet, 1995: 925–31; Tierney, 1982: 207–9).

A comparative analysis of Muslim countries in the Middle East, Asia and Africa finds that while the issues of domestic violence resonate with other societies, the Shari'a as the legal framework for administering marriage, divorce, custody and inheritance, and its various uses and interpretations shape the discourse of domestic violence. Transnational movements such as Islamization and human rights have shaped the progress of women's rights in these soceieties and consideration of 'whether *shari'a* is interpreted to construe violence against women as a *harm* or a *right*' (Hajjar, 2004: 7, emphasis in original). Many of the nations with majority Muslim populations that are signatories to the United Nations' Convention to Eliminate all forms of Discrimination Against Women (CEDAW) have made various reservations with the aim of preserving the reach of the Shari'a regarding personal status. The Shari'a in most Muslim soceieties is interpreted to permit some levels of violence within families in which men assume guardianship and control over women members who have a duty of obeisance. Individual states' policies regarding domestic violence will result from the interplay or jurisdictional struggle between different discourses and legal frames: international human rights edicts and religious or customary norms (Hajjar, 2004: 15–19).

The central aims of battered women's movements include the establishment of refuges, altering police behaviour to improve law-enforcement effectiveness and sensitivity to victims, providing more legal protection for the victims of domestic violence (for example restraining orders[2]) and reforming criminal laws to recognize and penalize domestic violence. An underlining theme in these reforms is that, at the very least, the criminal justice system should view domestic violence as a punishable offence and that perpetrators and victims should be viewed similarly to those in other assault cases. Both civil and criminal law can make important contributions to abused women, the perpetrators and the general community. Criminal justice policies which adopt surveillance and control through arrest and probation and include rehabilitation processes explicitly targeting violent behaviour and associated attitudes may provide the best chances for reducing violence and abuse (Lewis et al., 2001: 124).

While both laws and police attitudes reflect support for arresting offenders – with some advocating mandatory arrest policies – in battering cases there is often a discrepancy between the rhetoric and the reality of arrest. Some police continue to trivialize domestic complaints, believing that violence is a way of life for a particular couple, are reticent to intervene due to the low chances of arrest and eventual conviction, and may believe that domestic violence is not a real crime and therefore does not conform with their perceptions of real police work as crime control (Miller and Barberet, 1995: 936). Police are often reluctant to make arrests for domestic violence unless both disputants are present, the victim demands an arrest and signs the arrest warrant, the victim alleges violence and male alcohol consumption, the neighbours complain, or the suspect contests or confronts police authority (Berk and Loseke, 1981: 341–2; Ferraro, 1989: 61). Arrest is only one of the responses that police might make. They may negotiate or 'talk out' the dispute, threaten the disputants by asking one of the parties to leave the premises, or make an arrest (Sherman and Berk, 1984: 262). Nonintervention may be part of formal police policy because of a perception that domestic violence differs from other assault offences. Even where the official policy is to take formal action, police may make few arrests in assaults involving intimate partners. Experienced officers view women who conform to societal norms as more believable, less dangerous and more able to facilitate successful prosecution (Stalans and Finn, 1995: 307–13). Analyses of police records for domestic violence attendance show that arrest is no more effective than other police intervention in reducing further violence (Berk et al., 1992: 698; Pate and Hamilton, 1992: 695; Sherman et al., 1992: 686–8).

Recently, there has been attention paid to the ways in which the criminal law is applied to women who kill their abusive male partners. There is concern that the defences of provocation and self-defence (as traditionally developed and applied) are inadequate in cases where a woman kills her batterer. Feminists argue that a legal doctrine based on men's experiences and perceptions is unacceptable, as women defendants must fit into existing paradigms or become unable to avail themselves of those defences. For example, the paradigm of the law of self-defence is a situation where two men of roughly equal strength, possibly strangers, are engaged in a public brawl; thus, until recently, raising the defence in domestic settings has been particularly difficult for women (O'Donovan, 1993: 428–9; Sheehy et al., 1992: 370–80). Successfully arguing self-defence results in an acquittal, but the defendant must show that the amount of force used was proportionate to the imminent danger. This is a problem for many women, who are generally of a smaller size and strength than men. Demonstrating provocation reduces murder to manslaughter and requires the defendant to show that the victim's actions caused her/him to lose self-control and act in the heat of passion; the killing cannot be pre-meditated or carried out in 'cold blood'. Judges have been far more likely to recognize a woman's sexual taunts as sufficient provocation in cases of men killing their female partners (Howe, 1994: 232–5). They may or may not consider cumulative and extended violence and sexual abuse of female perpetrators to constitute provocation *(R v R* 1981: 321). Any lapse of time between the provocation and the killing has been an obstacle for the defence of women who kill violent partners. Nonetheless, the Court of Appeal (England and Wales) agreed that delay does not automatically exclude a provocation defence (Burton, 2001: 248; *R v Ahluwalia* 1992). In *R v Thornton* (1996) the Court stated:

> A defendant, even if suffering from that [battered woman] syndrome, cannot succeed in relying on provocation unless the jury consider she suffered or may have suffered a sudden and temporary loss of self-control at the time of the killing. That is not to say that a battered woman syndrome has no relevance to the defence of provocation. ... [I]t might be relevant in two ways. First, it may form an important background to whatever triggered the actus reus. A jury may more readily find there was a sudden loss of control triggered by even a minor incident, if the defendant has endured abuse over a period, on the 'last straw' basis. Secondly, depending on the medical evidence, the syndrome may have affected the defendant's personality so as to constitute a significant characteristic relevant (as we shall indicate) to the second question the jury has to consider in regard to provocation.

Reliance on the battered woman/wife syndrome and the use of expert witnesses to explain the syndrome to the court raise some dilemmas for feminist law reformers. Undoubtedly, courts' acceptance of the battered woman syndrome advances the position of women defendants, yet it also serves to psychologize or medicalize women's responses. Even though the introduction of evidence regarding the battered woman syndrome sought to counteract commonsense assumptions and negative stereotypes about women in abusive relationships, its incorporation into law has tended to reaffirm normative and everyday understandings of violent relationships

(Morgan, 1996: 56–75). A case study of the Ohio governor's 1990 decision to grant clemency to 26 women incarcerated for killing or assaulting abusive intimate partners or stepfathers demonstrates the direct influence of the battered woman's movement in achieving this outcome. Feminists used their careers and personal relationships to implement consciousness-raising groups within the women's prison, which established a collective identity among women inmates and created a social movement community (Gagné, 1996: 82–5).

In attempting to change legal practice or policy, feminists will adopt a wide range of strategies with varying degrees of success, depending, among other things, on the contexts in which they operate. Legal strategies can have very different short- and long-term effects, as some of the feminist activism around pornography and its regulation suggests.

Pornography

Feminist campaigns against pornography in North America, Europe and Australia in the late 1970s and 1980s aimed to replace laws on obscenity, which focus on protecting morality, with a conception of pornography as sex discrimination. Rather than raising issues of freedom of expression versus censorship, some feminists argue that pornography causes harm and violence to women and reinforces their subordination. They look to the law as an attempt to remedy gender inequality. Debates about pornography have been particularly controversial within the women's movement, reflecting widespread dissensus (Eckersley, 1987: 150–61).

Radical feminists have been at the forefront of efforts to revise the theory and practice of pornography. MacKinnon, for example, criticizes the way in which the abstractness of the legal concepts of obscenity and freedom of speech have made the pornographers' expression seem acceptable and even necessary to democratic society, at the same time as ignoring the subordination and dehumanization of women that pornography perpetuates (MacKinnon, 1986: 64–5). Moreover, obscenity law based on a male perspective constructs female sexuality (or the lack of it) from the standpoint of male dominance. Pornography turns a woman into a thing to be acquired and used (MacKinnon, 1989: 199). Women who are taken, used, bound, humiliated, battered and tortured become erotic from the male standpoint whereas, from women's view, this is evidence of inequality, violation, victimization, powerlessness and subordination. 'Pornography institutionalizes the sexuality of male supremacy, fusing the erotization of dominance and submission with the social construction of male and female' (MacKinnon, 1987: 172). Although the content and dynamic of pornography concern women, the law of obscenity has never even considered pornography a women's issue. Liberalism has never understood the reality of pornography: 'the free so-called speech of men silences the free speech of women' (MacKinnon, 1989: 205). MacKinnon argues that, from the feminist viewpoint, pornography is a form of forced sex, a practice of sexual politics and an institution of gender inequality, not a question of freedom of expression or morality. In this light, obscenity law treats morals from the male point of view (MacKinnon, 1989: 197). The availability of pornography does not just reinforce the ideological subordination of all women and the actual exploitation of the female participants in the industry, but is also directly linked to violence and rape.

Local antipornography movements in three US cities – Minneapolis in 1983, Indianapolis in 1984 and Bellingham in 1988 – proposed new legislation against pornography that largely relied on the concepts, writing and assistance of MacKinnon and Andrea Dworkin (a prominent feminist activist). The Campaign Against Pornography and Censorship, a British group established in 1989, also worked with lawyers to propose new laws against pornography modelled on the proposed US laws and the existing British race-relations legislation (Smith, 1993: 71). The proposed ordinances in the United States amended municipal civil-rights laws, conceptualized pornography as sex discrimination, and sought to further the equality of the sexes by enabling women to bring civil actions against those responsible for the production, sale, exhibition or distribution of pornography, and also for being coerced into pornographic performances. These ordinances defined pornography as:

> The graphic sexually explicit subordination of women through pictures or words that also includes women dehumanized as sexual objects, things, or commodities; enjoying pain or humiliation or rape; being tied up, cut up, mutilated, bruised, or physically hurt; in postures of sexual submission or servility or display; reduced to body parts, penetrated by objects or animals, or presented in scenarios of degradation, injury, torture; shown as filthy or inferior; bleeding, bruised, or hurt in a context that makes these conditions sexual. (MacKinnon, 1987: 176)[3]

This approach and legal strategy have been widely criticized. Four central issues are the subject of dispute among feminists: the definition of pornography; problems of causation between exposure to pornography and subsequent violence; the overlap between radical feminist and conservative perspectives on pornography; and a reliance on the law to remedy inequality.

1   The definition of pornography is so wide that it would encompass material central to the advancement of women and other subordinate groups, including gay and lesbian writing, experimental feminist art and birth-control information. The notion of 'sexually explicit subordination' would provide conservative forces with a tool to censor feminist writing and art that deal openly and explicitly with sexual themes (Hunter and Law, 1987–8: 108). Secondly, the attempt to develop a concrete 'objective' definition, while reducing the scope of subjective judicial assessments of whether something is obscene, contains no reference to context or the ways in which text or pictures have different meanings in different settings (Smith, 1993: 79). Thirdly, the definition presents a very narrow and stereotypical view of women's sexuality and parallels historical attempts to protect women from humiliating, degrading and offensive images. The conception of female sexuality treats women as victims with little agency or capacity to make choices (Duggan et al., 1984: 134–42; Hunter and Law, 1987–8: 105–8).

2   The connection between fantasy or symbolic representation and action in the real world is not simple, linear or causal. Sexual imagery and messages and their impact on the consumer are often multiple, contradictory, layered and highly contextual (Hunter and Law, 1987–8: 106). Treating sexually explicit material as the central factor in the oppression of women ignores other bases of sex discrimination, including the segmented labour market and pay discrimination (Smith, 1993: 81).

3   Many feminists have expressed unease and dismay regarding the coalitions formed by the radical feminists against pornography with conservative groups that are not primarily concerned with women's rights or equality. Only in Minneapolis was there support from local feminists. The other proponents of the antipornography laws included neighbourhood groups concerned about the effect of porn shops on residential areas and such conservative groups as Citizens for Decency opposed to the availability of sexually explicit materials for moral reasons (Duggan et al., 1984: 131–3).

4   Feminists also voiced surprise and concern about the reliance on legal remedies to promote social change, especially in the light of MacKinnon's own radical critique of the maleness of law (see Chapter 3). Many women's movement activists and commentators are also sceptical about the extent to which legal remedies can have the desired outcomes (Lacey, 1993: 107; Smart, 1989: 135–6).

None of the ordinances survived the legal contest. In Minneapolis, the mayor vetoed the proposed legal changes, while the other two cases were successfully challenged in the courts by book publishers and sellers. In a 1985 case – *American Booksellers Association v Hudnut* (the mayor of Indianapolis) – the court criticized the divergence between the proposed definition of pornography and legal precedents defining and prohibiting obscenity. The established legal definition requires that a publication, taken as a whole, must appeal to prurient interest, contain patently offensive depictions of sexual conduct and lack creative or scientific merit according to community standards (*Miller v California* 1973: 419). The new definition did not refer to any of these concepts. The court observed that the wider, new definition could encompass great literary works ranging from James Joyce's *Ulysses* to Homer's *Iliad*, both of which depict women as submissive objects for conquest and domination. The court had no difficulty in deciding that the proposed ordinance infringed the constitutionally guaranteed freedom of speech and opined:

The Constitution forbids the state to declare one perspective right and silence opponents. ... Speech that 'subordinates' women and also, for example, presents women as enjoying pain, humiliation, or rape, or even simply presents women in 'positions of servility or submission or display' is forbidden, no matter how great the literary or political value of the work taken as a whole. Speech that portrays women in 'positions of equality is lawful, no matter how graphic the sexual content. This is thought control. It establishes an 'approved' view of women, of how they may react to sexual encounters, of how the sexes may relate to each other. Those who espouse the approved view may use sexual images; those who do not, may not. (*American Booksellers v Hudnut* 1985: 325, 328)

Despite the failure of these specific attempts to change the law of obscenity, due in part to the virtually absolute protection of free speech in the USA, the legal discourse around pornography has changed. Framing pornography as sex discrimination prioritizes a feminist view of pornography focusing on gender inequality rather than traditional concerns with sin, moral depravity and family values (Lacey, 1993: 105–6).

Aspects of the feminist antipornography arguments have been adopted by the Canadian courts, which have been concerned with damage to the community and violence in general. In 1992, the Canadian Supreme Court unanimously upheld an antiobscenity law by focusing on the violence, degradation and dehumanization depicted in pornography *(R v Butler* 1992). In this case, the accused owned a shop selling and renting 'hardcore' videotapes and magazines and was charged with various counts of selling, possessing with the intention of distribution or sale, and exposing obscene material to the public contrary to the criminal code, which provides that 'any publication a dominant characteristic of which is the undue exploitation of sex, or of sex and any one or more of ... crime, horror, cruelty and violence shall be deemed to be obscene' (s 163(8) of the Criminal Code). The trial judge concluded that the obscene material was protected by the guarantee of freedom of expression in the 1982 Canadian *Charter of Rights and Freedoms.* On appeal, the Supreme Court reinterpreted the term obscenity; it replaced the previous emphasis on the prevailing standards of decency with a notion of gender-based harm (Scales, 1994: 357–8). The Court found that:

> Among other things, degrading or dehumanizing materials place women (and sometimes men) in positions of subordination, servile submission or humiliation. They run against the principles of equality and dignity of all human beings. ... This type of material would, apparently, fail the community standards test not because it offends against morals but because it is perceived by public opinion to be harmful to society, particularly to women. *(R v Butler* 1992: 479)

The court observed that the relevant section of the criminal code is designed to catch material that creates a risk of harm to society and that such serious social problems as violence against women require multiple government responses, including legislation and education. It agreed that avoiding harm to society is sufficiently important to warrant a minimum restriction on freedom of expression.

This Canadian decision has come closer than any other to an analysis of pornography in gender terms rather than in the traditional moral discourse. Concerns remain about its limitations and the ways in which it has been and will be used. For example, the decision retains the notion of community standards of tolerance.[4] A case decided after *Butler* (but brought before) involving a bookshop's challenge to customs official's seizure of various sexually explicit gay male materials purported to follow *Butler,* but the judge used a morality-based standard to conclude that all the publications were obscene. There have been subsequent police prosecutions of lesbian magazines and booksellers' challenging of customs' seizures of gay and lesbian material more because of the sexuality of the publishers or the targeted audience than the extent of harm. In one case, customs employees confiscated hundreds of books and magazines, including lesbian romance novels that contain no violence and almost no sex, as well as academic books about homosexuality and pornography (Scales, 1994: 362). Additionally, the *Butler* case retains the 'artistic' defence, observing that: 'Even material which by itself offends community standards will not be considered "undue" [exploitation], if it is required for the serious treatment of a theme' (*R* v *Butler* 1992: 482).

Reproductive rights

The legal arena and rights discourse have been important in lobbying for recognition of women's reproductive autonomy, especially in relation to abortion. In most western, industrial societies, abortion became a crime in the early nineteenth century, although certain terminations (if deemed therapeutic) were legal if carried out by a medical practitioner (Petersen, 1993). By the 1960s, access to abortion had become a central platform of the women's movement. Feminist proponents of decriminalization maintain that abortion is neither a medical nor a legal issue but a woman's right. They argue that women must have the right to control their own bodies and their reproductive lives in order to participate equally in society. Such arguments emphasize liberal legal values of choice, autonomy, freedom and privacy.

The shape of the abortion debates and strategies for change adopted by activists in various countries are affected by different political and legal structures and ideologies (Gibson, 1990: 181–5). Rights discourse is most salient in the USA due to its constitutional framework, the centrality of the courts in determining the status of abortion and the reliance on litigation strategies, including the use of test cases (Farr, 1993: 169). In the UK and some Australian jurisdictions, legislation permits therapeutic abortion and provides that an abortion will be legal only if performed by a registered medical practitioner after two other practitioners find that the duration of the pregnancy is within a specified time period, and that the termination is necessary to avoid injury to the physical or mental health (which often includes social factors) of the pregnant woman. Decriminalization does not provide women with an absolute right to abortion, but allows medical practitioners to perform abortions under certain circumstances; all other terminations of pregnancy remain criminal offences (Gibson, 1990: 181). In other Australian jurisdictions, abortion is legally available due to a judicial interpretation of state criminal statutes. Arguably, this is an example of effective litigation and of some courts' liberal attitude to women, and their recognition, although indirect, of women's rights or entitlements. However, the relevant cases were about allowing medical practitioners to perform the procedures and the decisions are vulnerable to appeal, as there has been no High Court or legislative affirmation of them.

In 1973, the US Supreme Court struck down all abortion laws, even those liberalizing abortion, as unconstitutional. In *Roe* v *Wade* (1973), the Court found that the right of privacy implicit in the Constitution 'is broad enough to encompass a woman's decision whether or not to terminate her pregnancy. The detriment that the State would impose upon the pregnant woman is altogether apparent' (*Roe* v *Wade* 1973: 153). The court did not agree that the woman's right to terminate her pregnancy is absolute and unqualified. First, the decision is made in consultation with 'her responsible physician'; and secondly, the state has interests in safeguarding health, in maintaining medical standards, and in protecting potential life that become more compelling than personal privacy as a pregnancy advances.

Following the *Roe* decision, abortion debates in the USA gathered momentum. The decision provided a major impetus to antiabortion activists with an expansion of their membership and resources (Luker, 1984: 137–44). The right-to-life-movement focused on the singular goal of having *Roe* v *Wade* overturned and abortion recriminalized. By the 1980s, abortion had become a site of contest over the meaning of motherhood, the role of women and men, the nature of the family, and the course of society in general (Ginsburg, 1989: 99; Petchesky, 1986: 242). Women's access to abortion in the USA has since been curtailed, although the right to choose remains. In a series of decisions the Supreme Court has dealt with this right in the abstract while downplaying the conditions under which the right can be realized. It has accepted the rights of states to prohibit the use of public funds to perform, inform or counsel about abortion and to require pre-abortion patients to be counselled on the negative consequences of abortion and then to wait 24 hours before the procedure (Farr, 1993: 177).

While the privacy doctrine successfully established the legal right to abortion, it became a tenuous foundation in the light of growing opposition to legal abortion and the increasing formalism of the US Supreme Court (Eisenstein, 1988: 187–9). Accordingly, pro-abortion or pro-choice arguments have shifted from privacy and choice to a focus on equality and the social and economic conditions that enable the 'right to choose' to be exercised rather than just possessed. In an amicus brief for the 1989 case *Webster* v *Reproductive Health Services,* the National Abortion Rights Action League (NARAL) argued that restrictive abortion laws deprive women of the freedom to control the course of their lives and thereby restrict their ability to participate in society equally with men. Equal participation rapidly erodes due to the financial constraints that childbearing and rearing place on women. Consequently, it is argued, the discourse of reproductive rights must recast the language of 'pro-choice' in terms of race, economic class, geographical location, age and other factors that determine access to equality (Eisenstein, 1991: 118–22). However, such concerns have not been adopted by the majority of the US Supreme Court, which emphasizes the existence of choice as distinct from the opportunities to exercise such 'choice'. So long as women do not rely on public health facilities, their 'choices' are unimpeded. Others can still choose to have a termination, but will have to fund it themselves if public facilities do not offer termination services. (Former) Chief Justice Rehnquist, delivering the judgement of the Court in *Webster,* declared:

> Missouri's refusal to allow public employees to perform abortions in public hospitals leaves a pregnant woman with the same choices as if the State had chosen not to operate any public hospitals at all. The challenged provisions only restrict a woman's ability to obtain an abortion to the extent that she chooses to use a physician affiliated with a public hospital. (1989: 3052)

In the abstract, this decision does not take away the right to abortion or limit the sphere of privacy, but by upholding states' right to restrict abortion services it reduces access for those women with few economic resources and without private health insurance who rely on public hospitals. This is a narrow, individualistic view of choice that does not take into account the social conditions under which choices can be implemented.

In *Planned Parenthood of Southeastern Pennsylvania v Casey* (1992), the Court upheld a state abortion statute requiring that a woman seeking an abortion give informed consent and that a minor seeking an abortion obtain the consent of one of her parents, but it rejected the spousal-notification provisions. The majority held:

> Though the woman has a right to choose to terminate or continue her pregnancy before viability, it does not at all follow that the State is prohibited from taking steps to ensure that this choice is thoughtful and informed. Even in the earliest stages of pregnancy, the State may enact rules and regulations designed to encourage her to know that there are philosophic and social arguments of great weight that can be brought to bear in favour of continuing the pregnancy to full term and that there are procedures and institutions to allow adoption of unwanted children as well as a certain degree of state assistance if the mother chooses to raise the child herself. ... It follows that States are free to enact laws to provide a reasonable framework for a woman to make a decision that has such profound and lasting meaning. *(Planned Parenthood* 1992: 711–12)

From this decision, it seems that the requirement of informed consent is satisfied even if only 'right-to-life' information is provided. According to the court, a state policy to persuade a woman to choose childbirth over abortion may not unduly burden her in making the decision. The court has shifted from a liberal view of women making the decision in private within the confidential doctor–patient relationship to a conception of women taking into account the interests of others – including the potential child, infertile couples seeking to adopt children, and other family members – when making the decision. The right to choose remains intact, but the conditions under which it can be exercised have been curtailed.

While the language of rights was instrumental in legalizing abortion, by the 1980s right-to-life organizations had developed a sophisticated rhetoric around the rights of the unborn. Advances in medical technology, especially ultrasound and electronic fetal monitoring, have facilitated a conception of the fetus as separate from the pregnant woman's body (Petchesky, 1987: 271). The success of right-to-life activists in the USA was aided by the neoconservative political regime prevalent during the 1980s and the rightward drift in the courts. According to fetal rights advocates, the interests of the woman and the fetus are not necessarily compatible; an adversarial relationship may exist in which the woman becomes liable for any birth defects or neonatal problems (Johnsen, 1986: 613). Fetal-rights discourse in the USA has justified court-ordered medical intervention, including caesarian sections and blood transfusions to benefit the fetus. Concern about fetal harm resulting from a pregnant woman's use of illegal drugs escalated during the 1980s and entailed attempts to prosecute pregnant drug users for harming the fetus by using statutes dealing with child abuse, neglect or endangerment and delivering controlled substances to minors (Farr, 1995: 236–7). Nevertheless, the emerging discourse of fetal rights and fetal personhood has not been deployed by courts unequivocally (De Gama, 1993; Diduck, 1993: 478).

Attempts to restrict abortion in the USA focus on the Supreme Court and so far have enjoyed far more success than in Australia or the UK, where antiabortion activists must lobby for legislative change. Numerous attempts to tighten existing criminal abortion statutes have failed in Australian legislatures (Coleman, 1988: 88–91). The concern of Australian and UK courts in abortion cases has been with maternal health and not with the health of the fetus as a separate entity. It seems that where abortion is largely accepted as a legitimate medical treatment, rebatable under national health schemes, it is less politicized and less vulnerable than where it is couched as a woman's constitutional right and the subject of high court decision making (Shaver, 1992: 21–2).

While feminists and right-to-life activists hold diametrically opposed viewpoints in the abortion debates, this is not the case in the debates on assisted conception, especially *in vitro* fertilization (IVF) and surrogacy. Despite different arguments and value orientations, the conclusions of some feminist and conservative critics converge: that medical scientists are self-interested and should not be trusted, and that IVF programmes are harmful and should be discontinued. For many feminists, harm is done to the women who undergo the often invasive and experimental procedures, while right-to-life activists are concerned primarily with the harm done to the embryo or fetus.

The meaning of reproductive autonomy is a point of disagreement among liberal and radical feminists. The latter suggest that, rather than extending women's choices and reproductive autonomy, assisted reproductive techniques actually narrow them, subject women to greater social control and further pathologize their bodies. The availability of such programmes reinforces pro-natalist ideals and places additional pressures on women who are unable to conceive; motherhood is reinforced as a necessary status for 'normal' women. Participants in IVF programmes may have little scope for making choices to refuse or vary treatments. Autonomy is reduced further, as the only sphere where women have some distinctive power and control – motherhood – is being steadily eroded by increasing medical intervention (Rothman, 1989: 152–8). Indeed, the whole notion of motherhood is being fragmented, especially visible in surrogacy arrangements where the genetic, gestational, social and legal mothers can all be different women, raising the question of who can make the most authentic claim to motherhood (Roach Anleu, 1993: 32–3).

On the other side, liberal feminists reject the image of women who participate in assisted reproduction programmes as victims unable or incapable of resisting male domination and passively complying with the desires of a husband to father children and the demands of mostly male medical doctors (Wikler, 1986: 1053). They maintain that such imagery trivializes women who have decided to participate in an IVF programme and denies that the desires of women who are unable to conceive are real and concrete, not merely ephemeral or socially constructed (Sandelowski, 1990: 41).

In some jurisdictions, legislation regulates the experimental and clinical application of assisted reproductive technologies. In some Australian states and the UK, statutes restrict the availability of assistance to married couples (or a legally defined equivalent), place restrictions on embryo experimentation and gamete donation, and outlaw commercial surrogacy. Despite the diverse issues raised by these technologies, public debate and the impetus for legislative regulation have focused primarily on three main themes (Roach Anleu, 1996: 182):

1   *the status of the embryo,* especially regarding experimentation, the existence of so-called spare or surplus embryos and their storage;
2   *the constitution of the family,* and the fate of traditional and legal conceptions of parenthood, which evince an assumption that marriage is the basis of family life. The historical fixation with marriage denotes a concern about fatherhood and paternity that becomes critical in the context of reproductive technology, as genetic/biological ties can no longer be automatically assumed (Smart, 1987: 101). It seems that marriage becomes more important in order to provide the appearance of genetic linkage and paternity, especially as medical technology may pose a greater threat to fatherhood than motherhood (De Gama, 1993: 123); and
3   *the role of medical science,* which is linked to concerns about the fate of embryos if experimentation and cryopreservation (freezing) remain unregulated, and to questions of the cost of the procedures and the importance of patients' rights to exercise informed consent.

In the USA, an analysis of court cases up to 1990 involving reproductive technologies demonstrates the ways in which judicial opinion attempts to alter social relationships. The cases tend not to recognize how social conditions shape reproductive choices; they promote fathers' rights; value men's biological contribution to childbearing; reflect assumptions about the proper role of mothers and fathers; and privilege the nuclear family. Nonetheless, judicial opinion is neither monolithic nor unidirectional; for example, in child-custody cases the courts recognized the influence of social conditions on reproductive choices and acknowledged the social as well as biological dimensions of parenting (Blankenship et al., 1993: 27–8).

Conclusion

A consistent pattern across the various areas of law reform canvassed in this chapter is that it has not had the desired effect nor brought the outcomes that many social movement activists expected. In part, this is because legal change neither necessarily nor directly translates into changed perceptions, practices and attitudes on the part of all the decision makers who are engaged in the application of new laws. Secondly, victims of discrimination or other harms are often reticent to use legal remedies to manage their situation, but will rather ignore the problem and do nothing, avoid the source of the harm or grievance, or deal with it through informal networks (Bumiller, 1987: 438). Thirdly, the failure of law reforms derives from the fact that laws are not the sole cause of pervasive gender inequalities, although they can certainly reinforce them. Moreover, statutory change and judicial decisions usually deal only with specific aspects of a problem.

It is naive to expect that simply reforming various statutes will directly transform discriminatory social practices and deep-seated attitudes regarding women. Nevertheless, it is unhelpful and highly reductionist to assert that despite antidiscrimination legislation, equal pay provisions and the broadening of the legal definition of rape, the situation of some women, at least, has not improved. Legal change can have important symbolic functions and is not necessarily unidirectional, incremental or cumulative. The actions and arguments of lawyers can improve the situation of individual women and, perhaps, even create important precedents. Smart's notion of the uneven development of law conceptualizes law as operating on a number of dimensions simultaneously. She refers to 'the possibility of seeing law both as a means of "liberation" and, at the same time, as a means of the reproduction of an oppressive social order. Law both facilitates change and is an obstacle to change' (Smart, 1986: 117). Viewing law as a complex of diverse and often contradictory pieces of legislation, judicial statements and enforcement practices, it is not surprising that advances in one area may be thwarted by various, including legal, impediments in another. For example, while abortion may be legally available in specific circumstances, the existence (or non-existence) of legislatively established national health schemes or private health insurance and personal income will restrict some women's access to abortion services.

Notes

1 In the USA, the EEOC guidelines issued in 1980 provide that:

> Unwelcome sexual advances, requests for sexual favours, and other verbal or physical conduct constitute sexual harassment when (1) submission to such conduct is made either explicitly or implicitly a term or condition of an individual's employment, (2) submission to or rejection of such conduct by an individual is used as the basis for employment decisions affecting such individual, or (3) such conduct has the purpose or effect of unreasonably interfering with an individual's work performance or creating an intimidating, hostile, or offensive working environment. (Equal Employment Opportunity Commission, 1980: 25)

2 Restraining or protection orders can be obtained by application to a court and are civil remedies. What is interesting is that violation of such an order is punished as a crime, not because the victim was endangered or actually assaulted but because a court order has been breached, constituting a serious offence.

3 Although the definition is framed in terms of depictions of women, both bylaws provided that the use of men, children or transsexuals in the place of women in these depictions also constitutes pornography.

4 The Court opined that:

> Pornography can be usefully divided into three categories: (1) explicit sex with violence, (2) explicit sex without violence but which subjects people to treatment that is degrading or dehumanizing, and (3) explicit sex without violence that is neither degrading or dehumanizing. ... Some segments of society would consider that all three categories of pornography cause harm to society because they tend to undermine its moral fibre. Others would contend that none of the categories cause harm. Furthermore there is a range of opinion as to what is degrading or dehumanizing. ... Because it is not a matter that is susceptible of proof in the traditional way and because we do not wish to leave it to the individual tastes of judges, we must have a norm that will serve as an arbiter in determining what amounts to an undue exploitation of sex. That arbiter is the community as a whole. (R v Butler 1992: 484)

8 Rights and Citizenship

Until recently, the topics of rights and citizenship had not received general sociological attention (Somers, 1994: 64; Turner, 1993). This absence can be partly attributed to sociologists' overwhelming concern with the social and their consequent focus on such collectivities as community, family and organizations, whereas rights have been interpreted as individual attributes. Secondly, the nation state, which for the most part of the twentieth century had been viewed as the source of citizenship, was of greater concern to political scientists, while sociologists studied such transnational processes as modernization, capitalism, industrialization, social class and bureaucratization. Thirdly, the view that any concept of rights is inevitably associated with morality, values and ethics and therefore beyond the realm of objective empirical investigation, or that rights are legal constructions or philosophical abstractions, perhaps rendered them outside the primary interests of the sociologist.

Nonetheless, rights and citizenship were not ignored by social theorists in the past (see for example Parsons, 1967). The current renewed interest in rights and citizenship follows the force of international events, especially the fall of communism in eastern Europe and the establishment of constitutional, democratic polities, the formation of the European Union, and the impossibility of viewing nation states as independent of supranational forces and relations, especially global capital and consumerism. Social movements and institutions that cross national boundaries have become the focus for claims about social rights and citizenship uncoupled from the nation state. Regardless of their position on the political spectrum, social movement activists usually adopt the language and discourse of rights and advocate the attainment or recognition of rights for particular constituencies.

This chapter examines recent elaborations on the concept of citizenship and associated rights among sociologists. While there is a general view that citizenship is more inclusive than such other traditional concepts as class and gender, there is little faith in the capacity of nation states to guarantee rights through domestic legal systems due to the weakening of national polities in the face of international economic forces, widespread telecommunications and large-scale migration. Some writers identify these trends as evidence of globalization and, instead of talking about citizenship rights underwritten by nation states, they shift attention to human rights being in an international context. Inevitably, the role of law is evident in these developments, especially the increasing impact of international law on the prerogatives of national legal systems. Even so, the concept of an international community that recognizes human rights remains utopian. The usual starting point for contemporary discussions of citizenship is T.H. Marshall's essay entitled 'Citizenship and Social Class', first published in 1950 but given as a series of lectures at Cambridge University the previous year.

The views of T.H. Marshall

For Marshall, citizenship is 'a status bestowed on those who are full members of a community' (1992: 18). It is an attribute or characteristic that people possess by virtue of belonging to a collectivity. Marshall extended the notion of citizenship from a narrow concept of formal rights to one that embraced social entitlements to include 'the whole range [of issues] from the right to a modicum of economic welfare and security to the right to share to the full in the social heritage and to live the life of a civilized being according to the standards prevailing in the society' (1992: 8). Citizenship requires a direct sense of community membership based on loyalty to a civilization, which is a common possession. Marshall identifies three elements of the concept of citizenship: civil, political and social.

1 *Civil rights* These include those rights necessary for individual freedom, namely liberty, freedom of speech, thought and faith, the right to own property and to conclude valid contracts, and the right to justice. The institutions most closely associated with civil rights are courts of justice that espouse the doctrines of the rule of law and due process. In the economic sphere, civil rights are characterized by free labour, that is, freedom from feudal ties and obligations, thus allowing social mobility, and the capacity to enter into employment contracts (which also requires geographical mobility). Marshall recognizes that such freedoms were limited and applied only to adult male members of the community, 'since the status of women, or at least of married women, was in some important respects peculiar' (1992: 12). Thus civil rights mean legal freedom, a formal status that may not be actually realized. Marshall specifies another subdimension of citizenship, namely industrial citizenship. Trade unionism has facilitated the advancement of collective civil rights that exist parallel with and supplementary to the system of political citizenship. While civil rights relate to individuals, trade unions are able to exercise vital civil rights collectively, therefore constituting a vehicle for raising the social and economic status of their members (Marshall, 1992: 26, 40). Industrial citizenship became significant as workers either did not possess or had not learned to use the political right of franchise.

2 *Political rights* These enable participation in the exercise of political power, either as a member of a body invested with political authority, for example the parliament and local government councils, or as an elector of the members of the

political body. In western capitalist democracies, political rights have expanded by paying a stipend to members of parliament to enable those members of society who do not have other sources of income or wealth to be involved, and by extending the franchise from male property owners to all adult male citizens, women, racial or ethnic minorities and to younger people.

3 *Social rights*   These refer to a minimum level of economic welfare, social security and living standards that are attendant on being a member of a collectivity. Social rights were the most clearly developed in the first two-thirds of the twentieth century, with the emergence of the welfare state and collective commitments to public education, housing, health, welfare and security in western capitalist democracies. The original source of social rights was membership of local communities and functional associations that were progressively replaced by the Elizabethan Poor Laws and a national system of wage regulation (Lockyer, 1964: 137–40). While the original Poor Laws championed the social rights of citizenship, by the nineteenth century they had come to do the opposite: poor relief was not an integral aspect of the rights of the citizen, but entailed forfeiting political rights and abrogating personal liberty by internment in the workhouse. Receipt of poor relief resulted in stigmatization and social exclusion. Possession of social rights did not guarantee other forms of citizenship. This was also the case with various Factory Acts that limited women's paid work during the nineteenth century: 'Women were protected because they were not citizens. If they wished to enjoy full and responsible citizenship, they must forgo protection' (Marshall, 1992: 14–15).

While the concept of citizenship existed in medieval times (and back to classical Greece and Rome), Marshall says that its history entails a differentiation of the elements, with citizenship growing from a local into a national institution. He considers that the evolution of citizenship has been in continuous progress over the past centuries and identifies the formative period of the different dimensions of citizenship with different centuries (acknowledging some overlap): civil rights belonged to the eighteenth century; political rights to the nineteenth; and social rights to the twentieth century (at least to the first two-thirds of it). Marshall's general conception of citizenship, then, emphasizes its sequential and cumulative nature, although he recognizes some unevenness, especially in relation to gender.

Marshall's primary interest is to assess the impact of citizenship on social inequality: the two forces emerged as a central contradiction during the twentieth century, yet are able to coexist. On the one side, all who possess citizenship status are equal with respect to the attached rights and duties, but social class is a system of inequality. While not arguing for direct causation, Marshall suggests that the growth of national citizenship coincides with the rise of capitalism by asking:

How is it that these two opposing principles could grow and flourish side by side in the same soil? ... The equality implicit in the concept of citizenship, even though limited in content, undermined the inequality of the class system, which was in principle a total inequality. (Marshall, 1992: 18–19)

Until the twentieth century, with the resurgence of social rights, citizenship and the social-class system remained compatible. Civil rights constituted the earliest forms of citizenship and were indispensable to a competitive, free-market economy that required the mobility of labour and capital. As civil rights were intensely individual in origin, they complemented the individualistic phase of capitalism and, indeed, were necessary to the maintenance of that particular form of inequality. This was especially salient in employment relations, which rely on contractual agreements between parties who are formally free and equal in status, though not necessarily equivalent in bargaining power. The blatant inequalities that emerged despite the equal possession of civil rights were not due to defects in civil rights but to an absence of social rights. Inability to enforce or implement rights derives from the unequal distribution of wealth, class prejudice and the very high cost of legal action. Ironically, civil rights, the possession of which might be more widespread or universal than other rights, are among the most difficult to realize because of a reliance on the legal system and the prohibitive cost of litigation (Marshall, 1992: 20–6). This resonates with Weber's discussion of the distinctiveness (and irrational dimensions) of the English legal system, which was able to deny substantive justice to economically weak segments and support, even reproduce, the interests of the capitalist classes while maintaining the ideology of formal legal equality (see Chapter 2).

A growing national consciousness and the extension of political rights enabled the establishment of social rights via the exercise of political power. By the beginning of the twentieth century, social rights were being incorporated into the status of citizenship, thus creating a universal right to real income not proportionate to the market value of the claimant. What is distinctive about social rights in the twentieth century is the shift in emphasis from ameliorating the conditions of the most disadvantaged individuals to attempting to modify the whole pattern of social inequality through governmental social insurance schemes, which are established legislatively and implemented bureaucratically (Hasenfeld et al., 1987: 397–401). Full citizenship requires the collective provision of certain services and benefits: 'The obligation of the state is towards society as a whole, whose remedy in case of default lies in parliament or a local council, instead of to individual citizens, whose remedy lies in a court of law, or at least in a quasi-judicial tribunal' (Marshall, 1992: 35). Schemes to remove the barriers between civil rights and their remedies include legal aid, guaranteed minimum wages, pensions, national health schemes and public housing provision.

Clearly, citizenship is not synonymous with equality. Citizenship operates as an instrument of social stratification, especially through education and in its relationship with the occupational structure. Members of the community have the right to equality of opportunity but not to equality of outcome (Marshall, 1992: 38–9). Status differences are compatible with democratic citizenship as long as they are not too vast, but exist within a population united in a single civilization or national identity, and are not the result of hereditary privilege. Inequalities can be tolerated and reproduced within an egalitarian society when they are neither too dynamic nor result in pressures for radical social change.

General criticisms

Marshall's conceptualization of citizenship as evolutionary, progressive, becoming more inclusive and ameliorating the negative, gross inequalities of the capitalist market has been widely criticized (Roche, 1987: 368–75). His view of citizenship is often unclear: he refers to three dimensions of citizenship at the outset, but then usually refers to different types of citizenship. The possession of some citizenship rights can weaken others, for example social rights based on family membership and actual or potential motherhood accorded to women in the workplace undermined their civil rights, especially their restriction from certain kinds of jobs, or paid employment altogether. With the shrinking of the welfare state since the 1970s, it is obvious that the achievement of rights is not cumulative or collectively guaranteed. Social rights provided by the welfare state are clearly reversible and not to be taken for granted (Turner, 1990: 192). Turner holds that: 'The Marshallian framework has been eroded because economic changes, technological innovation and globalization have transformed the nature of work, war and the social relations of reproduction. The three routes – employment, war service and family formation – to effective citizenship no longer provide a firm socio-economic framework within which social rights can be enjoyed' (2001: 203).

To be fair, however, Marshall (along with many others) could not have predicted the fate of the welfare state in the last quarter of the twentieth century. For Marshall, social class was the main dimension of inequality. He mentioned (but without theoretical attention) sex differences – specifically the exclusion of women from the occupational structure and from political rights – but did not attend to other dimensions of inequality, namely race, ethnicity and sexuality.

Marshall's discussion is entirely about England, which begs the question of whether he considered it to be the prototype of imminent development in capitalist, western democratic societies. His scheme may fit the English example (and there is some doubt about this), but it is historically and comparatively inappropriate to other societies (Mann, 1987: 339–40). While his concept of citizenship is tied by definition to the nation state, Marshall spent little time theorizing it (Roche, 1995: 716–19). Some commentators point out the decreasing capacity of the state to grant rights and realize citizenship and have moved toward discussing human rights in an international or global context. Many nation states do not reflect a notion of collective membership or a single, overriding national identity. National governments have explicitly and directly denied citizens access to resources and opportunities, engaged in political repression, acted contrary to international law and violated the rights of ethnic minorities. This is true of western democracies as well as nondemocratic states (Cohen, 1993: 102–3).

In developing a more contemporary concept of citizenship Turner treats 'citizenship as a particular case of social rights' (1997: 5). He views all economic, cultural and political rights as social rights (as distinct from human rights), because they all depend on membership of a nation state that grants or recognizes them. After examining the history of citizenship in a number of western nations, Turner proposes two essential factors: first, the passive or active nature of citizenship, that is, whether it is developed from above via the state, or from below through local associations; and second, the distinction between public and private arenas within civil society and the creation of a public domain of political activity. He then generates a model of four types of democratic polities as social contexts for the realization of citizenship rights:

1 *Revolutionary:* exemplified by the case of France, where popular struggle and a revolutionary conception of active citizenship combined with a strong public arena for citizen political participation and the achievement of new social rights following the French Revolution in 1789.
2 *Passive:* indicated by the English case, where citizenship derived from above after the constitutional settlement of 1688, which created the British citizen as the British subject and established a relatively strong public (or collective) domain allowing relatively active citizenship.
3 *Liberal:* adopted in the post-revolutionary USA, where the polity is constituted as participatory but is weakened by an emphasis on individualism and privacy.
4 *Plebiscitary democracy:* for example in Germany, where the individual citizen is submerged in the sacredness of the state while Lutheranism supports privacy and prioritized ethical and moral action within family life, thus resulting in a passive citizenship that collapsed into fascism (Turner, 1990: 206–10; 1997: 15–16).

From a Durkheimian perspective, Turner argues that in a secular society dominated by the nation state, public debates are no longer dominated by religious concerns and institutions; they are replaced by citizenship, which provides the common language or discourse, set of identities and value system. Thus citizenship is a form of social solidarity (Turner, 1997: 10). Turner has not relinquished the desire to articulate types or dimensions of citizenship nor forsaken an essentially evolutionary, albeit cross-cultural, perspective. He also expresses ambivalence about the concept of citizenship in his formulation of human rights that transcend, and may be in conflict with, national citizenship rights (Roche, 1995: 725).

Taking a very different approach, Somers argues that the development and precise character of modern citizenship are as much direct outcomes of medieval institutional and cultural foundations as they are based on the intervening forces of capitalist revolutions and class formation in the seventeenth and eighteenth centuries (Somers, 1994: 83). She disputes that the development of the civil, political and social components of citizenship coincided with epochs of economic development; denies that the supersession of local differences by national uniformity is a precondition of modern citizenship; and disagrees that citizenship practices vary according to categories of social actors, especially classes (Somers, 1993: 608). Her historical research points to the peculiarities of the English legal system and the regional and institutional conditions under which various rights are realized. She argues that virtually all English communities claimed, exercised, benefited and suffered from both the expansion and contraction of all three types of citizenship rights long before the triumph of their alleged capitalist cause (Somers, 1994: 77).

Somers adopts an institutional and narrative focus that uses a relational rather than a categorical approach to analysing social arrangements, viewed as indeterminate configurations of cultural and institutional relationships. From this perspective she proposes that:

> rather than in the transition to capitalism or in the 'birth of class society', the conditions for the possibility of citizenship rights can be located in the 12th–14th century legal revolution of medieval England that produced both national and local public (participatory) spheres as well as a national political culture based on the *idealized master narrative* of English legal and constitutional rights. (Somers, 1994: 73, emphasis in original)

Her central argument is that depending on their context or setting, laws that are applicable to all members of a nation state can be instruments of state or elite control or, alternatively, may represent popular citizenship rights.

Somers notes that the institutionalization of citizenship rights that does not correspond to the transition from feudalism to capitalism was a contingent and uneven process. Local legal processes generated different patterns of justice and rights in different types of English regions. She divides regions of eighteenth-century England into arable areas, characterized by strong manorial control and a weak capacity for local participation, and pastoral regions, which were the opposite.[1] England's nationwide legal institutions, and the universal legal discourses that emerged from Henry II's initial combination of the central state with local public (non-feudal) jurisdictional units to create a national public law with a local (and participatory) implementation, were still in place in the eighteenth century (Somers, 1993: 596). These cultural patterns formed part of the interaction between England's participatory legal institutions and the presence of contrasting regional political cultures. A culture of localism and participatory practices made the meaning of citizenship highly contested and variable, depending on the distribution of power to exercise those rights (Somers, 1993: 592–6; 1994: 98–9).

Only the people from the pastoral, later rural-industrial and eventually industrial villages from the fourteenth century onwards demonstrated explicitly positive expectations of their public political, social and civil rights. The absence of powerful social and political elites, the longer history of legal freedom and the presence of more solidaristic popular communities meant that civil liberties and public participatory law promoted more favourable outcomes for the labouring population. There is less evidence for such expectations on the part of labouring peoples located in the arable regions, comprised primarily of large commercial agricultural labour or unfree villeins. Indeed, the poor among these regions were more likely to view the law as oppressive. Thus the capacity for participatory association in the pastoral communities enabled greater interaction with national laws and their translation into citizenship rights (Somers, 1993: 593–5, 601–3; 1994: 81–2, 97).

Marshall implies that modern citizenship rights are society wide and universal in scope, that is, they are available to categories of people (by definition, because social rights are not individual rights). In contrast, Somers suggests that rather than being a category of social status, the rights of citizenship comprise a bundle of enforceable claims that are variably and contingently appropriated by members of small civil societies and differentiated legal cultures within one nation state. Rights are not logically attached to any one social category or persons, but are resources (cultural and institutional) that must be appropriated and in turn given meaning in the practical context of power and social relations (Somers, 1994: 78–9). Somers argues that England's formal national law produced highly localized and multiple practices of rights and enforcement practices. The conversion of laws to rights was local and contingent in effect and always adapted to local circumstances as a consequence of England's peculiar national hybrid legal infrastructure that conjoined national, county and local spheres. The English crown was able to achieve territorial-wide legal unification by forging institutional links with prefeudal public juridical units and local administrative centres. It was also able to construct a national legal sphere by incorporating into a single formal entity the pre-existing public legal and governing bodies, their political institutions and practices, resulting in an early national state that incorporated a majority of juridical and administrative units into a single entity without dismantling the original local bodies.

Public national institutions and local juries, the constabulary and the assizes (courts) mediated the relations between the crown and citizens. Political citizenship existed as a result of compulsory participation in local governance, administration and law. Social citizenship in the fourteenth century existed in a collection of national laws regulating labour relations and poor laws. The most significant feature of English welfare and industrial policies was that they were implemented through the normal channels and processes of government and law. For example, labour policies were implemented via the courts, which served as tribunals, while local justices and constables served as the administrative personnel to enforce regulations (Somers, 1993: 598; 1994: 77–8). The plasticity of England's legal structure enabled the formulation of national laws, with enforcement arrangements relying on local personnel in communities. This argument is compatible with Marshall's comments about a fusion between different types of rights before they became differentiated into his tripartite concept. Somers maintains that:

> citizenship practices emerge from the *articulation* of national organizations and universal rules with the particularism and varying political cultures of local environments (types of civil society). ... As such, citizenship practices are also a source of political identity – the translation of this identity into a rights-based positive citizenship identity depends entirely on the contexts of activation. (Somers, 1993: 589, emphasis in original)

Freedom and independence were conditional, not on freedom from the state, but on their rights as members of the English polity to make claims on the national state through local participation.

The tension that Somers identifies between the formal declaration and possession of rights and the conditions under which they can be mobilized or realized points to regional differences, thus suggesting that Marshall's observations about England and citizenship are too imprecise. The realization of citizenship rights also varies in terms of other social characteristics and associated resources, including gender and race.

Gender and citizenship

The assumption that civil and political rights are equally available to all citizens to use in securing greater social rights ignores gender differences in access to the realization of those rights. Social services can be a right of citizenship, or their level and type may depend on labour-force participation, marital or family status, or financial need. Feminist theory and research highlight the subjugation of women in the private sphere of the family which, according to liberal political and legal theory, ought to be free of state interference. Discussions of civil rights and contractual arrangements enacted in the public sphere did not resonate with the marriage contract (Pateman, 1988: 154–88). Social rights to welfare resources reflect and constitute relations between men and women in terms of sexuality, marriage, fertility, parenthood and kinship. Rights to control one's body and sexual person, as in marriage, consent to sexual activity and the control of fertility and reproduction, are contested issues for women. Relations of domination based on control of women's bodies and sexuality in the family, the workplace and public spaces compromise women's capacity to participate in the polity as citizens and affect their potential to assert and access social rights (Orloff, 1993: 309; 1996: 534; Shaver, 1990: 4–7).

Rather than having a universalistic or equal application, public social provision differentially affects women's material situations and shapes gender relations. Much discussion on the welfare state adopts explicitly gender-neutral concepts, but the categories of worker, state-market relations, stratification, citizenship and decommodification imply a male-based referent, or ideal-type employee. The male worker often serves as the ideal-typical citizen in analyses of social rights, with commentators addressing those dimensions of state social provision that are most relevant for male wage earners, for example programmes that compensate workers for losses incurred in the paid labour market, such as old-age pensions and unemployment benefits (Orloff, 1993: 307–8). Welfare provision is often viewed as deriving from the state or markets without recognizing the importance of families and women's unpaid work to the provision of social welfare. Women perform a disproportionate share of welfare work (which is often undervalued in terms of benefits and occupational status or credibility), whether it is provided by the state, private organizations, corporations or the family.

In many western systems of social provision, men's claims are based on paid work, while most women's claims derive from familial or marital roles, that is, on the basis of unpaid domestic and caring work and on their relationship to family members. In some countries, for example the USA, the social assistance programmes on which many single mothers rely are politically less legitimate, less generously funded and entail more surveillance than do contributory social insurance programmes on which most unemployed and retired wage-earning men rely (Orloff, 1993: 315). National differences and institutional arrangements shape the relationship between gender and welfare entitlements (Orloff, 1996: 64–8). For example, Australian welfare programmes are funded from general tax revenue, with entitlement independent of employment history. This noncontributory approach provides some women with a degree of financial and sexual independence not available under other social insurance schemes, where eligibility is attached to labour-market participation and benefits linked with labour-market performance. The shift in Australian social security over the past few decades has redefined the underlying basis of welfare assistance from a logic of gender difference to one of gender neutrality in the rules and conditions of entitlements (Bryson, 1995: 64–8; Shaver, 1990: 13; 1995: 143–5). However, this is also occurring at a time when the amounts and types of benefits available are in decline. In the USA, historical sources of gender bias linked to contributory social security benefits have declined, but race, class and marital-status disadvantages linked to noncontributory benefits remain. The gender gap in retired worker benefits persists as a result of gender differences in wages, female employees' tendency to interrupt paid employment for unpaid domestic responsibilities, and the elimination of minimum benefit levels (Meyer, 1996: 462).

Orloff proposes expanding the concept of social rights to include an examination of family law and the legal frameworks and social programmes dealing with legal personhood and the control of one's bodily capacities and functions. She suggests two new dimensions, namely access to paid work (affected by government employment policies) and the capacity to form and maintain an autonomous household. The state is woman friendly to the extent that it enhances women's leverage within marriage or increases the standards of living of woman-maintained families (Orloff, 1993: 318–21). Ironically, in the former socialist regimes of eastern Europe, women enjoyed more social rights than did their western counterparts. With the reunification of Germany, the disintegration of the Soviet Union and the establishment of market economies and constitutional democracies, women's rights to abortion and childcare, as well as their access to equal employment and political representation, have been severely curtailed (Ferree, 1994: 598; Rosenberg, 1991: 129; Ziélinska, 1993: 69–85).

Race and citizenship

Questions of race and citizenship have emerged in a number of contexts, many of which look to the law and legal institutions for remedies to effect social change. This section examines three such contexts: (i) institutionalized racism; (ii) hate crimes; and (iii) migration issues.

Institutionalized racism

The Stephen Lawrence Inquiry in the United Kingdom highlighted the pervasiveness of racism and racially motivated crime and documented the widespread distrust between police and minority ethnic communities (Bridges, 1999). A sudden, short, violent attack on an Afro-Caribbean man by a group of white youths in 1993 resulting in his death led to a public inquiry that concluded: 'Stephen Lawrence's murder was simply and solely and unequivocally motivated by racism' (Macpherson, 1999:

para 1.11). The police response and investigation were found to amount to institutional racism, defined by the inquiry as:

> the collective failure of an organization to provide an appropriate and professional service to people because of their colour, culture or ethnic origin. It can also be seen or detected in processes, attitudes and behaviour which amount to discrimination through unwitting prejudice, ignorance, thoughtlessness, and racist stereotyping which disadvantage minority ethnic people. (1999: para 6.34)

In a number of instances, indigenous peoples in Australia (and elsewhere) have sought redress for past wrongs in contemporary courts, with mixed results (Behrendt, 2004; Gale, 2005). The high point was the *Mabo* case (1992) in which the High Court agreed that the land rights of indigenous Australians were not nullified by British settlement and persisted where Aboriginal people and Torres Strait Islanders could demonstrate sufficient ties with the land. The litigants successfully drew on international law, in particular the concept of 'terra nullius', and the jurisprudence of other common-law countries to argue that Australia was not uninhabited or without law at the point of European settlement (Behrendt, 2004).

There has however been less success in regard to the 'stolen generation' litigation (Scott, 2004: 193–7). An analysis of two recent cases regarding indigenous legal claims for their compulsory removal from their families as children, state institutionalization and maltreatment shows the ways in which Eurocentric views and values permeate contemporary judicial reasoning (Marchetti and Ransley, 2005). In these cases the international law on genocide, as defined by the 1948 International Convention on the Prevention and Punishment of the Crime of Genocide, though argued by the litigants was not accepted. The High Court found no evidence supporting a conclusion that the removal of children policy amounted to an intention to destroy a racial group. Liberal legal formalism, legal doctrine and rules, Marchetti and Ransley argue, resulted in the evidence of indigenous witnesses being weighted less than that of non-indigenous witnesses and written not oral testimony being accorded relevance rendering indigenous witnesses less credible than their non-indigenous counterparts (2005: 549). The authors conclude: 'The Australian legal system being never intended to encompass the narratives of Indigenous people and the fact that it continues to operate in a hegemonic manner supports the view that racism in Australian courts exists, particularly at an unconscious level' (Marchetti and Ransley, 2005: 548).

Hate crimes

A hate crime can be defined as 'bias-motivated violence', relating to race, religion, colour, nationality, country of origin, ancestry, sexual orientation, gender, or disability (Grattet and Jenness, 2005: 906). Throughout the late 1980s and into the 1990s most US states passed at least one piece of legislation criminalizing 'hate-motivated intimidation and violence' (Grattet et al., 1998). Active social movement and professional groups also focused on the issue. However, the translation of the legal requirements into enforcement practices is mediated by the networks – professional, bureaucratic, political – within which enforcement agencies are situated. In different nations the emergence and enforcement of hate crime law can take different forms. Savelsberg and King (2005) argue that collective memories of hate and cultural trauma, differential exposure or a sensitivity to global scripts and local institutions can explain differences in the formation of hate crime law in the United States and Germany, suggesting that ideas about global convergence in laws are limited. Specifically, collective memory in the United States emphasizes domestic achievements, liberation from evil domestically and externally, and the contributions of the military. In contrast, the collective memory in Germany lacks a commemoration of the military and evil is linked with memories of failing states (Savelsberg and King, 2005: 609–11).

In their research on hate crime law implementation, Grattet and Jenness (2005) sought formal policy documents, known as 'hate crime general orders', from all 397 police and sheriffs' departments in California. The research aimed to generate a 'picture of how police and sheriff's departments in California envision hate crime as both a legal concept and a community problem' (2005: 909). Some of these departments did not have written policy documents; 197 provided a copy of their policy which showed that local agencies will adopt various responses to hate crime law. Some agencies had detailed policies and others a more limited approach, while many had not adopted anything. Considerable variation and overlap arise in the practical definitions of hate crime, in terms of the categories of persons covered, and in terms of the conduct and motivations described by these local police policies. Policies might be copied from other agencies, may take their cue from professional or social movement organizations or perhaps track the statutory language. Understanding hate crime enforcement also depends on interrelations between enforcement organizations and their immediate environments – constituted by crime rates, organized community groups, and human rights groups – which can affect the reporting of hate crimes and demand new police policy (McVeigh et al., 2003). Jenness and Grattet (2005: 339) explain that as organizations law enforcement agencies constitute the 'law-in-between' the law on the books and the law in action. Organizational structures and policies will mediate between legislation and police officers' everyday law enforcement discretion.

Migration issues

Debates in many countries regarding refugees and asylum seekers and the distinctions between legal and illegal entry affirm the salience of the nation state.[2] The flow of certain kinds of people or people from certain countries or regions has been linked to questions of national security and border control which many see as an important component of combating terrorism. There are implications for notions of citizenship: 'What happens to citizenship, as a potential force of justice, equality, and national cohesion, when large numbers of people from diverse linguistic, ethnic, racial, religious and cultural backgrounds cross state borders?' (Bloemraad et al., 2008: 154).

One example of where some of these issues have been manifest concretely is the French ban on the wearing of overt religious symbols which focused on headscarves worn by Muslim women (Wiles, 2007).

The nation state remains paramount in determining access to citizenship, or creating categories which allow temporary residence without the legal protections and rights accompanying citizenship. 'Immigration policy determines who stands inside or outside the law (or in between) and whether immigrants qualify as full participants in society, as it dictates whether they will have access to resources and, if they do, to what kind and for how long' (Menjívar, 2006: 102).

Since the September 11 (2001) terrorists attacks in the United States as well as bomb blasts on London (2005), Bali (2002), Madrid (2004), and Mumbai (2008) numerous governments have passed or strengthened their existing antiterrorism legislation. This response includes a reform of immigration and asylum laws and an unprecedented concern about border control, perceived to be essential for domestic and international security (Bosworth, 2008: Dauvergne, 2007; Feller, 2006). In addition a range of activities that could be linked with terrorism – such as financial transactions or the sale of certain chemical substances – are outlawed and procedures are in place for transnational policing, increased surveillance and a data tracking and a greater emphasis on international coordination and cooperation (Levi and Wall, 2004: 196–8).

Many western, liberal democracies, including the United Kingdom, Australia, New Zealand, Canada and the United States, have restricted the asylum process and limited most unskilled immigration while encouraging the migration of skilled and professional persons who have access to work and citizenship (Bosworth, 2008). Heighted security measures apply to potential asylum seekers from predominantly Muslim states, such as Iraq, Pakistan, Afghanistan, Iran and African countries (Dauvergne, 2007). Noncitizens, irrespective of their reasons for coming or mode of arrival, are denied access to various goods, services, and safeguards associated with the welfare state. For example, people without citizenship who were born outside the European Economic Area (EEA) cannot apply for child or housing benefits and in some cases will have no access to national health schemes (Calavita, 1998).

Discussions of refugees and asylum seekers are infused with the language and techniques of criminal justice: illegal migration, policing borders, and protecting security are more pervasive than displaced person, refugee, or persecution (Bosworth, 2008: 208; Pickering, 2004: 368). In *Al-Kateb* v *Godwin* (2004) the Australian High Court decided that the Migration Act's scheme of mandatory administrative detention was valid law, even though in the extant case the detention would likely have to be indefinite because it was unlikely that any country would grant Al-Kateb (a Palestinian born in Kuwait) entry. The Act envisages that detention will cease with the granting of an entry visa or by removal, and that parliament intends that a person's detention will continue until one of these two conditions occurs. The Court following the doctrine of the separation of powers concluded:

> As long as the detention is for the purpose of deportation or preventing aliens from entering Australia or the Australian community, the justice or wisdom of the course taken by Parliament is not examinable in this or any other

domestic court. It is not for the courts, exercising federal jurisdiction, to determine whether the course taken by Parliament is unjust or contrary to basic human rights. (*Al-Kateb* v *Godwin* 2004: para 74)

In Australia's northern borders, one type of forced migration – people smuggling – is a task for the Australian Federal Police who have contributed to the construction of people smuggling as a policing problem not just a political problem (Pickering, 2004: 365). (For a discussion of the rise of international policing see Deflem [2002]). Pickering (2004: 376) describes 'transversal' policing as arising from the blurring of immigration and criminal law, the fusing of domestic and transnational policing concerns, and the association of criminal (policing) and national security (military) issues.

Another form of geographic mobility which raises questions about citizenship and the associated rights and protections is that of transnational migration (not immigration), whereby foreign nationals from a few developing countries are recruited for employment in service industries, including hospitality and leisure, construction, and agriculture. A study in four US cities portrays the experiences of Salvadoran and Guatemalan entrants who were classified neither as strictly economic migrants nor as political refugees and permitted temporary work visas. Their experiences included a vulnerability to deportation, confinement to low wage jobs, a denial of basic needs, and limited access to decent housing, education, food and health care. Such temporary visas can be extended or not and thus result in long-term uncertainty inherent in their 'liminal' legal status (Menjívar, 2006: 1002). 'Legal categories mark immigrants not only as non-nationals but also as deportable, and these categories become marks of exclusion' (Menjívar, 2006: 1006).

New social movements and rights discourse

One of the hallmarks of contemporary social movements is a concern with obtaining rights for specific groups or classes of people, for example women, children, gay men and lesbians, indigenous people, disabled people, animals, fathers, fetuses and the victims of crime. Social movement activism involves making claims for more rights or at least for current political and social rights to be more inclusive, that is, available to the whole population and not just segments of it. Many would observe that central contemporary conflicts deal less with labour and economic problems and more with cultural and especially ethical problems. The key dimension of conflict is socio-cultural rather than socio-economic; it revolves around the control of knowledge and involves a resistance to technocratic domination (Bernstein, 2005: 53–5; Brigham, 1996: 129–54; Habermas, 1981: 34; Stychin, 1995).

In highlighting new forms of conflict, some students of social movements distinguish between 'old' and 'new' social movements, arguing that the latter seek to politicize the institutions of civil society in ways that are not constrained by the channels of representative-bureaucratic political institutions and thereby to reconstitute a civil society that no longer depends on increasing levels of regulation, control and intervention (Habermas, 1981; Offe, 1985: 820). The suggestion is that 'old' social movements, for example political parties and trade unions, accept the appropriateness of existing political and social institutions, but seek greater representation and inclusion. Examples of new social movements (NSMs) include the ecology or environmental movement, the women's movement, the gay rights movement, human rights movements, peace movements, land-rights movements, and movements advocating or engaging in alternative or communal modes of the production and distribution of goods and services. These social movements represent a special kind of conflict in the public arena that differs from conventional party politics and interest group lobbying; they are anti-institutional and transcend the system by questioning the very 'rules of the game' (Pakulski, 1991: 21–2).

Conflicts involving the participation of social movements will often commence with particular issues but then gradually coalesce to challenge principal institutional norms and socio-cultural patterns (Touraine, 1985: 772–7). Pakulski characterizes the 'eco-pax' (green) movement as being antibureaucratic and entailing a critique of current political and state structures. It is directed against centralism and calls for the reincorporation or, more importantly, the recognition of values in formal instrumental rationalism, which it considers permeate the contemporary social order. This social movement also challenges the boundaries of institutional politics. The eco-pax movements are about wilderness protection, nuclear disarmament, uranium mining, Aboriginal land rights and other contemporary issues. The remarkable coalescence of all these extremely diverse issues in protests, marches and rallies indicates the existence of a common denominator: a radical and broad challenge to modern trends (Pakulski, 1991: 164). Comparisons can also be made between the new social movements in the West and civil rights and oppositional movements in eastern Europe (Misztal, 1993: 452).

The content of citizenship in all western societies has been affected by the crisis of welfarism, the shrinking of the state and globalization, which hinder the expansion of social rights and redirect the claims for rights towards a new domain of cultural rights that involve the right to unhindered and legitimate representation, and the propagation of identities and lifestyles through information systems. These cultural rights are more in the form of negotiated claims than institutionalized legal entitlements. Claims for cultural citizenship involve not only a tolerance of diverse ethnic, race, sexual and other identities, but also claims to dignifying representation, normative accommodation and an active cultivation of these identities and their symbolic associations. These new claims entail arguments for the right to symbolic presence and visibility (versus marginalization); the right to dignifying representation (versus stigmatization); and the right to the propagation of identity and maintenance of lifestyles (versus assimilation) (Pakulski, 1997: 74–80).

One significant focus of social movement activity is sexuality and various organizations seek to have discriminatory laws repealed, thus enabling greater access to social resources and opportunities, and to have gay and lesbian rights recognized in law. There are also efforts to counter homophobic violence and harassment and to have criminal laws applied equally to all citizens, regardless of their sexuality (Manson and Tomsen, 1997; Stychin, 1995). Gamson's (1989) study of the AIDS activist movement, ACT UP (AIDS Coalition to Unleash Power), which formed in the

1980s in numerous US cities, shows that in many ways it is the archetypal new social movement (NSM). It has a broadly middle-class membership and combines instrumental, expressive and identity-oriented activities. Instrumental concerns relate to changing government policy and lobbying pharmaceutical companies; expressive pursuits include building a community and expressing collective anger and rage; and identity-oriented activities involve contesting cultural boundaries and assumptions by targeting the mass media, everyday language and other cultural representations and symbols of sexuality and AIDS. The focus of activism is less on state institutions and practices as sites of oppression and the need for transformation, but more on cultural scripts and practices that delineate 'normality' from 'abnormality', marginalizing the latter and attempting to normalize those so labelled. As a consequence, the focus of activism tends to be on abstract, invisible and disembodied entities that pervade everyday life and emphasize normalization (Gamson, 1989: 352–63).

Social movement participants do not rely for their self-identification on either the established political codes (left/right or liberal/conservative) or on the partly corresponding, socio-economic divisions (such as working class/middle class; poor/wealthy). Political conflict is articulated in terms of such identities as gender, ethnicity, age, locality and value orientations. Even so, the social base and political practice of these movements are not completely amorphous and heterogeneous in class and ideological terms. The following segments have been identified as important contributors to NSMs (Pakulski, 1991: 52–87):

1 *The new middle class,* especially those who work in the human service professions and/or the public sector. There appear to be relatively clear structural determinants of who is likely to support the new causes and engage in the practices of new politics, but the demands, and beneficiaries of the demands, are highly class unspecific and dispersed. New middle-class politics (in contrast to most working-class politics as well as 'old' middle-class politics) is typically a politics of a class, but not on behalf of a class. New middle-class social movement participants are characterized by a high educational status, relative economic security, experience of such security in their formative years and employment in personal-service occupations. The preponderance of such people has been well documented in such movements as the peace movement, environmental movements, various civil rights and feminist movements and urban citizens' initiatives.

2 *Elements of the old middle class,* the petit bourgeoisie, including farmers, self-employed businesspeople, artists and intellectuals. Their immediate economic interests often coincide with the concerns voiced by the protest politics of the new social movements.

3 A category of the population consisting of *people outside the labour market* or in a peripheral position to it, including unemployed workers, students, homemakers and retired persons. Members of these groups are not presently defined directly in their social situation by the labour market, their time constraints are more flexible, but some others, especially those receiving government benefits, are likely to be trapped by highly authoritarian and restrictive mechanisms of supervision, exclusion and social control. This often leads to a revolt against the bureaucratic or patriarchal regime of such institutions as government welfare departments.

A study of the green movement in Australia found that over half of the activists had tertiary education; one-third were in professional occupations (the largest category); over one-third enjoyed flexible working hours and almost half could regulate the pace of their work (Pakulski, 1991: 180–5). It also discerned that a large proportion of the activists had participated in anti-Vietnam protests and the women's movement during the 1960s and 1970s, suggesting a career trajectory of social activism. Other research agrees that support for environmentalism is socially located but only to a limited extent. The effects of social location vary in relation to different aspects of environmentalism and greater explanatory power regarding activism rather than a general environmental concern. This research suggests that the typical environmental supporter would be a tertiary-educated, social and cultural or human services professional, who is interested in art and literature, holds postmaterialist values (that is, supports freedom of speech and political participation), does not identify with a religious denomination but may consider nature to be sacred in itself (Tranter, 1996: 77). Men's involvement in the environmental movement seems to have been affected by the feminist movement, to the extent that they are concerned to be nonpatriarchal and nongendered in their activism (Connell, 1990: 473–7).

Social movement activists often adopt a discourse of rights and participate in the legal arena (courts and various quasi-legal or administrative tribunals) to achieve social reform at both national and international levels. In recent years, rights claims and discourse have moved beyond national polities and judicial systems to become a central aspect of international relations and global politics. This is especially true of human rights, as their denial or abrogation is precipitated by national governments and investigated by such supra-national, nongovernmental organizations as Amnesty International and Human Rights Watch.

Interestingly, not only do new social movements seek to influence law, but legal institutions and discourse will also inevitably shape the activities and orientation of the movements themselves. Rules made by governments and judicial language infuse and inform the movements themselves, becoming an essential part of their thought, their identity and their social boundaries. Movements are constituted in legal terms when they see the world in those terms and organize themselves accordingly. Legal forms are evident in the language, purposes and strategies of movement activity as political practices (Brigham, 1987; 1996: 1–27; Pedriana, 2006: 1720). For example, the gay movement uses the notions of rights and choice, feminists against pornography in the USA relied on the Constitution and judicial discussions about freedom of speech in order to criticize it, and the disadvantages of Australian Aboriginal people are often attributed to their lack of land rights, which demonstrates the way in which concepts deriving from Anglo-Australian property law can shape activists' claims and arguments.

Social movements based on identities and lifestyles can confront a difficult dilemma. On the one hand, expressing a collective identity is an important political strategy and source of strength, while on the other, identities can be unstable and shift. A social movement with an avowed identity may not be sensitive to the needs or incorporate the experiences of some who fall within its purview. For many women, for example, gender is not their primary experience of oppression and thus they will have a greater commitment to the ideals of other social movements and solidarity with some men than they do to the women's movement. Some activist movements involved in sexual politics, heavily influenced by postmodernist theories, are actively engaged in disrupting sex and gender identities and deconstructing identity categories, which result in disagreements about the meaning of labels and the boundaries of the collectivity. For example, Queer Nation, which was founded in 1990, does have a collective identity and level of organization, yet its identity is based on undermining sexual categories. Proponents of the term 'queer' and queer activists aim to be more inclusive than the terms 'gay' and 'lesbian' denote, as they wish to incorporate those people who do not identify with either male or female sexuality and do not define themselves as either homosexual or heterosexual. At the same time, queer activists will seek to undermine the veracity of the male/female and homosexual/heterosexual binary oppositions (Gamson, 1995: 390–4). Queer activists use the signs, symbols and artifacts of popular culture to subvert their meanings and construct their own identities. They also reconceptualize law as a discourse that both 'fixes' identity but also provides opportunities to contest those identities in a public arena. Law has the capacity to both facilitate and limit claims to identity (Bower, 1994: 1016–20). Nevertheless, some social movements will have more success than others in mobilizing the law for their own purposes and having their claims to citizenship recognized.

Human rights and rights discourse

Human rights have not long been a topic of sociological inquiry, in part because of the discipline's traditional scepticism towards the normative analysis of legal institutions, which is a legacy of classical (positivist) social theory. Sociology has previously not addressed the notion of human rights due to its rejection of a universal or natural conception of humanity or the human, and its greater attention to social roles and statuses shaped by such social institutions as economic relations, the level of industrialization, kinship networks, the occupational structure and the education system. Attention to cultural differences and particular social contexts, and an emphasis on the process of social construction, lead away from identifying a universal human actor with attendant (essential) rights and obligations. Secondly, in liberal political theory the concept of rights is an individual attribution or claim against the state and as such focuses on the integrity of the individual, whereas sociology by definition is more concerned with the larger social forces – class, family, gender, community, occupation – which shape individual action, values and life chances (Turner, 1993: 492, 500). As rights have generally been articulated as political or property rights (and, of course, historically the two have been indecipherable) their discussion has been successfully monopolized by the disciplines of politics and law.

Nevertheless, since World War II, issues of rights, especially human rights, have become topics of widespread discussion, particularly in western capitalist democracies, and sociology is unable to avoid their discussion. Increasing globalization, migration, the existence (perhaps more accurately, the recognition) of repressive regimes in many nation states and the expansion in the numbers of stateless people all point to the declining utility of a concept of citizenship that is based on the nation state and understood to reflect a national identity (Habermas, 1990: 492). Turner argues for a nonrelativistic conception of human rights that transcends nation-state boundaries. Distancing himself from natural-law theory, he nevertheless provides a foundationalist conception of human rights based on the presupposition that 'human beings are ontologically frail, and secondly that social arrangements, or social institutions, are precarious' (Turner, 1993: 501). He asserts that this frailty is a universal feature of human existence and that globalization increasingly escalates the risky nature of social life, the precariousness of social institutions and the inefficacy of nation states. Human beings are frail because our lives are finite and we typically exist under conditions of scarcity, disease and danger. Physical processes of ageing and decay, increasingly affected by environmental disasters, scarce resources and chronic disease, constrain human actors (Turner, 1993: 501–7).

This conception of human rights is admirable for requiring sociology to engage directly with topics of international discussion, but such a foundationalist view begs numerous questions:

1   Problems of inclusion: who or what is included in the notion of human or humanity? The category 'human' is neither self-evident nor uncontestable. For example, taking the pregnant woman's body, do we see two (or more) humans or one? The notion of frailty and the increasing precariousness of life can be equally applied to animals and even to plants; should they also be accorded human rights?
2   It is difficult to consider what human rights mean substantively outside of local, social contexts and political environments. Arguably, sociological theories of human rights must take a social constructionist point of view and recognize that the notion of human rights is a specific cultural and historical institution and the institutionalization of rights is a product of the balance of power between political interests (Waters, 1996: 593–5).
3   Problems of achievement and enforcement: to suggest that all humans have rights diverts attention from the political struggles that social movements have mounted to achieve some recognition of rights. Moreover, there is often a disjuncture between the possession of rights and their actualization or enforcement.
4   The concept of human rights as universal and based on all instances of human-ity renders other rights' claims particularistic and sectarian. One proponent advances that: 'Human rights have the particular advantage that in order to succeed no person can be excluded' (Waters, 1996: 598). Thus claims for civil rights for disadvantaged groups and reproductive rights for women may not be seen to apply universally to all humans.
5   Historically, the emergence of human-rights institutions and claims is a unique feature of western and twentieth-century development. Human-rights claims are often linked with political objectives and economic interests.

Globalization and the rise of international law

Widespread changes in Europe – especially the formation of new independent national states following the fall of the previous communist regimes and the estab-lishment of closer links between governments of Europe, including the promulgation of European laws that override domestic legislation and the European Court of Human Rights whose decisions are binding on member states – raise questions about the nature and scope of the nation state. There is also increasing recognition of the ineffectiveness, or at least the limitations, of individual nation states in determining or governing their internal or domestic affairs. The transnational nature of financial markets, communications, international trade, migration, disputes and even criminal activities, and such transnational organizations as the World Bank, the International Monetary Fund, the United Nations and multinational corporations, operates beyond the direct control of single nation states and yet these significantly affect national economies and policies. The increasing pervasiveness, importance and power of global economic, political and cultural relations are evidence of a growing globalization, which is also accompanied by an increasing concern with local identities, multiculturalism and pluralism within nation states. Some would argue that globalism and fragmentation tend to undermine the sovereignty of nation states, whereas others would maintain that globalization is not synonymous with world government or Americanization (Holton, 1997: 144).

Globalization, which refers to 'the increasing acceleration in both concrete global interdependence and consciousness of the global whole in the twentieth century' (Robertson, 1992: 8), was not recognized as a significant sociological concept until the mid-1980s. This set of processes breaks down the nexus between nation, state, societal community and territory, because it entails differentiating as well as homogenizing aspects. As discussed in Chapter 3, globalization recognizes the value of cultural niches and local abilities, allows for the formation of identities across national boundaries (sometimes these identities, especially among ethnic minorities, question the efficacy of the national boundaries) and enables a flow of information via telecommunications and tourism (Waters, 1994). It denotes the geographical and temporal expansion and deepening of social relations and institutions so that everyday, ordinary activities are increasingly influenced by events on the other side of the globe, and means that the practices and decisions of local groups and communities can have global reverberations. It suggests that many chains of political, economic and social activity are becoming worldwide in scope and that there is an intensification in levels of interaction and interconnectedness within and between states and societies (Held, 1995: 20–1).

While the term 'globalization' and the associated concepts of globalism and global have been taken up with alacrity by some sociologists, it tends to play down important social phenomena, most particularly politics and the reproduction of inequalities. It is a concept that is difficult to evaluate as it embraces so many ambiguities and contradictions, sometimes coming close to a tautology, and does not sufficiently attend to the sources and exercise of power and domination (Morris, 1997: 192–3; Silbey, 1997: 219–27). While globalization refers to supranational trends and forces, citizens' political participation still occurs at the level of the nation state. For example, European Union citizenship depends on citizenship of one of its member states, and the loss of primary citizenship also means the loss of one's derivative status (Morris, 1997: 198). The image of the global environment is one constituted by a free market of goods, services, communications and people. The role of law is central in this 'market' in the form of international contracts, the establishment of dispute-resolution procedures, and the regulation of relationships. However, the formulation of law is uncoupled from specific polities or local political participation.

The United Nations

Since World War II, there has been an extension of international law in the form of conventions and treaties that constrain the practices of nation states. This coincides with a shift in the conception of international relations as dealing solely with the relations between states, and international law as regulating those relations and having little import for the internal affairs or circumstances of people. There is greater recognition of the rights relating to individuals and obligations that exist beyond those established by their own legal systems. The most visible institution of international relations and international law is the United Nations (UN). The UN Charter established its main purposes as the prevention of aggression and the maintenance of international peace and security, the development of friendly relations between nations based on a respect for the principles of equal rights and self-determination, and 'to achieve international co-operation in solving international problems of an economic, social, cultural, or humanitarian character, and in promotion and encouraging respect for human rights and for fundamental freedoms for all without distinction as to race, sex, language, or religion' (United Nations, 1945: art. 1(3)). The sovereign state remains the central actor, as article 2(7) provides that 'nothing contained in the present Charter shall authorize the United Nations to intervene in matters which are essentially within the domestic jurisdiction of any state' (United Nations, 1945). Nevertheless, the activities of states are more and more constrained by increasing numbers of treaties and collective agreements and by customary international law; this is reflected in the practices of states and in *opinio juris,* that is, a consciousness of legal obligation as indicated by governmental declarations, resolutions or statements to international organizations (Charlesworth, 1991; Meron, 1987; *Nicaragua* v *United States of America* 1986: 97–101).

The UN Charter established a number of principal organs, including the General Assembly, the Security Council and the International Court of Justice (ICJ). One subject of eternal interest to international lawyers is the identification of what constitutes international law. The *Statute of the International Court of Justice* specifies the sources of international law as international conventions; international custom, evidence of a general practice accepted as law (in other words, when nation states act in a particular way they do so because their governments feel legally bound to do so); general principles of law recognized by civilized nations; and decisions by the ICJ (Article 38).

Problems of jurisdiction and problems of enforcement that have no parallel in domestic legal systems confront the operation of the ICJ. For example, in *Nicaragua* v *United States of America* 1986, Nicaragua argued that the USA – in recruiting, training, arming, equipping, financing, aiding and directing military and paramilitary actions in and against Nicaragua – violated express obligations under the UN

Charter. When the ICJ found that it had jurisdiction in the case, the USA argued that this was contrary to the law and fact and for political reasons refused to participate in any further proceedings (Franck, 1985). The ICJ found that the USA had breached customary international law obligations not to intervene in the affairs of another state, and it rejected the idea that violations of human rights by the Nicaraguan government could justify US military action. However, this decision did not affect the US government's foreign policy objectives in Central America.

The *Universal Declaration of Human Rights,* adopted in 1948 by the General Assembly of the United Nations, sets forth the basic human rights and fundamental freedoms to which all men and women in the world are entitled without discrimination. The articles of the *Declaration* deal with civil and political rights, as well as with economic, social and cultural rights. Its conception of human rights is essentialist, advocating that because humans are rational and moral beings they are entitled to certain rights and freedoms. Article 1 provides that: 'All human beings are born free and equal in dignity and rights. They are endowed with reason and conscience and should act towards one another in a spirit of brotherhood' (Center for Human Rights, 1994: 41). It establishes principles of equality and nondiscrimination, proclaims the right to life, the right to liberty and the right to security of person, advocates freedom from slavery and servitude, from torture and cruel, inhuman or degrading treatment or punishment, the right to a fair trial, freedom of movement, the right to own property, freedom of expression, the right of association and the right to participate in government. In addition, the United Nations has established the Human Rights Committee under the *International Covenant on Civil and Political Rights* (ICCPR) to monitor the implementation of the convention. The Human Rights Committee can receive allegations from individuals or states regarding noncompliance.

A recent issue confronting international law regards the use of armed intervention in a state to prevent such human rights' violations as widespread death or suffering among the population, even against the wishes of the government of that state. Traditionally, the view has been that this would be a violation of customary international law that has been shaped by the UN Charter's provisions that members must refrain from the use of force in a manner inconsistent with the purposes of the United Nations and the principle of nonintervention in the domestic jurisdiction of another state (Greenwood, 1993: 34–5). Numerous international incidents involving the repression and genocide of ethnic minority groups have highlighted this tension between state sovereignty and the human rights of citizens and the responsibility, if any, of other nations to intervene.

While there is increasing concern for human rights, or an increasing reliance on human rights' discourse, political objectives will often guide the practice of intervention and a justification for the use of force. For example, in 1991 the UN Security Council passed a resolution that condemned the repression of the Iraqi civilian population, especially the Kurds and Shi'ite Muslims, legitimating the policy of 'safe havens' and 'no-fly' zones whereby Iraq was required to cease military flights. These provisions were policed and enforced by a number of countries, including the USA and the UK. The Iraqi government however did not consent to this intervention and the Security Council did not make a formal determination, instead simply asserting that there was a threat to international peace and security in the region. One commentator suggests that it 'eschewed direct UN responsibility and accountability for the military force that ultimately was deployed, favouring, instead, a delegated, essentially unilateralist determination and orchestration of world policy, coordinated and controlled almost exclusively by the USA' (Weston, 1991: 517, emphasis deleted; see also Alston, 1992). On the other side, Human Rights Watch, an international human-rights monitoring group, claimed that the Security Council action represented 'the first time that the international community had formally limited a sovereign nation's authority over its own territory essentially on human rights grounds' (Alston, 1992: 107).

Similarly, in 1992 the UN Secretary General advised the Security Council that the UN peace-keeping forces were insufficient to contain all the warring factions in Somalia and that there was no alternative but to adopt more forceful measures to secure the humanitarian operations in Somalia. Subsequent Security Council resolutions placed an embargo on weapons and military equipment going to all the factions and advocated the use of all necessary means to establish a secure environment for humanitarian relief operations. There was not even the pretence that these resolutions were based on the consent of the government of Somalia, and arguably there was no government at the time. Again, the troops (which were separate from peace-keeping forces) who responded from various countries, including France and Belgium, acted under the unified command of the USA and, as such, were not directly controlled by the UN (Greenwood, 1993: 37–8).

Contemporary debates about human rights do not occur in an international sphere where all the participants are equal in terms of economic and political power. Institutions like the World Bank are able to place more pressure on newly industrializing nations and to tie loans and repayments into social and political reform, compared with their influence on such powerful global actors as the USA. World Bank policies can also target institutions that are not strictly in the economic sector. Its judicial reform projects in transition and developing countries in eastern Europe, Asia and Latin America presuppose that adherence to the rule of law, a separation of powers, strong courts and independent judicial officers and independent courts are essential for economic growth, good governance and trade liberalization (Messick, 1999; Williamson, 2000).

It is sometimes argued that the concept of rights as propounded in the west is founded on liberal individualism and thus has little relevance to other societies based on the primacy of family and community (Ghai, 1994: 1–6). Official views of human rights in such countries as Singapore, China, Malaysia and Indonesia stress a domestic jurisdiction, that is, they adopt the position that the recognition of rights is encapsulated in state sovereignty and that national treatment of human rights is no concern of other states or the international community. These views also stress the relativity of rights as determined by the historical, cultural, economic and political conditions of each country. For example, the Bangkok Governmental Declaration 'recognizes that while human rights are universal in nature, they must be considered in the context of a dynamic and evolving process of international norm-setting, bearing in mind the significance of national and regional peculiarities and various historical, cultural and religious backgrounds' (Ghai, 1994: 5–8).

Issues of political stability and the primacy of economic development will often restrict civil and political rights. During meetings hosted by ASEAN (Association of South-East Asian Nations) in 1997, the Malaysian Prime Minister Mahathir Mohamad, supported by Indonesia, the Philippines and South Korea, called for the UN to renegotiate the *Universal Declaration of Human Rights* on the ground that it was formulated by the superpowers and did not take into account the needs of developing countries. In response, a US official claimed that 'it is not a declaration that was imposed on the world by the West. It represents universal values against discrimination on the basis of race, religion, freedom of speech and assembly' (Greenlees, 1997: 1). Various nonwestern or nondemocratic governments have pointed to human rights abuses occurring in those nations that are the strongest advocates of the *Declaration*, for example the plight of indigenous people in Australia, the use of the death penalty in some states of the USA, and the existence of political prisoners in the UK. Advocates of universal human rights nevertheless will attempt to place economic and political pressure on governments, especially those that are authoritarian and that they view as jeopardizing human rights, and specifically where their political system does not conform to western notions of a participatory democracy.

There is no simple connection between the ratification of human rights' treaties and the enhanced protection of human rights. Ratificating human rights treaties is low cost with a high moral value, thus helping explain the disjunction between many states' propensity to join the international human rights' regime and their capacity, will, or commitment to comply domestically. Despite weak enforcement mechanisms such treaties can provide leverage for nongovernmental actors and social movements such as Amnesty International and Human Rights Watch to mobilize with reference to the human rights' instruments and pressure or shame governments to reduce violations. Human rights' activism can add to the normative power of the treaties and as Levy and Sznaider suggest: 'the current degree of institutionalization and juridification of human rights is a crucial source for state legitimacy' domestically as well as internationally (2006: 661). Merry's (2003) analysis of the *UN Convention on the Elimination of All Forms of Discrimination Against Women* (CEDAW) widely ratified shows that despite a lack of sanctions it forms part of an emerging global system of law through its educative function about the rights of women.

The specific and practical relationships between international law and domestic legislation is a topic of considerable vexation for governments, courts (both domestic and international), international jurists and political commentators (Crawford and Edeson, 1984; Duffy, 1992; Greig, 1976: 52–64). The general international law principle is that, to the extent that they are in conflict, then international law should override domestic legislation. For example, the Australian Commonwealth government's participation in such agreements as the *International Convention on the Elimination of all Forms of Racial Discrimination* (1965), the *Convention for the Protection of the World Cultural and Natural Heritage* (1972) and the *Convention on the Elimination of all Forms of Discrimination Against Women* (1979) has enabled it to legislate in such areas as race discrimination, protection of the environment and sex discrimination, which are ostensibly beyond the scope of its constitutionally defined powers. It has been able to do this as the High Court has increasingly adopted a wide definition of the external affairs' power in the Constitution to include a range of international activities and agreements, which, in turn, create obligations on the federal government. Some legal commentators interpret this development as weakening the power and integrity of the Australian state governments (Solomon, 1992: 29–33, 139–45). Nonetheless, the High Court does not agree that the adoption of treaties can be treated as mere devices to extend the substantive powers of the federal government *(Tasmania* v *Commonwealth of Australia* 1983: 489).

The contentious relationship between international and domestic law is evident in debates about war crimes and crimes against humanity. For example, German actions during World War II were legal according to German law, even though they were later condemned as history's most extensive war crimes. In the context of military law, much debate centres on the relationship between subordinates carrying out the orders of superiors and in identifying when there is a duty to disobey a superior order, the origin of that duty and the location of responsibility for illegal actions that occur under orders. Such issues were central to the Nuremberg tribunal and the trial of the Japanese general Yamashita, who was convicted and hanged for war crimes committed by his subordinates (Kelman and Hamilton, 1989: 71–5).

While the concept of war crimes already existed in international law via the Fourth Hague Convention in 1907, which expressly prohibited the killing of defenceless persons in occupied territory, crimes against humanity and crimes against peace were not explicitly formulated until the *Charter of the International Military Tribunal* (IMT) was developed to enable prosecution of Nazi war criminals at Nuremberg (Randall, 1988: 800–10; Steiner, 1991: 180; Wagner, 1989: 904). The IMT was created and jointly administered by the USA, Great Britain, France and the Soviet Union. Aggressive war was declared a crime against peace and genocidal policies against populations under one's own rule, including Nazi actions against German Jews or the nationals of subjugated countries, were declared crimes against humanity. Crimes against humanity include murder, extermination, enslavement, deportation and other inhumane acts committed against any civilian population or persecutions on political, racial or religious grounds, regardless of whether such actions are in violation of the domestic law of the country where they occur (Wagner, 1989: 902). These new crimes were formulated after the war, which deviates from the legal proscription against retrospective law and, perhaps, rather than indicating an international consensus, the formulation of new international criminal laws reflected the interests and concerns of the Allied victors.

Questions of responsibility for war crimes committed during World War II did not cease after these tribunals. Nonetheless, with the exception of Israel's Nazis and Nazi Collaborators (Punishment) Act of 1950 and the high-profile prosecution of Adolph Eichmann in 1961, the western allies became less willing to initiate trials themselves or to cooperate with Soviet authorities in seeking out alleged war criminals or extraditing them when their identity or location was known (Steiner, 1991: 181). In 1983, the UN adopted a resolution on principles of international cooperation in the detection, arrest, extradition and punishment of persons found guilty of war crimes and crimes against humanity (Green, 1988: 218). More than 40 years after the end of the war, a number of governments responded to public pressure from

Zionist groups, ex-service personnel, survivors and the families of victims by passing war-crimes legislation, for example Britain (1991), Canada (1987) and Australia (1988), with some instigating prosecutions, for example the prosecution of Klaus Barbie in France in 1987.

Another strategy for dealing with alleged war criminals is denaturalization (if the person has citizenship status) and deportation, which has been the strategy of the USA since 1978. The Australian government, after a 1987 report indicated that it was more than likely that about 70 current Australian residents had committed serious war crimes during World War II, decided not to adopt a policy of extradition but to make prosecution in domestic courts the mode of dealing with alleged war criminals. It established a Special Investigations Unit (now disbanded) and in 1988 substantially amended the War Crimes Act 1945 to provide that a person who committed a war crime between 1939 and 1945 is guilty of an indictable offence. It defined war crime as a serious crime including murder, manslaughter, rape and indecent assault. The definition of the offence incorporates both war crimes and crimes against humanity, by punishing crimes committed during war or occupation and the same actions in the form of political, racial or religious persecution not committed in the course of war but in a country involved in war or subject to occupation. As the former Chief Justice of the High Court observed: 'The Act makes criminal acts done by a person who, at the time of the commission of those acts, had no relevant connection with Australia ... [and it] makes conduct outside Australia unlawful thereby visiting that conduct with legal consequences under Australian law' (*Polyukhovich* v *Commonwealth of Australia*, 1991: 550, 553).

A number of war crimes trials have been initiated in the wake of more recent conflicts. For example, the International Criminal Tribunal for the Former Yugoslavia (ICTY) was established by the Security Council in 1994 and financed by the United Nations General Assembly. The first indictment charged Dragan Nikolic of Bosnia-Herzegovina with wilful killings, unlawful imprisonment, torture, persecution on discriminatory grounds and inhuman acts (Bergsmo, 1994: 40–9). The Court commenced on a small scale, was supported by the US Clinton Administration, and was then subjected to pressures from the Bush Administration to complete all investigations and trials by the end of the decade (Hagan et al., 2006).

The implementation of the new jurisdiction of the international criminal law at the ICTY involved day-to-day decisions, conflicting local and international demands and capacities as well as organizational imperatives. Successive prosecutorial regimes developed new legal practices enhancing the jurisdiction and moral authority of international law (Hagan et al., 2006: 1525). International criminal law is produced within a network of actors, institutions and practices as well as a changing political environment and new norms of criminality (Jenness, 2004).

Human rights' norms have become a generally available 'repertoire of legitimate claim making' in international law (Levy and Sznaider, 2006: 659). Globally accessible historical memories can politically and culturally frame various conflicts as issues of human rights and therefore as international and not just domestic issues. For example, Levy and Sznaider (2006) argue that inter-ethnic warfare in Kosovo with its

European geography and the television images resonated with Holocaust iconography, resulting in pressures for humanitarian intervention contrasting with the portrayal of genocide in Rwanda. Military intervention in Kosovo was constituted primarily as a moral obligation, girded by memories of the Nazi extermination policies, to combat atrocities and the Nuremberg concept of crimes against humanity to be tried in the ICTY. The Holocaust has become a symbol for the most extreme violation of human rights and state-sanctioned atrocities, and not just a concrete historical moment or the acts of a specific regime (Levy and Sznaider, 2006: 657). Similarly, the Spanish judge Baltasar Garzon demanded the arrests of Argentina's military dictators – arguing for crimes against humanity.

The image of international relations projected by the UN Charter (and related documents) is one of sovereign states linked together in a 'myriad of relations' under pressure to resolve disputes by peaceful means and according to legal criteria; subject in principle to tight restrictions on the use of force and constrained to observe 'certain standards' with regard to the treatment of all persons on their territory, including their own citizens (Held, 1995: 84–5). Held suggests that this guarding of the sovereign state means that, despite good intentions, the UN has effectively failed to generate a new principle of international organization that transcends the model of international relations to create new democratic mechanisms of political coordination and change. Also, it is susceptible to the agenda of the most powerful states, most evident in the Security Council and the veto powers of the five permanent members: the USA, France, Russia, China and the UK.

Held proposes the development of a cosmopolitan democratic law that is entrenched within and across national borders. This is a domain of law different in kind from the law of states and from international law. It transcends the particular claims of nations and states and extends to all in the 'universal community' (Held, 1995: 226–30). He is not contemplating the formation of a single, unified international structure of governance, but compliance and participation would be strongly normative: 'there would be a clear duty to obey the law. However, if those who governed flouted the terms of cosmopolitan law, the basis of political legitimacy would be eroded' (Held, 1995: 231). He envisages the emergence of a community of all democratic communities and the alignment of the different levels of law – national, regional, international – and believes that the rights and responsibilities of people as national citizens and as the subjects of cosmopolitan law would coincide, that democratic citizenship could become a truly universal status and that the nation state would eventually disappear. While this proposal takes the limitations of the nation state seriously and offers a utopian vision for individuals and the recognition of their rights, it underestimates the resilience of nation states to external forces and global pressures. Habermas similarly argues that only a democratic citizenship that does not close itself off in a particularistic fashion can pave the way for world citizenship that exists on a continuum with state citizenship. He proposes that democratic citizenship need not be rooted in the national identity of a people, but, regardless of the diversity of cultural forms of life, it does require that every citizen be socialized into a common political culture (1990: 500, 514–15). Levy and Sznaider maintain that

While states retain most of their sovereign functions, the basis for their legitimacy is no longer primarily conditioned by a contract with the nation, but also by their adherence to a set of nation-transcending human rights ideals. Legitimacy is mediated by how willing states are to engage with an emerging Human Rights regime. (2006: 659)

In varying ways UN multilateral treaties and conventions place obligations on signatories but states' interpretation, compliance and outright breaching will result in an uneven implementation. This is true across the spectrum from the most to the least developed nations. For example, following the invasion of Kuwait in 1990 the United Nations imposed sanctions on Iraq and later the Security Council established the UN controlled Oil-for-Food programme which prohibited the direct payment of hard currency to Iraq. In order to preserve the market for Australian wheat in Iraq the Australian Wheat Board (a statutory body granted a monopoly on Australian wheat sales) made payments to an Iraqi trucking company that were included in the wheat price and sought to cover up these payments while knowing that such a fee was prohibited by UN sanctions and Australian government policy. The report of the inquiry into certain Australian companies in relation to the UN Oil-for-Food Programme (Cole, 2006) identified complex arrangements aimed to misrepresent the true nature and purpose of the trucking fees which were flagrantly in breach of the UN convention. Commissioner Cole concluded: 'No one asked, "What is the right thing to do?"' because of the 'closed culture of superiority and impregnability, of dominance and self-importance' (Cole, 2006: xii). In this instance, global norms were insufficient to enforce the UN sanctions.

Citizenship in Europe

The European Union (EU) is one environment where postnational citizenship might be possible. However, EU citizenship resembles traditional nation-state citizenship; it is available only to those citizens of EU member countries. The webpage states that the European Union is based on the rule of law: 'This means that everything it does is derived from treaties, which are agreed on voluntarily and democratically by all Member States' (see http://europa.eu.abc/treaties/index_en. htm). Most recently, the Treaty of Lisbon was signed in 2007 and is awaiting ratification by all members before it can come into force. Its primary objectives are to make the EU more democratic and to provide further accountability and transparency in governance. Thus EU citizenship and its operation imply the nation state.

Of the 27 current (at 15 December 2008) EU member states, 10 are former Soviet bloc countries undergoing a broad transformation from communist to democratic regimes. While the specific changes vary in each country or new nation state, they generally include the privatization of public assets, property reforms, an official encouragement of private economic activity and investment, and the emergence of markets for labour, goods and services. Transition to a market economy also brings about new class formations and inequalities and perhaps places a greater emphasis or expectation on the new democratic laws and constitutional protections to advance citizens' rights (Nee, 1989: 665–7; Nee and Matthews, 1996: 429–31; Szelényi and Kostello, 1996: 1094).

It has become very clear that the effects of democratization and market economics are uneven. Women's participation in the new parliaments is much lower than under state socialism. While women had been active in public demonstrations and in initiating the process of reform, they did not enjoy equal inclusion in the actual decision-making or negotiation processes. Where new parliaments come to have a degree of real political power they become more clearly a male domain, and the achievement of emancipation on the part of men has also been accompanied by the sentimentalization of family and home and the clear (gender) segmentation of public and private spheres (Watson, 1993: 471–9). In the new Germany, ex-German Democratic Republic (GDR) women face disproportionately higher unemployment rates and the loss of many childcare and maternity benefits. Even though women in the former East Germany were not equal with men in terms of earnings, they had achieved equality with men regarding occupational qualifications and labour-force participation (Sørensen and Trappe, 1995: 399–400, 404). The former GDR was based on the principle that all citizens had a right and duty to paid employment, which entailed offering special benefits to women to facilitate motherhood and paid employment, and before unification most East German mothers remained in the workforce. By 1993, women's official unemployment rate was 20 per cent, roughly twice as high as men's, and they have reduced opportunities *vis-à-vis* men of gaining high-paid, more prestigious jobs (Ferree, 1993: 100–10; 1994: 612–16; 1995: 11).

Part of the transition to a market economy entails legal change. New political regimes will seek to establish new legal systems and all will tend to look towards the formal characteristics of western constitutional democracies, which seek to institutionalize such values as the rule of law, a separation of powers, civil rights and due process. In the former Soviet eastern European states the laws were especially draconian for those convicted of political crimes; lawyers and judges were subject to direct political control and intervention; many legal actors abused their power; there was an absence of due process; and investigations and punishments often involved torture and inhumane conditions. Interestingly, however, some research indicates that at least in some of the former Soviet states, the everyday operation of legal systems was not so very different from western legal systems. In East Germany, for example, judges were able to resist much of the routine political pressure and could decide cases on what they saw as the merits, except for the most politically sensitive cases involving people who sought to leave the country. Trial judges also tended to act more like mediators and were concerned to reconcile private interests and resolve disputes rather than rigidly adhere to procedural issues (Scheppele, 1996: 630). In Hungary, the legal arena had some relative autonomy from state directives and political objectives (Scheppele, 1996: 644). Moreover, western legal systems and laws are not entirely independent of politics, as a broader concept than party politics.

Two central issues now confront the democratizing governments of eastern Europe, as well as those in Latin American countries and other places where politically repressive regimes have been displaced: the role of law in the process of transition; and what to do about officials of the former regimes who enforced the repressive laws, committed human-rights abuses and acceded to political compromise and corruption. Each country going through the democratization process has to decide what should be done with the previous regime's secret police, torturers, death squads, informers and collaborators, as well as their political superiors. New governments will generally proclaim their allegiance to human rights, civil liberties and the rule of law. This raises a range of legal and moral issues about accountability for actions that were once legalized government policy, about due process, retrospective justiciability and enforcement, and questions about the scope of international law and its impact on national legal policies (Cohen, 1995: 9). Three strategies have been adopted: punishment, compensation and lustration (Cohen, 1995: 23–8).

1 *Legal punishment* involves identifying those with an individual or collective responsibility and organizing a civilian criminal trial. Following German reunification, west German courts argued that east German judges and prosecutors should have declared the border regime invalid because the statutory law in the GDR had ignored human rights, thus establishing a duty of civil disobedience on the basis of human rights (Blankenburg, 1995: 229–30). Supra-national courts have also been established which try individuals, including current or former heads of state. For example the International Criminal Court was established by a United Nations treaty, located in The Hague and inaugurated in 2003 (see www.icc.int). Criminal courts in other countries have also been used to prosecute individuals accused of serious war crimes and crimes against humanity.

2 *Compensation and restoration* entail using variants on the civil-law model to provide material compensation and restore dignity to victims and their families. This entails returning property and other assets, including deposits kept in Swiss banks, which had been confiscated under the previous political regime.

3 *Lustration* entails identifying, unmasking and denouncing individuals or whole categories of people who had colluded with the previous regime by maintaining silence, informing or collaborating (rather than individual crimes or gross human rights violations) and removing them from any government positions or employment. For example, in (the former) Czechoslovakia the 1991 Lustration Law barred former members of the secret police, former high-level Communist Party officials, and members of the voluntary People's Militia and other groups from any high-level government employment and required job applicants to produce a document declaring that they did not belong to any of the listed categories (Cohen, 1995: 26). In East Germany the situation was rather different as, rather than establishing new democratic and legal institutions, the existing institutions were absorbed into the political and legal system of West Germany. Lustration of former communist leaders occurred under the principles of the West German constitution and in courts staffed primarily by West German legal personnel (Blankenburg, 1995: 225). Following reunification, all law professors, judges and prosecutors had to reapply for their jobs and provide information on their party membership, political activities, and participation in cases of political injustice (Blankenburg, 1995: 239–43).

The role of law in the process of transition

In the process of transformation, the rule of law or *Rechtsstaat-type* legalism is emphasized, both as a means to protect society and human rights against an all-pervasive state (party) domination, and to promote or further a market economy that is believed to be the solution to the present crisis (Sajo, 1990: 229). Prior socialist legal systems viewed laws as commands used to implement socialist policies. This social engineering approach underscored the law as instrumental to social and economic planning, with legislation having a lesser role than regulation by governmental decrees. Modernization in eastern Europe relied to a great extent on the state and the state in turn used its law to promote modernization. Socialist law is not based on a concept of individual rights, but claims to be a collective-interest-oriented system emphasizing the reciprocity of rights and obligations. There remained a general scepticism about the legal system: it was often ambiguous and a source of oppression, especially of political opposition (Massell, 1968; Sajo, 1990: 331–3). In this climate, the rule of law came to symbolize the protection of individual rights and independence from political parties; it was seen as nonbureaucratic, clear and predictable, and thus as a complete break from socialist legal institutions. The establishment of constitutional reforms was a clear symbolic act on the part of the new postcommunist governments committed to democratic reform (Sajo, 1990: 335).

Anticommunist opposition in the east European countries criticized the legal system much less in terms of technical concepts or models of western constitutionalism and the rule of law than in relation to universal human rights (Sajo, 1990: 333). Democratic oppositions in Poland, Hungary and Czechoslovakia emphasized the importance of civil society, where the autonomy of civil (private) action presupposes a legally bounded state. Following 'democratic transformations', many eastern and central European states moved rapidly to ratify international treaties on human and political rights, for example the *European Convention on Human Rights* (ECHR). The ECHR subjects domestic legal systems to highly sophisticated judicial control mechanisms and assessments of the extent to which domestic law and practice conform with its requirements (Drzemczewski, 1995). Laws are now enacted with the intention of repealing some of the most discriminatory and oppressive rules of the former regimes, especially the abolition of antifree-speech rules in criminal law, creating an effective freedom of association for people in those countries (Sajo, 1990: 334–5).

Legislation is also important in establishing new property relations. Property transformation in postsocialist societies involves the decentralized reorganization of assets and the centralized management of liabilities. In Hungary, property transformation occurred without conventional privatization, which is contrary to predictions of a rapid transfer of assets from state-owned enterprises to private ownership (Stark, 1996: 996–8). Whereas in the state socialist economy the state attempted to manage assets centrally, in the first years of the postsocialist economy the state attempted to manage liabilities centrally. In 1991, the Hungarian government fundamentally modified three important laws regulating the accounting of assets and liabilities in its quest to maintain a lead in the regional competition for foreign investments and international credits. The aim of the laws was to require enterprises to switch to western-style accounting principles and bankruptcy provisions and to put the domestic banks on a western footing. One effect of this was a crisis in the banking system due to an enormous increase in bankruptcies and liquidation. The state proceeded to acquire the banks, not via a process of nationalization but as the dominant shareholder (Stark, 1996: 1010–12). This example demonstrates that there is not necessarily a clear distinction between public and private ownership; many firms can have different kinds of owners and specific legislation furthers such an outcome. Legislation and policies that clarify property rights may be more important contributors to the dynamism of local enterprises and entrepreneurs than the privatization of assets.

Conclusion

This chapter provides an overview of the recent sociological discussion of citizenship, human rights and globalization. Law is present in the formulation of each of these concepts. It is through law that governments articulate or recognize citizenship rights and social movement activists engage with the legal arena (as well as others) to make rights' claims for various groups and constituencies. Increasingly, the efficacy of the nation state to guarantee citizenship is being questioned. Such global forces as the flow of goods, services, communications and people are often unimpeded by national boundaries and not amenable to national control, yet will still have a direct impact on domestic affairs. Even where new nation states are emerging, particularly in the former Soviet Europe, their formation is being constrained by the force of broader events, particularly international law and its obligations. Often constitutional democracies that formally guarantee the rule of law and equal rights are being adopted as the most egalitarian forms of legal system and are perceived to constitute radical departures from the previous arbitrary, *ad hoc* and overtly political legal regimes. However, as many commentators point out, formal legal equality is not tantamount to actual equality, and in fact may even reproduce substantive inequalities.

Notes

1   There is some debate about the accuracy of Somers' classification of an area as either arable or pastoral. Hopcroft, for example, argues that regional differences in political culture and participation stemmed less from the nature of the local agricultural economy than from regional differences in social institutions (1995: 792–5).
2   An excellent source of information and research on refugees, asylum seekers, human rights and international law is the *International Journal of Refugee Law*.

9 Conclusion

This book provides a sociological approach to law and social change. It has mapped out important global changes which can have varying impacts on national legal systems and local laws. These changes are also significant for the perceptions, among various actors, of the availability or utility of law as a route to, or symbol of, reform. There is some evidence of convergence in substantive laws and legal institutions, as many countries legislate on similar topics sometimes following their participation in multilateral conventions or treaties. Countering the simple convergence thesis, much empirical research identifies the diverse ways in which legislation is implemented and enforced locally. As Carruthers and Halliday suggest: 'national experiences influence global norm making and global norms constrain national lawmaking' (2006: 1187).

The book also offers an expansive conception of law. Law is presented as a complex of practices and institutions, generally oriented towards social control, regulation or dispute resolution. Law is not viewed primarily as a contained body of knowledge accessible only to legal practitioners and judicial personnel. Determining what the law is in relation to a particular dispute is one minute facet of its operation in social life. Nor is the law constituted simply by the structures and processes of the formal legal system and the activities of legal personnel, including police officers, lawyers, judges and court administrators. For some theorists, the distinctiveness of law derives from its mode of enforcement or source of authority; others will consider it an interpretive scheme that categorizes and regulates social relationships; while for others it is its discrete language based on rights discourse and notions of property ownership. Law is an integral component of social organization and cannot be understood in a vacuum and isolated from other social institutions and social forces. It shapes and is shaped by market relations, the structure of social inequality, the level of industrialization, cultural values, processes of socialization, governmental structures and political ideology, as well as by other social phenomena.

The preceding chapters are less concerned with addressing the question of what law is or arriving at a simple or single conception of law than with inquiring into how sociologists define or conceptualize law and its interrelationships with other forms of social control, dispute resolution and regulation. The discussion addresses the interrelationships between law and social change by critically examining contemporary developments in the interdisciplinary field of socio-legal theory combined with analyses of empirical and comparative case studies. For many social movements and activists, law is a critical strategy for social reform, yet it is constrained by social institutions, cultural values, everyday practices and legal consciousness. Law is an important constitutive force moulding social relations and identities, which in turn constitute and shape law (Brigham, 1996: 129–54). Law provides resources for social change, for example legal language and the power of legal concepts that can be used to articulate identities or claims, but it also limits the capacity for social activism (Bower, 1994).

While the term 'the law' is often used by social researchers, legal practitioners and citizens alike, it usually means different things to the different people using it (Ewick and Silbey, 1998). In order to capture some of the diversity of law and legal practice in social life, this book first canvasses various conceptions of law and surveys legal theorists' articulations of law, especially in the perspectives of legal formalism, legal realism and natural law. In contrast, a sociological approach to law is more concerned with substantive empirical issues in which law varies in its level of significance, than with abstract notions of the law. This is shown in the overview of Durkheim, Weber and Marx's sociological theories of social structure, action and social change. The diversity of conceptions of law and interconnections with social life is clearly apparent in current social theories of law, which tend to emphasize the multiplicity of legal norms, the complexity and instability of law, the importance of subjectivity and the transformative capacity of law. Postmodern approaches, often following Foucault, and pluralistic discussions of law do not focus on legal institutions but on regulation and discipline, the deployment of legal imagery and rights discourses and the infusion and pervasiveness of law in everyday life. In this context, lawyers are important, but not the sole, actors in interpreting, transforming, or even manipulating, the law and thus affecting access to legal remedies.

Two important areas of law and legal action are dispute resolution and social control and both are discussed in reference to global, national and local changes and challenges. Of course, not all resolutions of disputes or social control entail law, and a goal of this book is to assess the interrelationships between law and other mechanisms for resolving conflict and attempting to achieve social control or regulation. To investigate the ways in which social contexts, cultural values, political institutions and history can structure such interrelationships, numerous empirical and comparative case studies from a variety of societies are incorporated. The final, substantive chapters of the book examine the ways in which social movements, especially the women's movement and rights activists, focus on law as an important strategy for social change. These chapters also demonstrate how legal institutions and discourse will shape the nature of social activism, as well as providing resources to marginalized groups (as well as other interests) for the assertion (or denial) of citizenship and equality.

Following Durkheim, the book generally distinguishes between law as dispute resolution and law as social control and devotes a chapter to each, largely because legal institutions in common-law countries reflect such a distinction. However, the difference is more analytical than empirical. Many criminal-law practices, for example, entail informal negotiations and mediation and eschew litigation and adversarial courtroom tactics. Changes in the legal system can indicate wider shifts and orientations on the part of the general public or, at least, political elites. Criminal laws and the criminal justice system, perhaps more than other areas, are particularly subject to 'moral' panics (Cohen, 1980) and electoral politics, often resulting in more severe penalties, the criminalization of new types of behaviour and harsher policies toward certain categories of offender.

One significant shift in the legal systems of many western, democratic nations is the expansion of alternative dispute resolution (ADR) as an organized and desirable reform. Its rationale has followed widespread criticism of legal institutions' failure to provide justice to the many litigants and victims of crime, the expense, the time involved in any court action and the whole structure of adversarialism, which discounts opportunities for compromise, mediation, negotiation and more informal approaches. Many would assert that the new tribunals facilitate the local resolution of disputes, are faster, more informal, more efficient and less costly than court action. Rather than being an alternative to the formal legal system, the new fora for dispute resolution and some criminal justice issues are usually connected with more formal procedures and do involve legal personnel. The extent to which the ADR movement offers an alternative to the formal legal system, the relationship between different forms of dispute processing and the degree to which reformers' aspirations have been realized are topics of ongoing empirical research.

The book's overarching theme is the interrelationship between law and social change. The oft-called classical social theorists – Durkheim, Weber and Marx – were centrally concerned with the question of social change and to varying degrees did theorize the significance of law in epochal social transformations, including the emergence of market economies, the rise of rationality as a key principle of social organization, and the growth and increasing complexity of social life. Marx and Weber were particularly interested in the interconnections between economic conditions and the form of law, as well as issues relating to access to justice and the role of law in the reproduction of social stratification. For Durkheim, identifying the dominant form of law in a society is an important indicator of the type of society, thus mapping social change requires mapping legal change. Of these three theorists, Weber's theory of law is the most coherent and detailed and he explicitly links the rise of formal rational law with the pervasiveness of rationality (goal-oriented action) in western economic and social life. His typology of law implies an evolutionary legal development, with formally rational law being the most advanced type; and, while cognizant of the significance of economic forces, he does not attribute causality to modern capitalism and modern legal systems. He assigns particular significance to the self-interested legal profession and its links with the capitalist class system to explain why the English legal system was impervious to the development of fully rational law. For Weber, the distinctive character of law derives from its mode of enforcement by legally empowered actors, thus suggesting that the operation of law depends on particular, established, legitimate institutional arrangements.

For many contemporary social and political movements, legal institutions and doctrine are important avenues for social reform. At an institutional level, the focus is often on securing progressive change via litigation and judicial decisions. For example, civil rights groups, women's movements, and indigenous activists have sought social reform and greater legal rights and protections, redress for past wrongs through litigation and the establishment of favourable interpretations of the constitution or bills of rights, where these exist. Legislation has also been important in such areas as sex and race discrimination, industrial relations and the establishment of welfare programmes. Indeed, during the twentieth century most western democratic nations established social policy programmes via legislation.

Many writers have described some of the consequences of the statutory establishment and administrative implementation of welfare states as the legalization or juridification of everyday life and social relations. The state provision of benefits and pensions in the areas of income maintenance, health and education ostensibly aims to enhance recipients' economic independence and reduce a reliance on charities and informal or family sources of assistance, in order to achieve a minimum economic status and standard of living as a social right. These entitlements aim to enhance citizens' autonomy; however, they also entail high levels of governmental regulation and surveillance. Enforcement of eligibility criteria is not carried out by legal personnel, but by state-employed (or at least funded) managers, administrators and welfare personnel. The welfare state presents a paradox: it enhances autonomy by buffering the effects of an unregulated market, but the formation of legislation and bureaucracies to administer legal entitlements (usually in the form of monetary compensation) result in a greater regulation of everyday life, that is, less autonomy (Habermas, 1987).

Aside from social movement activism in the legal arena, a reliance on law emerges at a more local or everyday level, where people deploy rights discourses and notions of ownership and property in attempts to realize their interests or resolve dilemmas. Such activities and interactions may occur without any recourse to the formal institutions of law or to legal personnel. Arguments that something is legal or illegal and claims to possess certain legal entitlements can be deployed for their moral suasion rather than as indicating any intention to initiate legal action (Ewick and Silbey, 1998: 18–19). Law also pervades everyday life via cultural representations, especially the widespread use of legal language and imagery to describe social interactions and relationships. In popular culture, law-and-order television programmes and movies and the profusion of contemporary literature dealing with the criminal justice system and the legal profession attest to the salience of legal phenomena. On the other side, the televising of criminal trials often dissipates the distinction between fiction and nonfiction.

Viewing law as an important strategy or resource for social change can easily lead to an instrumentalist conception and the inevitable question of whether or not specific instances of legislation or court decisions have been successful in achieving an expected or desired social change. Numerous difficulties exist when determining how to measure the success or failure of particular law reforms, especially when apparent failures might result in long-term change, or victories might have symbolic effects that were not anticipated. Many legal reforms are assessed as having failed. Researchers point out that sex discrimination legislation and judicial decisions recognizing or upholding women's rights to equal employment opportunities have not resulted in widespread gender equality. In the criminal justice area, considerable research demonstrates that, despite legal changes providing the victims of sexual offences (mostly women) with more protections, the incidence of rape remains high and the difficulties that victims have during the prosecution process remain. Similarly, laws against race discrimination and those guaranteeing civil rights to many marginalized groups have not been translated into greater social equality or the absence of discrimination. While it might be a useful political strategy to focus on law reform, an instrumentalist conception of law is far too simplistic. Any legal change requires interpretation, application and enforcement, which can all undermine the changes anticipated by social activists. Law reforms can be overtaken by political forces and events, defined by enforcement personnel or administrators as not economically or practically viable, and may create incentives for opponents to mobilize and seek to overturn them.

Rather than talking about the success or failure of law reform or its inevitable role in reproducing economic and social inequalities, or alternatively viewing law as an unfolding corpus of doctrine that is impervious to social movement strategies or policy imperatives, it is more fruitful to conceptualize law as an arena, with porous boundaries. Various interest groups and actors can participate in the legal arena or juridical field and seek to have their worldviews and experiences translated into law. This involves competition for the right to control law (Bourdieu, 1987). The law provides opportunities and resources for social movement activism. The juridical field becomes a social space oriented towards the conversion of direct conflict between actors into a juridically regulated debate between professions acting by proxy. The legal arena also constrains social action, as it requires social problems and complaints to be translated or transformed into legal concepts and legal remedies. Agreement to participate in this field indicates an acceptance of conflict resolution according to legal rules, conventions and discourse: interests and needs become rights and duties; social arrangements become contracts; and harms and damages are translated into crimes.

Many of the foregoing chapters discussed examples of research that entailed some empirical social science methodologies. The final sections of this chapter provide an overview of some significant issues regarding socio-legal research.

Social research and law

First, a note on what is meant by the term 'research'. Research for the social scientist and the lawyer will typically mean different things and involve different methods. Legal research entails searches of decided cases and statutes to ascertain the current law or legal reasoning on a particular issue. Lawyers and jurists will analyse, debate, discuss and theorize law as doctrine – norms, rules, principles, concepts – and analyse the modes of their interpretation and validation (Cotterrell, 1998: 171). Law schools will train students to identify and analyse the legal principles – *ratio decidendi* – underlying judicial, mostly appellate, decisions. The aim of much legal scholarship then, is to clarify and influence legal reasoning in terms of a self-referential system rather than to further the public understanding of law, legal institutions or processes (Hillyard, 2007: 275).

Broadly, empirical social research relies on a range of methodologies, including surveys, interviews, observation, experimentation and various written material and documents, in order to study 'the operation and effects of the law' in multiple settings (Baldwin and Davis, 2003: 880). However, 'it is principally through empirical study of the *practice* of law (especially of the preliminary and apparently more mundane aspects), and in studying the way legal processes and decisions impact upon the citizen, that the disciplines of sociology and, to a lesser degree, philosophy, psychology, and economics have entered into and enriched the study of law' (Baldwin and Davis, 2003: 881, emphasis in original).

Despite these broad differences in social and legal research, in many ways the logic of science and of law, as traditionally constructed, have many similarities. They share common social and intellectual origins in seventeenth-century Enlightenment England. This period emphasized the search for rational modes of reasoning distinct from customary or traditional practices and beliefs, the quest to uncover or discover underlying laws and principles, and an interest in facts. Law and social science articulate distinctive conceptions of fact and evidence and are sites of contest, argument, debate, disagreement, competition and deconstruction (Fuchs and Ward, 1994). They are both socially situated and influenced by contexts and human action (Peneff, 1988). Science and law 'include local negotiations on what counts as evidence and fact, political struggles over priority and property rights, and the skilful use of textual and nontextual resources to produce artifacts and convincing narratives' (Fuchs and Ward, 1994: 485).

Social research in legal settings

Legal institutions, organizations and settings can present distinct challenges to the social scientist (Banakar and Travers, 2005a, 2005b). One significant challenge is that of access. If gatekeepers do not consider the research project or questions of value or interest or not of direct practical relevance to them or their organization, then researchers' access can be denied or restricted. On the other side, following Ewick and Silbey (1998) all social settings have legal dimensions, law is infused in everyday life, there is no space without law, thus any social issue, setting or process can evince law or legal issues or be subject to juridification. 'Law constitutes social life to a significant degree by influencing the meanings of basic categories (such as property, ownership, contract, trust, responsibility, guilt, and personality) that colour or define social relations' (Cotterrell, 1998: 177). However, it is useful to distinguish between institutionalized legal settings and law in ordinary or everyday settings.

Banakar (2000) goes further and suggests that sociological studies of the law are limited in their potential to capture the 'truth' of law as legal practitioners experience it, especially in relation to legal doctrine. In other words, sociological concepts and legal concepts and understandings of the world are different, and 'the question is whether sociology is able to climb out of its own skin and get inside the law to understand and explain the law's "truth", namely, the motives and meanings of legal phenomena from within' (2000: 274). While not directly drawing on the work of Luhmann (1985, see Chapter 3) this question echoes his theoretical concerns. To the extent that social researchers rely on sociological concepts to understand or explain legal settings, processes, actors and so on, then the experience of those participants will necessarily be refracted through artificial (sociological) concepts and not communicated through insider descriptions and perspectives. This tension, to varying degrees, emerges in all social research (Becker, 1998), but Banakar suggests it is magnified in socio-legal research because of the power of law as a discourse or form of knowledge, its strength as an institution and closure as a profession. Law is well-placed to protect its identity and jurisdiction when confronted with external and what it considers to be intrusive knowledge and expertise.

Regardless of the way in which this epistemological problem is resolved or managed there are a number of important practical issues in social research in the legal sphere.

1 *Access and gatekeepers* Legal organizations or settings are porous to social research to different degrees (Baldwin and Davis, 2003: 893). Some topics are not easily available for study. Research in legal settings can entail 'studying up', that is obtaining access to powerful, influential, busy people who may not wish to or do not have time to participate by completing a survey, being interviewed or observed, or by providing other information to the researcher (Smart, 1984). For example, social researchers will often perceive judges as 'hard to reach' (Cowan and Hitchings, 2007; Hunter et al., 2005), or a 'difficult population' due to 'the high status and professional remoteness of the judiciary in American society, [and others] judicial time constraints, assumed resentment or unwillingness to be tested, concerns by judges about confidentiality of responses, and perhaps a distrust, dislike, or perceived irrelevance of social and behavioral science and scientists' (Dobbin et al., 2001: 287). Dobbin and colleagues offer practical advice for conducting survey research with difficult populations. They found that most of the US state trial court judges they contacted for their research on the admissibility of expert evidence were interested in the topic and they obtained high response rates to their telephone and mail survey instruments. Drawing on Dillman's Total Design Method (Dillman, 2007), they emphasize the importance of constructing a detailed and well thought-out plan for project administration which includes sufficient flexibility to manage the inevitable, unanticipated events and situations that will arise in the field.

   Some legal subjects are more accessible to the non-lawyer and will hold greater intuitive appeal (Baldwin and Davis, 2003: 884). The technical intricacies of trust or contract have not been as appealing as the criminal law, though the focus of criminological research is typically on the institutions of the criminal law – police, courts, lawyers, corrections, and so on – or on the effects of criminal laws on segments of the populations rather than the substantive law itself. Undertaking social science research in legal and criminal justice settings can also raise special questions of ethics (Israel, 2004).

2 *Legal discourse* Both law and sociology are concerned with similar topics of social control, regulation and social relations and both disciplines use such concepts as a norm, rule, crime, sanction, punishment, and dispute. However, it is this similarity and overlap which lead to competition, disagreement and debate between social and legal knowledge as law's dominant professional and academic position resists

external argument and criticism (Banakar, 2000: 286). In contrast, social research has had more acceptance and credibility in the medical, health and illness sphere. As medicine's concerns are with concepts of health and illness which rely on biochemistry, anatomy, physiology and so on there is no overlap or similarity with sociological concepts, thus reducing the potential for contest, debate, and disagreement. The respective spheres of expertise of the medical practitioner or scientist and the social researcher are more delineated than is the case with law and social science. Moreover, legal discourse is adversarial. Lawyers are trained to debate, argue, contest the meaning of terms, and to challenge evidence of various kinds and not accept research findings as fact, but will often seek to delimit its relevance, value or applicability.

Nonetheless, in recent years the demand for socio-legal research has increased, especially for applied or evaluation research, which has a potential value for policy makers. An increasing government inclination to assess or monitor legal innovations and to evaluate consequences, or success however it is defined, has increased the scope and capacity of socio-legal research (Baldwin and Davis, 2003: 888). For example, the UK Ministry of Justice, and formerly the Department of Constitutional Affairs, commissions research, including evaluation research, on a wide range of socio-legal topics and also provides various statistics on the civil and criminal justice systems (see www.justice.gov.uk and www.dca.gov.uk; see for example Hester et al., 2008; Shapland et al., 2008).

Legal reforms or new legal programmes – such as mediation centres or services, specialist or problem-solving courts, new arrangements for legal aid funding, and new sentencing provisions – are typically established as pilot programmes with explicit expectations that the reforms will be evaluated via empirical research before longer-term implementation. Other changes, for example sentencing reforms, might be subject to socio-legal research which is evaluative but not explicitly evaluation research.

Evaluation research raises a number of issues for socio-legal and social science researchers more generally, mostly relating to the political environment in which evaluation research occurs. This has been a source of particular discussions in criminology (Pawson and Tilley, 1994; Travers, 2005a, 2005b; Weatherburn, 2005).

First, questions emerge about the independent nature of such research. As various agencies – governmental and non-governmental – commission research they will usually define the parameters and extent of the research, by setting the terms of reference, specifying the budget and making decisions about the availability of the findings and relevance of conclusions. The need to provide organizations with recommendations they can understand and implement within a budget makes evaluation research distinctive: 'evaluation methods often represent a compromise between the ideal and the feasible' (Weiss, 1998: 18).

Second, commissioners of research may not publicly release findings which are critical of the organization's policies or practices and that do not support agency initiatives or agendas. The researchers (depending on the nature of the contractual agreement with the commissioning agency) may not have the capacity to publish or use the research findings independent of the decisions of the commissioners of the research. There might also be self-censorship, as researchers might avoid criticizing programmes or agencies because of an over-identification with the organization or its personnel or a desire to maintain relations to ensure future evaluation research opportunities (Travers, 2005a: 40).

Third, evaluation research may not need to be as rigorous as academic peer-reviewed research. It may not be intellectually fulfilling or extend knowledge and opportunities for theoretical development to the same degree as basic research.

Fourth, evaluation research design often relies on quantitative research methods and may not attend to more qualitative aspects of the operation of a programme. Moreover, the methodology and time frame of much evaluation research cannot assess longer term or deeper consequences of the innovations. Pawson and Tilley suggest that the dominant quasi-experimental research model of evaluation is inappropriate for gauging change within social programmes and that more attention must be paid to the underlying mechanisms and political contexts of any innovation (1994: 292). Evaluating the effects of a particular programme or intervention in isolation from the circumstances that might facilitate or impede its effectiveness, implementation or transformation will mean that the findings of evaluation research are necessarily limited .

Governments and other agencies may decide to have a programme or innovation evaluated for a variety of overt and covert purposes, including:

(a) a need for information on which to base decisions;
(b) political ammunition or leverage;
(c) to delay decision making;
(d) to provide legitimacy or the justification for a decision;
(e) to avoid taking responsibility for a decision;
(g) to gain kudos for a successful innovation;
(g) to discredit a disliked policy, and/or;
(h) to maintain prestige by commissioning independent research (Weiss, 1998: 22–5).

Some commentators point to the problem of evaluation research in the field of criminal justice in which 'inconsistent *results, non-replicability, partisan disagreement* and above all, *lack of cumulation* remain to dash the hopes of evaluators seeking to establish clear, unequivocal guidelines to policy making' (Pawson and Tilley, 1994: 292, emphases in original). A similar conclusion is drawn from a review of evaluation studies in ADR (Mack, 2003). The research question was to identify 'whether empirical research establishes specific criteria, or identifies key features about disputes and-or ADR programs, which might provide a checklist to guide a court in making a referral to ADR' (2003: 1). This review concludes that few criteria exist which can be widely identified by empirical research in a range of settings and that the most important criteria can be framed in general, abstract terms, providing little concrete guidance to courts in different settings. What works in local settings depends on the particular goals, location, resources, organizational imperatives, type of cases and personnel (Mack, 2003: 8).

A recent UK inquiry considered the current capacity for empirical legal research among lawyers and social scientists (Genn et al., 2006). 'The explicit focus of the Inquiry was the capacity of the academy to undertake *empirical* research on law and legal processes, defined as the study through direct methods of the operation and impact of law and legal processes in society, with a particular emphasis on non-criminal law and processes' (2006: 3, emphasis in original). The scope of the report was limited to non-criminal law topics and processes, because unlike many other substantive areas of law and legal issues, criminal law and processes – crime, policing, and criminal justice – have received more funding and public attention. Criminology has become a field of scholarship and distinct occupation with a stronger empirical research capacity than other areas of law (Genn et al., 2006: 6; Hillyard, 2007: 68, 71). The report identifies the low number of grant applications dealing with socio-legal topics, evidence of little interest among academic researchers in tendering for socio-legal research, and an apparent lack of interest in empirical legal research within the socio-legal community which seems to prefer 'purely theoretical and textual analyses rather than theoretically informed empirical legal research' (Genn et al., 2006: 9).

One of the causes of the current lack of capacity in socio-legal research is identified as the limitations of law school education and training which emphasizes teaching legal doctrine and professional practice requirements that constrain law school curricula. There is little opportunity for teaching social science research methods which do not fit into the legal paradigm of research and scholarship. 'For commissioners of research, the capacity problem manifests itself in a shortage of researchers with the skills to conduct good quality empirical research in the civil law and policy field' (Genn et al., 2006: 9). In a context where the amount and complexity of new legislation are increasing, governments consider legislation as central for policy change and implementation, law plays an increasing regulatory role in contemporary socieities, and the number of legal personnel continues to grow, the lack of good quality social legal research measuring the effects of some of these changes in the field is problematic. As Hillyard suggests:

> The need for high quality and rigorous empirical research to investigate the form, substance, and operation of the law in modern society could not be greater. At the same time, it is clear that legally trained personnel are playing an expanding role in modern society and more research is needed to understand not only the work they do but to analyse the impact that legal training and thinking may have on different areas of life. (2007: 274)

In conclusion, the law is dynamic and flexible and continuously subject to contestation and change; it is in perpetual motion. The law's 'power of form' lies in its constitutive tendency to formalize and codify everything that enters its field. This conception also underpins Smart's (1986) notion regarding the uneven development of law. Even though the law is not a single, coherent unitary phenomenon, aspects of it may facilitate or reflect social change, but such developments may not be implemented or occur elsewhere. Consequently, an engagement with the law must be one strategy for social reform, but legal change does not depend on social movement activism. The role of law in social change or the way in which new social environments or activism impact on the formation of legislation and implementation of legal mandates are empirical questions amenable to social science investigation.

References

Abadinsky, Howard (1991) *Law and Justice: An Introduction to the American Legal System*, 2nd edn, Chicago, Nelson-Hall.

Abbott, Andrew (1981) 'Status and strain in the professions', *American Journal of Sociology*, 86: 819–35.

Abbott, Andrew (1983) 'Professional ethics', *American Journal of Sociology*, 88: 855–85.

Abbott, Andrew (1986) 'Jurisdictional conflicts: a new approach to the development of the legal professions', *American Bar Foundation Research Journal*, Spring: 187–224.

Abbott, Andrew (1988) *The System of Professions: An Essay on the Division of Expert Labor*, Chicago, University of Chicago Press.

Abel, Richard L. (1981) 'Conservative conflict and the reproduction of capitalism: the role of informal justice', *International Journal of the Sociology of Law*, 9: 245–67.

Abel, Richard L. (1982a) 'The contradictions of informal justice', in Abel, R.L. (ed.), *The Politics of Informal Justice*, New York, Academic Press.

Abel, Richard L. (1982b) 'Introduction', in Abel, R.L. (ed.), *The Politics of Informal Justice*, New York, Academic Press.

Abel, Richard L. (1985) 'Comparative sociology of legal professions: an exploratory essay', *American Bar Foundation Research Journal*, Winter: 5–79.

Abel, Richard L. (1989) 'Between market and state: the legal profession in turmoil', *Modern Law Review*, 52: 285–25.

Abel, Richard L. and Lewis, Philip S. C. (eds) (1988a) *Lawyers in Society: Comparative Theories*, Berkeley, University of California Press.

Abel, Richard L. and Lewis, Philip S. C. (eds) (1988b) *Lawyers in Society: The Civil Law World*, Berkeley, University of California Press.

Abel, Richard L. and Lewis, Philip S. C. (eds) (1988c) *Lawyers in Society: The Common Law World*, Berkeley, University of California Press.

Abercrombie, Nicholas, Hill, Stephen and Turner, Bryan S. (eds) (2006) *The Penguin Dictionary of Sociology*, London, Penguin.

Acker, Joan (1990) 'Hierarchies, jobs, bodies: a theory of gendered organizations', *Gender & Society*, 4: 139–58.

Adams, Kenneth (1983) 'The effect of evidentiary factors in charge reduction', *Journal of Criminal Justice*, 11: 525–37.

Albonetti, Celesta A. (1991) 'An integration of theories to explain judicial discretion', *Social Problems*, 38: 247–66.

Albrow, Martin (1975) 'Legal positivism and bourgeois materialism: Max Weber's view of the sociology of law', *British Journal of Law & Society*, 2: 14–31.

Allars, Margaret (1990) *Introduction to Australian Administrative Law*, Sydney, Butterworths.

Alschuler, Albert W. (1975) 'The defense attorney's role in plea bargaining', *Yale Law Journal*, 84: 1170–314.

Alschuler, Albert W. (1979) 'Plea bargaining and its history', *Law & Society Review*, 13: 211–45.

Alston, Philip (1992) 'The Security Council and human rights: lessons to be learned from the Iraq–Kuwait crisis and its aftermath', *Australian Year Book of International Law*, 13: 107–76.

Andrews, Lori B. (1981) 'Lawyer advertising and the First Amendment', *American Bar Foundation Research Journal*, Fall: 67–102.

Arjomand, Saïd Amir (2004) 'Social theory and the changing world: mass democracy, development, modernization and globalization', *International Sociology*, 19: 321–53.

Arnold, Bruce L. and Hagan, John (1992) 'Careers of misconduct: the structure of prosecuted professional deviance among lawyers', *American Sociological Review*, 57: 771–80.

Arnold, Bruce L. and Hagan, John (1994) 'Self-regulatory responses to professional misconduct within the legal profession', *Canadian Review of Sociology & Anthropology*, 31: 168–83.

Aronson, Mark (1992) *Managing Complex Trials: Reform of the Rules of Evidence and Procedure*, Melbourne, Australian Institute of Judicial Administration.

Arthurson, Kathy and Jacobs, Keith (2006) 'Housing and anti-social behaviour in Australia', in Flint, J. (ed.), *Housing, Urban Governance and Anti-Social Behaviour*, Bristol, The Policy Press.

Ashworth, Andrew (1992a) *Sentencing and Criminal Justice*, London, Weidenfeld and Nicolson.

Ashworth, Andrew (1992b) 'Sentencing reform structures', *Crime & Justice: an Annual Review of Research*, 16: 181–241.

Ashworth, Andrew (1993) 'Victim impact statements and sentencing', *Criminal Law Review*: 498–509.

Ashworth, Andrew (2002) 'Responsibilities, rights and restorative justice', *British Journal of Criminology*, 42: 578–96.

Astor, Hilary (1990) 'Domestic violence and mediation', *Australian Dispute Resolution Journal*, 1: 143–53.

Astor, Hilary (2007) 'Mediator neutrality: making sense of theory and practice', *Social & Legal Studies*, 16: 221–39.

Astor, Hilary and Chinkin, Christine (2002) *Dispute Resolution in Australia*, 2nd edn, Sydney, Butterworths.

Atkins, Susan and Hoggett, Brenda (1984) *Women and the Law*, Oxford, Basil Blackwell.

Atkinson, Rowland (2006) 'Spaces of discipline and control: the compounded citizenship of social renting', in Flint, J. (ed.), *Housing, Urban Governance and Anti-Social Behaviour*, Bristol, The Policy Press.

Auerbach, Jerold S. (1976) *Unequal Justice: Lawyers and Social Change in Modern America*, New York, Oxford University Press.

Australian Law Reform Commission (1980) *Sentencing Federal Offenders*, Canberra, Australian Government Publishing Service.

Australian Law Reform Commission (1988) *Sentencing*, Report No. 44, Canberra, Australian Government Publishing Service.

Australian Law Reform Commission (1994) *Equality Before the Law: Women's Equality*, Report No. 69, Part II, Sydney, ALRC.

Australian Law Reform Commission (2005) *Sentencing of Federal Offenders*, Discussion paper 70, Sydney, ALRC.

Auyero, Javier and Swistun, Debora (2008) 'The social production of toxic uncertainty', *American Sociological Review*, 73: 357–79.

Bacchi, Carol Lee (1990) *Same Difference: Feminism and Sexual Difference*, Sydney, Allen & Unwin.

Balbus, Isaac D. (1977) 'Commodity form and legal form: an essay on the "relative autonomy" of the law', *Law & Society Review*, 11: 571–88.

Baldwin, John and Davis, Gwynn (2003) 'Empirical research in law', in Cane, P. and Tushnet, M. (eds), *The Oxford Handbook of Legal Studies*, Oxford, Oxford University Press.

Baldwin, John and McConville, Michael (1977) *Negotiated Justice: Pressures to Plead Guilty*, London, Martin Robertson.

Baldwin, John and McConville, Michael (1979) 'Plea bargaining and plea negotiation in England', *Law & Society Review*, 13: 287–307.

Bamford, David (2004) 'Litigation reform 1980–2000: a radical challenge?', in Prest, W.R. and Roach Anleu, S. (eds), *Litigation: Past and Present*, Sydney, University of New South Wales Press.

Banakar, Reza (2000) 'Reflections on the methodological issues of the sociology of law', *Journal of Law & Society*, 27: 273–95.

Banakar, Reza and Travers, Max (2005a) 'Law, sociology and method', in Banakar, R. and Travers, M. (eds), *Theory and Method in Socio-Legal Research*, Oxford, Hart Publishing.

Banakar, Reza and Travers, Max (eds) (2005b) *Theory and Method in Socio-Legal Research*, Oxford, Hart Publishing.

Barnes, J. A. (1966) 'Durkheim's *Division of Labor in Society*' *Man* (new series), 1: 158–75.

Barnett, Larry D. (1993) *Legal Construct, Social Concept: A Macrosociological Perspective on Law*, New York, Aldine de Gruyter.

Bartholomew, Amy and Hunt, Alan (1991) 'What's wrong with rights?', *Law & Inequality*, 9: 1–58.

Bartky, Sandra Lee (1988) 'Foucault, femininity and the modernization of patriarchal power', in Diamond, I. and Quinby, L. (eds), *Femininity and Foucault: Reflections of Resistance*, Boston, Northeastern University Press.

Bartlett, Katharine T. (1990) 'Feminist legal methods', *Harvard Law Review*, 103: 829–88.

Bauman, Z. (1998) *Globalization: The Human Consequences*, New York, Columbia University Press.

Baxter, Hugh (1996) 'Bringing Foucault into law and law into Foucault', *Stanford Law Journal*, 48: 449–79.

Beamish, Thomas D. (2000) 'Accumulating trouble: complex organization, a culture of silence, and a secret spill', *Social Problems*, 47: 473–98.

Beck, Ulrich (1992) *Risk Society: Towards a New Modernity*, London, Sage.

Beck, Ulrich (1996) 'World risk society as cosmopolitan society?: Ecological questions in a framework of manufactured uncertainties', *Theory, Culture & Society*, 13: 1–32.

Beck, Ulrich and Lau, Christoph (2005) 'Second modernity as a research agenda: theoretical and empirical explorations in the "meta-change" of modern society', *British Journal of Sociology*, 56: 525–57.

Becker, Howard S. (1978) 'Arts and crafts', *American Journal of Sociology*, 83: 863–89.

Becker, Howard S. (1998) *Tricks of the Trade: How to Think About Your Research While You're Doing It*, Chicago, IL: University of Chicago Press.

Behrendt, Larissa (2004) 'Challenging the status quo: indigenous activism and the rule of law in Australia', in Prest, W.R. and Roach Anleu, S. (eds), *Litigation: Past and Present*, Sydney, University of New South Wales Press.

Beirne, Piers (1979) 'Empiricism and the critique of Marxism on law and crime', *Social Problems*, 26: 373–85.

Beirne, Piers and Sharlet, Robert (1980) *Pashukanis: Selected Writings on Marxism and Law*, London, Academic Press.

Benson, Michael L. and Walker, Esteban (1988) 'Sentencing the white collar offender', *American Sociological Review*, 53: 294–302.

Berger, Ronald J., Searles, Patricia and Neuman, W. Lawrence (1988) 'The dimensions of rape reform legislation', *Law & Society Review*, 22: 329–57.

Bergmann, Barbara (1986) *The Economic Emergence of Women*, New York, Basic Books.

Bergsmo, Morten (1994) 'International Criminal Tribunal for the former Yugoslavia: recent developments', *Human Rights Law Journal*, 15: 405–10.

Berk, Richard A., Campbell, Alec, Klap, Ruth and Western, Bruce (1992) 'The deterrent effect of arrest in incidents of domestic violence: a Bayesian analysis of four field experiments', *American Sociological Review*, 57: 698–708.

Berk, Sarah Fenstermaker and Loseke, Donileen R. (1981) 'Handling family violence: situational determinants of police arrest in domestic disturbances', *Law & Society Review*, 15: 317–46.

Berman, Greg and Feinblatt, John (2001) 'Problem solving courts: a brief primer', *Law & Policy*, 23: 125–40.

Berman, Harold J. (1968) 'Legal reasoning', in David, S. (ed.), *International Encyclopedia of the Social Sciences*, New York, Free Press.

Berman, Jesse (1969) 'The Cuban popular tribunals', *Columbia Law Review*, 69: 1317–54.

Bernstein, Mary (1997) 'Celebration and suppression: the strategic uses of identity by the lesbian and gay movement', *American Journal of Sociology*, 103: 531–65.

Bernstein, Mary (2005) 'Identity politics', *Annual Review of Sociology*, 31: 47–74.

Birnbaum, N. (1953) 'Conflicting interpretations of capitalism: Marx and Weber', *British Journal of Sociology*, 4: 25–41.

Black, Donald (1970) 'Production of crime rates', *American Sociological Review*, 35: 733–48.

Black, Donald (1976) *The Behavior of Law*, New York, Academic Press.

Black, Donald (1993) *The Social Structure of Right and Wrong*, San Diego, Academic Press.

Blankenburg, Erhard (1994) 'The infrastructure for avoiding civil litigation: comparing cultures of legal behavior in the Netherlands and West Germany', *Law & Society Review*, 28: 789–808.

Blankenburg, Erhard (1995) 'The purge of lawyers after the breakdown of the East German Communist regime', *Law & Social Inquiry*, 20: 223–43.

Blankenship, Kim M., Rushing, Beth, Onorato, Suzanne, A. and White, Renee (1993) 'Reproductive technologies and the U.S. courts', *Gender & Society*, 7: 8–31.

Bloemraad, Irene, Korteweg, Anna and Yurdakul, Gökçe (2008) 'Citizenship and immigration: multiculturalism, assimilation, and challenges to the nation-state', *Annual Review of Sociology*, 34: 153–79.

Blumberg, Abraham S. (1967) 'The practice of law as a confidence game: organizational cooptation of a profession', *Law & Society Review*, 1: 15–39.

Bohman, James (1994) 'Complexity, pluralism and the constitutional state: on Habermas's *Faktizitat und Geltung*', *Law & Society Review*, 28: 897–930.

Bolton, Sharon C. and Muzio, Daniel (2007) 'Can't live with 'em; can't live without 'em: gendered segmentation in the legal profession', *Sociology*, 41: 47–65.

Bordo, Susan (1993) *Unbearable Weight: Feminism, Western Culture, and the Body*, Berkeley, University of California Press.

Bosworth, Mary (2008) 'Border control and the limits of the sovereign state', *Social & Legal Studies*, 17: 199–215.

Bottomley, Anne (1985) 'What is happening to family law? A feminist critique', in Brophy, J. and Smart, C. (eds), *Women in Law: Explorntions in Law, Family and Sexuality*, London, Routledge & Kegan Paul.

Bourdieu, Pierre (1987) 'The force of law: toward a sociology of the juridical field', *Hastings Law Journal*, 38: 814–53.

Bower, Lisa C. (1994) 'Queer acts and the politics of "direct address": rethinking law, culture, and community', *Law & Society Review*, 28: 1009–33.

Brady, David, Beckfield, Jason and Zhao, Wei (2007) 'The consequences of economic globalization for affluent democracies', *Annual Review of Sociology*, 33: 313–34.

Braithwaite, John (1989) *Crime, Shame and Reintegration*, Cambridge, Cambridge University Press.

Braithwaite, J. and Drahos, P. (2000) *Global Business Regulation*, Cambridge, Melbourne, Cambridge University Press.

Braithwaite, John and Petit, Philip (1994) 'Republican criminology and victim advocacy', *Law & Society Review*, 28: 765–76.

Brazier, Margaret, Lovecy, Jill, Moran, Michael and Potton, Margaret (1993) 'Falling from a tightrope: doctors and lawyers between the market and the state', *Political Studies*, 41: 197–213.

Bredemeier, Harry C. (1962) 'Law as an integrative mechanism', in Evan, W. M. (ed.), *The Law and Sociology*, New York, Free Press.

Brereton, David and Casper, Jonathan D. (1981) 'Does it pay to plead guilty? Differential sentencing and the functioning of criminal courts', *Law & Society Review*, 16: 45–70.

Brewer, Laura (1996) 'Bureaucratic organisation of professional labour', *Australian & New Zealand Journal of Sociology*, 32: 21–38.

Bridges, Lee (1999) 'The Lawrence inquiry – incompetence, corruption, and institutional racism', *Journal of Law & Society*, 26: 298–322.

Brigham, John (1987) 'Right, rage and remedy: forms of law in political discourse', *Studies in American Political Development*, 2: 3–16.

Brigham, John (1996) *The Constitution of Interests: Beyond the Politics of Rights*, New York, New York University Press.

Brigham, John and Harrington, Christine (1989) 'Realism and its consequences: an inquiry into contemporary socio-legal research', *International Journal of the Sociology of Law*, 17: 41–62.

Broadhurst, Roderic and Loh, Nini (1993) 'The phantom of deterrence: the Crime (Serious and Repeat Offender) Sentencing Act', *Australian & New Zealand Journal of Criminology*, 26: 251–71.

Brody, S. R. (1976) *The Effectiveness of Sentencing: A Review of the Literature*, London, Her Majesty's Stationery Office.

Brooks, Christopher W. (2004) 'The longitudinal study of civil litigation in England 1200–1996', in Prest, W.R. and Roach Anleu, S. (eds), *Litigation: Past and Present*, Sydney, University of New South Wales Press.

Brown, Imogen and Hullin, Roy (1992) 'A study of sentencing in the Leeds Magistrates' Courts: the treatment of ethnic minority and white offenders', *British Journal of Criminology*, 32: 41–53.

Brown, Jeff (1994) 'Review of *Politics and Plea Bargaining*: victims' rights in California', *Hastings Law Journal*, 45: 697–705.

Brown, Nathan J. (1995) 'Law and imperialism: Egypt in comparative perspective', *Law & Society Review*, 29: 103–25.

Bryson, Lois (1995) 'Two welfare states: one for women, one for men', in Edwards, A. and Magarey, S. (eds), *Women in a Restructuring Australia: Work and Welfare,* Allen & Unwin, Sydney.

Buck, Trevor (2005) *Administrative Justice and Alternative Dispute Resolution: The Australian Experience*, DCA Research Series 8/05, UK, Department for Constitutional Affairs.

Buerger, Michael and Green Mazerolle, Lorraine (1996) 'Third-party policing: a theoretical analysis of an emerging trend', unpublished manuscript.

Bumiller, Kristin (1987) 'Victims in the shadow of the law: a critique of the model of legal protection', *Signs: Journal of Women in Culture and Society*, 12: 421–39.

Bumiller, Kristin (1990) 'Fallen angels: the representation of violence against women in legal culture', *International Journal of the Sociology of Law*, 18: 125–42.

Burger, Warren E. (1982) 'Isn't there a better way?', *American Bar Association Journal*, 68: 274–7.

Burman, Sandra B. and Harrell-Bond, Barbara E. (1979) *The Imposition of Law*, New York, Academic Press.

Burns, Stacy Lee and Peyrot, Mark (2003) 'Tough love: nurturing and coercing responsibility and recovery in California drug courts', *Social Problems*, 50: 416–38.

Burstein, Paul (1991) 'Legal mobilization as a social movement tactic: the struggle for equal employment opportunity', *American Journal of Sociology*, 96: 1201–25.

Burton, Mandy (2001) 'Intimate homicide and the provocation defence – endangering women *R* v. *Smith*', *Feminist Legal Studies*, 9: 247–58.

Byrne, Dominic (1984) 'An unequal right to equal pay', *Journal of Law & Society*, 11: 247–57.

Cable, Sherry, Shriver, Thomas E. and Mix, Tamara L. (2008) 'Risk society and contested illness: the case of nuclear weapons workers', *American Sociological Review*, 73: 380–401.

Cahn, Naomi R. (1991) 'Defining feminist litigation', *Harvard Women's Law Journal*, 14: 1–20.

Cain, Maureen (1974) 'The main themes of Marx' and Engels' sociology of law', *British Journal of Law & Society*, 1: 136–48.

Cain, Maureen (1983) 'The general practice lawyer and the client: towards a radical conception', in Dingwall, R. and Lewis, P. (eds), *The Sociology of the Professions: Lawyers, Doctors, and Others*, London, Macmillan.

Cain, Maureen (1994) 'The symbol traders', in Cain, M. and Harrington, C. B. (eds), *Lawyers in a Postmodern World: Translation and Transgression*, Buckingham, Open University Press.

Cain, Maureen and Hunt, Alan (1979) *Marx and Engels on Law*, London, Academic Press.

Calavita, Kitty (1998) 'Immigration, law, and marginalization in a global economy: notes from Spain', *Law & Society Review*, 32: 529–66.

Cappelletti, Mauro (1993) 'Alternative dispute resolution processes within the framework of the world-wide access to justice movement', *Modern Law Review*, 56: 282–96.

Carlin, Jerome (1962) *Lawyers on their Own*, New Brunswick, Rutgers University Press.

Carlin, Jerome E. (1966) *Lawyers' Ethics: A Survey of the New York City Bar*, New York, Russell Sage Foundation.

Carrington, Kerry (1993) *Offending Girls*, Sydney, Allen & Unwin.

Carr-Saunders, A. M. and Wilson, P. A. (1933) *The Professions*, Oxford, Oxford University Press.

Carruthers, Bruce G. and Halliday, Terence C. (2006) 'Negotiating globalization: global scripts and intermediation in the construction of Asian insolvency regimes', *Law & Social Inquiry*, 31: 521–84.

Cass, Bettina (1985) 'Rewards for women's work', in Goodnow, J. and Pateman, C. (eds), *Women, Social Science and Public Policy*, Sydney, Allen & Unwin.

Center for Human Rights (1994) *United Nations Action in the Field of Human Rights*, New York & Geneva, United Nations.

Chambliss, William J. (1964) 'A sociological analysis of vagrancy', *Social Problems*, 12: 67–77.

Chambliss, William J. (1967) 'Types of deviance and the effectiveness of legal sanctions', *Wisconsin Law Review*, Summer: 703–19.

Chambliss, William J. (1969) *Crime and the Legal Process*, New York, McGrawHill.

Chambliss, William (1974) 'The state, the law, and the definition of behavior as criminal or delinquent', in Glaser, D. (ed.), *Handbook of Criminology*, Chicago, Rand McNally.

Chambliss, William J. (1979) 'Contradictions and conflicts in law creation', *Research in Law and Sociology*, 2: 3–27.

Chan, Janet and Zdenkowksi, George (1986) 'Just alternatives – Part II', *Australian & New Zealand Journal of Criminology*, 19: 131–54.

Chancer, Lynn S. (1987) 'New Bedford, Massachusetts, March 6, 1983–March 22, 1984: the "before and after" of a group rape', *Gender & Society*, 1: 239–60.

Charlesworth, H. C. M. (1991) 'Customary international law and the Nicaragua case', *Australian Year Book of International Law*, 11: 1–31.

Cheh, Mary M. (1991) 'Constitutional limits on using civil remedies to achieve criminal law objectives: understanding and transcending the criminal–civil law distinction', *Hastings Law Journal*, 42: 1325–413.

Chesney-Lind, Meda (1973) 'Judicial enforcement of the female sex role: the family court and the female delinquent', *Issues in Criminology*, 8: 51–69.

Chesney-Lind, Meda (1978) 'Chivalry re-examined: women and the criminal justice system', in Bowker, L.H. (ed.), *Women, Crime and the Criminal Justice System*, Lexington, Lexington Books.

Chiu, Charlotte (1998) 'Do professional women have lower job satisfaction than professional men? Lawyers as a case study', *Sex Roles*, April: 521–37.

Chiu, Charlotte and Leicht, Kevin (1999) 'When does feminization increase equality? The case of lawyers', *Law & Society Review*, 33: 557–94.

Church, Thomas (1976) 'Plea bargains, concessions and the courts: analysis of a quasi-experiment', *Law & Society Review*, 10: 373–401.

Church, Thomas W. Jr. (1985) 'Examining local legal culture', *American Bar Foundation Research Journal*, 10: 449–510.

Churches, Christine (2004) 'Some figures behind the numbers: going to law in early-modern England', in Prest, W.R. and Roach Anleu, S. (eds), *Litigation: Past and Present*, Sydney, University of New South Wales Press.

Clarke, Ronald V. (1992) *Situational Crime Prevention: Successful Case Studies*, New York, Harrow and Heston.

Cobb, Neil (2007) 'Governance through publicity: Anti-Social Behavior Orders, young people, and the problematization of the right to anonymity', *Journal of Law & Society*, 34: 342–73.

Cocozza, Joseph J. and Steadman, Henry J. (1978) 'Prediction in psychiatry: an example of misplaced confidence in experts', *Social Problems*, 25: 265–76.

Coffey, Michelle (1995) 'Lawyers condemn plans for overhaul', *The Weekend Australian*, July 15–16: 8.

Cohen, Albert K. (1955) *Delinquent Boys: The Culture of the Gang*, New York, Free Press.

Cohen, Stanley (1979) 'The punitive city: notes on the dispersal of social control', *Contemporary Crises*, 3: 39–63.

Cohen, Stanley (1980) *Folk Devils and Moral Panics: The Creation of the Mods and Rockers*, Oxford: Basil Blackwell.

Cohen, Stanley (1985) *Visions of Social Control: Crime, Punishment and Classification*, Cambridge, Polity Press.

Cohen, Stanley S. (1993) 'Human rights and crimes of the state: the culture of denial', *Australian & New Zealand Journal of Criminology*, 26: 97–115.

Cohen, Stanley (1995) 'State crimes of previous regimes: knowledge, accountability and the policing of the past', *Law & Social Inquiry*, 20: 7–50.

Cole, George F. (1970) 'The decision to prosecute', *Law & Society Review*, 4: 331–43.

Cole, The Honourable Terence R. H. (2006) *Report of the Inquiry into Certain Australian Companies in Relation to the UN Oil-For-Food Programme*. Canberra, Commonwealth of Australia.

Coleman, Karen (1988) 'The politics of abortion in Australia: freedom, church and state', *Feminist Review*, 29: 75–97.

Coles, Frances S. (1986) 'Forced to quit: sexual harassment complaints and agency response', *Sex Roles*, 14: 81–95.

Collins, Eliza G. C. and Blodgett, Timothy B. (1981) 'Sexual harassment ... some see it ... some won't', *Harvard Business Review*, 59: 76–95.

Collins, Hugh (1982) *Marxism and Law*, Oxford, Oxford University Press.

Connell, Robert W. (1990) 'A whole new world: remaking masculinity in the context of the environmental movement', *Gender & Society*, 40: 452–78.

Connell, R. W. (1997) 'Why is classical theory classical?', *American Journal of Sociology*, 102: 511–57.

Constable, Marianne (1995) 'A new conception of laws?', *Law & Society Review*, 29: 593–7.

Cornell, Drucilla (1991) 'Sexual difference, the feminine, and equivalency: a critique of MacKinnon's *Toward a Feminist Theory of the State*', *Yale Law Journal*, 100: 247–75.

Corns, Christopher (1990) 'Destructuring sentencing decision-making in Victoria', *Australian & New Zealand Journal of Criminology*, 23: 145–57.

Coser, Lewis A. (1982) 'The notion of control in sociological theory', in Gibbs, J.P. (ed.), *Social Control: Views from the Social Sciences*, Beverly Hills, Sage.

Cossins, Anne (1995) 'On stone throwing from the feminist sidelines: a critique of Helen Garner's book, *The First Stone*', *Melbourne University Law Review*, 20: 528–58.

Cotterrell, Roger (1991) 'The Durkheimian tradition in the sociology of law', *Law & Society Review*, 25: 923–45.

Cotterrell, Roger (1992) *The Sociology of Law*, 2nd edn, London, Butterworths.

Cotterrell, Roger (1986) 'Law and sociology: notes on the constitution and confrontations of disciplines', *Journal of Law & Society*, 13: 9–34.

Cotterrell, Roger (1998) 'Why must legal ideas be interpreted sociologically?', *Journal of Law & Society*, 25: 171–92.

Cowan, Dave and Hitchings, Emma (2007) '"Pretty boring stuff": district judges and housing possession proceedings', *Social & Legal Studies*, 16: 363–82.

Cowan, Dave, Blandy, Sarah, Hitchings, Emma, Hunter, Caroline and Nixon, Judy (2006) 'District judges and possession proceedings', *Journal of Law & Society*, 33: 547–71.

Crawford, Adam (2003) '"Contractual governance" of deviant behaviour', *Journal of Law & Society*, 30: 479–505.

Crawford, Adam (2006) 'Policing and community safety in residential areas: the mixed economy of visible patrols', in Flint, J. (ed.), *Housing, Urban Governance and Anti-Social Behaviour*, Bristol, The Policy Press.

Crawford, James and Edeson, W. R. (1984) 'International law and Australian law ', in Ryan, K.W. (ed.), *International Law in Australia*, 2nd edn, Sydney, Lawbook Co.

Crompton, Rosemary (1990) 'Professions in the current context', *Work, Employment & Society*, Special Issue: 147–66.

Crompton, Rosemary and LeFeuvre, Nicky (1996) 'Paid employment and the changing system of gender relations: a cross-national comparison', *Sociology*, 30: 427–45.

Curran, B., Rosich, K. J., Carson, C. N. and Puccetti, M. (1985) *The Lawyer Statistical Report: a Statistical Profile of the U.S. Legal Profession in the 1980s*, Chicago, American Bar Association.

Curtis, Dennis E. (1992) 'The fake trial', *Southern California Law Review*, 65: 1523–30.

D'Alessio, Stewart J. and Stolzenberg, Lisa (1995) 'The impact of sentencing guidelines on jail incarceration in Minnesota', *Criminology*, 33: 283–302.

Dalrymple, James (1994) 'She done me wrong: why Mike Tyson is smearing the rape victim between him and $1 billion', *The Australian Magazine*, November 5–6: 14–20, 22.

Daly, Kathleen (1989a) 'Neither conflict nor labeling nor paternalism will suffice: intersections of race, ethnicity, gender, and family in criminal court decisions', *Crime & Delinquency*, 35: 136–68.

Daly, Kathleen (1989b) 'Rethinking judicial paternalism: gender, work-family relations, and sentencing', *Gender & Society*, 3: 9–36.

Daly, Kathleen and Hayes, Hennessey (2002) 'Conferencing and re-offending in Queensland', *Australian & New Zealand Journal of Criminology*, 37: 167–91.

Daly, Kathleen and Immarigeon, Russ (1998) 'The past, present, and future of restorative justice: some critical reflections', *Contemporary Justice Review*, 1: 21–45.

Daniel, Ann (1998) *Scapegoats for a Profession: Uncovering Procedural Injustice*, Amsterdam, Harwood Academic Publishers.

Danzig, Richard (1973) 'Toward the creation of a complementary, decentralized system of criminal justice', *Stanford Law Review*, 26: 1–54.

Danzig, Richard and Lowy, Michael J. (1975) 'Everyday disputes and mediation in the United States: a reply to Professor Felstiner', *Law & Society Review*, 9: 675–94.

Darbyshire, Penny (2007) 'Where do English and Welsh judges come from?', *Cambridge Law Journal*, 66: 365–88.

Dauvergne, Catherine (2007) 'Security and migration law in the less Brave New World', *Social & Legal Studies*, 16: 533–49.

Davies, Celia (1996) 'The sociology of professions and the profession of gender', *Sociology*, 30: 661–79.

Davies, Margaret (1994) 'Feminist appropriations: law, property and personality', *Social & Legal Studies*, 3: 365–91.

Davies, Margaret (2008) *Asking the Law Question*, 3rd edn, Sydney: Thomson Law Book Company.

Davis, Robert C. (1982) 'Mediation: the Brooklyn experiment', in Tomasic, R. and Feeley, M.M. (eds), *Neighborhood Justice: Assessment of an Emerging Idea*, New York, Longman.

De Gama, Katherine (1993) 'A brave new world? Rights discourse and the politics of reproductive autonomy', *Journal of Law & Society*, 20: 114–30.

Deflem, Mathieu (1996) 'Introduction: law in Habermas's theory of communicative action', in Deflem, M. (ed.), *Habermas, Modernity and Law*, London, Sage.

Deflem, Mathieu (1997) 'Surveillance and criminal statistics: historical foundations of governmentality', *Studies in Law, Politics and Society*, 17: 149–84.

Deflem, Mathieu (1998) 'The boundaries of abortion law: systems theory from Parsons to Luhmann and Habermas', *Social Forces*, 76: 775–818.

Deflem, Mathieu (2002) *Policing World Society: Historical Foundations of International Police Cooperation*, Oxford and New York, Oxford University Press.

Derber, Charles (1983) 'Managing professionals: ideological proletarianization and post-industrial labor', *Theory & Society*, 2: 309–41.

Dezalay, Yves (1990) 'The big bang and the law: the internationalization and restructuration of the legal field', *Theory, Culture & Society*, 7: 279–93.

Dezalay, Yves and Garth, Bryant (1995) 'Merchants of law as moral entrepreneurs: constructing international justice from the competition for transnational business disputes', *Law & Society Review*, 29: 27–64.

Dezalay, Yves and Garth, Bryant G. (1996a) *Dealing in Virtue: International Commercial Arbitration and the Construction of a Transnational Legal Order*, Chicago and London, University of Chicago Press.

Dezalay, Yves and Garth, Bryant G. (1996b) 'Fussing about the forum: categories and definitions as stakes in a professional competition', *Law & Social Inquiry*, 21: 285–312.

Dezalay, Yves and Garth, Bryant (1997) 'Law, lawyers and social capital: "rule of law" versus relational capitalism', *Social & Legal Studies*, 6: 109–41.

Dezalay, Yves and Garth, Bryant G. (2002) *The Internationalization of Palace Wars*, Chicago and London, University of Chicago Press.

Di Tomaso, Nancy (1989) 'Sexuality in the workplace: discrimination and harassment', in Hearn, J., Sheppard, D.L., Tancred-Sheriff, P. and Burrell, G. (eds), *The Sexuality of Organizations*, London, Sage.

Diamond, A. S. (1951) *The Evolution of Law*, London, Watts.

Diduck, Alison (1993) 'Legislating ideologies of motherhood', *Social & Legal Studies*, 2: 461–85.

Dietrich, Joachim (2005) 'Giving content to general concepts', *Melbourne University Law Review*, 29: 218–41.

Dillman, Don A. (2007) *Mail and Internet Surveys: The Tailored Design Method*, 2nd edn, Hoboken, John Wiley.

Dine, Janet and Watt, Bob (1995) 'Sexual harassment: moving away from discrimination', *Modern Law Review*, 58: 343–63.

Dinovitzer, Ronit, Garth, Bryant G., Sander, Richard, Sterling, Joyce and Wilder, Gita Z. (2004) *After the JD: First Results of a National Study of Legal Careers*, Chicago, NALP Foundation for Law Career Research and Education and the American Bar Foundation.

Dixon, Jo (1995) 'The organizational context of criminal sentencing', *American Journal of Sociology*, 100: 1157–98.

Dixon, Jo and Seron, Carroll (1995) 'Stratification in the legal profession: sex, sector and salary', *Law & Society Review*, 29: 381–412.

Dobbin, Shirley A., Gatowski, Sophia I., Ginsburg, Gerald P., Merlino, Mara l., Dahir, Veronica and Richardson, James T. (2001) 'Surveying difficult populations: lessons learned from a national survey of state trial court judges', *Justice System Journal*, 22: 287–307.

Donoghue, Jane (2008) 'Antisocial Behaviour Orders in Britain: contextualizing risk and reflexive modernization', *Sociology*, 42: 333–55.

Dotan, Yoav (1999) 'Public lawyers and private clients: an empirical observation on the relative success rates of cause lawyers', *Law & Policy*, 21: 401–25.

Doyle, Daniel P. and Luckenbill, David (1991) 'Mobilizing law in response to collective problems: a test of Black's theory of law', *Law & Society Review*, 25: 103–16.

Dror, Yehezkel (1968) 'Law and social change', in Simon, R.J. (ed.), *The Sociology of Law: Interdisciplinary Readings*, Scranton, Chandler Publishing Company.

Drzemczewski, Andrew (1995) 'Ensuring compatibility of domestic law with the European Convention on Human Rights prior to ratification: the Hungarian model/Introduction to a reference document', *Human Rights Law Journal*, 16: 241–60.

Duffy, Michael (1992) 'Practical problems of giving effect to treaty obligations – the cost of consent', *Australian Year Book of International Law*, 12: 16–21.

Duggan, Lisa, Hunter, Nan and Vance, Carole S. (1984) 'False promises: feminist antipornography in the U.S. Women Against Censorship', in Burstyn, V. (ed.), *Women Against Censorship*, Vancouver, Douglas & McIntyre.

Durkheim, Emile (1973) 'Two laws of penal evolution', *Economy and Society*, 2: 285–308.

Durkheim, Emile (1974) *Sociology and Philosophy*, New York, Free Press.

Durkheim, Emile (1984) *The Division of Labor in Society*, New York, Free Press.

Durkheim, Emile (1986) 'The positive science of morality in Germany', trans. Frank Pearce, *Economy and Society*, 15: 346–54.

Duxbury, Neil (1991) 'Jerome Frank and the legacy of legal realism', *Journal of Law & Society*, 18: 175–205.

Eckersley, Robyn (1987) 'Whither the feminist campaign? An evaluation of feminist critiques of pornography', *International Journal of the Sociology of Law*, 15: 149–78.

Edwards, Anne and Heenan, Melanie (1994) 'Rape trials in Victoria: gender, sociocultural factors and justice', *Australian & New Zealand Journal of Criminology*, 27: 213–36.

Edwards, Mark Evan (1996) 'Pregnancy discrimination litigation: legal erosion of capitalist ideology under equal employment opportunity law', *Social Forces*, 75: 247–69.

Eekelaar, John and Dingwall, Robert (1988) 'The development of conciliation in England', in Robert Dingwall and John Eekelaar (eds) *Divorce, Mediation and the Legal Process*, Oxford, Clarendon Press.

Eisenstein, Zillah R. (1988) *The Female Body and the Law*, Berkeley, University of California Press.

Eisenstein, Zillah (1991) 'Privatizing the state: reproductive rights, affirmative action, and the problem of democracy', *Frontiers*, 12: 98–125.

Elliott, Anthony (2002) 'Beck's sociology of risk: a critical assessment', *Sociology*, 36: 293–316.

Elliott, Anthony and Lemert, Charles (2006) *The New Individualism: the Emotional Costs of Globalization*, Oxford, Routledge.

Engen, Rodney L. and Steen, Sara (2000) 'The power to punish: discretion and sentencing reform in the war on drugs', *American Journal of Sociology*, 105: 1357–95.

Epstein, Cynthia Fuchs (1968) *Women and Professional Careers: The Case of the Woman Lawyer*, Ann Arbor, University Microfilms International.

Epstein, Cynthia Fuchs (1970) *Woman's Place: Options and Limits in Professional Careers*, Berkeley, University of California Press.

Epstein, Cynthia Fuchs (1983) *Women in Law*, Garden City, Anchor Books.

Equal Employment Opportunity Commission (1980) *Code of Federal Regulations, Vol 29, Labor*, Washington, DC, Federal Register.

Erez, Edna and Tontodonato, Pamela (1990) 'The effect of victim participation in sentencing on sentencing outcome', *Criminology*, 28: 451–74.

Erez, Edna, Roeger, Leigh and Morgan, Frank (1994) *Victim Impact Statements in South Australia: an Evaluation*, Adelaide, Office of Crime Statistics.

Etzioni, Amitai (1966) *Studies in Social Change*, New York, Chicago, San Francisco, Toronto, London, Holt, Rinehart and Winston, Inc.

Evan, William M. (1990) *Social Structure and Law: Theoretical and Empirical Perspectives*, Newbury Park, Sage.

Ewald, François (1991) 'Insurance and risk', in Burchell, G., Gordon, C. and Miller, P. (eds), *The Foucault Effect: Studies in Governmentality*, London, Harvester Wheatsheaf.

Ewick, Patricia and Silbey, Susan S. (1998) *The Common Place of Law: Stories from Everyday Life*, Chicago, University of Chicago Press.

Ewing, Sally (1987) 'Formal justice and the spirit of capitalism: Max Weber's sociology of law', *Law & Society Review*, 21: 487–512.

Fain, T. and Anderton, D. (1987) 'Sexual harassment: organizational context and diffuse states', *Sex Roles*, 15: 291–311.

Faris, Ellsworth (1934) 'Book review: *Emile Durkheim and the Division of Labor*', *American Journal of Sociology*, 40: 376–7.

Farr, Kathryn Ann (1984) 'Administration and justice: maintaining balance through an institutionalized plea negotiation process', *Criminology*, 22: 291–319.

Farr, Kathryn Ann (1993) 'Shaping policy through litigation: abortion law in the United States', *Crime & Delinquency*, 39: 167–83.

Farr, Kathryn Ann (1995) 'Fetal abuse and the criminalization of behavior during pregnancy', *Crime & Delinquency*, 41: 235–44.

Faulconbridge, James and Muzio, Daniel (2008) 'Organizational professionalism in globalizing law firms', *Work, Employment & Society*, 22: 7–25.

Faulkes, Wendy (1990) 'The modern development of alternative dispute resolution in Australia', *Australian Dispute Resolution Journal*, 1: 61–8.

Feeley, Malcolm M. (1979) 'Perspectives on plea bargaining', *Law & Society Review*, 13: 199–209.

Feeley, Malcolm M. and Simon, Jonathan (1992) 'The new penology: notes on the emerging strategy of corrections and its implications', *Criminology*, 30: 449–74.

Feenan, Dermot (2005) *Applications by women for silk and judicial office in Northern Ireland*. A Report commissioned by the Commissioner for Judicial Appointments for Northern Ireland.

Feenan, Dermot (2007) 'Understanding disadvantage partly through an epistemology of ignorance', *Social & Legal Studies*, 16: 509–31.

Feinman, Jay M. and Gabel, Peter (1990) 'Contract law as ideology', in Kairys, D. (ed.), *The Politics of Law: a Progressive Critique*, rev edn, New York, Pantheon.

Feller, Erika (2006) 'Asylum, migration and refugee protection: realities, myths and the promise of things to come', *International Journal of Refugee Law*, 18: 509–36.

Felstiner, William L.F. (1974) 'Influences of social organization on dispute processing', *Law & Society Review*, 9: 63–94.

Felstiner, William L.F. and Williams, Lynne A. (1982) 'Community mediation in Dorchester, Massachusetts', in Tomasic, R. and Feeley, M.M. (eds), *Neighborhood Justice: Assessment of an Emerging Idea*, New York, Longman.

Felstiner, William L.F., Abel, Richard L. and Sarat, Austin (1980–81) 'The emergence and transformation of disputes: naming, blaming, claiming …', *Law & Society Review*, 15: 631–54.

Ferraro, Kathleen J. (1989) 'Policing woman battering', *Social Problems*, 36: 61–74.

Ferree, Myra Marx (1993) 'The rise and fall of mommy politics: feminism and unification in (East) Germany', *Feminist Studies*, 19: 89–115.

Ferree, Myra Marx (1994) '"The time of chaos was the best": feminist mobilization and demobilization in East Germany', *Gender & Society*, 8: 597–623.

Ferree, Myra Marx (1995) 'After the wall: explaining the status of women in the Former G.D.R.', *Sociological Focus*, 28: 9–22.

Ferree, Myra Marx and Martin, Patricia Yancey (1995) 'Doing the work of the movement: feminist organizations', in Ferree, M.M. and Martin, P.Y. (eds), *Feminist Organizations: Harvest of the New Women's Movement*, Philadelphia, Temple University Press.

Fineman, Martha (1988) 'Dominant discourse, professional language and legal change in child custody decision-making', *Harvard Law Review*, 101: 727–74.

Fineman, Martha A. (1991) 'Introduction', in Fineman, M.A. and Thomadson, N.S. (eds), *At the Boundaries of Law: Feminism and Legal Theory*, New York, Routledge.

Finkelstein, Michael O. (1975) 'A statistical analysis of guilty plea practices in the federal courts', *Harvard Law Review*, 89: 293–315.

Finley, Lucinda M. (1986) 'Transcending equality theory: a way out of the maternity and workplace debate', *Columbia Law Review*, 86: 1118–82.

Fiss, Peer C. and Hirsch, Paul M. (2005) 'The discourse of globalization: framing and sensemaking of an emerging concept', *American Sociological Review*, 70: 29–52.

FitzGerald, Jeffrey (1983) 'Grievances, disputes & outcomes: a comparison of Australia and the United States', *Law in Context*, 1: 15–45.

FitzGerald, J. M. (1984) 'Thinking about law and its alternatives: Abel et al. and the debate over informal justice', *American Bar Foundation Research Journal*, 3: 637–57.

Fitzgerald, Jacqueline (2008) 'Does circle sentencing reduce Aboriginal offending?', *Crime & Justice Bulletin*, 115: 1–12.

Fitzpatrick, Peter (1983) 'Marxism and legal pluralism', *Australian Journal of Law and Society*, 1: 45–59.

Flint, John (2006a) 'Introduction', in Flint, J. (ed.), *Housing, Urban Governance and Anti-Social Behaviour*, Bristol, The Policy Press.

Flint, John (ed.) (2006b) *Housing, Urban Governance and Anti-Social Behaviour: Perspectives, Policy and Practice*, Bristol, The Policy Press.

Flood, John (1989) 'Megalaw in the U.K.: Professionalism or corporatism? A preliminary report', *Indiana Law Journal*, 64: 569–92.

Flood, John (1991) 'Doing business: the management of uncertainty in lawyers work', *Law & Society Review*, 25: 41–71.

Flood, John and Caiger, Andrew (1993) 'Lawyers and arbitration: the juridification of construction disputes', *Modern Law Review*, 56: 412–40.

Foucault, Michel (1979) *Discipline and Punish: The Birth of the Prison*, New York, Vintage Books.

Foucault, Michel (1980) 'Two lectures', in Gordon, C. (ed.), *Power/Knowledge: Selected Interviews and Other Writings 1972–1977 by Michel Foucault*, New York, Pantheon.

Foucault, Michel (1981) *The History of Sexuality: An Introduction*, Harmondsworth, Penguin.

Foucault, Michel (1991) 'Governmentality', in Burchell, G., Gordon, C. and Miller, P. (eds), *The Foucault Effect: Studies in Governmentality*, London, Harvester Wheatsheaf.

Fourcade, Marion and Savelsberg, Joachim J. (2006) 'Introduction: global processes, national institutions, local bricolage: shaping law in an era of globalization', *Law & Social Inquiry*, 31: 513–19.

Franck, Thomas M. (1985) 'Icy day at the ICJ', *American Journal of International Law*, 79: 379–84.

Freeman, Jody (1993) 'The disciplinary function of rape's representation: lessons from the Kennedy Smith and Tyson trials', *Law & Social Inquiry*, 18: 517–46.

Freiberg, Arie (2001) 'Problem-oriented courts: innovative solutions to intractable problems', *Journal of Judicial Administration*, 11: 8–27.

Freidson, Eliot (1983) 'The reorganization of the professions by regulation', *Law & Human Behavior*, 7: 279–90.

Freidson, Eliot (1994) *Professionalism Reborn: Theory, Prophecy and Policy*, Cambridge, Polity Press.

Friedman, Lawrence (1979) 'Plea bargaining in historical perspective', *Law & Society Review*, 13: 247–59.

Frohmann, Lisa (1991) 'Discrediting victims' allegations of sexual assault: prosecutorial accounts of case rejections', *Social Problems*, 38: 213–26.

Frohmann, Lisa (1997) 'Convictability and discordant locales: reproducing race, class, and gender ideologies in prosecutorial decisionmaking', *Law & Society Review*, 31: 531–56.

Fuchs, Stephan and Ward, Steven (1994) 'What is deconstruction, and where and when does it take place? Making facts in science, building cases in law', *American Sociological Review*, 59: 481–500.

Fudge, Judy (1989) 'The effect of entrenching a bill of rights upon political discourse: feminist demands and sexual violence in Canada', *International Journal of the Sociology of Law*, 17: 445–63.

Fuller, Lon L. (1978) 'The forms and limits of adjudication', *Harvard Law Review*, 92: 353–409.

Gabel, Peter (1980) 'Reification in legal reasoning', *Research in Law and Sociology*, 3: 25–51.

Gabel, Peter and Harris, Paul (1982–83) 'Building, power and breaking images: critical legal theory and the practice of law', *New York University Review of Law and Social Change,* 11: 369–411.

Gabel, Peter and Kennedy, Duncan (1984) 'Roll over Beethoven', *Stanford Law Review*, 36: 1–55.

Gagné, Patricia (1996) 'Identity, strategy, and feminist politics: clemency for battered women who kill', *Social Problems*, 43: 77–93.

Galanter, Marc (1974) 'Why the "haves" come out ahead: speculations on the limits of legal change', *Law & Society Review*, 9: 95–160.

Galanter, Marc (1983a) 'Mega-law and mega-lawyering in the contemporary United States', in Dingwall, R. and Lewis, P. (eds), *The Sociology of the Professions: Lawyers, Doctors and Others*, London, Macmillan.

Galanter, Marc (1983b) 'Reading the landscape of disputes: what we know and don't know about our allegedly contentious and litigious society', *UCLA Law Review*, 31: 4–71.

Galanter, Marc (1985) '"... A settlement judge, not a trial judge": judicial mediation in the United States', *Journal of Law & Society*, 12: 1–18.

Galanter, Marc (1988) 'The life and times of the big six: or, the federal courts since the good old days', *Wisconsin Law Review*, 6: 921–54.

Galanter, Marc (1992) 'Law abounding: legalisation around the North Atlantic', *Modern Law Review*, 55: 1–24.

Galanter, Marc and Palay, Thomas (1991) *Tournament of Lawyers: The Transformation of the Big Law Firm*, Chicago, University of Chicago Press.

Gale, Peter (2005) *The Politics of Fear: Lighting the Wik*, Frenchs Forest, NSW, Pearson Longman.

Gamson, Josh (1989) 'Silence, death, and the invisible enemy: AIDS activism and social movement "newness"', *Social Problems*, 36: 351–67.

Gamson, Josh (1995) 'Must identity movements self-destruct? A queer dilemma', *Social Problems*, 42: 390–407.

Garland, David (1990) 'Frameworks of inquiry in the sociology of punishment', *British Journal of Sociology*, 41: 1–15.

Garland, David (2001) *The Culture of Control: Crime and Social Order in Contemporary Society*, Oxford, Oxford University Press.

Garth, Bryant G. (2003) 'Law and society as law and development', *Law & Society Review*, 37: 305–14.

Geertz, Clifford (1983) *Local Knowledge: Further Essays in Interpretive Anthropology*, New York, Basic Books.

Gelb, Joyce (1987) 'Social movement "success": a comparative analysis of feminism in the United States and the United Kingdom', in Katzenstein, M.F. and Mueller, C.M. (eds), *The Women's Movements of the United States and Western Europe: Consciousness, Political Opportunity, and Public Policy*, Philadelphia, Temple University Press.

Genn, Hazel (1993) 'Tribunals and informal justice', *Modern Law Review*, 56: 393–411.

Genn, Hazel G., Beinart, Sarah, Finch, Steven, Korovessis, Christos and Smith, Patten (1999) *Paths to Justice: What People Do and Think about Going to Law*, Oxford and Portland, OR, Hart Publishing.

Genn, Hazel, Partington, Martin and Wheeler, Sally (2006) *Law in the Real World: Improving Our Understanding of How Law Works*, London, Nuffield Inquiry on Empirical Legal Research.

Gerth, H. H. and Mills, C. Wright (1977) *From Max Weber: Essays in Sociology*, London, Routledge and Kegan Paul.

Ghai, Yash (1994) 'Human rights and governance: the Asia debate', *Australian Year Book of International Law*, 15: 1–34.

Gibbs, Jack P. (1965) 'Norms: the problem of definition and classification', *American Journal of Sociology*, 70: 586–94.

Gibbs, Jack P. (1966) 'The sociology of law and normative phenomena', *American Sociological Review*, 31: 315–25.

Gibbs, Jack P. (1982) 'The notion of social control', in Gibbs, J.P. (ed.), *Social Control: Views from the Social Sciences*, Beverly Hills, Sage.

Gibbs, James L., Jr. (1963) 'The Kpelle moot: a therapeutic model for the informal settlement of disputes', *Africa*, 33: 1–10.

Gibson, Suzanne (1990) 'Continental drift: the question of context in feminist jurisprudence', *Law & Critique*, 1: 173–200.

Giddens, A. (1976) *New Rules of Sociological Method: A Positive Critique of Interpretative Sociologies*, London, New York, Harper & Row.

Giddens, Anthony (1990) *The Consequences of Modernity*, Stanford, CA, Stanford University Press.

Giddens, Anthony (1999) *Runaway World: How Globalisation is Reshaping Our Lives*, London, Profile.

Gilligan, Carol (1982) *In a Different Voice: Psychological Theory and Women's Development*, Cambridge, Harvard University Press.

Ginn, Jay, Arber, Sara, Bannen, Julia, Dale, Angela, Dex, Shirley, Elias, Peter, Moss, Peter, Pahl, Jan, Roberts, Ceridwen and Rubery, Jill (1996) 'Feminist fallacies: a reply to Hakim on women's employment', *British Journal of Sociology*, 47: 167–74.

Ginsburg, Faye D. (1989) *Contested Lives: The Abortion Debate in an American Community*, Berkeley, University of California Press.

Ginsburg, Ruth Bader (1981) 'Inviting judicial activism: a "liberal" or "conservative" technique?', *Georgia Law Review*, 15: 539–58.

Glasser, Cyril and Roberts, Simon (1993) 'Dispute resolution: civil justice and its alternatives', *Modern Law Review*, 56: 277–81.

Glendon, Mary Ann (1989) *The Transformation of Family Law: State, Law and Family in the United States and Western Europe*, Chicago, University of Chicago Press.

Glenn, H. Patrick (2003) 'A transnational concept of law', in Cane, P. and Tushnet, M. (eds), *The Oxford Handbook of Legal Studies*, Oxford, Oxford University Press.

Goodale, Mark (2005) 'Empires of law: discipline and resistance within the transnational system', *Social & Legal Studies*, 14: 553–83.

Goode, William J. (1969) 'The theoretical limits of professionalization', in Etzioni, A. (ed.), *The Semi-Professions and their Organization: Teachers, Nurses, Social Workers*, New York, Free Press.

Goode, William J. (1957) 'Community within a community: the professions', *American Sociological Review*, 20: 194–200.

Gordley, James (1984) 'Legal reasoning: an introduction', *California Law Review*, 72: 138–77.

Gorman, Elizabeth H. (2005) 'Gender streotypes, same-gender preferences, and organizational variation in the hiring of women: evidence from law firms', *American Sociological Review*, 70: 702–28.

Gorman, Elizabeth H. (2006) 'Work uncertainty and the promotion of professional women: the case of law firm partnership', *Social Forces*, 85: 865–91.

Gottfredson, Michael R. and Hindelang, Michael J. (1979a) 'A study of *The Behavior of Law*', *American Sociological Review*, 44: 3–18.

Gottfredson, Michael R. and Hindelang, Michael J. (1979b) 'Theory and research in the sociology of law', *American Sociological Review*, 44: 27–37.

Grattet, Ryken and Jenness, Valerie (2005) 'The reconstitution of law in local settings: agency discretion, ambiguity, and a surplus of law in the policing of hate crime', *Law & Society Review*, 39: 893–941.

Grattet, Ryken, Jenness, Valerie and Curry, Theodore R. (1998) 'The homogenization and differentiation of hate crime law in the United States, 1978 to 1995: innovation and diffusion in the criminalization of bigotry', *American Sociological Review*, 63: 286–307.

Graycar, Regina and Morgan, Jenny (2002) *The Hidden Gender of Law*, 2nd edn, Annandale, Federation Press.

Grbich, Judith E. (1991) 'The body in legal theory', in Fireman, M.A. and Thomadsen, N.S. (eds), *At the Boundaries of Law: Feminism and Legal Theory*, New York, Routledge.

Green, L. C. (1988) 'Canadian law, war crimes and crimes against humanity', *British Year Book of International Law*, 59: 217–35.

Green, Lorraine (1996) *Policing Places with Drug Problems*, Thousand Oaks, Sage.

Greenberg, David F. (1983) 'Donald Black's sociology of law: a critique', *Law & Society Review*, 17: 337–68.

Greenlees, Don (1997) 'Great divide on human rights', *The Australian*, Wednesday, July 30: 1–7.

Greenwood, C. (1957) 'Attributes of a profession', *Social Work*, 2: 45–55.

Greenwood, Christopher (1993) 'Is there a right of humanitarian intervention?', *The World Today*, 49: 34–40.

Greig, D. W. (1976) *International Law*, Sydney, Butterworths.

Grillo, Tina (1991) 'The mediation alternative: process dangers for women', *Yale Law Journal*: 545–610.

Griset, Pamala (1994) 'Determinate sentencing and the high cost of overblown rhetoric: the New York experience', *Crime & Delinquency*, 40: 532–48.

Grundy, Sue and Jamieson, Lynn (2007) 'European identities: from absent-minded citizens to passionate Europeans', *Sociology*, 41: 663–81.

Gusfield, J. (1967) 'Moral passage: the symbolic process in public designations of deviance', *Social Problems*, 15: 175–88.

Habermas, Jurgen (1981) 'New social movements', *Telos*, 49: 33–7.

Habermas, Jurgen (1984) *Reason and the Rationalization of Society*, Boston, Beacon Press.

Habermas, Jurgen (1987) *Lifeworld and System: a Critique of Functionalist Reason*, Boston, Beacon Press.

Habermas, Jurgen (1990) 'Citizenship and national identity' in Habermas, J. (ed.), *Between Facts and Norms: Contributions to a Discourse Theory of Law and Democracy*, Cambridge, Polity.

Habermas, Jurgen (1996) *Between Facts and Norms: Contributions to a Discourse Theory of Law and Democracy*, Cambridge, Polity.

Hagan, John and Kay, Fiona (2007) 'Even lawyers get the blues: gender, depression, and job satisfaction in legal practice', *Law & Society Review*, 41: 51–78.

Hagan, John and Parker, Patricia (1985) 'White-collar crime and punishment: the class structure and legal sanctioning of securities violations', *American Sociological Review*, 50: 302–16.

Hagan, John, Levi, Ron and Ferrales, Gabrielle (2006) 'Swaying the hand of justice: the internal and external dynamics of regime change at the International Criminal Tribunal for the Former Yugoslavia', *Law & Social Inquiry*, 31: 585–616.

Hajjar, Lisa (2004) 'Religion, state power, and domestic violence in muslim societies: a framework for comparative analysis', *Law & Social Inquiry*, 29: 1–38.

Hakim, Catherine (1995) 'Five feminist myths about women's employment', *British Journal of Sociology*, 46: 429–55.

Hale, Sir Matthew (1971) *Historia Placitorum Coronae*, vol. 1, London, Professional Books.

Haley, John Owen (1978) 'The myth of the reluctant litigant', *Journal of Japanese Studies*, 4: 359–90.

Haley, John O. (1982) 'Sheathing the sword of justice in Japan: an essay on law without sanctions', *Journal of Japanese Studies*, 8: 265–81.

Hall, Richard H. (1968) 'Professionalization and bureaucratization', *American Sociological Review*, 33: 92–104.

Halliday, Terence C. and Osinsky, Pavel (2006) 'Globalization of law', *Annual Review of Sociology*, 32: 447–71.

Halliday, Terence C. and Carruthers, Bruce G. (2007) 'The recursivity of law: global norm making and national lawmaking in the globalization of corporate insolvency regimes', *American Journal of Sociology*, 112: 1135–202.

Hallinan, Maureen T. (1997) 'The sociological study of social change: 1996 Presidential Address', *American Sociological Review*, 62: 1–11.

Haltom, William and McCann, Michael J. (2004) *Distorting the Law: Politics, Media, and the Litigation Crisis*, Chicago, University of Chicago Press.

Hamilton, V. Lee and Sanders, Joseph (1992) *Everyday Justice: Responsibility and the Individual in Japan and the United States*, New Haven, Yale University Press.

Handler, Joel F. (1978) *Social Movements and the Legal System: A Theory of Law Reform and Social Change*, New York: Academic Press.

Hanlon, Gerard (1997) 'A profession in transition? Lawyers, the market and significant others', *Modern Law Review*, 60: 798–822.

Hanlon, Gerard (1998) 'Professionalism as enterprise: service class politics and the redefinition of professionalism', *Sociology*, 32: 43–64.

Harrington, Christine B. (1982) 'Delegalization reform movements: a historical analysis', in Abel, R. (ed.), *The Politics of Informal Justice*, New York, Academic Press.

Harrington, Christine B. (1984) 'The politics of participation and non participation in dispute processes', *Law & Policy*, 6: 203–30.

Harrington, Christine B. (1985) *Shadow Justice: The Ideology and Institutionalization of Alternatives to Court*, Greenwich, Greenwood Press.

Harrington, Christine B. and Merry, Sally Engle (1988) 'Ideological production: the making of community mediation', *Law & Society Review*, 22: 709–35.

Harris, Alexes (2007) 'Diverting and abdicating judicial discretion: cultural, political, and procedural dynamics in California juvenile justice', *Law & Society Review*, 41: 387–427.

Harris, Angela (1990) 'Race and essentialism in feminist legal theory', *Stanford Law Review*, 42: 581–616.

Hart, Herbert L. A. (1961) *The Concept of Law*, Oxford, Clarendon Press.

Hart, H. L. A. (1980) 'Positivism and the separation of law and morals', in Feinberg, J. and Gross, H. (eds), *Philosophy of Law*, 2nd edn, Belmont, Wadsworth.

Hasenfeld, Yeheskel , Rafferty, Jane A. and Mayer, N. Zald (1987) 'The welfare state, citizenship and bureaucratic encounters', *Annual Review of Sociology*, 13: 387–415.

Haug, Marie (1973) 'Deprofessionalization: an alternative hypothesis for the future', *Sociological Review Monograph*, 20: 195–211.

Hay, Douglas (1975) 'Property, authority and the criminal law', in Hay, D., Linebaugh, P., Rule, J.G., Thompsson, E.P. and Winslow, C. (eds), *Albion's Fatal Tree: Crime and Society in Eighteenth-Century England*, London: Allen Lane.

Heath, Mary and Naffine, Ngaire (1994) 'Men's needs and women's desires: feminist dilemmas about rape law reform', *Australian Feminist Law Journal*, 3: 30–52.

Heinz, John and Laumann, Edward O. (1982) *Chicago Lawyers: The Social Structure of the Bar*, New York, Russell Sage.

Heinz, John P., Paik, Anthony and Southworth, Ann (2003) 'Lawyers for conservative causes: clients, ideology, and social distance', *Law & Society Review*, 37: 5–50.

Heinz, John P., Nelson, Robert L., Sandefur, Rebecca L. and Laumann, Edward O. (2005) *Urban Lawyers: The New Social Structure of the Bar*, Chicago, University of Chicago Press.

Held, David (1995) *Democracy and the Global Order: From the Modern State to Cosmopolitan Governance*, Cambridge, Polity.

Henham, Ralph (1995) 'Sentencing policy and the role of the Court of Appeal', *Howard Journal*, 34: 218–27.

Henham, Ralph (2002) 'Sentencing policy and guilty plea discounts', in Tata, C. and Hutton, N. (eds), *Sentencing and Society: International Perspectives*, Aldershot, Ashgate.

Herman, Didi (1993) 'Beyond the rights debate: a note on plea bargaining and case pressure', *Social & Legal Studies*, 2: 23–43.

Hester, Marianne, Pearce, Julia and Westmarland, Nicole (2008) *Early Evaluation of the Integrated Domestic Violence Court*, Croydon, London, Ministry of Justice.

Heumann, Milton (1975) 'A note on plea bargaining and case pressure', *Law & Society Review*, 9: 515–28.

Heumann, Milton and Loftin, Colin (1979) 'Mandatory sentencing and the abolition of plea bargaining: the Michigan felony firearm statute', *Law & Society Review*, 13: 393–429.

Hilbink, Thomas M. (2004) 'You know the type...: categories of cause lawyering', *Law & Social Inquiry*, 29: 657–98.

Hillyard, Paddy (2007) 'Law's empire: socio-legal empirical research in the twenty-first century', *Journal of Law & Society*, 34: 266–79.

Hindess, Barry and Hirst, Paul (1977) *Mode of Production and Social Formation: An Autocritique of Pre-capitalistic Modes of Production*, London, Macmillan.

Hinton, Martin (1995) 'Expectations dashed: victim impact statements in South Australia', *University of Tasmania Law Review*, 14: 81–99.

Hirst, Paul (1972) 'Marx and Engels on law, crime and morality', *Economy and Society*, 1: 28–56.

Hofrichter, Richard (1982) 'Justice centers raise basic questions', in Tomasic, R. and Feeley, M.M. (eds), *Neighborhood Justice: Assessment of an Emerging Idea*, New York, Longman.

Hofrichter, Richard (1987) *Neighborhood Justice in Capitalist Society: The Expansion of the Informal State*, Westport, Greenwood Press.

Holmes, Malcolm D., Daudistel, Howard C. and Taggart, William A. (1992) 'Plea bargaining and state district court case loads: an interrupted time series analysis', *Law & Society Review*, 26: 139–59.

Holmes, O. W. (1897) 'The path of the law', *Harvard Law Review*, 10: 457–78.

Holton, R. J. (1987) 'The idea of crisis in modern society', *British Journal of Sociology*, 38: 502–20.

Holton, Robert J. (1997) 'Four myths about globalisation', *Flinders Journal of History and Politics*, 19: 141–56.

Holton, Robert J. (2008) *Global Networks*, Houndmills, Basingstoke, Palgrave Macmillan.

Hopcroft, Rosemary L. (1995) 'Conceptualising regional differences in eighteenth century England', *American Sociological Review*, 60: 791–7.

Howe, Adrian (1994) 'Provoking comment: the question of gender bias in the provocation defence – a Victorian case study', in Grieve, N. and Burns, A. (eds), *Australian Women: Contemporary Feminist Thought*, Melbourne, Oxford University Press.

Hughes, Everett C. (1971) *The Sociological Eye*, New York, Aldine.

Hunt, Alan (1978) *The Sociological Movement in Law*, London, Macmillan.

Hunt, Alan (1981) 'Dichotomy and contradiction in the sociology of law', *British Journal of Law & Society*, 8: 47–77.

Hunt, Alan (1983) 'Behavioral sociology of law: a critique of Donald Black', *Journal of Law & Society*, 10: 19–46.

Hunt, Alan (1985) 'The ideology of law: advances and problems in recent applications of the concept of ideology to the analysis of law', *Law & Society Review*, 19: 11–37.

Hunt, Alan (1987) 'The critique of law: what is "critical" about critical legal theory', *Journal of Law & Society*, 14: 5–19.

Hunt, Alan (1990) 'Rights and social movements: counter-hegemonic strategies', *Journal of Law & Society*, 17: 309–28.

Hunt, Alan (1992) 'Foucault's expulsion of law: toward a retrieval', *Law & Social Inquiry*, 17: 1–38.

Hunt, Alan (1993) *Explorations in Law and Society: Toward a Constitutive Theory of Law*, New York, Routledge.

Hunt, Alan and Wickham, Gary (1994) *Foucault and Law: Toward a Sociology of Law as Governance*, London, Pluto Press.

Hunter, Caroline (2006) 'The changing legal framework: from landlords to agents of social control', in Flint, J. (ed.), *Housing, Urban Governance and Anti-Social Behaviour*, Bristol, Policy Press.

Hunter, Caroline, Blandy, Sarah, Cowan, Dave, Nixon, Judy, Hitchings, Emma, Pantazis, Christina and Parr, Sadie (2005) *The Exercise of Judicial Discretion in Rent Arrears Cases*, DCA Research Series 6/05, UK, Department for Constitutional Affairs.

Hunter, Nan D. and Law, Sylvia (1987–8) 'Brief amici curiae of Feminist AntiCensorship Taskforce et al. in *American Booksellers Association* v *Hudnut*', *Journal of Law Reform*, 21: 69–136.

Hunter, Rosemary (1988) 'Women workers and federal industrial law: from Harvester to comparable worth', *Australian Journal of Labour Law*, 1: 147–72.

Hunter, Rosemary (2002) 'Talking up equality: women barristers and the denial of discrimination', *Feminist Legal Studies*, 10: 113–30.

Hunter, Rosemary (2005) 'Discrimination against women barristers: evidence from a study of court appearances and briefing practices', *International Journal of the Legal Profession*, 12: 3–49.

Hurst, James Willard (1980) 'The functions of courts in the United States, 1950–1980', *Law & Society Review*, 15: 401–71.

Ingleby, Richard (1993) 'Court sponsored mediation: the case against mandatory participation', *Modern Law Review*, 56: 441–51.

Ishii, Yoneo (1994) 'Thai Muslims and the royal patronage of religion', *Law & Society Review*, 28: 453–60.

Israel, Mark (2004) 'Strictly confidential? Integrity and the disclosure of criminological and socio-legal research', *British Journal of Criminology*, 44: 715–40.

Jenness, Valerie (2004) 'Explaining criminalization: from demography and status politics to globalization and modernization', *Annual Review of Sociology*, 30: 147–72.

Jenness, Valerie and Grattet, Ryken (2005) 'The law-in-between: the effects of organizational perviousness on the policing of hate crime', *Social Problems*, 52: 337–59.

Jessop, Bob (1980) 'On recent Marxist theories of law, the state, and juridico-political ideology', *International Journal of the Sociology of Law*, 8: 39–68.

Johnsen, Dawn E. (1986) 'The creation of fetal rights: conflicts with women's constitutional rights to liberty, privacy, and equal protection', *Yale Law Journal*, 95: 599–625.

Johnson, Terence J. (1972) *Professions and Power*, London, Macmillan.

Johnstone, Quintin and Wenglinsky, Martin (1985) *Paralegals: Progress and Prospects of a Satellite Occupation*, Westport, Greenwood Press.

Jones, T. Anthony (1981) 'Durkheim, deviance and development: opportunities lost and regained', *Social Forces*, 59: 1009–24.

Jordan, Emma Coleman (1992) 'Race, gender and social class in the Thomas sexual harassment hearings: the hidden fault lines in political discourse', *Harvard Women's Law Journal*, 15: 1–24.

Kagan, Robert A. (1988) 'What makes Uncle Sammy sue?', *Law & Society Review*, 21: 717–42.

Kairys, David (1990) 'Introduction', in Kairys, D. (ed.), *The Politics of Law: A Progressive Critique*, rev. edn, New York, Pantheon Books.

Kanter, Rosabeth M. (1977) *Men and Women of the Corporation*, New York, Basic Books.

Katz, Jack (1988) *Seductions of Crime: Moral and Sensual Attractions in Doing Evil*, New York, Basic Books.

Katzenstein, Mary Fainsod (1987) 'Comparing the feminist movements of the United States and Western Europe: an overview', in Katzenstein, M.F. and Muller, C.M. (eds), *The Women's Movements of The United States and Western Europe: Consciousness, Political Opportunity, and Public Policy*, Philadelphia, Temple University Press.

Kawashima, Takeyoshi (1963) 'Dispute resolution in contemporary Japan', in von Mehren, A.T. (ed.), *Law in Japan: The Legal Order in a Changing Society*, Cambridge, Harvard University Press.

Kay, Fiona M. and Hagan, John (1995) 'The persistent glass ceiling: gendered inequalities in the earnings of lawyers', *British Journal of Sociology*, 46: 278–310.

Kay, Fiona M. and Hagan, John (1998) 'Raising the bar: the gender stratification of law-firm capital', *American Sociological Review*, 63: 728–43.

Kaye, Tim (1987) 'Natural law theory and legal positivism: two sides of the same practical coin', *Journal of Law & Society*, 14: 303–19.

Kelly, Erin and Dobbin, Frank (1999) 'Civil rights law at work: sex discrimination and the rise of maternity leave policies', *American Journal of Sociology*, 105: 455–92.

Kelman, Herbert C. and Hamilton, V. Lee (1989) *Crimes of Obedience: Toward a Social Psychology of Authority and Responsibility*, New Haven, Yale University Press.

Kennedy, Duncan (1990) 'Legal education as training for hierarchy', in Kairys, D. (ed.), *The Politics of Law: A Progressive Critique*, rev. edn, New York, Pantheon Books.

Kidder, Robert L. (1983) *Connecting Law and Society*, Englewood Cliffs, Prentice-Hall.

King, Michael (1993) 'The "truth" about autopoiesis', *Journal of Law & Society*, 20: 218–36.

King, Michael S. (2003) 'Applying therapeutic jurisprudence from the bench', *Alternative Law Journal*, 28: 172–5.

Klegon, D. (1978) 'The sociology of the professions: an emerging perspective', *Work & Occupations*, 5: 259–83.

Kostiner, Idit (2003) 'Evaluating legality: toward a cultural approach to the study of law and social change', *Law & Society Review*, 37: 323–68.

Kritzer, Herbert M. (2007) 'Toward a theorization of craft', *Social & Legal Studies*, 16: 321–40.

Kronman, Anthony T. (1983) *Max Weber*, Stanford, Stanford University Press.

Kruttschnitt, Candace (1982) 'Women, crime, and dependency: an application of the theory of law', *Criminology*, 19: 495–513.

Krygier, Martin (1990) 'Marxism and the rule of law: reflections after the collapse of communism', *Law & Social Inquiry*, 15: 633–63.

Lacey, Nicola (1993) 'Theory into practice: pornography and the public/private dichotomy', *Journal of Law & Society*, 20: 93–113.

Lacey, Nicola and Zedner, Lucia (1995) 'Discourses of community in criminal justice', *Journal of Law &Society*, 22: 301–25.

Ladinsky, Jack (1963) 'Careers of lawyers, law practice and legal institutions', *American Sociological Review*, 28: 47–54.

Lancaster, H. (1982) 'Companies expanding legal staffs as the cost of outside work soars', *Wall Street Journal*, 1 March: 25.

Land, Hilary (1980) 'The family wage', *Feminist Review*, 6: 55–77.

Langbein, John H. (1979) 'Understanding the short history of plea bargaining', *Law & Society Review*, 13: 261–72.

Larson, Magali S. (1977) *The Rise of Professionalism: A Sociological Analysis*, Berkeley, University of California Press.

Lasser, William (1988) *The Limits of Judicial Power: The Supreme Court in American Politics*, Chapel Hill, University of North Carolina Press.

Law Reform Commission of Victoria (1986) *Rape and Allied Offences: Substantive Aspects*, Discussion Paper no. 2, Melbourne, Government Printer.

Law Society of British Columbia (1992) *Gender Equality in the Justice System: A Report of the Law Society of British Columbia Gender Bias Committee*, Vancouver, Law Society of British Columbia.

Lee, R. G. (1992) 'From profession to business: the rise and rise of the city law firm', *Journal of Law & Society*, 19: 31–48.

Lenman, Bruce and Parker, Geoffrey (1980) 'The state, the community and the criminal law in early modern Europe', in Gartrell, V.A.C., Lenman, B. and Parker, G. (eds), *Crime and the Law: The Social History of Crime in Western Europe since 1500*, London, Europa Publications.

Lerman, Lisa G. (1984) 'Mediation of wife abuse cases: the adverse impact of informal dispute resolution on women', *Harvard Women's Law Journal*, 7: 57–113.

Lessan, Gloria T. and Sheley, Joseph F. (1992) 'Does law behave? A macrolevel test of Black's propositions on change in law', *Social Forces*, 70: 655–78.

Levi, Michael and Wall, David S. (2004) 'Technologies, security and privacy in the post-9/11 European information society', *Journal of Law & Society*, 31: 194–220.

Levy, Daniel and Sznaider, Natan (2006) 'Sovereignty transformed: a sociology of human rights', *British Journal of Sociology*, 57: 657–76.

Lewis, Ruth, Dobash, Rebecca Emerson, Dobash, Russell P. and Cavanagh, Kate (2001) 'Law's progressive potential: the value of engagement with the law for domestic violence', *Social & Legal Studies*, 10: 105–30.

Lianos, Michaelis and Douglas, Mary (2000) 'Dangerization and the end of deviance: the institutional environment', *British Journal of Criminology*, 40: 261–78.

Ligertwood, Andrew (1993) *Australian Evidence*, 2nd edn, Sydney, Butterworths.

Lister, Diane (2006) 'Tenancy agreements: a mechanism for governing anti-social behaviour?', in Flint, J. (ed.), *Housing, Urban Governance and Anti-Social Behaviour*, Bristol, The Policy Press.

Lloyd, Lord and Freeman, M.D.A. (eds) (1985) *Lloyd's Introduction to Jurisprudence*, 5th edn, London, Stevens.

Lockyer, Roger (1964) *Tudor and Stuart Britain 1471–1714*, London, Longmans.

Luhmann, Niklas (1985) *A Sociological Theory of Law*, London, Routledge & Kegan Paul.

Luhmann, Niklas (1986) 'The self-reproduction of law and its limits', in Teubner, G. (ed.), *Dilemmas of Law in the Welfare State*, New York, Walter de Gruyter.

Luhmann, Niklas (1988a) 'The third question: the creative use of paradoxes in law and legal history', *Journal of Law & Society*, 15: 153–65.

Luhmann, Niklas (1988b) 'The unity of the legal system', in Teubner, G. (ed.), *Autopoietic Law: A New Approach to Law and Society*, New York, Walter de Gruyter.

Luhmann, Niklas (1992) 'Operational closure and structural coupling: the differentiation of the legal system', *Cardozo Law Review*, 13: 1419–41.

Luker, Kristin (1984) *Abortion and the Politics of Motherhood*, Berkeley, University of California Press.

Lukes, Steven (1975) *Emile Durkheim*, Harmondsworth, Penguin.

Lukes, Steven and Scull, Andrew (1983) *Durkheim and the Law*, Oxford, Basil Blackwell.

Lupton, Deborah (1999) *Risk*, Routledge, London.

Lynch, David (1994) 'The impropriety of plea agreements: a tale of two counties', *Law & Social Inquiry*, 19: 115–34.

Macaulay, Stewart (1963) 'Non-contractual relations in business: a preliminary study', *American Sociological Review*, 28: 55–67.

Macaulay, Stewart (1979) 'Lawyers and consumer protection laws', *Law & Society Review*, 14: 115–71.

MacCorquodale, Patricia and Jensen, Gary (1993) 'Women in the law: partners or tokens?', *Gender & Society*, 7: 582–93.

Macdonald, Keith M. (1995) *The Sociology of the Professions*, London, Sage.

Macdonald, S. (2006) 'A suicidal woman, roaming pigs and a noisy trampolinist: refining the ASBO's definition of "anti-social behaviour"', *Modern Law Review*, 69: 183–213.

Mack, Kathy (1993) 'Continuing barriers to women's credibility: a feminist perspective on the proof process', *Criminal Law Forum*, 4: 327–53.

Mack, Kathy (1994) '*B. v R.*: Negative stereotypes and women's credibility', *Feminist Legal Studies*, 11: 183–94.

Mack, Kathy (1995) 'Alternative dispute resolution and access to justice for women', *Adelaide Law Review*, 17: 123–46.

Mack, Kathy (1998) '"You should scrutinize the evidence with great care": corroboration of women's testimony about sexual assault', in Easteal, P. (ed.), *Balancing the Scales: Rape, Law Reform and Australian Culture*, Sydney, Federation Press.

Mack, Kathy (2003) *Court Referral to ADR: Criteria and Research*, Melbourne, Australian Institute of Judicial Administration.

Mack, Kathy and Roach Anleu, Sharyn (1995) *Pleading Guilty: Issues and Practices*, Melbourne, Australian Institute of Judicial Administration.

Mack, Kathy and Roach Anleu, Sharyn (1997) 'Sentence discount for a guilty plea: time for a new look', *Flinders Journal of Law Reform*, 1: 128.

Mack, Kathy and Roach Anleu, Sharyn (2007) '"Getting through the list": judgecraft and legitimacy in the lower courts', *Social & Legal Studies*, 16: 341–61.

Mack, Kathy and Roach Anleu, Sharyn (2008) 'The National Survey of Australian Judges: an overview of findings', *Journal of Judicial Administration*, 18: 5–21.

Mackenzie, Geraldine (2005) *How Judges Sentence*, Sydney, Federation Press.

MacKinnon, Catharine (1979) *Sexual Harassment of Working Women: A Case of Sex Discrimination*, New Haven, Yale University Press.

MacKinnon, Catharine (1982) 'Feminism, Marxism, method, and the state: an agenda for theory', *Signs: Journal of Women in Culture and Society*, 7: 515–44.

MacKinnon, Catharine (1983) 'Feminism, Marxism, method, and the state: toward feminist jurisprudence', *Signs: Journal of Women in Culture and Society*, 8: 635–58.

MacKinnon, Catharine (1986) 'Pornography: not a moral issue', *Women's Studies International Forum*, 9: 63–78.

MacKinnon, Catharine (1987) *Feminism Unmodified: Discourses on Life and Law*, Cambridge, Harvard University Press.

MacKinnon, Catharine (1989) *Toward a Feminist Theory of the State*, Cambridge, Harvard University Press.

Macpherson, William (1999) *The Stephen Lawrence Inquiry. Report of an inquiry by Sir William Macpherson of Cluny*, London, The Stationery Office.

Maine, Henry Sumner, Sir (1888) *Ancient Law: Its Connection with the Early History of Society and its Relation to Modern Ideas*, 12th edn, London, Murray.

Malinowski, Bronislaw (1961) *Crime and Custom in Savage Society*, London, Routledge & Kegan Paul.

Malleson, Kate (2003) 'Justifying gender equality on the Bench: why difference won't do', *Feminist Legal Studies*, 11: 1–24.

Malleson, Kate (2006) 'Rethinking the merit principle in judicial selection', *Journal of Law & Society*, 33: 126–40.

Mann, Michael (1987) 'Ruling class strategies and citizenship', *Sociology*, 21: 339–54.

Marchetti, Elena and Daly, Kathleen (2007) 'Indigenous sentencing courts: towards a theoretical and jurisprudential model', *Sydney Law Review*, 29: 415–43.

Marchetti, Elena and Ransley, Janet (2005) 'Unconscious racism: scrutinizing judicial reasoning in "stolen generation" cases', *Social & Legal Studies*, 14: 533–52.

Marshall, T. H. (1992) 'Citizenship and social class', in Marshall, T.H. and Bottomore, T. (eds), *Citizenship and Social Class*, London, Pluto.

Martin, Patricia Yancey (1990) 'Rethinking feminist organizations', *Gender & Society*, 4: 182–206.

Martin, Patricia Yancey and Powell, Marlene R. (1995) 'Accounting for the "second assault": legal organizations' framing of rape victims', *Law & Social Inquiry*, 19: 853–90.

Martin, Patricia Yancey, Reynolds, John R. and Keith, Shelley (2002) 'Gender bias and feminist consciousness among judges and attorneys: a standpoint theory analysis', *Signs: Journal of Women in Culture and Society*, 27: 665–705.

Martinson, Robert (1974) 'What works–questions and answers about prison reform', *The Public Interest*, 35: 22–54.

Marx, Karl (1975) 'Debates on the law on thefts of wood', in Marx, K. and Engels, F. (eds), *Collected Works vol.1: Karl Marx, 1835–43*, London, Lawrence and Wishart.

Marx, Karl and Engels, Friedrich (1948) *Communist Manifesto: Socialist Landmark, with a New Appreciation, written for the Labour Party by Harold J. Laski*, London, George Allen and Unwin.

Mason, Gail and Tomsen, Stephen (1997) *Homophobic Violence*, Sydney, Hawkins Press.

Massell, Gregory J. (1968) 'Law as an instrument of revolutionary change in a traditional milieu', *Law & Society Review*, 2: 179–228.

Mastura, Michael (1994) 'Legal pluralism in the Philippines', *Law & Society Review*, 28: 461–75.

Mather, Lynn (1995) 'The fired football coach (or, how trial courts make policy)', in Epstein, L. (ed.), *Contemplating Courts*, Washington, DC, CQ Press.

Mather, Lynn (1998) 'Theorizing about trial courts: lawyers, policymaking, and tobacco litigation', *Law & Social Inquiry*, 23: 897–940.

Mather, Lynn and Yngvesson, Barbara (1980) 'Language, audience, and the transformation of disputes', *Law & Society Review*, 15: 775–821.

Mathews, Jane M. (1982) 'The changing profile of women in the law', *Australian Law Journal*, December: 634–42.

Matoesian, Gregory M. (1995) 'Language, law and society: policy implications of the Kennedy Smith rape trial', *Law & Society Review*, 29: 669–701.

Matrix Justice Group (2008) *Dedicated Drug Court Pilots: A Process Report*, Ministry of Justice Research Series 7/08, UK, Ministry of Justice.

Mauer, Marc (1995) 'The international use of incarceration', *Prison Journal*, 75: 113–23.

Mazerolle, Lorraine and Ransley, Janet (2005) *Third Party Policing*, Cambridge, Cambridge University Press.

Mazerolle, Lorraine, Soole, David and Rombouts, Sacha (2006) 'Street-level drug law enforcement: a meta-analytical review', *Journal of Experimental Criminology*, 2: 409–35.

Mazerolle, Lorraine, Soole, David and Rombouts, Sacha (2007) 'Drug law enforcement: a review of the evaluation literature', *Police Quarterly*, 10: 115–53.

McBarnett, Doreen (1994) 'Legal creativity: law, capital and legal avoidance', in Cain, M. and Harrington, C.B. (eds), *Lawyers in a Postmodern World: Translation and Transgression*, Buckingham, Open University Press.

McCallum, David and Laurence, Jennifer (2008) 'Psy-knowledge, history and the sociology of law: the case of juvenile justice', *Journal of Sociology*, 44: 115–31.

McCann, Michael W. (1991) 'Legal mobilization and social reform movements: notes on theory and its application', *Studies in Law, Politics and Society*, 11: 225–54.

McCann, Michael W. (1994) *Rights at Work: Pay Equity Reform and the Politics of Legal Mobilization*, Chicago, University of Chicago Press.

McConville, Michael (1998) 'Plea bargaining: ethics and politics', *Journal of Law & Society*, 25: 562–87.

McConville, Mike and Mirsky, Chester (1993) 'Looking through the guilty plea glass: the structural framework of English and American state courts', *Social & Legal Studies*, 2: 173–93.

McConville, Mike and Mirsky, Chester (1995) 'The rise of guilty pleas: New York, 1800–1865', *Journal of Law & Society*, 22: 443–74.

McCoy, Candace (1993) *Politics and Plea Bargaining: Victims' Rights in California*, Philadelphia, University of Pennsylvania Press.

McEvoy, Kieran, Mika, Harry and Hudson, Barbara (2002) 'Introduction: practice, performance and prospects for restorative justice', *British Journal of Criminology*, 42: 469–75.

McEwen, Craig A., Mather, Lynn and Maiman, Richard J. (1994) 'Lawyers, mediation and the management of divorce practice', *Law & Society Review*, 28: 149–86.

McHugh, Michael (1988a) 'The law-making function of the judicial process – Part II', *Australian Law Journal*, 62: 116–27.

McHugh, Michael (1988b) 'The law making function of the judicial process – Part I', *Australian Law Journal*, 62: 15–31.

McHugh, M. H. (1995) 'The growth of legislation and litigation', *Australian Law Journal*, 69: 37–48.

McLellan, David (1977) *Karl Marx: Selected Writings*, Oxford, Oxford University Press.

McVeigh, Rory, Bjarnason, Thoroddur and Welch, Michael R. (2003) 'Hate crime reporting as a successful social movement outcome', *American Sociological Review*, 68: 843–67.

McWhinney, Edward (1968) 'Legal systems: common law systems', in Sills, D. (ed.), *International Encyclopedia of the Social Sciences*, New York, Free Press.

Meeker, James W. and Pontell, Henry N. (1985) 'Court caseloads, plea bargains and criminal sanctions: the effects of Section 17 P.C. in California', *Criminology*, 23: 119–43.

Menjívar, Cecilia (2006) 'Liminal legality: Salvadoran and Guatemalan immigrants' lives in the United States', *American Journal of Sociology*, 111: 999–1038.

Menkel-Meadow, Carrie (1987) 'Portia in a different voice: speculating on a women's lawyering process', *Berkeley Women's Law Journal*, 1: 39–63.

Menkel-Meadow, Carrie (1989a) 'Exploring a research agenda of the feminization of the legal profession: theories of gender and social change', *Law & Social Inquiry*, 14: 289–319.

Menkel-Meadow, Carrie (1989b) 'Feminization of the legal profession: the comparative sociology of women lawyers', in Abel, R.L. and Lewis, P.S.C. (eds), *Lawyers in Society: Comparative Theories*, Berkeley, University of California Press.

Meron, Theodor (1987) 'The Geneva Conventions on customary international law', *American Journal of International Law*, 81: 348–70.

Merry, Sally Engle (1979) 'Going to court: strategies of dispute management in an American urban neighborhood', *Law & Society Review*, 13: 891–925.

Merry, Sally Engle (1982) 'Defining "success" in the neighborhood justice movement' in Tomasic, R. and Feeley, M.M. (eds), *Neighborhood Justice: Assessment of an Emerging Idea*, New York, Longman.

Merry, Sally Engle (1988) 'Legal pluralism', *Law & Society Review*, 22: 869–96.

Merry, Sally Engle (1990) 'The discourses of mediation and the power of naming', *Yale Journal of Law & the Humanities*, 2: 1–36.

Merry, Sally Engle (1991) 'Law and colonialism', *Law & Society Review*, 25: 889–922.

Merry, Sally Engle (2003) 'Constructing a global law – violence against women and the human rights system', *Law & Social Inquiry*, 28: 941–78.

Merry, Sally Engle (2006) *Human Rights and Gender Violence: Translating International Law into Local Justice*, Chicago, University of Chicago Press.

Merton, Robert K. (1934) 'Durkheim's *Division of Labor in Society*', *American Journal of Sociology*, 40: 319–28.

Merton, Robert K. (1936) 'The unanticipated consequences of purposive social action', *American Sociological Review*, 1: 894–904.

Merton, Robert K. (1968) *Social Theory and Social Structure*, New York, The Free Press.

Mertz, Elizabeth (1992) 'Language, law and social meanings: linguistic/anthropological contributions to the study of law', *Law & Society Review*, 26: 413–45.

Messick, Richard E. (1999) 'Judicial reform and economic development: a survey of the issues', *World Bank Research Observer*, 14: 117–36.

Meyer, John W. (2000) 'Globalization: sources and effects on national states and societies', *International Sociology*, 15: 233–48.

Meyer, John W., Boli, John, Thomas, George M. and Ramirez, Francisco O. (1997) 'World society and the nation-state', *American Journal of Sociology*, 103: 144–82.

Meyer, Madonna Harrington (1996) 'Making claims as workers or wives: the distribution of social security benefits', *American Sociological Review*, 61: 449–65.

Miethe, Terence D. (1987) 'Charging and plea bargaining practices under determinate sentencing: an investigation of the hydraulic displacement of discretion', *Journal of Criminal Law & Criminology*, 78: 155–76.

Milkman, Ruth (1986) 'Women's history and the Sears case', *Feminist Studies*, 12: 375–400.

Miller, Richard E. and Sarat, Austin (1980–81) 'Claims and disputes: assessing the adversary culture', *Law & Society Review*, 15: 525–66.

Miller, Susan L. and Barberet, Rosemary (1995) 'A cross-cultural comparison of social reform: the growing pains of the battered women's movements in Washington, D.C. and Madrid, Spain', *Law & Social Inquiry*, 19: 923–66.

Milner, Neal (1989) 'The denigration of rights and the persistence of rights talk: a cultural portrait', *Law & Social Inquiry*, 14: 631–75.

Mirchandani, Rekha (2005) 'What's so special about specialized courts? The state and social change in Salt Lake City's Domestic Violence Court', *Law & Society Review*, 39: 379–417.

Misztal, Barbara A. (1993) 'Understanding political change in Eastern Europe: a sociological perspective', *Sociology*, 27: 451–70.

Miyazawa, Setsuo (1987) 'Taking Kawashima seriously: a review of Japanese research on Japanese legal consciousness and disputing behavior', *Law & Society Review*, 21: 219–41.

Monachesi, Elio (1960) 'Cesare Beccaria', in Mannheim, H. (ed.), *Pioneers in Criminology*, London, Stevens & Sons.

Monsma, Karl and Lempert, Richard (1992) 'The value of counsel: 20 years of representation before a public housing eviction board', *Law & Society Review*, 26: 627–67.

Mooney, Linda A. (1986) 'The behavior of law in a private legal system', *Social Forces*, 64: 733–50.

Moore, Dawn (2007) 'Translating justice and therapy: the drug treatment court networks', *British Journal of Criminology*, 47: 42–61.

Moorhead, Richard (2007) 'The passive arbiter: litigants in person and the challenge to neutrality', *Social & Legal Studies*, 16: 405–24.

Moorhead, Richard, Sefton, Mark and Scanlan, Lesley (2008) *Just satisfaction? What drives public and participant satisfaction with courts and tribunals*, Ministry of Justice Research Series 5/08, UK, Ministry of Justice.

Moorhead, Richard, Sherr, Avrom and Paterson, Alan (2003) 'Contesting professionalism: legal aid and nonlawyers in England and Wales', *Law & Society Review*, 37: 765–808.

Morgan, Megan (1996) 'Battered woman syndrome: women's experiences, expert evidence and legal discourse', Adelaide, Flinders University.

Morison, John and Leith, Philip (1992) *The Barrister's World: And the Nature of Law*, Milton Keynes, Open University Press.

Morris, Allison and Maxwell, Gabrielle M. (1993) 'Juvenile justice in New Zealand: a new paradigm', *Australian & New Zealand Journal of Criminology*, 26: 72–90.

Morris, Lydia (1997) 'Globalization, migration and the nation-state: the path to a post-national Europe?', *British Journal of Sociology*, 48: 192–209.

Mossman, Mary J. (1990) 'Women lawyers in twentieth century Canada: rethinking the image of "Portia"', in Graycar, R. (ed.), *Dissenting Opinions: Feminist Explorations in Law and Society*, Sydney, Allen & Unwin.

Mulcahy, Aogán (1994) 'The justifications of "justice": legal practitioners' accounts of negotiated case settlements in magistrates' courts', *British Journal of Criminology*, 34: 411–30.

Mulcahy, Linda (2001) 'The possibilities and desirability of mediator neutrality – towards an ethic of partiality?', *Social & Legal Studies*, 10: 505–27.

Münch, Richard (1992) 'Autopoiesis by definition', *Cardozo Law Review*, 13: 1463–71.

Mungham, Geoff and Bankowski, Zenon (1976) 'The jury in the legal system', in Carlen, P. (ed.), *Sociology of Law*, Sociological Review Monograph no. 23, Keele, University of Keele.

Murphy, Kristina (2005) 'Regulating more effectively: the relationship between procedural justice, legitimacy, and tax non-compliance', *Journal of Law & Society*, 32: 562–89.

Murphy, W. T. (1991) 'The oldest social science? The epistemic properties of the common law tradition', *Modern Law Review*, 54: 182–215.

Muzio, Daniel (2004) 'The professional project and the contemporary re-organisation of the legal profession in England and Wales', *International Journal of the Legal Profession*, 11: 33–50.

Muzio, Daniel and Ackroyd, Stephen (2005) 'On the consequences of defensive professionalism: recent changes in the legal labour process', *Journal of Law & Society*, 32: 615–42.

Nader, Laura (1979) 'Disputing without the force of law', *Yale Law Journal*, 88: 998–1021.

Nader, Laura and Metzger, Duane (1963) 'Conflict resolution in two Mexican communities', *American Anthropologist*, 65: 584–92.

Naffine, Ngaire (1990) *Law and the Sexes: Explorations in Feminist Jurisprudence*, Sydney, Allen & Unwin.

Naffine, Ngaire (1992) 'Windows on the legal mind: the evocation of rape in legal writings', *Melbourne University Law Review*, 18: 741–67.

Naffine, Ngaire (1997) *Feminism and Criminology*, Sydney, Allen and Unwin.

Naffine, Ngaire and Owens, Rosemary J. (eds) (1997) *Sexing the Subject of Law*, London, Sweet & Maxwell.

Nardulli, Peter (1979) 'The caseload controversy and the study of criminal courts', *Journal of Criminal Law & Criminology*, 70: 89–101.

Nash, Mike (1992) 'Dangerousness revisited', *International Journal of the Sociology of Law*, 20: 337–49.

National Crime Prevention Council (1996) *Working with Local Laws to Reduce Crime*, Washington, National Crime Prevention Council.

Nee, Victor (1989) 'A theory of market transition: from redistribution to markets in state socialism', *American Sociological Review*, 54: 663–81.

Nee, Victor and Matthews, Rebecca (1996) 'Market transition and societal transformations in reforming state socialism', *Annual Review of Sociology*, 22: 401–35.

Nelson, Robert L. (1981) 'Practice and privilege: social change and the structure of large law firms', *American Bar Foundation Research Journal*, Winter: 97–140.

Nelson, Robert L. (1983) 'The changing structure of opportunity: recruitment and careers in large law firms', *American Bar Foundation Research Journal*, Winter: 109–42.

New South Wales Law Reform Commission (1982) *Third Report on the Legal Profession: Advertising and Specialization*, Sydney, Law Society.

NJC Project Team (2007) *The Neighbourhood Justice Centre: Community Justice in Action in Victoria*, Victoria, Neighbourhood Justice Centre.

O'Donovan, Katherine (1993) 'Law's knowledge: the judge, the expert, the battered woman, and her syndrome', *Journal of Law & Society*, 20: 427–37.

O'Donovan, Katherine and Szyszczak, Erika (1988) *Equality and Sex Discrimination Law*, Oxford, Blackwell.

Offe, Claus (1985) 'New social movements: challenging the boundaries of institutional politics', *Social Research*, 52: 817–68.

O'Malley, Pat (1983) *Law, Capitalism and Democracy*, Sydney, George Allen & Unwin.

O'Malley, Pat (1987) 'Marxist theory and Marxist criminology', *Crime & Social Justice*, 29: 70–87.

Oppenheimer, Martin (1973) 'The proletarianization of the professional', in Halmos, P. (ed.), *Professionalisation and Social Change*, Sociological Review Monograph no. 20, Keele, University of Keele.

Orloff, Ann (1993) 'Gender and the social rights of citizenship: the comparative analysis of state policies and gender relations', *American Sociological Review*, 58: 303–28.

Orloff, Ann (1996) 'Gender in the welfare state', *Annual Review of Sociology*, 22: 51–78.

Packer, Herbert L. (1969) *The Limits of the Criminal Sanction*, Stanford, Stanford University Press.

Padgett, John E. (1985) 'The emergent organization of plea bargaining', *American Journal of Sociology*, 90: 753–800.

Padgett, John E. (1990) 'Plea bargaining and prohibition in the federal courts', *Law & Society Review*, 24: 413–50.

Pakulski, Jan (1991) *Social Movements: The Politics of Moral Protest*, Melbourne, Longman Cheshire.

Pakulski, Jan (1997) 'Cultural citizenship', *Citizenship Studies*, 1: 73–86.

Parker, Christine (1994) 'The logic of professionalism: stages of domination in legal service delivery to the disadvantaged', *International Journal of the Sociology of Law*, 22: 145–68.

Parker, Christine (1997) 'Converting the lawyers: the dynamics of competition and accountability reform', *Australian & New Zealand Journal of Sociology*, 33: 39–55.

Parsons, Talcott (ed.) (1947) *Max Weber, The Theory of Social and Economic Organisation*, New York, Free Press.

Parsons, Talcott (1951) *The Social System*, New York, Free Press.

Parsons, Talcott (1954) *Essays in Sociological Theory*, New York, Free Press.

Parsons, Talcott (1962) 'The law and social control', in Evan, W. M. (ed.), *The Law and Sociology: Exploratory Essays*, New York, Free Press.

Parsons, Talcott (1964a) 'Evolutionary universals in society', *American Sociological Review*, 29: 339–57.

Parsons, Talcott (1964b) 'Introduction', in Parsons, T. (ed.), *Max Weber: The Theory of Social and Economic Organizations*, New York, Free Press.

Parsons, Talcott (1967) 'Full citizenship for the Negro American? A sociological problem', in Parsons, T. and Clark, K.B. (eds), *The Negro American*, Boston, Beacon Press.

Parsons, Talcott (1971) 'Valued freedom and objectivity', in Stammer, O. (ed.), *Max Weber and Sociology Today*, Oxford, Basil Blackwell.

Parsons, Talcott (1976) 'Social structure and the symbolic media of interchange', in Blau, P.M. (ed.), *Approaches to the Study of Social Structure*, London, Open Books.

Parsons, Talcott (1978) 'Law as an intellectual stepchild', in Johnson, H.M. (ed.), *Social System and Legal Process*, San Francisco, Jossey-Bass.

Pate, Antony M. and Hamilton, Edwin E. (1992) 'Formal and informal deterrents to domestic violence: the Dade County spouse assault experiment', *American Sociological Review*, 57: 691–7.

Pateman, Carole (1988) *The Sexual Contract*, Cambridge, Polity-Press.

Pawson, R. and Tilley, N. (1994) 'What works in evaluation research', *British Journal of Criminology*, 34: 291–306.

Pedriana, Nicholas (2006) 'From protective to equal treatment: legal framing processes and transformation of the women's movement in the 1960s', *American Journal of Sociology*, 111: 1718–61.

Peneff, Jean (1988) 'The observers observed: French survey researchers at work', *Social Problems*, 35: 520–35.

Petchesky, Rosalind Pollack (1986) *Abortion and Woman's Choice: The State, Sexuality, and Reproductive Freedom*, London, Verso.

Petchesky, Rosalind Pollack (1987) 'Fetal images: the power of visual culture in the politics of reproduction', *Feminist Studies*, 13: 263–92.

Petersen, Kerry A. (1993) *Abortion Regimes*, Aldershot, Dartmouth.

Pettit, Becky and Western, Bruce (2004) 'Mass imprisonment and the life course: race and class inequality in U.S. incarceration', *American Sociological Review*, 69: 151–69.

Pickering, Sharon (2004) 'The production of sovereignty and the rise of transversal policing: people-smuggling and federal policing', *Australian & New Zealand Journal of Criminology*, 37: 362–80.

Pierce, Jennifer (1996) 'Rambo litigators: emotional labor in a male-dominated occupation', in Chery, C. (ed.), *Masculinities in Organizations*, London, Sage.

Plotnikoff, Joyce and Woolfson, Richard (2005) *Review of the Effectiveness of Specialist Courts in Other Jurisdictions*, DCA Research Series 3/05, UK, Department of Constitutional Affairs.

Polan, Diane (1982) 'Toward a theory of law and patriarchy', in Kairys, D. (ed.), *The Politics of Law: A Progressive Critique*, New York, Pantheon Books.

Popovic, Jelena (2002) 'Judicial officers: complementing conventional law and changing the culture of the judiciary', *Law in Context*, 20: 121–36.

Poulantzas, Nicos (1978) *State, Power, Socialism*, London, NLB.

Powell, Michael J. (1985) 'Developments in the regulation of lawyers: competing segments and market, client, and government controls', *Social Forces*, 64: 281–305.

Powell, Michael J. (1993) 'Professional innovation: corporate lawyers and private law making', *Law & Social Inquiry*, 18: 423–52.

Prest, Wilfrid R. (1986) *The Rise of the Barristers: A Social History of the English Bar 1590–1640*, Oxford, Clarendon Press.

Quinney, Richard (1970) *The Social Reality of Crime*, Boston, Little Brown.

Quinney, Richard (1975) 'Crime control in capitalist society: a critical philosophy of legal order', in Taylor, I., Waldon, P. and Young, J. (eds), *Critical Criminology*, London, Routledge & Kegan Paul.

Quinney, Richard (1977) *Class, State, and Crime: On the Theory and Practice of Criminal Justice*, New York, Longman.

Quinney, Richard (1978) 'The production of a Marxist criminology', *Contemporary Crises*, 2: 277–92.

Rackley, Erika (2006) 'Difference in the House of Lords', *Social & Legal Studies*, 15: 163–85.

Randall, Kenneth C. (1988) 'Universal jurisdiction under international law', *Texas Law Review*, 66: 785–841.

Rehg, William (1996) 'Translator's introduction', in Habermas, J. (ed.), *Between Facts and Norms: Contributions to a Discourse Theory of Law and Democracy*, Cambridge, Polity Press.

Reichman, Nancy (1986) 'Managing crime risks: toward an insurance based model of social control', *Research in Law, Deviance and Social Control*, 8: 51–72.

Renner, Karl (1969) 'The development of capitalist property and the legal institutions complementary to the property norm', in Aubert, V. (ed.), *Sociology of Law*, Harmondsworth, Penguin.

Reskin, Barbara and Padavic, Irene (1994) *Women and Men at Work*, Thousand Oaks, Pine Forge Press.

Reynolds, Frank E. (1994) 'Dhamma in dispute: the interactions of religion and law in Thailand', *Law & Society Review*, 28: 433–51.

Rheinstein, Max (1954) 'Introduction', in *Max Weber on Law in Economy and Society*, Cambridge, Harvard University Press.

Rifkin, Janet (1980) 'Toward a theory of law and patriarchy', *Harvard Women's Law Journal*, 3: 83–95.

Ritzer, George (1975) 'Professionalization, bureaucratization, and rationalization: the views of Max Weber', *Social Forces*, 53: 627–34.

Roach Anleu, Sharyn L. (1992a) 'Critiquing the law: themes and dilemmas in Anglo-American feminist legal theory', *Journal of Law & Society*, 19: 423–40.

Roach Anleu, Sharyn L. (1992b) 'The legal profession in the United States and Australia: deprofessionalization or reorganization?', *Work & Occupations*, 19: 184–204.

Roach Anleu, Sharyn L. (1993) 'Reproductive autonomy: infertility, deviance and conceptive technology', *Law in Context*, 11: 17–40.

Roach Anleu, Sharyn L. (1996) 'Regulating new reproductive technologies: an examination of the emergence of legislation in two Australian states', *Perspectives on Social Problems*, 8: 175–97.

Roach Anleu, Sharyn L. (1998) 'The role of civil sanctions in social control: a sociolegal examination', in Mazerolle, L.G. and Roehl, J. (eds), *Civil Remedies*, New York, Criminal Justice Press.

Roach Anleu, Sharyn (2006) *Deviance, Conformity and Control*, 4th edn, Frenchs Forest, NSW, Pearson Education Australia.

Roach Anleu, Sharyn and Mack, Kathy (2007) 'Magistrates, magistrates courts and social change', *Law & Policy*, 29: 183–209.

Roach Anleu, Sharyn and Mack, Kathy (2009) 'Gender, judging and job satisfaction', *Feminist Legal Studies*, 17: 183–209.

Roach Anleu, Sharyn and Prest, Wilfrid R. (2004) 'Litigation: historical and contemporary dimensions', in Prest, W.R. and Roach Anleu, S. (eds), *Litigation: Past and Present*, Sydney, University of New South Wales Press.

Roberts, Simon (1992) 'Mediation in the lawyers' embrace', *Modern Law Review*, 55: 258–64.

Roberts, Simon (1993) 'Alternative dispute resolution and civil justice: an unresolved relationship', *Modern Law Review*, 56: 452–70.

Roberts, Michael and Michael Palmer (2005) *Dispute Processes: ADR and the Primary Forms of Decision-Making*, 2nd edn, Cambridge, Cambridge University Press.

Robertson, Roland (1992) *Globalization: Social Theory and Global Culture*, London, Sage.

Roche, Maurice (1987) 'Citizenship, social theory and social change', *Theory & Society*, 16: 363–99.

Roche, Maurice (1995) 'Review article: citizenship and modernity', *British Journal of Sociology*, 46: 715–33.

Rock, Paul (1998) 'Rules, boundaries and the courts: some problems in the neo-Durkheimian sociology of deviance', *British Journal of Sociology*, 49: 586–601.

Roehl, Janice A. and Cook, Roger A. (1982) 'The neighborhood justice centers field test', in Tomasic, R. and Feeley, M.M. (eds), *Neighborhood Justice: Assessment of an Emerging Idea*, New York, Longman.

Rose, Vicki McNickle (1977) 'Rape as a social problem: a byproduct of the feminist movement', *Social Problems*, 25: 75–89.

Rosenberg, Dorothy J. (1991) 'Shock therapy: GDR women in transition from a socialist welfare state to a social market economy', *Signs: Journal of Women in Culture and Society*, 17: 129–51.

Rosenberg, Gerald N. (2008) *The Hollow Hope: Can Courts Bring About Social Change?*, 2nd edn, Chicago, University of Chicago Press.

Rosenberg, Janet, Perlstadt, Harry and Phillips, William R.E. (1993) 'Now that we are here: discrimination, disparagement, and harassment at work and the experience of women lawyers', *Gender & Society*, 7: 415–33.

Ross, Edward Alsworth (1896) 'Social control', *American Journal of Sociology*, 1: 513–35.

Ross, Susan Deller (1992) 'Proving sexual harassment: the hurdles', *Southern California Law Review*, 65: 1451–8.

Roth, Julius A. (1974) 'Professionalism: the sociologist's decoy', *Sociology of Work & Occupations*, 1: 6–23.

Rothman, Barbara K. (1989) *Recreating Motherhood: Ideology and Technology in a Patriarchal Society*, New York, Norton.

Rothman, Robert A. (1984) 'Deprofessionalization: the case of law in America', *Work & Occupations*, 11: 183–206.

Rottleuthner, Hubert (1988) 'Biological metaphors in legal thought', in Teubner, G. (ed.), *Autopoietic Law: A New Approach to Law and Society*, New York, Walter de Gruyter.

Rubinstein, Michael L. and White, Teresa J. (1979) 'Alaska's ban on plea bargaining', *Law & Society Review*, 13: 367–83.

Sajo, Andras (1990) 'New legalism in east central Europe: law as an instrument of social transformation', *Journal of Law &Society*, 17: 329–42.

Sallmann, Peter A. (1991) 'In search of the holy grail of sentencing: an overview of some recent trends and developments', *Journal of Judicial Administration*, 1: 125–47.

Sandefur, Rebecca L. (2001) 'Work and honor in the law: prestige and the division of lawyers' labor', *American Sociological Review*, 66: 382–403.

Sandefur, Rebecca L. (2008) 'Access to civil justice and race, class, and gender inequality', *Annual Review of Sociology*, 34: 339–58.

Sandelowski, Margarete (1990) 'Fault lines: infertility and imperiled sisterhood', *Feminist Studies*, 16: 33–51.

Sander, Frank E. A. (1985) 'Alternative methods of dispute resolution: an overview', *University of Florida Law Review*, 37: 1–18.

Sander, Richard H. and Williams, Douglass E. (1989) 'Why are there so many lawyers? Perspectives on a turbulent market', *Law & Social Enquiry*, 14: 431–79.

Santos, Boaventura de Sousa (1987) 'Law: a map of misreading. Toward a post-modern conception of law', *Journal of Law & Society*, 14: 279–302.

Santos, Boaventura de Sousa (1995) 'Three metaphors for a conception of law: the frontier, the baroque and the south', *Law & Society Review*, 29: 569–84.

Sarat, Austin (1976) 'Alternatives in dispute processing: litigation in a small claims court', *Law & Society Review*, 10: 339–75.

Sarat, Austin and Felstiner, William L. (1986) 'Law and strategy in the divorce lawyer's office', *Law & Society Review*, 20: 93–134.

Sarat, Austin and Grossman, Joel (1975) 'Courts and conflict resolution: problems in the mobilization of adjudication', *American Political Science Review*, 69: 1200–17.

Savelsberg, Joachim J. (1992) 'Law that does not fit society: sentencing guidelines as a neoclassical reaction to the dilemmas of substantivized law', *American Journal of Sociology*, 97: 1346–81.

Savelsberg, Joachim J. (1994) 'Knowledge, domination, and criminal punishment', *American Journal of Sociology*, 99: 911–43.

Savelsberg, Joachim J. and King, Ryan D. (2005) 'Institutionalizing collective memories of hate: law and law enforcement in Germany and the United States', *American Journal of Sociology*, 111: 579–616.

Scales, Ann (1994) 'Avoiding constitutional depression: bad attitudes and the fate of Butler', *Canadian Journal of Women and the Law/Revue Femmes et Droit*, 7: 349–92.

Scheingold, Stuart A. (1974) *The Politics of Rights: Lawyers, Public Policy and Political Change*, New Haven, Yale University Press.

Scheingold, Stuart A., Olson, Toska and Pershing, Jana (1994) 'Sexual violence, victim advocacy, and republican criminology: Washington state's Community Protection Act', *Law & Society Review*, 28: 729–63.

Scheppele, Kim Lane (1992) 'Just the facts, Ma'am: sexualized violence, evidentiary habits, and the revision of truth', *New York Law School Review*, 37: 123–72.

Scheppele, Kim Lane (1995) 'Manners of imagining the real', *Law & Social Inquiry*, 20: 995–1022.

Scheppele, Kim Lane (1996) 'The history of normalcy: rethinking legal autonomy and the relative dependence of law at the end of the Soviet Empire', *Law & Society Review*, 30: 627–50.

Schmid, Carol (1988) 'The Supreme Court, civil rights and racial equality: a sociological interpretation', *Research in Law, Deviance and Social Control*, 9: 63–84.

Schneider, Beth E. (1991) 'Put up and shut up: workplace sexual assaults', *Gender & Society*, 5: 533–48.

Schneider, Elizabeth M. (1986) 'The dialectic of rights and politics: perspectives from the women's movement', *New York University Law Review*, 61: 589–652.

Schneider, Elizabeth M. (1988) 'Task force reports on women in the courts: the challenge for legal education', *Journal of Legal Education*, 38: 87–95.

Schuck, Peter H. (1987) *Agent Orange on Trial: Mass Toxic Disasters in the Courts*, Cambridge, Belknap Press.

Schulhofer, Stephen J. (1984) 'Is plea bargaining inevitable?', *Harvard Law Review*, 97: 1037–107.

Schulhofer, Stephen J. (1985) 'No job too small: justice without bargaining in the lower criminal courts', *American Bar Foundation Research Journal*, Summer: 519–98.

Schultz, Ulrike and Shaw, Gisela (eds) (2003) *Women in the World's Legal Professions*, Oxford and Portland, OR, Hart Publishing.

Schultz, Ulrike and Shaw, Gisela (2008) 'Editorial: Gender and judging', *International Journal of the Legal Profession*, 15: 1–5.

Schwartz, Richard D. (1965) 'Introduction', *Law and Society*, Summer: 1–3.

Schwartz, Richard D. (1974) 'Legal evolution and the Durkheim hypothesis: a reply to Professor Baxi', *Law & Society Review*, 8: 645–68.

Schwartz, Richard D. and Miller, James (1964) 'Legal evolution and societal complexity', *American Journal of Sociology*, 70: 159–69.

Sciulli, David (1995) 'Donald Black's positivism in law and social control', *Law & Social Inquiry*, 20: 805–28.

Scott, Shirley V. (2004) 'International law as litigation strategy for indigenous Australians: a comparison of the *Mabo* and *Nulyarimma* cases', in Prest, W.R. and Roach Anleu, S. (eds), *Litigation: Past and Present*, Sydney, University of New South Wales Press.

Scott, W. R. (1966) 'Professionals in bureaucracies – areas of conflict', in Vollmer, H.M. and Mills, D.L. (eds), *Professionalization*, Englewood Cliffs, Prentice-Hall.

Scutt, Jocelynne A. (1988) 'The privatisation of justice: power differentials, inequality and the palliative of counselling and mediation', *Women's Studies International Forum*, 11: 503–20.

Selznick, Philip (1982) 'Sociology and natural law', in Black, D. and Mileski, M. (eds), *The Social Organization of Law*, New York, Seminar Press.

Senate Standing Committee on Legal and Constitutional Affairs (1994) *Gender Bias and the Judiciary*, Canberra, Government of Australia.

Seron, Carroll (1996) *The Business of Practicing Law: The Work Lives of Solo and Small Firm Attorneys*, Philadelphia, Temple University Press.

Seron, Carroll and Ferris, Kerry (1995) 'Negotiating professionalism: the gendered social capital of flexible time', *Work & Occupations*, 22: 22–48.

Sewell, William H., Jr. (1992) 'A theory of structure: duality, agency, and transformation', *American Journal of Sociology*, 98: 1–30.

Shamir, Ronen (1990) '"Landmark cases" and the reproduction of legitimacy: the case of Israel's High Court of Justice', *Law & Society Review*, 24: 781–805.

Shapland, Joanna, Atkinson, Anne, Atkinson, Helen, Dignan, James, Edwards, Lucy, Hibbert, Jeremy, Howes, Marie, Johnstone, Jennifer, Robinson, Gwen and Sorsby, Angela (2008) *Does restorative justice affect reconviction? The fourth report from the evaluation of three schemes*, Ministry of Justice Research Series 10/08, Ministry of Justice, UK.

Shaver, Sheila (1990) *Gender, Social Policy Regimes and the Welfare State*, Discussion Papers, Sydney, University of New South Wales Social Policy Research Centre.

Shaver, Sheila (1992) *Body Rights, Social Rights and the Liberal Welfare State*, Discussion Papers, Sydney, University of New South Wales Social Policy Research Centre.

Shaver, Sheila (1995) 'Women, employment and social security', in Edwards, A. and Magarey, S. (eds), *Women in a Restructuring Australia: Work and Welfare*, Sydney, Allen & Unwin.

Shaw, Jo (2003) 'The European Union: discipline building meets polity building', in Cane, P. and Tushnet, M. (eds), *The Oxford Handbook of Legal Studies*, Oxford, Oxford University Press.

Sheehy, Elizabeth A., Stubbs, Julie and Tolmie, Julia (1992) 'Defending battered women on trial: the battered woman syndrome and its limitations', *Criminal Law Journal*, 16: 369–94.

Sheleff, Leon Shaskolsky (1975) 'From restitutive to repressive law: Durkheim's *Division of Labor in Society* revisited', *Archives Européennes de Sociologie*, 16: 16–45.

Sherman, Lawrence W. and Berk, Richard A. (1984) 'The specific deterrent effects of arrest for domestic assault', *American Sociological Review*, 49: 261–71.

Sherman, Lawrence W., Smith, Douglas with Schmidt, Janell D. and Rogan, Dennis P. (1992) 'Crime, punishment, and stake in conformity: legal and informal control of domestic violence', *American Sociological Review*, 57: 680–90.

Sieder, Rachel (2007) 'The judiciary and indigenous rights in Guatemala', *I-Con*, 5: 211–41.

Silbey, Susan S. (1991) 'Loyalty and betrayal: Cotterrell's discovery and reproduction of legal ideology', *Law & Social Inquiry*, 16: 809–33.

Silbey, Susan S. (1997) '"Let them eat cake": globalization, postmodern colonialism, and the possibilities of justice', *Law & Society Review*, 31: 207–35.

Silbey, Susan and Sarat, Austin (1989) 'Dispute processing in law and legal scholarship: from institutional critique to the reconstruction of the juridical subject', *Denver University Law Review*, 66: 437–98.

Simon, Jonathan (1987) 'The emergence of a risk society: insurance, law and the state', *Socialist Review*, 95: 61–89.

Simon, Jonathan (1988) 'The ideological effects of actuarial practices', *Law & Society Review*, 22: 771–800.

Skrbis, Zlatko, Kendall, Gavin and Woodward, Ian (2004) 'Locating cosmopolitanism: between humanist ideal and grounded social category', *Theory, Culture & Society*, 21: 115–36.

Skrentny, John D. (2006) 'Law and the American state', *Annual Review of Sociology*, 32: 213–45.

Smart, Carol (1984) *The Ties that Bind: Law, Marriage and the Reproduction of Patriarchal Relations*, London, Routledge and Kegan Paul.

Smart, Carol (1986) 'Feminism and law: some problems of analysis and strategy', *International Journal of the Sociology of Law*, 14: 109–23.

Smart, Carol (1987) '"There is of course the distinction dictated by nature": law and the problem of paternity', in Stanworth, M. (ed.), *Reproductive Technologies: Gender, Motherhood and Medicine*, Cambridge, Polity Press.

Smart, Carol (1989) *Feminism and the Power of Law*, London, Routledge.

Smart, Carol (1990) 'Law's power, the sexed body, and feminist discourse', *Journal of Law & Society*, 17: 194–210.

Smart, Carol (1991) 'Penetrating women's bodies: the problem of law and medical technology', in Abbott, P. and Wallace, C. (eds), *Gender, Power and Sexuality*, London, Macmillan.

Smigel, Erwin O. (1960) 'The impact of recruitment on the organization of the large firm', *American Sociological Review*, 25: 56–66.

Smigel, Erwin O. (1964) *The Wall Street Lawyer: Professional Organization Man?*, Glencoe, Free Press.

Smith, Anna Marie (1993) '"What is pornography?" An analysis of the policy statement of the Campaign Against Pornography and Censorship', *Feminist Review*, 43: 71–87.

Smith, Philip (2008a) 'Durkheim and criminology: reconstructing the legacy', *Australian & New Zealand Journal of Criminology*, 41: 333–44.

Smith, Philip (2008b) *Punishment and Culture*, Chicago, Chicago University Press.

Snyder, Francis G. (1981) 'Anthropology, dispute processes and law: a critical introduction', *British Journal of Law & Society*, 8: 41–80.

Sokoloff, Natalie J. (1992) *Black Women and White Women in the Professions: Occupational Segregation by Race and Gender, 1960–1980*, New York, Routledge.

Solomon, David (1992) *The Political Impact of the High Court*, Sydney, Allen & Unwin.

Somers, Margaret R. (1993) 'Citizenship and the place of the public sphere: law, community and political culture in the transition to democracy', *American Sociological Review*, 58: 587–620.

Somers, Margaret R. (1994) 'Rights, relationality and membership: rethinking the making and meaning of citizenship', *Law & Social Inquiry*, 19: 63–112.

Sommerlad, Hilary (2002) 'Women solicitors in a fractured profession: intersections of gender and professionalism in England and Wales', *International Journal of the Legal Profession*, 9: 213–34.

Sommerlad, Hilary and Sanderson, Peter (1998) *Gender, Choice and Commitment: Women Solicitors in England and Wales and the Struggle for Equal Status*, Dartmouth, Ashgate.

Soothill, Keith, Sylvia, Walby and Bagguley, Paul (1990) 'Judges, the media, and rape', *Journal of Law & Society*, 17: 211–23.

Sørensen, Annemette and Trappe, Heike (1995) 'The persistence of gender inequality in earnings in the German Democratic Republic', *American Sociological Review*, 60: 398–406.

Spangler, Eve (1986) *Lawyers for Hire: Salaried Professionals at Work*, New Haven, Yale University Press.

Spelman, Elizabeth V. (1988) *Inessential Woman: Problems of Exclusion in Feminist Thought*, Boston, Beacon Press.

Spitzer, Steven (1975a) 'Punishment and social organization: a study of Durkheim's theory of penal evolution', *Law & Society Review*, 9: 613–35.

Spitzer, Steven (1975b) 'Toward a Marxian theory of deviance', *Social Problems*, 22: 638–51.

Spitzer, Steven (1979) 'Notes toward a theory of punishment and social change', *Research in Law and Sociology*, 2: 207–29.

Spohn, Cassia, Gruhl, John and Welch, Susan (1981) 'The effect of race and sentencing: a re-examination of an unsettled question', *Law & Society Review*, 16: 71–88.

Stager, David A.A. and Foot, David (1988) 'Changes in lawyers' earnings: the impact of differentiation and growth in the Canadian legal profession', *Law & Social Inquiry*, 13: 71–85.

Staggenborg, Suzanne (1989) 'Organizational and environmental influences on the development of the pro-choice movement', *Social Forces*, 68: 204–40.

Staggenborg, Suzanne (1995) 'Can feminist organizations be effective?', in Ferree, M.M. and Martin, P.Y. (eds), *Feminist Organizations: Harvest of the New Women's Movement*, Philadelphia, Temple University Press.

Stalans, Loretta J. and Finn, Mary A. (1995) 'How novice and experienced officers interpret wife assaults: normative and efficiency frames', *Law & Society Review*, 29: 287–321.

Stark, David (1996) 'Recombinant property in East European capitalism', *American Journal of Sociology*, 101: 993–1027.

Steffensmeier, Darrell, Kramer, John and Streifel, Cathy (1993) 'Gender and imprisonment decisions', *Criminology*, 31: 411–46.

Steiner, Eva (1991) 'Prosecuting war criminals in England and France', *Criminal Law Review*: 180–8.

Stewart, Iain (1990) 'The critical legal science of Hans Kelsen', *Journal of Law & Society*, 17: 273–308.

Stolzenberg, Lisa and D'Alessio, Stewart J. (1994) 'Sentencing and unwarranted disparity: an empirical assessment of the long-term impact of sentencing guidelines in Minnesota', *Criminology*, 32: 301–10.

Stone, Alan (1985) 'The place of law in the Marxian structure-superstructure archetype', *Law & Society Review*, 19: 39–67.

Stychin, Carl (1995) *Law's Desire: Sexuality and the Limits of Justice*, London, Routledge.

Sudnow, David (1965) 'Normal crimes: sociological features of the penal code in a public defender's office', *Social Problems*, 12: 255–76.

Sullivan, Rohan (1994) 'Wife joins storm over sex remarks', *The Australian*, Wednesday, January 13: 1–2.

Sumner, Colin (1979) *Reading Ideologies: an Investigation into the Marxist Theory of Ideology and Law*, London, Academic Press.

Symonds, Michael and Pudsey, Jason (2008) 'The concept of "paradox" in the work of Max Weber', *Sociology*, 42: 223–52.

Szelényi, Ivan and Kostello, Eric (1996) 'The market transition debate: toward a synthesis?', *American Journal of Sociology*, 101: 1082–96.

Tait, David (2002) 'Sentencing as performance: restoring drama to the courtroom', in Tata, C. and Hutton, N. (eds), *Sentencing and Society: International Perspectives*, Aldershot, Ashgate.

Tannen, Ricki Lewis (1990) 'Report of the Florida Supreme Court Gender Bias Study Commission', *Florida Law Review*, 42: 803–997.

Tata, Cyrus (2002) 'Accountability for sentencing decision process – Towards a new understanding', in Tata, C. and Hutton, N. (eds), *Sentencing and Society: International Perspectives*, Aldershot, Ashgate.

Tata, Cyrus (2007a) 'In the interests of clients or commerce? Legal aid, supply, demand, and "ethical indeterminacy" in criminal defence work', *Journal of Law & Society*, 34: 489–519.

Tata, Cyrus (2007b) 'Sentencing as craftwork and the binary epistemologies of the discretionary decision process', *Social & Legal Studies*, 16: 425–47.

Tata, Cyrus and Hutton, Neil (eds) (2002) *Sentencing and Society: International Perspectives*, Aldershot, Ashgate.

Tata, Cyrus and Stephen, Frank (2006) '"Swings and roundabouts": do changes to the structure of legal aid remuneration make a real difference to criminal case management and case outcomes?', *Criminal Law Review*, 8: 722–41.

Taub, Nadine and Schneider, Elizabeth M. (1982) 'Perspectives on women's subordination and the role of law', in Kairys, D. (ed.), *The Politics of Law: A Progressive Critique*, New York, Pantheon.

Taylor, Ian, Walton, Paul and Young, Jock (1973) *The New Criminology: For a Social Theory of Deviance*, London, Routledge & Kegan Paul.

Terdiman, R. (1987) 'Translator's introduction to "The force of law: toward a sociology of the juridical field" by Pierre Bourdieu', *Hastings Law Journal*, 38: 805–13.

Teubner, Gunther (1983) 'Substantive and reflexive elements in modern laws', *Law & Society Review*, 17: 239–85.

Teubner, Gunther (1984) 'After legal instrumentalism? Strategic models of postregulatory law', *International Journal of the Sociology of Law*, 12: 375–400.

Teubner, Gunther (1986) 'The transformation of law in the welfare state', in Teubner, G. (ed.), *Dilemmas of Law in the Welfare State*, New York, Walter de Gruyter.

Teubner, Gunther (1987) 'Juridification – concepts, aspects, limits, solutions', in Teubner, G. (ed.), *Juridification of Social Spheres: A Comparative Analysis in the Areas of Labor, Corporate, Antitrust and Social Welfare Law*, New York, Walter de Gruyter.

Teubner, Gunther (1989) 'How the law thinks: toward a constructivist epistemology of law', *Law & Society Review*, 23: 727–57.

Thomas, D. A. (1970) *Principles of Sentencing: The Sentencing Policy of the Court of Appeal Criminal Division*, London, Heinemann.

Thompson, E. P. (1975) *Whigs and Hunters: The Origin of the Black Act*, New York, Pantheon.

Thornton, Margaret (1986) 'Feminist jurisprudence: illusion or reality?', *Australian Journal of Law and Society*, 3: 5–29.

Thornton, Margaret (1990) *The Liberal Promise: Anti-Discrimination Legislation in Australia*, Melbourne, Oxford University Press.

Thornton, Margaret (1991) 'Feminism and the contradictions of law reform', *International Journal of the Sociology of Law*, 19: 453–74.

Thornton, Margaret (2007) '"Otherness" on the bench: how merit is gendered', *Sydney Law Review*, 29: 391–413.

Thornton, Margaret and Bagust, Joanne (2007) 'The gender trap: flexible work in corporate legal practice', *Osgoode Hall Law Journal*, 45: 773–811.

Tierney, Kathleen (1982) 'The battered women movement and the creation of the wife beating problem', *Social Problems*, 29: 207–20.

Tocqueville, Alexis de (1969) *Democracy in America*, Garden City, Doubleday.

Tomasic, Roman (1982) 'Mediation as an alternative to adjudication: rhetoric and reality in the neighborhood justice movement', in Tomasic, R. and Feeley, M.M. (eds), *Neighborhood Justice: Assessment of an Emerging Idea*, New York, Longman.

Tomasic, R. and Bullard, C. (1978) *Lawyers and their Work*, Sydney, Law Association of New South Wales.

Tomasic, Roman and Feeley, Malcolm M. (1982) 'Introduction', in Tomasic, R. and Feeley, M.M. (eds), *Neighborhood Justice: Assessment of an Emerging Idea*, New York, Longman.

Tomaskovic-Devey, Donald and Roscigno, Vincent J. (1996) 'Racial economic subordination and white gain in the U.S. South', *American Sociological Review*, 61: 565–89.

Tombs, Jacqueline and Jagger, Elizabeth (2006) 'Denying responsibility: sentencers' accounts of their decisions to imprison', *British Journal of Criminology*, 46: 803–21.

Tomsen, Stephen (1992) 'Professionalism and state engagement: lawyers and legal aid policy in Australia in the 1970s and 1980s', *Australian & New Zealand Journal of Sociology*, 28: 307–29.

Tonry, Michael H. (1987) 'Sentencing guidelines and sentencing commissions: the second generation', in Wasik, M. and Pease, K. (eds), *Sentencing Reform: Guidance or Guidelines*, Manchester, Manchester University Press.

Tonry, Michael (1991) 'The politics and processes of sentencing commissions', *Crime & Delinquency*, 37: 307–29.

Tonry, Michael (1993) 'The failure of the US Sentencing Commission's guidelines', *Crime & Delinquency*, 39: 131–49.

Touraine, Alain (1985) 'An introduction to the study of social movements', *Social Research*, 52: 749–87.

Trade Practices Commission (1994) *Study of the Professions – Legal: Summary of Final Report*, Canberra, Australian Government Publishing Service.

Tranter, Bruce (1996) 'The social bases of environmentalism in Australia', *Australian & New Zealand Journal of Sociology*, 32: 61–84.

Travers, Max (1993) 'Putting sociology back into the sociology of law', *Journal of Law & Society*, 20: 438–51.

Travers, Max (2005a) 'Evaluation research and criminal justice: beyond a political critique', *Australian & New Zealand Journal of Criminology*, 38: 39–58.

Travers, Max (2005b) 'Evaluation research and legal services', in Banakar, R. and Travers, M. (eds), *Theory and Method in Sociol-Legal Research*, Oxford, Hart Publishing.

Travers, Max (2007a) 'Sentencing in the Children's Court: an ethnographic perspective', *Youth Justice*, 7: 21–35.

Travers, Max (2007b) *The New Bureaucracy: Quality Assurance and its Critics*, Bristol, Policy.

Treiman, Donald J. and Hartmann, Heidi I. (1981) *Women, Work and Wages: Equal Pay for Jobs of Equal Value*, Washington, National Academy Press.

Trubek, David M. (1972) 'Max Weber on law and the rise of capitalism', *Wisconsin Law Review*, 3: 720–53.

Trubek, David M. (1984) 'Where the action is: critical legal studies and empiricism', *Stanford Law Review*, 36: 575–622.

Trubek, David M. (1986) 'Max Weber's tragic modernism and the study of law in society', *Law & Society Review*, 20: 573–98.

Tunc, André (1984) 'The not so common law of England and the United States, or, precedent in England and in the United States, a field study by an outsider', *Modern Law Review*, 47: 150–70.

Turner, Bryan S. (1981) *For Weber: Essays on the Sociology of Fate*, Boston, Routledge & Kegan Paul.

Turner, Bryan S. (1990) 'Outline of a theory of citizenship', *Sociology*, 24: 189–217.

Turner, Bryan S. (1993) 'Outline of a theory of human rights', *Sociology*, 27: 489–512.

Turner, Bryan S. (1997) 'Citizenship studies: a general theory', *Citizenship Studies*, 1: 1–18.

Turner, Bryan S. (2001) 'The erosion of citizenship', *British Journal of Sociology*, 52: 189–209.

Tushnet, Mark (1984) 'An essay on rights', *Texas Law Review*, 62: 1363–403.

Twining, William (1993) 'Alternative to what? Theories of litigation, procedure and dispute settlement in Anglo-American jurisprudence: some neglected classics', *Modern Law Review*, 56: 380–92.

Tyler, Tom R. (1990) *Why People Obey the Law*, New Haven, Yale University Press.

Tyler, Tom R. and Boeckmann, Robert J. (1997) 'Three strikes and you are out, but why? The psychology of public support for punishing rule breakers', *Law & Society Review*, 31: 237–65.

United Nations (1945) *Charter of the United Nations*, Geneva, UN.

United States Bureau of the Census (1994) *Statistical Abstract of the United States: 1994*, US Government Printing Office.

United States District Court (1986) 'Offer of proof concerning the testimony of Dr. Rosalind Rosenberg in *EEOC v Sears Roebuck*', *Signs: Journal of Women in Culture and Society*, 11: 757–66.

Upham, Frank K. (1976) 'Litigation and moral consciousness in Japan: an interpretative analysis of four Japanese pollution suits', *Law & Society Review*, 10: 579–619.

Van Hoy, Jerry (1995) 'Selling and processing law: legal work at franchise law firms', *Law & Society Review*, 29: 703–29.

Vaughan, Diane (1998) 'Rational choice, situated action, and the social control of organizations', *Law & Society Review*, 32: 23–61.

Vaughan, Diane (1999) 'The dark side of organizations: mistake, misconduct, and disaster', *Annual Review of Sociology*: 271–305.

Villmoore, Adelaide H. (1991) 'Women, differences and rights as practices: an interpretive essay and a proposal', *Law & Society Review*, 25: 385–410.

Vincent, Andrew (1993) 'Marx and law', *Journal of Law & Society*, 20: 371–97.

Vogel, David (1986) *National Styles of Regulation: Environmental Policy in Great Britain and the United States*, Ithaca, Cornell University Press.

Vogel, Lise (1990) 'Debating difference: feminism, pregnancy and the workplace', *Feminist Studies*, 16: 9–32.

von Hirsch, Andrew (1976) *Doing Justice: The Choice of Punishments*, New York, Hill & Wang.

Wagatsuma, Hiroshi and Rosett, Arthur (1986) 'The implications of apology: law and culture in Japan and the United States', *Law & Society Review*, 20: 461–98.

Wagner, J. M. (1989) 'U.S. prosecution of past and future war criminals and criminals against humanity: proposals for reform based on the Canadian and Australian experience', *Virginia Journal of International Law*, 29: 887–936.

Waller, L. and Williams, C. R. (1993) *Criminal Law: Texts and Cases*, Sydney, Butterworths.

Waters, Malcolm (1989) 'Collegiality, bureaucratization, and professionalization: a Weberian analysis', *American Journal of Sociology*, 94: 945–72.

Waters, Malcolm (1994) 'A world of difference', *Australian & New Zealand Journal of Sociology*, 30: 229–34.

Waters, Malcolm (1995) 'Globalisation and the social construction of human rights', *Australian & New Zealand Journal of Sociology*, 31: 29–36.

Waters, Malcolm (1996) 'Human rights and the universalisation of interests: towards a social constructionist approach', *Sociology*, 30: 593–600.

Watson, Irene and Heath, Mary (2004) 'Growing up the space: a conversation about the future of feminism', *Australian Feminist Law Journal*, 20: 95–111.

Watson, Peggy (1993) 'Eastern Europe's silent revolution: gender', *Sociology*, 27: 471–87.

Weatherburn, Don (1985) 'Appellate review, judicial discretion and the determination of minimum periods', *Australian & New Zealand Journal of Criminology*, 18: 272–83.

Weatherburn, Don (2005) 'Critical criminology and its discontents: a response to Travers' critique of criminal justice evaluation', *Australian & New Zealand Journal of Criminology*, 38: 416–20.

Weber, Max (1947) *The Theory of Social and Economic Organisation*, New York, Free Press.

Weber, Max (1978) *Economy and Society: An Outline of Interpretive Sociology*, Berkeley, University of California Press.

Webley, Lisa and Duff, Liz (2007) 'Women solicitors as a barometer for problems within the legal profession – time to put values before profits?', *Journal of Law & Society*, 34: 374–402.

Weeks, Elaine Lunsford, Boles, Jacqueline M., Garbin, Albeno P. and Blount, John (1986) 'The transformation of sexual harassment from a private trouble into a public issue', *Sociological Inquiry*, 56: 432–55.

Weisbrot, David and Davis, Ian (2004) 'Litigation and the Federal justice system', in Prest, W.R. and Roach Anleu, S. (eds), *Litigation: Past and Present*, Sydney, UNSW Press.

Weisburd, David, Waring, Elin and Wheeler, Stanton (1990) 'Class, status, and the punishment of white-collar criminals', *Law & Social Inquiry*, 15: 223–43.

Weiss, Carol H. (1998) *Evaluation: Methods for Studying Programs and Policies*, 2nd edn, Upper Saddle River, NJ, Prentice Hall.

Wells, Celia (2002) 'Women law professors – negotiating and transcending gender identities at work', *Feminist Legal Studies*, 10: 1–38.

West, Robin (1988) 'Jurisprudence and gender', *University of Chicago Law Review*, 55: 1–72.

West, Robin (1991) 'The difference in women's hedonic lives: a phenomenological critique of feminist legal theory', in Fineman, M.A. and Thomadson, N.S. (eds), *At the Boundaries of Law: Feminism and Legal Theory*, New York, Routledge.

Weston, Burns H. (1991) 'Security Council Resolution 678 and Persian Gulf decision making: precarious legitimacy', *American Journal of International Law*, 85: 516–35.

Wikler, Norma Juliet (1986) 'Society's response to the new reproductive technologies: the feminist responses', *Southern California Law Review*, 59: 1043–57.

Wilensky, Harold L. (1964) 'The professionalization of everyone?', *American Journal of Sociology*, 70: 137–58.

Wiles, Ellen (2007) 'Headscarves, human rights, and harmonious multicultural society: implications of the French ban for interpretations of equality', *Law & Society Review*, 41: 699–736.

Williams, Linda S. (1984) 'The classic rape: when do victims report?', *Social Problems*, 31: 459–67.

Williams, Patricia (1987) 'Alchemical notes: reconstructing ideals from deconstructed rights', *Harvard Civil Rights–Civil Liberties Law Review*, 22: 401–33.

Williams, Patricia (1991) *The Alchemy of Race and Rights*, Cambridge, Harvard University Press.

Williams, Wendy W. (1984–5) 'Equality's riddle: pregnancy and the equal treatment/special treatment debate', *New York University Review of Law & Social Change*, 13: 325–80.

Williamson, John (2000) 'What should the World Bank think about the Washington consensus?', *World Bank Research Observer*, 15: 251–64.

Wissler, Roselle L. (1995) 'Mediation and adjudication in the small claims court: the effects of process and case characteristics', *Law & Society Review*, 29: 323–58.

Wolfe, Alan (1992) 'Sociological theory in the absence of people: the limits of Luhmann's systems theory', *Cardozo Law Review*, 13: 1729–43.

Wright, Ted and Melville, Angela (2004) '"Hey, but who's counting": the metrics and politics of trends in civil litigation', in Prest, W.R. and Roach Anleu, S. (eds), *Litigation Past and Present*, Sydney, UNSW Press.

Yale Law Journal (1979) 'Dispute resolution', *Yale Law Journal*, 88: 905–9.

Yngvesson, Barbara (1984) 'What is a dispute about? The political interpretation of social control', in Black, D. (ed.), *Toward a General Theory of Social Control* vol. 2, New York, Academic Press.

Young, Gary (1979) 'Marx on bourgeois law', *Research in Law and Sociology*, 2: 133–67.

Zander, Michael (1989) *A Matter of Justice: the Legal System in Ferment*, Oxford, Oxford University Press.

Zdenkowski, George (1994) 'Contemporary sentencing issues', in Chappell, D. and Wilson, P. (eds), *The Australian Criminal Justice System: the Mid 1990s*, Sydney, Butterworths.

Zelizer, Viviana (1989) 'The social meaning of money: "special monies"', *American Journal of Sociology*, 95: 342–77.

Zerner, Charles (1994) 'Through a green lens: the construction of customary environmental law and community in Indonesia's Maluku Islands', *Law & Society Review*, 28: 1079–123.

Zevnick, Nola and Davis, Ronni (1993) 'Price Waterhouse revisited: will the Civil Rights Act of 1991 cure the defects?', *Women's Rights Law Reporter*, 15: 87–100.

Ziélinska, Eleonora (1993) 'Recent trends in abortion legislation in Eastern Europe, with particular reference to Poland', *Criminal Law Forum*, 4: 47–93.

Cases Cited

ACTV v *Commonwealth* (1992) 108 ALR 577.

Al-Kateb v *Godwin* (2004) 219 CLR 562.

American Booksellers Association v *Hudnut* (1985)771 F 2d 323.

Brown v *Board of Education* (1954) 347 US 483.

Cameron v *R* (2002) 209 CLR 339.

Mabo & Others v *Queensland* (no.2) (1992) 175 CLR 1.

Meritor Savings Bank v *Vinson* (1986) 91 L Ed 49.

Miller v *California* (1973) 37 L Ed 419.

Nationwide News v *Wills* (1992) 108 ALR 681.

Nicaragua v *United States of America* (1986) ICJR 14.

Planned Parenthood of Southeastern Pennsylvania v *Casey* (1992) 120 L Ed 674.

Polyukhovich v *Commonwealth of Australia* (1991) 101 ALR 545.

R v *Ahluwalia* [1992] 4 All ER 889.

R v *Butler* (1992) 1 SCR 452.

R v *R* (1981) 28 SASR 321.

R v *Thomson; R v Houlton* (2000) 49 NSWLR 383.

R v *Thornton* (No2) [1996] 2 All ER 1023.

R v *Turner* (1970) 2 QB 321.

R v *Williscroft* (1975) VR 292.

Roe v *Wade* (1973) 410 US 113.

Tasmania v *Commonwealth of Australia* (1983) 57 ALJR 450.

Theophanous v *Herald & Weekly Times* (1994) 124 ALR 1.

Webster v *Reproductive Health Services* (1989) 109 S Ct 3040.

Internet citations

Australian Government, Equal Opportunity for Women in the Workplace Agency, 'Overview of the Act', http://www.eowa.gov.au/About_EOWA/Overview_of_the_Act.asp [accessed 09.12.2008].

Department of Justice, Victoria, 'Neighbourhood Justice Centre', http://www.justice.vic.gov.au/wps/wcm/connect/DOJ+Internet/Home/The+Justice+System/Neighbourhood+Justice/ [accessed 30.11.2008].

European Union, http://europa.eu.abc/treaties/index_en.htm [accessed 15.12.2008].

International Chamber of Commerce, ADR Dispute Resolution Services, 'ICC ADR – Suggested clauses' http://www.iccwbo.org/court/adr/id5346/index.html [accessed 25.07.2008].

International Chamber of Commerce, 'What is ICC?' http://www.iccwbo.org/id93/index.html [accessed 25.07.2008].

International Criminal Court, http://www.Icc.int [accessed 18.12.2008]

Ministry of Justice (UK) (Formerly Department for Constitutional Affairs, www.dca.gov.uk) www.justice.gov.uk [accessed 09.12.2008].

Sentencing Advisory Council (Victoria), www.sentencingcouncil.vic.gov.au [accessed 09.12.2008].

United Nations, 'Declaration of Basic Principles of Justice for Victims of Crime and Abuse of Power' adopted by General Assembly resolution 40/34 of 29 November 1985 www2.ohchr.org/English/law/pdf/victims.pdf. [accessed 09.12.2008]

Index

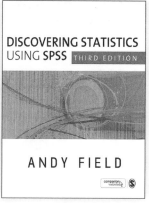
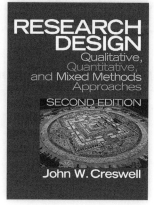

Supporting researchers for more than forty years

Research methods have always been at the core of SAGE's publishing. Sara Miller McCune founded SAGE in 1965 and soon after she published SAGE's first methods book, *Public Policy Evaluation*. A few years later, she launched the Quantitative Applications in the Social Sciences series – affectionately known as the 'little green books'.

Always at the forefront of developing and supporting new approaches in methods, SAGE published early groundbreaking texts and journals in the fields of qualitative methods and evaluation.

Today, more than forty years and two million little green books later, SAGE continues to push the boundaries with a growing list of more than 1,200 research methods books, journals, and reference works across the social, behavioural, and health sciences.

From qualitative, quantitative and mixed methods to evaluation, SAGE is the essential resource for academics and practitioners looking for the latest in methods by leading scholars.

www.sagepublications.com